COMPANION TO HYMNS OF FAITH AND LIFE

by

Lawrence R. Schoenhals, Ph.D., Mus.D.

Light and Life Press
Winona Lake, Indiana

All rights reserved.
No part of this book
may be reproduced in any form,
except for brief quotations in reviews,
without the written permission
of the publisher.

Printed in the United States of America
by Light and Life Press, Winona Lake, Indiana 46590

**Copyright 1980 by
Light and Life Press**

ISBN 0-89367-040-5

To the Memory of Mildred

Beloved wife,
mother, and source of inspiration to all who knew her.

TABLE OF CONTENTS

Preface 7
Introduction by Paul N. Ellis 9
Part One
   Historical Background 15
   Christian Doctrine and Christian Hymnody 19
   Hymns of Faith and Life — An Overview 25
Part Two
   Notes on the Hymns
Bibliography 31
Indexes
   Authors, Translators, and Sources 398
   Composers, Arrangers, and Sources 400
   Alphabetical Index of Tunes 403
   Scriptural References in Hymns 406
   Complete Index of First Lines and Titles 410

PREFACE

Hymns are meant to be sung. They are *most* effective when wedded to appropriate music and sung by a body of believers. As Cervantes wrote in *Don Quixote:* "The proof of the pudding is the eating." It is not enough to read about hymns. They must be sung to be fully appreciated. But they *can* exert a powerful impact also when quoted or when read responsively or antiphonally. Using them with a bit of imagination can add zest to corporate and private worship.

For the first six months following the publication of *Hymns of Faith and Life,* my wife and I used it exclusively in our evening devotions. We read the congregational readings responsively or in unison. We did the same with the hymns. We searched for parallels between the readings and the hymns. For example, we noted that hymn No. 40, "The Man Who Once Has Found Abode," is a metrical version of Psalm 91 and that congregational reading No. 641 is an excerpt from the same psalm.

We reveled in the flights of poetic expression which somehow opened up new spiritual insights. Some of the hymns provided illuminating commentary on illusive biblical truths. Other hymns jarred our complacency. Hymn No. 504, "The City Is Alive, O God," and No. 25, "God of Grace and God of Glory," do not permit casual reflection. They demand a response.

It is my hope that this manual will be a useful tool for pastors and, for laypersons, a means of unlocking the devotional treasures of the hymnal so often only superficially explored.

Not all the material included will be equally valuable to all readers. The sophisticated professional will know already or have available in his library much of the information. The advantage of including here the commonly known facts is for the sake of convenience. This is a companion to a *particular* hymnal. Still, some information is included for the first time, and in that sense the researcher cannot ignore it. At some points my findings contradict those of my professional colleagues. I invite their comments. Even with careful proofreading, some errors will have crept in. I welcome correspondence pointing these out.

In the first section, I deal in elementary fashion with some basic things in hymnody. The reader who is conversant with the field may wish to skip these paragraphs. For those who find the material too brief, I invite their attention to the bibliography in the back of the book.

In the second section, I deal with each song in *Hymns of Faith and Life*. A reasonably consistent pattern will be followed although the amount of information differs widely. A limited amount of biographical information is included when it has a bearing on the hymn being discussed.

Since the publication of the first historical companion to *Hymns Ancient and Modern,* most major hymnals have generated companion volumes. Ours does not differ greatly from many of these. I have benefited from the work done by earlier authors. Their contributions to our knowledge of hymnody are greatly appreciated. I have used many of the same sources they used. I have tried to give proper acknowledgement where they uncovered information not generally known. All writers of hymnal manuals must acknowledge indebtedness to the monumental (no other term adequately describes it) *Dictionary of Hymnology* edited by John Julian (1836-1913). In addition to this marvelous compendium of information, those of us who have done extensive research in the British Museum have had the added benefit of using Julian's personal library which was deposited there some years ago.

Finally, I would acknowledge the encouragement and assistance of my son, G. Roger Schoenhals, editorial director of Light and Life Press, and his associates, and to my secretary Margery Brubaker and those who helped her in preparing the manuscript for publication.

INTRODUCTION

In the eighteenth century, Charles Wesley's religious lyrics became popular during the spiritual revival that resulted in Methodism. John Newton's *Olney Hymns,* which included sixty-eight hymns by the poet William Cowper, was published late in that century and influenced greatly the evangelical ideal of the hymn. The gospel song and folk tunes have been included more recently in the hymnody of the church.

Singing has a long history in Judeo-Christian worship in spite of the hesitancy of English churchmen to accept lyrics of human composition. The deliverance of Israel from slavery in Egypt inspired the majestic hymn of praise which "Moses and the people of Israel sang" and is recorded in Exodus 15. The Psalms were written to be sung, recited, or chanted in corporate worship. In the time of spiritual renewal under Hezekiah's reign, the people of Judah gathered in celebration and "The whole assembly worshiped, and the singers sang, and the trumpeters sounded. . . . The king and the princes commanded the Levites to sing praises to the Lord with the words of David and of Asaph" (see II Chronicles 29:28-30, RSV).

Jesus and His disciples sang hymns together (Mark 14:26). Paul and Silas sang hymns in the prison (Acts 16:25). The common use of hymn singing in the early church is implied and its character defined in Paul's word to the Corinthians: "I will sing with the spirit and I will sing with the mind also" (I Corinthians 14:15, RSV). We know from the Dead Sea Scrolls that songs were being composed in the second and first centuries before Christ.

For many centuries, we can be sure, religious lyrics have been used to sing (or shout) praise and adoration to God. The Scottish church may have considered as heresy all lyrics except the Psalms, and the English church may have thought the singing of songs in worship to be fanaticism; but Christian faith and experience demand affirmation and expression. And even in England, hymns and carols were used long before the Reformation.

The Reformation in Germany developed a rich hymnody in the sixteenth century. Luther gave an important place to the metrical hymn in public worship. He differed with Calvin in this. Calvin insisted on the singing of only the Psalms or transpositions of Scripture selections. Nevertheless, whether they used the Psalms or lyrics of poets, the Reformers sang!

We must conclude that spiritual renewal, revival, and reformation in every age evoke singing. Christian worship may be properly described as celebration. And celebration demands song.

The purpose and use of song may differ according to the occasion. When religious faith is vital and spiritual experience meaningful, various needs may be met by the singing of hymns. The expression of adoration, praise, and thanksgiving to God is plainly served by appropriate lyrics and tunes. The hymn may give voice to petition and intercession. Glad testimony to personal trust, confidence, and victory may be given in song. Singing can be used to articulate our vows and commitment or to affirm our creed. The hymns have been used from the earliest history of God's people to teach the great truths about God and His dealing with mankind.

Whether the hymns are used in private or public worship, therefore, they should be used intelligently. Every effort should be made to gain understanding in worship. This is the import of Paul's determination to sing both "with the spirit" and "with the mind." Music artfully expresses authentic emotion, if it is good. Inexpressible depths of feeling may be interpreted in melody and rhythm. Paul seeks to avoid, however, the perils of Hellenistic mysticism. Singing should do more than express feeling. Teaching and meaningful worship always have been goals of worthy hymns.

Each hymn in *Companion to Hymns of Faith and Life* has been researched by Dr. Schoenhals, and material has been selected to inform both mind and spirit. Interesting and pertinent facts provided regarding the lyrics and the music will add to our appreciation of the hymn.

The pastor will find *Companion to Hymns of Faith and Life* useful in selecting hymns for public worship. A careful choice of songs will aid in creating the spirit of worship and will lead the thoughts of the worshipers toward the biblical truth to be proclaimed. The pastor can reinforce the message God has for the people by the illustrations and instructions available to him in this book.

Companion to Hymns of Faith and Life will be a rich resource for those who direct the music of the church. Students of sacred music will benefit from the careful study of this companion to the hymnal. All of us can use the book wisely for our private devotions and personal enrichment.

Dr. Lawrence R. Schoenhals is eminently qualified to make this significant contribution to the hymnody of the church. He served as the executive editor of *Hymns of Faith and Life*, published jointly by the Wesleyan and the Free Methodist Churches, in 1976. He was music director of the "Light and Life Hour" international broadcast for twenty-one years and was the associate editor of *Hymns of the Living Faith* (1951). Dr. Schoenhals is a loyal churchman, a sensitive Christian gentleman, who has spent all his professional career in Christian higher education in music and administration. A member of the Hymn Society of America, he is a recognized scholar in sacred music.

John Wesley, in his preface to *A Collection of Hymns for the Use of the People Called Methodists* (London, 1780), defended vigorously the quality of the poetry in the hymnal. He protested that others had freely changed the lyrics, with some frequency, much to the detriment of the original verse. In his opinion, however, there was something more important than the quality of the verse. He wrote: "That which is of infinitely more moment than the spirit of poetry is the spirit of piety." He desired the Methodist hymns to contribute to the assurance of the believer and the "perfecting [of] holiness in the fear of God."

The purpose and emphasis of the author of *Companion to Hymns of Faith and Life* concur with Wesley's desire. He is concerned with authentic spiritual life and "the beauty of holiness" in Christian experience and worship. *Hymns of Faith and Life* and this *Companion* are two volumes that should be off your bookshelf daily as you use them as tools of the Spirit for personal and corporate edification.

Paul N. Ellis, Bishop
Free Methodist Church of North America
Winona Lake, Indiana

PART ONE

Historical Background Christian Doctrine and Christian Hymnody
Hymns of Faith and Life — An Overview

HISTORICAL BACKGROUND

"Psalms and hymns and spiritual songs" (Ephesians 5:19) describes the philosophy and intent of the compilers of the hymnal, *Hymns of Faith and Life*. There are metrical versions of psalms and paraphrases of psalms. There are the standard hymns which have graced the worship experiences of Christians for many generations. Wesleyan hymns, the peculiar heritage of Methodists everywhere, are well represented. In the "spiritual songs" category, there are gospel songs, spirituals, and folk songs. Depending on one's definition, perhaps half the songs fall into this classification.

In his well-documented history of the Free Methodist denomination, *From Age to Age a Living Witness,* Bishop Leslie Ray Marston focused attention on the commitment of early Free Methodists "to earnest congregational singing." From the beginning, the church firmly believed that the most important church music was that performed by the congregation itself. To that end, Free Methodists were exhorted to cultivate singing in every society.

The earliest Free Methodist congregations used the Methodist Episcopal hymnal of 1849. As the fledgling denomination developed an awareness of its own identity, demands grew for a Free Methodist hymnody. The first answer to this demand was *Spiritual Songs and Hymns for Pilgrims,* compiled and published in 1868, apparently as a private venture, by B. T. Roberts, first general superintendent of the Free Methodist Church.

The General Conference of 1878 appointed a committee of fifteen to compile a hymnbook. One stipulation: The church was not to be involved financially. Although the committee worked long hours and agreed on a selection of 600 hymns, the book was not published.

Four years later, the 1882 General Conference appointed a smaller committee of six to complete the task. They used the Methodist hymnal of 1849 as a basis for their selections, supplemented by other hymnals and by the list compiled by the 1878 committee. The result was *The Hymn Book of the Free Methodist Church,* published by B. T. Roberts in 1883. This book contained no music. However, there is evidence that congregations used the *Metrical Tune Book* as a source of music. This latter book was published by Philip Phillips in 1873. Phillips was a Methodist and editor of the 1867 *New Hymn and Tune Book: An Offering of Praise for the Methodist Episcopal Church.*

The Reverend J. G. Terrill, general missionary secretary of the Free Methodist Church, evidently took Phillips's *Metrical Tune*

Book and adapted it for use in conjunction with the Free Methodist hymnal. This new version of the *Tune Book* was copyrighted in 1890. Terrill was in the process of revising and enlarging it to include all the hymns in the Free Methodist hymnal when he died in 1895.

Thomas B. Arnold, the church's first publishing agent, took over the project and added a supplement of 290 miscellaneous songs, which he designated *Light and Life Songs*. Some of this latter group are now found in most standard hymnals (e.g., "My Jesus, I Love Thee" and "What a Friend We Have in Jesus"). The new publication was titled *Metrical Tune Book with Supplement* and bore the names of Phillips, Terrill, and Arnold on the title page. Copyright date was 1896. An intricate cross-numbering system related the hymns in the *Tune Book* to the numbers in the 1883 *Hymn Book*.

The 1903 General Conference appointed a hymnal revision committee. It met once, organized itself, and scheduled a second meeting. None was held and no further work on the revision was done.

The General Conference of 1903 also authorized the publication of a Sunday school songbook. Using, perhaps, the supplement of *Light and Life Songs* in the *Metrical Tune Book* as a model, *Light and Life Songs* was issued in 1904. It was followed by other gospel songbooks at periodic intervals: *Voices of Praise* (1909); *Light and Life Songs,* No. II (1914); No. III (1918); No. IV (1928); *Inspirational Songs* (1924); *Worship in Song* (1935); and *Choice Light and Life Songs* (1950).

In 1907, the General Conference ordered a new hymnal to be prepared. The Executive Committee was instructed to name a Hymnal Commission. Thirteen persons were appointed with Bishop Wilson T. Hogue as chairman. The Wesleyan Methodist Church was invited to participate and responded by naming one member, the Reverend A. T. Jennings, editor of *The Wesleyan Methodist*. The commission proceeded to organize itself by electing three of its members to serve as editors. The Wesleyan representative was among the three. A music editor outside the commission, Thoro Harris, was appointed. The resulting publication was the *Free Methodist Hymnal* of 1910. The Wesleyan Methodist Church adopted the same book as its official hymnal under the title *Wesleyan Methodist Hymnal*.

The 1910 *Free Methodist Hymnal* served well for forty-one years. It would probably have been revised sometime in the 1930s had it not been for the severe economic depression. Denominations tend to revise their hymnody about every twenty years.

It was not until the General Conference of 1947 that a new hymnal was authorized. Similar action was taken by the Wesleyan Methodist Church. In due time, a Joint Hymnal

Commission was named consisting of ten Free Methodists and five Wesleyans. At a later time, the commission was enlarged by the addition of two Free Methodists and two Wesleyans.

The Commission and its smaller editorial committee finished the work and produced *Hymns of the Living Faith* in time for the Free Methodist General Conference of 1951. Free Methodists added the subtitle *Hymnal of the Free Methodist Church*. Wesleyans identified the book similarly for their use.

Hymns of the Living Faith gained wide acceptance both within and outside the two denominations. It was acclaimed by no less authority than the editor of the 1933 Methodist Episcopal hymnal as "one of the finest hymnals which has appeared in this century."

Hymns of Faith and Life (1976) has now joined the fine tradition established by earlier Free Methodist hymnals. It is the product of nine years of work by another Joint Hymnal Commission authorized by both the Free Methodist and the Wesleyan denominations. The commission numbered forty, twenty from each denomination. In addition to the bishops and general superintendents, there were ministers and laymen from all sections of both Canada and the United States. The denominational colleges were well represented, and missionaries and our ministers in the United Kingdom also made suggestions.

Nine years may seem like a long time, but denominational hymnals generally take about that long to produce. There's a good reason why such projects tend to "stretch out." Commission members are professional people for whom hymnal work is an "add on." Also, it takes a good deal of time to reconcile differences of opinion. The democratic process cannot be hurried.

Earlier hymnal revision committees expressed concern about the integrity of the hymn texts. They complained about the indiscriminate alteration that often changed the intention of the authors.

The Joint Hymnal Commission for the 1976 hymnal established some basic principles to guide in the revision. These included the intention to restore texts to their original forms as far as practicable and also to require a majority vote for all decisions.

A denominational hymnal ought to reflect the tastes, aspirations, and concerns of its communicants. *Hymns of Faith and Life* does this. There is enough of the traditional to make most people feel comfortable in using it. But there are also new resources to stretch the imagination and resourcefulness of clergy and laity alike. It is a hymnal for this dynamic period in Free Methodist history.

CHRISTIAN DOCTRINE AND CHRISTIAN HYMNODY

In all too many cases, hymns are used because of their familiarity and/or for their "pretty tunes." It is true that the act of singing corporately can be a unifying and an exhilarating experience. Rotarians and Kiwanians, among secular groups, employ group singing for this very purpose. The use of hymns in church ought to have a more noble purpose.

The content of the hymn and its relation to the larger objective of the service need most careful and prayerful consideration. The indiscriminate omission of stanzas by some ministers and song leaders, leaving incomplete thoughts dangling, is a measure of the thoughtlessness with which hymns are often employed.

A Few Examples:
HFL No. 184 "God Is Gone up on High"
Stanza 6 cannot be omitted.

HFL No. 248 "God Calling Yet! Shall I Not Hear?"
Stanzas 4 and 5 are affirmations for questions raised in earlier stanzas.

HFL No. 304 "O Thou Who Camest from Above"
Stanza 4 is a continuation of stanza 3.

HFL No. 308 "I Gave My Life for Thee"
Stanza 5 should not be omitted.

HFL No. 315 "Come, Holy Spirit, God and Lord"
All stanzas should be sung.

HFL No. 341 "O for that Flame of Living Fire"
Stanza 5 must not be omitted.

HFL No. 374 "O for a Faith that Will Not Shrink"
No stanza should be omitted.

HFL No. 419 "Am I a Soldier of the Cross?"
Stanza 4 is the affirmation that follows the questions raised in the preceding stanzas.

HFL No. 506 "Where Cross the Crowded Ways of Life"
Stanza 5 is a continuation of stanza 4.

HFL No. 511 "When I Survey the Wondrous Cross"
All stanzas should be sung.

In preparing this official hymnal to be shared by the Free Methodist and the Wesleyan denominations, doctrinal integrity was of real concern. A committee was charged with the responsibility of examining all texts to make sure the theological statements expressed were consistent with the doctrinal positions of the two denominations. It was the conviction of the Commission that heresy set to music is still heresy and that we should be as careful of the doctrine we sing as we are of the doctrine we preach.

I have attempted in the following pages to focus attention on the doctrinal content of our hymns. Hymns have an important teaching function, and we should welcome this available reinforcement to our oral and written pastoral exhortations. The peculiar hold on one's memory of words set to music is well known.

Frederick W. Faber, author of "Faith of Our Fathers" and himself a convert to Roman Catholicism, wrote: "There is scarcely anything which takes so strong a hold upon people as religion in metre, hymns or poems on doctrinal subjects.... Catholics even are said to be sometimes found poring with a devout and unsuspecting delight over the verses of the Olney Hymns, which the Author himself can remember acting like a spell upon him for years, strong enough to be for long a counter influence to very grave convictions, and even now to come back from time to time unbidden into the mind."

In my own experiences, I recall a journalist, attached to a major metropolitan newspaper, who became a personal friend because of our mutual interest in hymns. Although long disassociated with our denomination, he still had fond memories of the songs learned in his youth in a Free Methodist minister's home and could quote them at length. He felt a kinship to his former communion by way of its hymnody.

John Julian, speaking of Christopher Wordsworth, nephew of William Wordsworth, reported that he "looked upon hymns as a valuable means of stamping permanently upon the memory the great doctrines of the Christian church. He held it to be 'the first duty of a hymnwriter to teach sound doctrine, and thus to save souls.'" (See hymns 51, 57, 135, and 337.)

The essential truths of much of the New Testament and significant portions of the Old Testament can be traced in the allusions and paraphrases in our hymnody. Henry Bett, in *The*

Hymns of Methodism in Their Literary Relations, is even more forthright: "There can hardly be a single paragraph anywhere in the Scriptures that is not somewhere reflected in the writings of the Wesleys. The hymns, in many cases, are a mere mosaic of biblical allusions."

There can be no doubt that John and Charles Wesley used hymns as doctrinal statements.

It is an instructive exercise to take some accepted evangelical "Statement of Faith" and find hymns that illustrate each article. Probably the most venerable and widely accepted of all formulations of belief is "The Apostles' Creed." It is an excellent statement for this purpose. We know there is at least one hymn which will serve as a commentary on each article. The nineteenth-century hymnwriter, Samuel J. Stone, wrote such a series. Only one has remained in common usage, however, "The Church's One Foundation."

"The Apostles' Creed" may be the oldest of the major creeds. It is so named because of the widespread but unsubstantiated medieval assumption that it was composed by the apostles themselves. Customarily, we recognize twelve divisions or articles, although it is possible to further divide some of them to make a total of sixteen.

Our hymnal includes a metrical version of "The Apostles' Creed" (No. 58, "We All Believe in One True God"), written by Tobias Clausnitzer (1668) and translated by Catherine Winkworth (1863). The tune *Wir Glauben All' An Einen Gott* is the traditional tune for Clausnitzer's hymn. This is a good place to begin.

Article I. *I Believe in God the Father Almighty, Maker of heaven and earth.*

Illustrative hymn: "I Sing Th'almighty Power of God" (No. 16). Many hymns might be chosen, but I think it is appropriate to select one written by Isaac Watts, a contemporary of J. S. Bach. By universal agreement, Watts is regarded as the "Father of English hymnody." This assertion is made, not because there were no English hymns written before his time, but because he possessed the genius to break the stranglehold that metrical psalms held on public worship in the Reformed churches from the time of Calvin onward.

This particular hymn was written especially for young people but it speaks meaningfully to Christians of all ages. (See also page 46.)

Article II: *And in Jesus Christ His only Son our Lord.*

Almost any hymn of praise to Christ will illustrate this article. A particularly appropriate one is "Beautiful Saviour" (No. 74). There are at least three translations in common use. One of them begins "Fairest Lord Jesus," popularized in Richard Storrs Willis's *Church Chorals and Choir Studies,* 1850. Our translation is by Joseph Augustus Seiss from *The Sunday School Book,* 1873, of the American Lutheran General Council. (See also page 89.)

Article III: *Who was conceived by the Holy Ghost, born of the Virgin Mary.*

The Advent and Nativity sections of the hymnal are rich with illustrative hymns. William Billings's "A Virgin Unspotted" (No. 120) is of some historical interest. The text appears anonymously and in various forms in a number of early English and American collections. The tune *Judea* was composed by the first American to make music his profession. There has been a revival in recent years of the use of Billings's music. (See also page 117.)

Article IV: *Suffered under Pontius Pilate, was crucified, dead, and buried. He descended into hell.*

Illustrative hymn: "Go to Dark Gethsemane" (No. 150) is a moving portrayal of "Christ, Our Example in Suffering," the title Montgomery used as a heading. (See also page 134.)

I also call your attention to hymns 162-168, in the section *The Words from the Cross,* which are particularly suitable for use in a Good Friday service. (See also page 143.)

Article V: *The third day He rose again from the dead.*

Illustrative hymn: "The Day of Resurrection" (No. 171) is a powerful wedding of text and tune in praise of the risen Christ. (See also page 144.)

Article VI: *He ascended into heaven, and sitteth on the right hand of God the Father Almighty.*

Charles Wesley's "God Is Gone up on High" (No. 184), is taken from his *Hymns for Ascension Day.* (See also page 151.)

Article VII: *From thence He shall come to judge the quick and the dead.*

There are two hymns in our hymnal that address the subject of judgment. One is No. 238 by Charles Wesley, "Thou Judge of Quick and Dead." The other is one of the seven great hymns of the medieval church, *Dies Irae*. Our translation by Sir Walter Scott is No. 237, "That Day of Wrath, That Dreadful Day." (See also pages 180 and 182.)

Article VIII: *I Believe in the Holy Ghost.*
The most famous hymn on this subject is also one of the seven great hymns of the medieval church, *Veni Creator Spiritus*. Our hymnal uses "Creator Spirit! By Whose Aid" (No. 204), which is John Wesley's adaptation of John Dryden's translation. (See also page 161.)

Our hymnal has many hymns on the Holy Spirit. Each should be studied for its own particular emphasis.

Article IX: *The Holy catholic church, the communion of saints.*
The first part of this article is perhaps best illustrated by hymn No. 501, "The Church's One Foundation," although a number of other hymns commend themselves (e.g., No. 467, "Christ Is Made the Sure Foundation"; No. 473, "Built on the Rock"; and No. 476, "I Love Thy Kingdom, Lord").

The meaning of the second phrase of this article is less clear. One interpretation is the "fellowship of believers with each other." This concept may not be grasped easily by children unless taught through the use of the delightful hymn "I Sing a Song of the Saints of God" (No. 535).

All congregations ought to become thoroughly acquainted with hymn No. 462, "For All the Saints," which invites joint participation with the choir, and with Charles Wesley's "Christ from Whom All Blessings Flow" (No. 472).

Article X: *The forgiveness of sins.*
Congregations with Methodist heritage will respond enthusiastically to the two hymns written by Charles Wesley at the time of his conversion, No. 272, "Where Shall My Wondering Soul Begin?" and No. 273, "And Can It Be?" (See also pages 203 and 205.)

Article XI: *The resurrection of the body.*
There are a number of hymns that proclaim the truth "... because I live, ye shall live also" (John 14:19). One I like particularly is No. 461, "Ten Thousand Times Ten Thousand," written by a former dean of Canterbury Cathedral in the

nineteenth century. (See also page 333.)

Article XII: *And the life everlasting. Amen.*

Swedish congregations sing No. 466, "In Heaven Above," with great appreciation. The text and tune will readily fix themselves in the minds and hearts of all worshipers regardless of national origin.

> In heaven above, in heaven above,
>   Where God our Father dwells,
> How boundless there the blessedness!
>   No tongue its greatness tells;
> There face to face, and full and free,
> Ever and evermore we see —
> We see the Lord of Hosts!

HYMNS OF FAITH AND LIFE — AN OVERVIEW

The religious songs a congregation sings tell us something of the depth and the intensity of its devotional life. In fact, such songs actually help determine the quality of devotional life. It is important, therefore, that we choose our songs carefully and with prayer.

The trivial and often tasteless songs tolerated in some evangelical churches are an affront to most spiritually sensitive worshipers. We may safely take our position with John Wesley who soundly condemned "nonsense" and "doggerel" in hymns.

Free Methodist-Wesleyan hymnody is at a level a few notches above that used in many churches. At least officially it is. Practically, there is great room for improvement. A good place to start is to become acquainted with the devotional treasures in *Hymns of Faith and Life*.

William Cowper said it well in hymn No. 222:

> Sometimes a light surprises
> The Christian while he sings.

The surprise is more likely to be experienced by the worshiper whose awareness has been aroused by singing with the spirit and with the understanding also. (I Corinthians 14:15)

With *Hymns of Faith and Life* in our hands, we begin our tour of discovery.

I. Creeds

Although many denominations regularly use the recitation of creeds in their public worship services, Free Methodists and Wesleyans have not traditionally done so. The Hymnal Commission chose to make two creeds available for ready reference by printing them inside the front cover. They are "The Apostles' Creed" and "An Affirmation in the Words of Saint John." The traditional form of "The Apostles' Creed" was chosen. Note that "the holy catholic church" does not refer to the Roman church but to the "Church Universal."

In the preceding chapter we discussed the doctrinal content of hymns and related them to the various sections of "The Apostles' Creed."

II. Title Page

The quotation from Charles Wesley is the second stanza of his hymn "Ye Servants of God, Your Master Proclaim," which is discussed in part two of the *Companion*.

III. Explanatory Notes
Read these to help you understand the principles that guided the editing of the hymns and the symbols used.

IV. Preface
Here you will find a concise statement of the philosophy of Free Methodist-Wesleyan hymnody together with important historical material, including the membership of the Joint Hymnal Commission.

V. Table of Contents
This should be studied in conjunction with the Topical Index beginning on page 567 of the hymnal. The comprehensive range of themes covered in the hymnal is impressive. The grouping of the hymns under the major topical headings (The Worship of God, The Christian Life, The Living Church, The Nation, Service Music, etc.) has both logical and theological bases.

VI. Page Arrangement
At this point it might be appropriate to call your attention to the fact that no page numbers are assigned to the hymnal proper. The reason is obvious. Sometimes there are two short hymns on a given page. Longer hymns often require more than one page. It is proper, therefore, to identify a particular hymn by number and not by page. Page numbers are used in the latter part of the hymnal, however, for ease in locating features other than hymns.

We have followed the practice of assigning separate numbers to alternate tunes set to the same text, for example, "All Hail the Power of Jesus' Name!" which has three tunes.

Turn now to hymn No. 1, "O for a Thousand Tongues to Sing," for an explanation of the types of information included for each hymn.

Hymn Title (First line of first stanza. This pattern is followed consistently except where the copyright owner has stipulated otherwise, as in hymn No. 39.)

Source of text and dates (Upper left)

Tune title and metric pattern (Upper right. C.M. stands for common meter. Its metric pattern is 8.6.8.6., meaning the first line has eight syllables, the second has six, and so on. Other meters that are assigned names are: S.M., short meter, 6.6.8.6.; and L.M., long meter, 8.8.8.8. When "D" appears, as in hymn No. 5, it stands for "doubled" and means that the pattern is repeated. See the Metrical Index beginning on page 560.)

Source of music and dates (Upper right)

Explanatory Notes (Occasionally, a short historical note is added at the bottom of the page.)

Key Scripture (An effort was made to locate a Scripture verse that encapsulated the central theme of each hymn. See also the Scriptural Index beginning on page 563.)

Topical Notations (These are derived from the Table of Contents.)

Copyrights (Many of the hymns are still protected by copyrights. Most of these are noted, beginning on page 550. In a few instances, the copyright owner required that the notation be given on the page with the hymn.)

VII. Rituals and Worship Aids

A. *The Sacrament of the Lord's Supper.* Two forms of the ritual are given. One is predominantly clergy-directed. The other provides for congregational participation. (See pages 494-497.)

B. *The John Wesley Covenant Service.* Beginning in 1755, John Wesley conducted a covenant service on numerous occasions. It came to be a regular part of watch night services that he led. By 1780, he published the text in pamphlet form and the practice became well established among Methodists.

Following Wesley's death, a series of revisions of the service left very little of the original language intact. We have restored large portions of the service and have introduced congregational participation. In fact, ours is the only contemporary hymnal to include the covenant service in something that approximates the authentic language and form of the original. John Wesley still speaks powerfully to this generation, even though some expressions will seem quaint upon first reading.

We have restricted our editorial changes to additions made necessary by the introduction of congregational participation and to deletions required because of the excessive length of the original. The hymns were chosen with care, but others may be substituted if desired.

In the relatively short time *Hymns of Faith and Life* has been available, the John Wesley Covenant Service has won wide acceptance and high praise. For instance, participants in the annual Graduate Students Theological Consultation, conducted jointly by the Free Methodist and Wesleyan denominations, have requested that their final session shall always conclude with the covenant service preceding the Sacrament of the Lord's Supper (See pages 498-503).

C. *Congregational Readings.* The use of a number of standard versions of Scripture and an imaginative division of the texts make this section especially useful. Note the effect of reading No. 602 responsively. Two additional psalms are printed opposite hymn No. 1.

A topical index of the readings and a scriptural index are provided on pages 548 and 549.

D. *Indexes.* A comprehensive set of indexes is included. Special attention is called to the Scriptural Index and to the Topical Index of the hymns. Judicious use of these will help pastors and laypersons make wider use of the hymnic resources of the hymnal.

The Metrical Index lists the hymns according to their metrical patterns. It is often possible to select a more familiar tune than the one printed with a given text.

E. *The Hymns.* Part II of this volume gives historical, biographical, and anecdotal information on most of the hymns and their writers.

PART TWO

Notes on the Hymns

1 O for a Thousand Tongues to Sing

Charles Wesley (1707-1788)

In the judgment of James Montgomery, Charles Wesley was excelled as a hymnwriter only by Isaac Watts.

This hymn, included in John and Charles Wesley's *Hymns and Sacred Poems,* 1740, originally had eighteen 4-line stanzas and bore the title: "For the Anniversary Day of One's Conversion." In his *Journal,* Charles Wesley dated his conversion May 21, 1738. It is assumed that this hymn was written about one year later.

Our six stanzas are 7-12 in the original. When John Wesley used this as the first hymn in his *Collection of Hymns for the Use of the People Called Methodists,* 1780, the so-called "Large Hymnbook," he printed stanzas 7-10, 12, 13, 14, 17, and 18. Stanza 7 is often thought to have been inspired by a remark Moravian Peter Böhler made to Charles Wesley: "Had I a thousand tongues, I would praise Him with them all."

The first stanza in the complete hymn read:

> Glory to God, and praise, and love
>   Be ever, ever given,
> By saints below and saints above
>   The Church in earth and heaven.

Charles Wesley was well-nigh overpowered by a flood of emotion as he realized in a personal way the redemptive power of Christ's atonement. This is reflected in the original stanza 5, shown by his use of italics:

> I felt my Lord's atoning blood
>   Close to *my* soul applied;
> *Me, me* He loved — the Son of God
>   For *me,* for *me,* He died.

The Free Methodist hymnal of 1883 and the Free Methodist-Wesleyan hymnals of 1910, 1951, and 1976 all print the same six stanzas. In 1883 and 1910, the suggested tune is a "fuguing tune," called *Northfield* by Jeremiah Ingalls (1764-1828). *Azmon* is used in 1951 and 1976.

This hymn was sung at the reopening of Wesley's Chapel on November 1, 1978, exactly 200 years to the day after John Wesley preached his first sermon there. Queen Elizabeth II and representatives of Methodist bodies from five continents were in attendance. It was the first time Her Majesty had worshiped in a Methodist church. Bishop Elmer E. Parsons was the official Free Methodist representative.

AZMON was composed in 1828 by Carl Gotthelf Gläser (1784-1829). It appeared anonymously in Lowell Mason's *The Modern Psalmist,* 1839. In a later collection, Mason identified the tune as composed by "C. G." There he named the tune *Denfield*, but later changed it to AZMON, a name found in Numbers 34:4-5. The harmonization is undoubtedly by Lowell Mason. In various collections, the tune has appeared in 4/4, 6/8, 3/4, and 3/2 meters.

2   O Worship the King

Sir Robert Grant (1779-1838)

This hymn is based on William Kethe's version of Psalm 104 in the Anglo-Genevan *Psalter* of 1561, using the same meter. Stanza 1, by Kethe, shows the relationship:

> My soule praise the Lord, speake good of his Name
> O Lord our great God how doest thou appeare,
> So passing in glorie, that great is thy fame,
> Honour and majestie, in thee shine most cleare.

As published in Edward H. Bickersteth's *Christian Psalmody*, 1833, there were six stanzas. The omitted sixth stanza reads as follows:

> O Lord of all might, how boundless Thy love!
> While angels delight to hymn Thee above,
> The humbler creation, though feeble their lays,
> With true adoration shall lisp to Thy praise.

The first three stanzas of the hymn are a faithful paraphrase of the opening verses of Psalm 104. The remaining stanzas expound on the principal theme of the psalm, emphasizing God's care, love, and mercy toward His children.

The hymn has been in Free Methodist-Wesleyan hymnals since 1910. In 1910 and in 1951, the four stanzas used are: 1, 2, 4, and 5. In 1976 all stanzas except Grant's sixth are used, and the authorized text has been restored.

Grant was born in Bengal, India, probably in 1779, rather than in 1785 as given by Julian, and died in Dalpoorie, India, in 1838. He was educated at Cambridge, became a member of Parliament, Director of the East India Company, Governor of Bombay, knighted in 1834.

LYONS is sometimes credited to Johann Michael Haydn (1736-1806), younger brother of Franz Joseph, but the evidence is inconclusive. It appeared first, anonymously, in William Gardiner's *Sacred Melodies*, 1815. Oliver Shaw's *Sacred Melodies*, 1818, was the first American collection to include it.

3 Immortal, Invisible, God Only Wise
Walter Chalmers Smith (1824-1908)

This hymn first appeared in the author's *Hymns of Christ and the Christian Life,* 1867, included in the section "Hymns of the Holy Trinity." At the suggestion of the British hymn book editor, William Garrett Horder (1841-1922), Smith made a number of changes in the text; and the hymn, thus altered, was introduced into English hymnody in Horder's *Congregational Hymns,* 1884. This is the version printed in our 1976 hymnal. The 1951 hymnal included the hymn's first appearance in Free Methodist-Wesleyan hymnody.

There were six 4-line stanzas originally. In our hymnal we use stanzas 1, 2, 3, and a combination of the opening lines of stanzas 5 and 6. The omitted fourth stanza reads:

> Today and Tomorrow with Thee still are Now;
> Nor trouble, nor sorrow, nor care, Lord, hast Thou;
> Nor passion doth fever, nor age can decay,
> The same God for ever as on yesterday.

Smith was born in Aberdeen, took his theological education in Edinburgh, and subsequently served several pastorates in London and elsewhere. In 1876, he became minister of the Free High Church in Edinburgh, remaining there until his retirement in 1893.

ST. DENIO is a Welsh hymn melody, apparently founded on a folksong. The earliest use as a hymn tune is in *Caniadau y Cyssegr,* 1839, produced by John Roberts. In Wales the tune is known as *Joanna.* Note that the tenor imitates the melody in the last score of the music.

4 Let All the World in Every Corner Sing
George Herbert (1593-1632)

The author of the text was a poet greatly admired by John Wesley. This particular poem written c. 1632 is one of 164 poems comprising *The Temple,* 1633. There it is entitled "Antiphon." If we sing it in antiphonal fashion we can better achieve the effect the poet desired.

Izaak Walton, the famous seventeenth-century author and contemporary of Herbert, praised *The Temple* highly when he wrote:

> A book in which, by declaiming his own spiritual conflicts, Herbert hath comforted and raised many a dejected and

discomposed soul and charmed them with sweet and great thoughts.

Walton, who wrote the famous book on fishing *The Compleat Angler,* mentions Herbert in that book where he refers to him as "the holy Herbert." In his biography of Herbert, Walton states: "Thus he lived, and thus he died like a saint, full of alms-deeds, full of humility, and all the examples of a virtuous life."

Another beautiful hymn by George Herbert, also taken from *The Temple,* is the following, originally in seven 4-line stanzas, now generally in abbreviated form. It is found in a number of contemporary British hymnals.

1. King of glory, King of peace,
    I will love Thee;
And, that love may never cease,
    I will move Thee.
Thou hast granted my request,
    Thou hast heard me;
Thou didst note my working breast,
    Thou hast spared me.

2. Wherefore with my utmost art
    I will sing Thee,
And the cream of all my heart
    I will bring Thee,
Though my sins against me cried,
    Thou didst clear me;
And alone, when they replied,
    Thou didst hear me.

3. Seven whole days, not one in seven,
    I will praise Thee;
In my heart, though not in heaven,
    I can raise Thee.
Small it is, in this poor sort
    To enrol Thee:
E'en eternity's too short
    to extol Thee.

UNIVERSAL PRAISE was composed for this text by Walter Grenville Whinfield (1865-1919), an Anglican curate. It was published in *The English Hymnal,* 1906.

5 Joyful, Joyful, We Adore Thee
Henry Van Dyke (1852-1933)

This hymn was written in 1907 according to Tertius Van Dyke, son of the author. The occasion was during a preaching visit to Williams College in the Berkshires. At breakfast one morning, Van Dyke placed a manuscript before the college president James Garfield and said, "Here is a hymn for you. Your mountains were my inspiration. It must be sung to the music of Beethoven's 'Hymn to Joy.' "

This hymn entered Free Methodist-Wesleyan hymnody in 1951.

HYMN TO JOY, also called BONN and JOY, composed by Ludwig van Beethoven (1770-1827), is derived from the principal theme in the last movement of his *Symphony No. 9*, the *Choral Symphony*. Its use as a hymn tune dates from mid-nineteenth century.

The *Choral Symphony* was written after Beethoven was totally deaf. At the first performance in Vienna, he stood by the orchestra conductor to indicate to him the tempo of each movement but heard neither the music nor the applause.

6 From All That Dwell Below the Skies
Isaac Watts (1674-1748), stanzas 1 and 2
Anonymous, c. 1780, stanzas 3 and 4

In the preface to *The Christian Psalmist or Hymns, Selected and Original,* 1825, James Montgomery wrote:

> Dr. Watts may almost be called the inventor of hymns in our language; for he so far departed from all precedent, that few of his compositions resemble those of his fore-runners — while he so far established a precedent to all his successors, that none have departed from it. . . .

Isaac Watts was born in Southampton, the son of an Independent layman and proprietor of a successful boarding school. He was a precocious youngster, drilled by his father in Latin at four years of age, in Greek at about eight, in French at eleven, and in Hebrew at thirteen. Young Watts chose to attend a nonconformist academy rather than Oxford, for he did not wish to become an Anglican.

Watts's skill as a rhymster was demonstrated at an early age. The story is often told about his dissatisfaction with the psalm singing of his day. The criticism apparently nettled his father who challenged the youth to produce something better. The result was a hymn beginning:

> Behold the glories of the Lamb
> Before His Father's throne.
> Prepare new honors for His Name
> And songs before unknown.

Although in frail health, he was ordained and became minister of Mark Lane Independent Chapel in London, serving for ten years. Forced to relinquish this post because of his health, he went to live in the home of one of his parishioners, Sir Thomas Abney, Lord Mayor of London, intending to stay but a short time. Instead he remained thirty-six years, until his death.

Although known today primarily for his many hymns, Watts's brilliance was recognized during his lifetime for his scholarly writings in many fields, including theology, logic, ethics, astronomy, and pedagogy. An honorary doctorate was conferred on him by the University of Edinburgh.

Watts's *Divine and Moral Songs,* published in 1720, provided religious and moral instruction for generations of children. They contained such oft-quoted lines as "How doth the busy little bee / Improve each shining hour?" and:

> In works of labor or of skill
> I would be busy too;
> For Satan finds some mischief still
> For idle hands to do.

Isaac Watts is buried in the nonconformist cemetery at Bunhill Fields across from Wesley's City Road Chapel in London. Others buried nearby are Susannah Wesley, William Blake, and John Bunyan.

"From All That Dwell Below the Skies," a paraphrase of Psalm 117, appeared in Watts's *Psalms of David, Imitated in the Language of the New Testament,* 1719, in two long-meter stanzas. Later on, it was reprinted in a hymnbook published in York by R. Spence, c. 1780, together with eight additional lines. In this form it was reprinted in John Wesley's *Pocket Hymnbook for the Use of Christians of All Denominations,* 1786. The author of the additional lines is not identified. In the eighth edition, dated 1791, it is hymn number 113 and carries a notation that it is to be sung to the tune STANTON.

"From All That Dwell" has appeared in all Free Methodist hymnals since 1883. It was hymn number 1 in 1883 and 1910. In 1883, 1910, and 1951, a fifth stanza was added consisting of Bishop Ken's doxology, "Praise God from Whom All Blessings Flow."

OLD HUNDREDTH appeared first in the enlarged edition of

the French-Genevan *Psalter*, 1551, to accompany Psalm 134. It has been attributed to Louis Bourgeois, the editor of that edition of the *Psalter*. Kethe's version of Psalm 100 was undoubtedly written for this tune.

Our hymnal has restored the original rhythmic pattern of the Bourgeois tune.

Although we think of such tunes as being somewhat solemn, they were regarded in earlier times as "jocund and lively." Henry Wilder Foote in *Three Centuries of American Hymnody* quotes a nineteenth-century writer as saying, "strange, indeed, that the very tunes that send us to sleep caused our forefathers to dance."

J. S. Bach made at least two harmonizations of OLD HUNDREDTH *in triple time* to German chorale texts. The one for "Herr Gott, dich loben alle wir" gives the melody in this fashion.

An early harmonized version appeared in Day's *Psalter*, 1561, where it accompanied the text "Al peopull y^t on earth do dwel," Note that the melody is in the tenor voice.

7 All People That on Earth Do Dwell
Version of William Kethe (c. 1530-1594), *Scottish Psalter,* 1650
Doxology by John Mason Neale (1818-1866)

This metric version of Psalm 100, called by Longfellow in *The Courtship of Miles Standish* "that grand old Puritan anthem," appeared first in Daye's incomplete *Psalter,* 1561, where it is unsigned. Later evidence indicates that the author was undoubtedly William Kethe. It did not appear in the first complete edition of the Sternhold and Hopkins psalter (Old Version) 1562, but was included in the appendix of the 1564 edition and in the main body of the edition of 1565. It is thus the oldest surviving English metrical psalm still in use that also appeared in Sternhold and Hopkins.

Psalm 100 is one of the few psalms specifically mentioned by William Shakespeare. In *The Merry Wives of Windsor* [II:1] he wrote:

> ...they do no more adhere and keep place together than the Hundredth Psalm to the tune of *Green Sleeves.*

Since Shakespeare's day, *Green Sleeves* has become an acceptable addition to many hymnals, including our 1951 hymnal, but not as a setting for a psalm.

There are a number of textual changes from the 1560-61 *Psalter.*

- 1:3 *fear* changed to *mirth* in the *Scottish Psalter,* 1650, and in a number of older English psalters.
- 2:1 "The Lord ye know" changed to "know that the Lord" in the same sources as the change in stanza 1.
- 2:3 "Folck" changed to "flock," possibly as a result of a printer's error, as early as 1585. It has continued to be the accepted form since that time, because it relates more appropriately to the context.
- 5   John Mason Neale derived this doxology from Tate and Brady (New Version) and it was included in Thring's *Collection,* 1882.

The hymnal of 1951 was the first Free Methodist-Wesleyan hymnal to use this hymn, but without the changes incorporated in the present hymnal.

OLD HUNDREDTH (See No. 6.)

8 We Praise Thee, O God, Our Redeemer
Julia Bulkley Cady Cory (1882-1963)

According to William J. Reynolds in *Hymns of Our Faith,* this hymn was written by Mrs. Cory in 1902 in response to a request by J. Archer Gibson, the organist of Brick Presbyterian Church in New York. It was written to be sung to KREMSER and was first used at Thanksgiving, 1902, in Brick Presbyterian Church and also in another New York City church, the Church of the Covenant.

This is the first appearance in Free Methodist-Wesleyan hymnody.

KREMSER is derived from a Netherlands folk song which appeared in Adrian Valerius's *Nederlandtsch Gedenckelanck,* 1626. From this collection Edward Kremser, the director of a Vienna male choral society, selected six tunes and published them in his *Sechs altniederländische Volkslieder,* 1877, of which *Kremser* is one. There it accompanied a German translation of the Dutch text "We Gather Together to Ask the Lord's Blessing."

9 Now Thank We All Our God
Martin Rinkart (1586-1649)
Translated by Catherine Winkworth (1827-1878)

"Nun danket alle Gott" appeared in Rinkart's *Jesu Hertz-Büchlein* in the edition of 1663. It is assumed that it was also included in the first edition (1636), although no copy is extant. This hymn, known as the German *Te Deum,* was written as a short grace to be sung at the table, *Tisch-Gebetlein,* with a metrical version of the *Gloria Patri,* added as a third stanza. The first two stanzas are based on the Apocryphal Book of Ecclesiasticus (50:22-24). It has been suggested that the choir sing the thanksgiving (stanza 1), the congregation the prayer (stanza 2), and all join in the doxology (stanza 3).

The excellent translation by Catherine Winkworth was published in her *Lyra Germanica,* Second Series, 1858. The reference to the Holy Ghost in the third stanza does not appear in the original German nor in Winkworth's translation.

The 1951 hymnal was the first Free Methodist-Wesleyan hymnal to include the hymn, printing it without alteration. The present hymnal adopted the change in stanza 3 from the *Anglican Hymn Book,* 1965.

Relating it to stanza 1 of this hymn, Dr. Howard A. Smith, Presbyterian minister in Warsaw, Indiana, gave an effective

Thanksgiving address using Psalm 116:12, "What shall I render unto the Lord for all his benefits toward me?" We should render our thanks with "heart and hands and voices."

NUN DANKET appeared in Johann Crüger's *Praxis Pietatis Melica,* 1647, with the Rinkart text. Crüger is usually regarded as the composer. The present form of the melody and much of the harmonization are derived from a chorale in Mendelssohn's *Lobegesang (Hymn of Praise),* 1840.

10 When All Thy Mercies, O My God
Joseph Addison (1672-1719)

Although Addison held a number of important posts in government, his influence was probably most widely felt through writings in *The Spectator, The Tatler, The Guardian,* and *The Freeholder.* It is in the first of these that his five hymns appeared, all within the span of three months in the year 1712. The five are: "The Lord My Pasture Shall Prepare" *(HFL* 402), "When All Thy Mercies, O My God" *(HFL* 10), "The Spacious Firmament on High" *(HFL* 35), "How Are Thy Servants Blest, O Lord" *(HFL* 52), and "When Rising from the Bed of Death."

In *The Spectator* for August 9, 1712, Addison wrote an essay "On Gratitude" which concluded with this paragraph:

> I have already obliged the public with some pieces of divine poetry which have fallen into my hands, and as they have met with the reception which they deserve, I shall, from time to time, communicate any work of the same nature which has not appeared in print, and may be acceptable to my readers.

Then followed the hymn "When All Thy Mercies" in thirteen 4-line stanzas. Our hymnal prints stanzas 1, 6, 7, 11, 13. Stanzas 10 and 12 are worth noting:

> 10. Ten thousand, thousand precious gifts
>   My daily thanks employ;
>   Nor is the least a cheerful heart,
>   That tastes those gifts with joy.
>
> 12. When nature fails, and day and night
>   Divide Thy works no more,
>   My ever grateful heart, O Lord,
>   Thy mercy shall adore.

John Wesley greatly admired Addison and in conversation with Adam Clarke, shortly before his own death, paid this tribute to Addison.

God raised up Mr. Addison, and his associates, to lash the prevailing vices, and ridiculous and profane customs of the country, and to show the excellence of Christianity and Christian institutions.

Addison challenged the writers of his day: "A writer does not have to be obscene to be brilliant."

When Addison was on his deathbed he is reported to have called his wayward step-son the Earl of Warwick to his bedside and exhorted him gently: "See in what peace a Christian can die!"

"When All Thy Mercies" entered Free Methodist hymnody in 1883, using the same five stanzas as in 1976. The suggested tune was *Peterborough* by Ralph Harrison, 1786. The 1910 hymnal used *Geneva*, a tune in fugal style by John Cole (c. 1774-1855). In 1951 the tune used was *Manoah* from Greatorex's *Collection*, 1851.

BANGOR, a Scottish psalm tune, is taken from *The Compleat Melody: or Harmony of Sion*, 1734, by William Tans'ur (1706-1783). This is its first appearance in a Free Methodist hymnal. The tune is mentioned by Robert Burns in his poem "The Ordination."

Tans'ur became an accepted authority by early American composers through the publication of an American edition of *A Compleat Melody in Three Parts*, 1755. No doubt William Billings got his ideas for his "fuguing" pieces by reading the obscure and inaccurate explanations of *canon* and *fugue* by Tans'ur.

One of the tunes from *A Compleat Melody* . . . was included in John Wesley's *Foundery Tune-Book*. There it is called "Tans'ur's Tune."

11 My God, the Spring of All My Joys

Isaac Watts (1674-1748)
Altered by John Wesley (1703-1791)

First published in Book II of *Hymns and Spiritual Songs*, 1707, by Watts, this hymn bore the heading "God's Presence is Light in Darkness." There were five 4-line stanzas originally. Stanza 4, which is omitted in our hymnal, reads:

> My soul would leave this heavy clay
>   At that transporting word,
> Run up with joy the shining way,
>   T'embrace my dearest Lord.

John Wesley's alterations in *Psalms and Hymns,* 1741, changed it from a hymn "about God" to one addressed "to God." Thus, stanza 2 in Watts, read:

> In darkest shades, if *He* appear,
>   My dawning is begun;
> *He* is my soul's sweet morning star,
>   And *He* my rising sun.

It is interesting that Wesley did not include the hymn in the "Large Hymnbook," 1780, but it was inserted, after Wesley's death, in the eighteenth edition, 1805.

The hymn has been included in all Free Methodist hymnals since 1883. All except in 1976 use five stanzas.

Watts's *Hymns and Spiritual Songs,* 1707, is in three books or sections: "I. Collected from the Scriptures; II. Compos'd on Divine Subjects; III. Prepared for the Lord's Supper." There is a preface in the form of an essay "Towards the Improvement of Christian Psalmody, by the Use of Evangelical Hymns in Worship, as well as the Psalms of David."

"My God, the Spring of All My Joys" appears in Book II. "When I Can Read My Title Clear" *(HFL* 450) is also found in Book II. Three other hymns from Book II are "Come, Ye That Love the Lord" *(HFL* 50) "Come, Holy Spirit, Heavenly Dove" *(HFL* 200) and "Alas, and Did My Savior Bleed?" *(HFL* 513). "When I Survey" *(HFL* 510) is found in Book III.

An excerpt from the preface might as well be addressed to many twentieth-century worshipers.

> While we sing the Praises of our God in his Church, we are employ'd in that part of Worship which of all others is the nearest a-kin to Heaven; and 'tis pity that this of all others should be perform'd the worst upon Earth.... To see the dull indifference, the negligent and the thoughtless Air that sits upon the Faces of a whole Assembly while the Psalm is on their Lips, might tempt even a charitable Observer to suspect the fervency of Inward Religion, and 'tis much to be fear'd that the minds of most of the Worshippers are absent or unconcern'd.

ST. MARTIN'S by William Tans'ur, Sr. (1706-1783) has been associated with this hymn in all the Free Methodist hymnals since 1883. It is still sung by the alumni at Harvard commencements to the Tate and Brady version of Psalm 78. The first appearance of *St. Martin's* was in Tans'ur's *The Compleat Melody,* or *Harmony of Sion,* published in England in 1734. It ran through many editions including American editions beginning in 1755 under the title *The Royal Melody Compleat.* An early form was published in Newburyport in 1769.

12 Through All the Changing Scenes of Life
Nahum Tate (1652-1715) and Nicholas Brady (1659-1726)

This version of Psalm 34 first appeared in *A New Version of the Psalms of David, Fitted to the Tunes Used in Churches,* 1696, in eighteen 4-line stanzas. In the second edition of 1698 the hymn was revised. We have drawn our hymn from that revised form, using stanzas 1, 3, 8, and 18 together with Tate and Brady's doxology. The 1976 hymnal is the first Free Methodist-Wesleyan hymnal to include it.

The Psalter is dedicated to "His Most Excellent Majesty / William III / of / Great Britain, France, / and Ireland / KING, / Defender of the Faith...." The presentation page reads in part as follows:

> At the Court at Kensington
> December 3, 1696
> Present
> The King's Most Excellent Majesty
> in Council

Upon the Humble Petition of Nicholas Brady and Nahum Tate, this Day read at the Board, setting forth, that the Petitioners have, with their utmost Care and Industry, compleated A New Version of the Psalms of David in English Metre, fitted for Publick Use; and humbly praying His Majesty's Royal Allowance, that the said Version may be used in such Congregations as shall think fit to receive it.

His Majesty taking the same into His Royal consideration, is pleased to Order in Council, that the said New Version ... be, and the same is hereby Allowed and Permitted to be used in all Churches, Chappels and Congregations, as shall think fit to receive the Same.

IRISH was first published in *A Collection of Hymns and Poems* (Dublin, 1749), probably edited by John Frederick Lampe (1703-1751). Lampe was an excellent German bassoonist and composer who, after settling in England, came under the influence of the Wesleys. His book *Hymns on the Great Festivals, and Other Occasions,* 1746, was the first book of tunes written expressly for the hymns of Charles Wesley. It contained twenty-four hymn tunes.

In Ireland the tune IRISH is sung to the text "O God Our Help in Ages Past." This marks its first appearance in a Free Methodist-Wesleyan hymnal.

13 Great God of Nations
Alfred Alexander Woodhull (1810-1836)

In its original form this American Thanksgiving hymn began "God of the Passing Year to Thee." The author was a medical doctor practicing in Princeton, New Jersey. His hymn appeared in the official edition of the Presbyterian *Psalms & Hymns,* Princeton, 1829. In the 1849 Methodist hymnal this hymn appears anonymously under the heading "National Blessings."

The hymn entered Free Methodist hymnody in 1883 in five stanzas. Stanza 3, omitted in 1951 and 1976, read as follows:

> Here freedom spreads her banner wide
> And casts her soft and hallowed ray;
> Here thou our fathers' steps didst guide
> In safety through their dangerous way.

The hymn did not appear in the 1910 hymnal.

MENDON was first observed in Ephraim Reed's *Musical Monitor,* third edition, 1824, according to Leonard Ellinwood, editor of *The Hymnal 1940 Companion.* Then it was included in the supplement of Samuel Dyer's *New Selection of Sacred Music,* third edition, 1825. Lowell Mason is credited with assigning the name "Mendon," after a town by that name in Massachusetts.

In our hymnal of 1883 the suggested tune was *Bridgewater,* a "fuguing" tune by Lewis Edson, 1800.

14 Great God, We Sing that Mighty Hand
Philip Doddridge (1702-1751)

This hymn was written in 1740 and published posthumously in 1755 by the author's friend Job Orton in *Hymns Founded on Various Texts in the Holy Scriptures. By the late Reverend Philip Doddridge, D.D. Published from the Author's Manuscript....* It appeared under the general heading "Help obtained of God, Acts 26:22. For the New Year."

This is the first inclusion of this hymn in a Free Methodist-Wesleyan hymnal.

Doddridge was well acquainted with Isaac Watts. One of his books is dedicated to Watts. It is *The Rise and Progress of Religion in the Soul...,* 1744, and apparently was written at the insistence of Dr. Watts.

WAREHAM is taken from *A Sett of New Psalm Tunes and Anthems in Four Parts,* 1738, by William Knapp (1698-1768), where it was set to a portion of Psalm 36. There it is headed "for ye holy Sacrament." Wareham is the name of Knapp's birthplace. Except for one skip the melody is entirely diatonic.

The original form of the melody, which was in the tenor, is as follows:

15 The God of Abraham Praise

Daniel ben Judah (14th century)
Paraphrased version of <i>The Yigdal</i> by Thomas Olivers (1725-1799)</div>

The thirteen articles of the Hebrew Creed were drawn up by Moses Maimonides (1130-1205 A.D.). The metrical form of the *Yigdal* was believed to be the work of Daniel ben Judah in about the fourteenth century.

It is said that Thomas Olivers, an associate of the Wesleys, heard the *Yigdal* sung in the Great Synagogue, Duke's Place, Aldgate, London, and was so moved by the experience that he rendered the Hebrew text into English. He gave it, as he told a friend, "as far as I could, a Christian character." The actual writing of the hymn is believed to have been done in the home of John Bakewell in Greenwich.

In the estimate of James Montgomery *(The Christian Psalmist,* (1825), "There is not in our language a lyric of more majestic style, more elevated thought, or more glorious imagery...."

Olivers's original paraphrase consisted of twelve 8-line stanzas.

This hymn appeared in the Free Methodist hymnals of 1883 (stanzas 1-4, unaltered, suggested tune *John Street* by George Coles); 1910 (stanzas 1-4, unaltered, tune *John Street);* 1951 (text greatly altered, tune *Leoni);* 1976 (stanzas 1, 2, 4, 12, unaltered).

Thomas Olivers was, for all his humble origin, a self-taught scholar who was entrusted with the correction of many of John Wesley's publications while in the process of printing. John Fletcher said that he, Olivers, was

> twenty-five years ago, a mechanic, and, like "one" Peter, "alias" Simon the fisherman, and like "one" Saul, "alias" Paul a tent-maker, he had the honour of being promoted to the dignity of a Preacher of the Gospel; and his talents as a

writer, a logician, a poet, and a composer of sacred music, are known to those who have looked into his publications.

Olivers died in 1799 and is buried in John Wesley's tomb in the small burying ground behind City Road Chapel in London.

LEONI (YIGDAL) is named after Meyer Lyon, or Leoni (1751-1797), the chief singer of the Great Synagogue where Olivers first heard the Hebrew Doxology. Lyon provided Olivers with the melody and it was by Olivers's instructions that the tune was named *Leoni*.

Rabbi Francis L. Cohen supplied Julian with a copy of the melody as it was sung at that time. In Cohen's opinion the hymn was sung in unison in the Synagogue of Leoni's day, with an accompaniment provided by specially appointed singers. Cohen's version follows:

16 I Sing the Almighty Power of God
Isaac Watts (1674-1748)

This hymn appeared first in Watts's *Divine Songs Attempted in Easy Language, for the Use of Children,* 1715, in eight 4-line stanzas. It bore the title "Praise for Creation and Providence."

The 1951 hymnal introduced this hymn to Free Methodist-Wesleyan hymnody. (See also comments at No. 6.)

ELLACOMBE, named for a village in Devonshire, England, appeared first in *Gesangbuch der Herzogl Wirtemburgischen katholischen Hofkapelle,* 1784. This collection was made for use in the private chapel of the Duke of Wirtemburg.

17 God the Omnipotent
Henry Fothergill Chorley (1808-1872)

This hymn was written for Lvov's tune by Henry F. Chorley, music critic for the London *Times,* and published in John

Hullah's *Part Music,* 1842, in four 4-line stanzas. Our hymnal prints stanzas 2-4. The omitted first stanza is:

> God the all-terrible! King, who ordainest
> Great winds Thy clarions, the lightnings Thy sword,
> Show forth Thy pity on high where Thou reignest:
> Grant to us peace, O most merciful Lord.

John Ellerton wrote an imitation of this hymn in 1870 during the Franco-Prussian war. His first stanza begins, "God the Almighty One, wisely ordaining." A number of hymnals combine centos from the Chorley and the Ellerton versions.

Our 1910 hymnal prints the Chorley version in its entirety with the last line of the first three stanzas altered. The 1951 hymnal follows 1910 except stanza 1 is omitted.

In 1976 stanza 1 is also omitted. The remaining stanzas use the form of the text found in *Hymns Ancient and Modern.* Our stanza 3 is Chorley's fourth.

RUSSIAN HYMN, by Alexis Feodorovich Lvov (1799-1870), was written in 1833 at the request of Tsar Nicholas I who wanted a national anthem for Russia. In his *Memoirs,* Lvov told of accompanying Emperor Nicholas on a trip to Prussia and Austria in 1833. On returning, he wrote:

> I heard that the Emperor had expressed regret that Russia had no national hymn, and as he was tired of the English tune that had been used, I was asked to write a national anthem for Russia.

The tune has been used as a motif in a number of symphonic compositions including the *1812 Overture* by Tchaikovsky.

18 Praise My Soul, the King of Heaven
Henry Francis Lyte (1793-1847)

This paraphrase of Psalm 103 was first printed in Lyte's *Spirit of the Psalms,* 1834, in five 6-line stanzas. It entered Free Methodist hymnody in 1883 in three stanzas (1-3). The suggested tune was *Sicilian Mariners' Hymn.* It was omitted in 1910. In 1951 it was printed with the fourth stanza omitted and set to the *Lauda Anima* tune. The hymn is printed in its entirety in our present hymnal. The only alteration is the substitution of "Alleluia! Alleluia!" for "Praise Him! Praise Him!" in each stanza. Stanza 4 may be omitted according to the suggestion included in the original publication in 1834.

This hymn was sung at the wedding of King George VI and Queen Mary on April 26, 1923.

An interesting effect can be achieved by singing the alleluias in canon. The second part will begin on the third syllable of the first alleluia.

LAUDA ANIMA was written by Sir John Goss (1800-1880) for this text and published in 1869 in The Brown-Borthwick, *Supplemental Hymn and Tune Book, third edition, with New Appendix.* A notation on the original manuscript indicates it was composed on July 15, 1868.

Goss was organist at St. Paul's in London from 1838 until his retirement in 1872. According to Stanley L. Osborne in *If Such Holy Song,* 1976, Goss was knighted in 1872 and received an honorary D.Mus. degree from Cambridge in 1876.

19 Jesus, We Look to Thee

Charles Wesley (1707-1788)

This hymn appeared in our hymnals in 1883 and 1910 but was omitted in 1951. It is now restored in 1976. It was written by Charles Wesley and included in *Hymns and Sacred Poems,* Vol II, Part II, 1749, in four 8-line stanzas. It is headed "At Meeting of Friends." *HFL* follows the original text except that the first half of Wesley's stanza 2 is omitted as well as all of stanza 4.

The omitted sections are:

2a. Not in the name of pride
    Or selfishness we meet;
From nature's paths we turn aside,
    And worldly thoughts forget,
4. Thou wilt to us make known
    Thy nature and Thy name,
Us who our utmost Savior own,
    From every touch of blame,
From every word and deed,
    From every thought unclean,
Our Jesus till our souls are freed
    From all remains of sin.

DOMINICA was composed by Sir Herbert Stanley Oakeley (1830-1903) for the 1875 edition of *Hymns Ancient and Modern.* Oakeley was professor of music in the University of Edinburgh for a number of years. He was knighted in 1876 and made Composer of Music to Her Majesty in Scotland.

20 Stand Up and Bless the Lord
James Montgomery (1771-1854)

This hymn was written for the anniversary of Red Hill Wesleyan Sunday School, Sheffield, March 15, 1824. It was altered slightly, changing "children" to "people" in the second line, when Montgomery included it in his *Christian Psalmist*, 1825, in six 4-line stanzas.

The hymn was altered to begin "Arise and Bless the Lord" in the hymnals of 1883, 1910, and 1951. The 1976 hymnal restores Montgomery's opening line. In all four hymnals the fourth stanza is omitted. It reads:

> There with benign regard
>   Our hymns He deigns to hear;
> Though unrevealed to mortal sense,
>   The spirit feels them near.

ST. THOMAS is thought to have been written by Aaron Williams (1731-1776) since it appears in his *New Universal Psalmodist*, 1770. It had been published earlier in *The Universal Psalmodist*, 1763, in a considerably longer version. Williams was a man of various talents — composer, music teacher, and music engraver. On Sundays he was clerk of a Scottish church in London Wall.

Another tune, also called ST. THOMAS, does not resemble the Williams tune.

21 We Worship Thee, Almighty God
Johan Olof Wallin (1779-1839)
Translated by Charles Wharton Stork (b. 1881)

Johan Olof Wallin is regarded as Sweden's greatest hymnwriter and a hymnbook editor of eminence. The official Psalmbook of the Church of Sweden, *Den Swenska Psalmboken*, for which he was largely responsible, served virtually without revision from 1819 to 1937.

Longfellow mentions Wallin in his translation of Tegnér's Swedish poem "Children of the Lord's Supper":

> And with one voice
> Chimed in the congregation, and sang an anthem
>   immortal
> of the sublime Wallin, of David's harp in the
>   Northland.

Wallin's philosophy of hymnody demanded that every hymn meet high standards:

> A new hymn, aside from the spiritual considerations, which must never be compromised in any way, should be so correct, simple, and lyrical in form and so free from inversions and other imperfections in style, that after the lapse of a hundred years, a father may be able to say to his son, "Read the Psalmbook, my boy, and you will learn your mother tongue!"

(Quoted by J. Irving Erickson in *Twice-Born Hymns*)

Wallin earned a Ph.D. degree at age twenty-four, received the chief prize for poetry at the university on two occasions, went on to be ordained, become a pastor, then a bishop, and finally, in 1837, Archbishop of Sweden.

"We Worship Thee, Almighty God," known as the Swedish *Te Deum*, is the first appearance of a Wallin hymn in Free Methodist-Wesleyan hymnody.

TER SANCTUS is taken from the *Rostockerhandboken*, 1529.

22 Lo, God Is Here!

Gerhardt Tersteegen (1697-1769)
Translated by John Wesley (1703-1791)

This hymn and the following one are translations of the same German hymn by Tersteegen, *Gott ist gegenw*ärtig. In its original form it appeared in *Geistliches Blumeng*ärtlein, 1729, in eight 10-line stanzas. It was headed "Remembrance of the Glorious and Delightful Presence of God." It was hymn number 581 in the *Herrnhut Collection*, and it was probably from this source that John Wesley made his translation. One German writer called it "A hymn of deepest adoration of the All Holy God, and a profound introduction to blessed fellowship with Him."

"Lo, God Is Here" is a rather free translation by John Wesley in six 6-line stanzas and is included in his *Hymns and Sacred Poems*, Part II, 1739. The single alteration is given below:

> 1:2 And own how *dreadful* is this place!

Stanza 6 which is omitted in *HFL* reads as follows:

> As flowers their opening leaves display,
>   And glad drink in the solar fire,
> So may we catch Thy every ray,
>   So may Thy influence us inspire:
> Thou Beam of the Eternal Beam,
> Thou purging Fire, Thou quickening Flame!

The 1910 hymnal also included this hymn to the tune

Monmouth from Joseph Klug's *Geistliche Lieder,* 1535, using stanzas 1, 2, and 4.

VATER UNSER (OLD 112th) derives its name from its association with Martin Luther's version of The Lord's Prayer. Its first appearance was in a manuscript part-book given by Johann Walther to Luther in 1530. In 1539 it was published in Valten Schumann's *Geistliche Lieder.*

In English psalters it was associated with Psalm 112, hence the name OLD 112th. It was said to be a favorite of John Wesley and was included by him in the *Foundery Collection,* 1742, calling it *Playford's Tune,* set to the text "Thou Hidden Love of God, Whose Height."

Johann Sebastian Bach based his Cantata No. 101 on the tune VATER UNSER and used it also in a number of other compositions. Mendelssohn used it as the basis for his *Sixth Organ Sonata.*

John Wesley was responsible for the printing of more than one tune book. The first of these was a *Collection of Tunes as they are sung at the Foundery,* 1742, the so-called *Foundery Tune-Book.* It was, as Lightwood remarks in his *Hymn Tunes and their Story,* "one of the worst printed books ever issued from the press ... full of extraordinary mistakes...." It was nevertheless a remarkable book for it revealed something of John Wesley's taste in hymn tunes. Among the forty-two tunes are several still in popular usage, including OLD 112th, OLD 113th *(HFL* No. 27), and HANOVER *(HFL* No. 80).

The large number of hymns coming from the pen of Charles Wesley with their diversity of meters made a new tune book necessary. One issued by a friend of the Wesleys was not considered adequate. John wrote: "I want the People called Methodists to sing true the Tunes which are in *common Use* among them. At the same time I want them to have in One Volume the *best Hymns* which we have printed: and one of an *easy* Price." The result was *Sacred Melody: or a Choice Collection of Psalm and Hymn Tunes,* 1761. It was in the preface of this volume that John Wesley gave his famous rules for singing:

I. Learn these *Tunes* before you learn any others; afterwards learn as many as you please.

II. Sing them exactly as they are printed here, without altering or mending them at all; and if you have learned to sing them otherwise, unlearn it as soon as you can.

III. Sing *All*. See that you join with the congregation as frequently as you can. Let not a slight degree of weakness or weariness hinder you. If it is a cross to you, take it up, and you will find it a blessing.

IV. Sing *lustily* and with a good courage. Beware of singing as if you were half dead, or half asleep; but lift up your voice with strength. Be no more afraid of your voice now, nor more ashamed of its being heard, than when you sung the songs of *Satan*.

V. Sing *modestly*. Do not bawl, so as to be heard above or distinct from the rest of the congregation, that you may not destroy the harmony; but strive to unite your voices together, so as to make one clear melodious sound.

VI. Sing *in Time*. Whatever time is sung be sure to keep with it. Do not run before nor stay behind it; but attend close to the leading voices, and move therewith as exactly as you can; and take care not to sing *too slow*. This drawling way naturally steals on all who are lazy; and it is high time to drive it out from us, and sing all our tunes just as quick as we did at first.

VII. Above all sing *spiritually*. Have an eye to God in every word you sing. Aim at pleasing *Him* more than yourself or any other creature. In order to do this attend strictly to the sense of what you sing, and see that your *Heart* is not carried away with the sound, but offered to God continually; so shall your singing be such as the *Lord* will approve of here, and reward you when He cometh in the clouds of heaven.

Charles Wesley has a hymn entitled "The True Use of Music" (*Hymns and Sacred Poems,* Vol. II, Pt. II, 1749) that is worth comparing with John Wesley's "Rules."

> 1. Listed into the cause of sin
>   Why should a good be evil?
>   Music, alas! too long has been
>   Press'd to obey the devil:
>   Drunken, or lewd, or light the lay
>   Flow'd to the soul's undoing,
>   Widen'd, and strew'd with flowers the way
>   Down to eternal ruin.
>
> 2. Who on the part of God will rise,
>   *Innocent sound* recover,
>   Fly on the prey, and take the prize,
>   Plunder the carnal lover,
>   Strip him of every moving strain,
>   Every melting measure,
>   Music in virtue's cause retain,
>   Rescue the holy pleasure?
>
> 3. Come let us try if Jesu's love
>   Will not as well inspire us:
>   This is the theme of those above,
>   This upon earth shall fire us.
>   Say, if your hearts are tuned to sing,
>   Is there a subject greater?
>   Harmony all its strains may bring,
>   Jesus's name is sweeter.

5. Who hath a right like us to sing,
      Us whom His mercy raises?
   Merry our hearts, for Christ is King,
      Cheerful are all our faces:
   Who of His love doth once partake
      He evermore rejoices:
   Melody in our hearts we make,
      Melody with our voices.

6. He that a sprinkled conscience hath,
      He that in God is merry,
   Let him sing psalms, the Spirit saith,
      Joyful, and never weary,
   Offer the sacrifice of praise,
      Hearty, and never ceasing,
   Spiritual songs and anthems raise,
      Honour, and thanks, and blessing.

7. Then let us in His praises join,
      Triumph in His salvation,
   Glory ascribe to love Divine,
      Worship, and adoration:
   Heaven already is begun,
      Open'd in each believer;
   Only believe, and still sing on,
      Heaven is ours for ever.

The *Minutes of the Conferences,* e.g., those for 1763, 1765, and 1768, contain further injunctions on proper congregational singing. (Extracted in Curwen's *Studies in Worship-Music,* 1880).

Sacred Melody was followed by *Sacred Harmony, or A Choice Collection of Psalm and Hymn Tunes in Two or Three Parts for the Voice, Harpsichord, and Organ,* 1781. In this collection the hymn "Christ the Lord Is Risen Today," *(HFL* No. 172), is set to the Handel tune for "See the Conquering Hero Comes" from *Judas Maccabeus* (See *HFL* No. 178).

23 God Reveals His Presence

Gerhardt Tersteegen (1697-1769)
Translated by Frederick William Foster (1760-1835)
and John Miller, or Mueller (1756-1790)
Altered by William Mercer (1811-1873)

This hymn and the preceding one represent two different versions of the same German hymn. The Foster and Miller translation is in the *Moravian Hymn-Book,* 1789. William Mercer, in his *Church Psalter and Hymn Book,* 1855, omitted one stanza, retained thirteen lines of the original translation, slightly altered another stanza, and rewrote the rest with, as Julian says, "little regard to the German."

Several modern hymnals include this hymn with a number of further alterations. The most common change is to use as an opening line "God Himself Is with Us."

This is the first appearance of this hymn and tune in a Free Methodist-Wesleyan hymnal.

WUNDERBARER KÖNIG, also called ARNDBERG and GRÖNIGEN, first appeared in Joachim Neander's *Glaub-und Liebes-übung,* 1680, and is thought to have been composed by him. Neander (1650-1680) is credited with some sixty hymns and about nineteen hymn tunes. This tune was written by Neander for his hymn beginning with the words "Wunderbarer König," based on Psalm 150:6, entitled "Inciting Oneself to the Praise of God."

24 God of Our Fathers
                              Daniel Crane Roberts (1841-1907)

Roberts was an Episcopalian hymnwriter, born at Bridgehampton, Long Island. This hymn was written in 1876 for the "Centennial" Fourth of July celebration at Brandon, Vermont, in which town Roberts was rector of St. Thomas Episcopal Church at the time. Later he became vicar of St. Paul's Church, Concord, New Hampshire. This is the first Free Methodist-Wesleyan hymnal to include it.

NATIONAL HYMN was composed for these words by George William Warren (1828-1902), organist of St. Thomas Church, New York City. It was included in a musical edition of the 1892 Episcopal hymnal, produced by J. Ireland Tucker and William W. Rosseau in 1894, under the title *Hymnal with Tunes Old and New.* This tune entered Free Methodist-Wesleyan hymnody in 1951 to accompany the text "Heralds of Christ, Who Bear the King's Commands."

25 God of Grace and God of Glory
                              Harry Emerson Fosdick (1878-1970)

This hymn was written at Boothbay Harbor, Maine, for the opening service of Riverside Church in New York City, October 5,

1930. It was sung again at the dedication service, February 8, 1931. Its first publication was in H. Augustine Smith's *Praise and Service,* 1932. This is its first inclusion in a Free Methodist-Wesleyan hymnal.

Fosdick was a Baptist minister and hymnwriter born at Buffalo, New York; professor of practical theology, Union Theological Seminary; minister at Park Avenue and Riverside churches, New York (1926-1946).

CWM RHONDDA was composed by John Hughes (1873-1932). The tune, originally called RHONDDA, was written for the annual Baptist Singing Festival at Capel Rhondda, Pontypridd, Wales, in 1907 (1905 according to some sources). The tune entered Free Methodist-Wesleyan hymnody in 1951. *Cwm* means "low valley." *Rhondda* is the name of a river in Wales. Fosdick is said to have been displeased with this Welsh setting for his hymn. His preference was REGENT SQUARE. He blamed the change on the Methodists! *The Methodist Hymnal,* 1935, edited by Robert Guy McCutchan, wedded the text to this tune.

26 All Creatures of Our God and King
Metrical version of St. Francis's *Canticle of the Sun,* 1225
Translated by William Henry Draper (1855-1933)

The poem *Canticle of the Sun,* also known as *Canticle of the Creatures,* was written by Giovanni Bernardone, commonly known as Francesco. He was born in Assisi in 1182 and died in 1226. He was sainted by Pope Gregory IX in 1228. St. Francis's love of nature is beautifully expressed in this famous poem.

The original Italian text may be examined in Vlastimil Kybal's *Francis of Assisi* (Notre Dame, 1954). Matthew Henry in his critical essay *Pagan and Christian Religious Sentiment* speaks of it thus: "... artless in language, irregular in rhythm, it matches with the childlike genius that produced it, and the simple natures that loved and repeated it...." He then gives a literal translation of the poem of which the following is an excerpt:

O most high, almighty, good Lord God, to thee belong praise, glory, honour and all blessing!
Praised be my Lord God with all his creatures; and specially our brother the sun, who brings us the day, and who brings us the light; fair is he, and shining with a very great splendour: O Lord, he signifies to us thee!
Praised be my Lord for our sister the moon, and for the stars, the which he has set clear and lovely in heaven.

Praised be my Lord for our brother the wind, and for air and cloud, calms and all weather, by the which thou upholdest in life all creatures.

Our metrical version of the poem was written by William Henry Draper when he was Anglican rector of a Yorkshire parish. The exact date is unknown. It was written for a Whitsuntide Festival for children at Leeds. Originally there were seven stanzas, of which we print 1, 2, 3, 5, and 7.

This is the first appearance of the text in Free Methodist-Wesleyan hymnody.

LASST UNS ERFREUEN, also called EASTER SONG, ST. FRANCIS, and VIGILES ET SANCTI, was originally set to the Easter text "Lasst uns erfreuen herzlich sehr." It comes from the *Catholische Geistliche Kirchengesäng,* 1623. Ralph Vaughan Williams is generally credited with taking this German tune, lengthening it, harmonizing it, and including it with the text, "Ye Watchers and Ye Holy Ones," in *The English Hymnal,* 1906.

27 I'll Praise My Maker While I've Breath
Isaac Watts (1674-1748)
Altered by John Wesley (1703-1791)

This hymn was published in Watts's *The Psalms Imitated...,* 1719, in six 6-line stanzas. It was headed "Praise to God for His Goodness and Truth." It is based on Psalm 146. John Wesley had a high regard for this hymn and was heard repeating parts of it on his deathbed. He included it in at least three of his collections: *The Charles-Town Collection,* 1737; *A Collection of Psalms and Hymns,* 1744; and in the *Wesleyan Hymnbook,* 1780.

The 1883 Free Methodist hymnal printed four stanzas of the hymn. The suggested tune was *Jefferson Street* by Isaac B. Woodbury. The 1910 hymnal also used four stanzas to the tune *Southhampton*. It was omitted in 1951.

The alterations made by John Wesley have been widely adopted. As Watts wrote the hymn:

1:1 "with my breath"
2* Why should I make a Man my Trust?
Princes must die and turn to Dust;
Vain is Help of Flesh and Blood;
Their Breath departs, their Pomp and Power
And Thoughts all vanish in an Hour;
Nor can they make their Promise good.
3 (no change)

> 4:1 "The Lord hath Eyes to give the blind;"
> :2 "The Lord supports the sinking Mind;"
> 5* He loves His Saints; he knows them well,
>   But turns the Wicked down to Hell:
>   Thy God O Zion ever reigns:
>   Let every Tongue, let every Age
>   In this exalted Work engage;
>   Praise him in everlasting Strains.
> 6 (no change)
> *Stanzas omitted by Wesley.

(See also comments at No. 6.)

OLD 113th, also known as LUCERNE, can be traced to the Strassburg *Kirchenampt*, 1525. From there it was taken into Calvin's *Aulcuns pseaulmes*, 1539, from thence into the French-Genevan psalters. It is attributed to Matthäus Greiter, a musician serving in the Strassburg Cathedral. The first English psalter to include it was *Fourscore and Seven Psalmes*, 1561.

John Wesley was fond of this tune and included it in his "Foundery" Tune Book, 1742. It was to this tune that he sang Watts's "I'll Praise My Maker" on the day before his death. (See comments at No. 22.)

28 What Shall I Do, My God, to Love
Charles Wesley (1707-1788)

This hymn which was included in the 1883 and 1910 hymnals, omitted in 1951, is now restored in 1976. It was originally written in eighteen 4-line stanzas. Included here are stanzas 11, 12, 13, 14, and 17. Its first appearance was in *Hymns and Sacred Poems*, 1742, with the heading "Holiness desired." Stanza 1 read as follows:

> O what an evil heart have I,
>   So cold, and hard, and blind,
> With sin so ready to comply,
>   And cast my God behind!

MANCHESTER NEW was written by Robert Wainwright (1748-1782) who was organist at The Old Collegiate Church of Manchester and later at St. Peter's in Liverpool. Dr. Wainwright, an unusually facile organist, once competed for the position of organist of Halifax parish church where a new organ had just been built. James T. Lightwood, in *The Music of the Methodist Hymn-Book*, reports the annoyance of the old organ builder with Wainwright's virtuosity: "Te tevil, te tevil, he run over the key like one cat, he vil not give my pipes room for to shpeak."

This is the first appearance of this tune in a Free Methodist-Wesleyan hymnal.

29, 30 The Lord's My Shepherd, I'll Not Want
Scottish Psalter, 1650

Paraphrases and metrical versions of Psalm 23 abound. This traditional form was derived from a number of earlier versions, each one contributing words, phrases or lines. The 1650 form is preserved unaltered in our 1951 and 1976 hymnals and with a slight change in the 1910 hymnal.

Between the years 1414 and 1889 no fewer than 326 complete or partial versions of the psalter in English were published. All of them are listed in Julian's *Dictionary of Hymnology.* Among the intriguing titles is one by William Hunnis, *Seven Sobs of a Sorrowful Soule for Sinne...*, 1585. Only a few of the many versions attained wide acceptance. A comparison with the opening lines of Psalm 23 as it appeared in other well-known English psalters is instructive.

> My shepherd is the living God,
>   nothing therefore I neede,
> In pastures faire with waters calme
>   he set me for to feede.
> —Sternhold and Hopkins, 1562 (Old Version)

> Jehovah feedeth me, I shall not lack.
> In grassy folds, he down doth make me lye:
>   he gently-leads me, quiet waters by.
> —*Ainsworth Psalter,* 1612

> The Lord to mee a shepheard is,
>   want therefore shall not I.
> Hee in the folds of tender-grasse
>   doth cause me down to lie:
> —*The Bay Psalm Book,* 1640

> Since God does me, his worthless Charge,
>   Protect with tender Care,
> As watchful Shepherds guard their Flocks,
>   What can I want or fear?
> —Tate and Brady, 1696 (New Version)

CRIMOND, melody generally ascribed to Jessie Seymour Irvine (1836-1887), appeared first in William Carnie's *Northern Psalter,* Aberdeen, 1872. The harmonization is by David Grant. The tune is gaining in acceptance as the proper setting for this metrical psalm. It was used at the wedding of Queen Elizabeth II and Prince Philip in Westminster Abbey.

BROTHER JAMES' AIR was written by James Leith Bain (d. 1925). It was incorporated in a choral composition by Gordon Jacob (b. 1895) from which this hymn arrangement is adapted. Ours may be the first hymnal to include it in this form. Dr. Jacob is an English composer and teacher and authority on orchestration.

31 O God, for Thy Redeeming Love
Edwin J. Rix (b. 1928)

The words and music of this hymn were written in April 1970, by an Ontario physician and churchman Edwin J. Rix. It was conceived during the weekly Communion Service in Erindale Bible Chapel and completed, with music, a few days later. Stanzas 1 and 2 relate to Romans 3:24-25; 5:8; and 8:32. Stanza 3 relates to Exodus 25:21-22; Romans 3:25; and Hebrews 10:19-22.

Dr. Rix was born in Norwich, Norfolk, England, December 9, 1928. He is married and has four children. He met his wife through involvement in InterVarsity Fellowship. His medical training was in Birmingham Medical School. About a year after graduation he emigrated to Newfoundland and subsequently to Ontario.

Dr. Rix is a violinist and violist and currently plays viola with the Mississauga Symphony. In addition to active involvement in his church he is a member of the Gideons and serves on the IVCF Area Committee.

ERINDALE is the tune title selected by Dr. Rix. It gets its name from Erindale Bible Chapel in Mississauga, Ontario, with which Dr. Rix is associated.

32 My God, How Wonderful Thou Art
Frederick William Faber (1814-1863)

This was first published in the author's *Jesus and Mary*, 1849, in nine 4-line stanzas. It bore the title "The Eternal Father." It entered Free Methodist hymnody in 1883 using seven of the nine stanzas, omitting stanzas 6 and 8. It was omitted in 1910 but restored in 1951. In 1976, stanzas 1, 3, 4, and 5 were chosen. The only alterations are in stanza 2 where Faber wrote: "How beautiful, how beautiful" and "awful purity."

Faber, priest of the Oratory of St. Philip Neri, London, had two purposes, he said, in composing his hymns:

> ... first, to furnish some simple and original hymns for singing; secondly, to provide English Catholics with a hymn-book for reading, in the simplest and least involved metres; and both these objects have not unfrequently required considerable sacrifice in a literary point of view.

Just as St. Ambrose, Martin Luther, and Charles Wesley, among others, wrote hymns to promote true doctrine and to combat heresy, Faber wrote hymns to counteract what he regarded as the heresy of Protestantism. He wrote that "There is scarcely anything which takes so strong a hold upon people as religion in metre, hymns or poems on doctrinal subjects." Then he mentions the influence of Wesley's hymns and the Olney collection.

Evangelicals in every denomination might be instructed in the use of hymns by Faber's further comment:

> Catholics even are said to be sometimes found poring with a devout and unsuspecting delight over the verses of the Olney Hymns, which the Author himself can remember acting like a spell upon him for years, strong enough to be for long a counter influence to very grave convictions, and even now to come back from time to time unbidden into the mind.

ST. STEPHEN, also called NAYLAND, by William Jones (1726-1800) was included in his *Ten Church Pieces for the Organ, with Four Anthems in Score, Composed for the Use of the Church of Nayland, in Suffolk, and Published for its Benefit,* 1789. It was set to the Sternhold version of Psalm 23.

33 For the Beauty of the Earth
Folliott Sandford Pierpoint (1835-1917)

This hymn was included in the second edition of Orby Shipley's *Lyra Eucharistica,* 1864, in eight 6-line stanzas, where it was entitled "The Sacrifice of Praise." It was intended as a hymn to be sung at the celebration of Holy Communion. Our restoration of much of Pierpoint's original language confirms its appropriateness as a Communion hymn. Note Hebrews 13:15: "By him therefore let us offer the sacrifice of praise to God continually, that is, the fruit of our lips giving thanks to his name." It has been used extensively as a children's hymn also.

In the present hymnal, stanzas 1, 2, 3, 4, 5, and 6 are used, with 5 and 6 interchanged and 5 considerably altered. Originally it read:

> For each perfect gift of thine,
>   To our race so freely given,
> Graces human and divine,
>   Flowers of earth and birds of heaven,
> Christ, our God, . . .

This hymn entered Free Methodist-Wesleyan hymnody in 1951.

DIX by Conrad Kocher (1786-1872) was included in his collection of tunes, *Stimmen aus dem Reiche Gottes,* 1838. Kocher was organist of the Stiftskirche in Stuttgart for nearly forty years. The tune name and the shortened form of the tune derive from its association with the hymn "As with Gladness Men of Old" by William Chatterton Dix in the original musical edition of *Hymns Ancient and Modern,* 1861, where it was arranged by William Henry Monk (1823-1889).

34 God of Concrete, God of Steel
Richard Granville Jones (b. 1926)

This fine contemporary hymn was written in 1964 for a youth group. The author is a Methodist clergyman in England. One of the first hymnals to include it was *100 Hymns for Today: A Supplement to Hymns Ancient and Modern,* 1969, where it is headed "The Earth is the Lord's." In the same year, it was published in *Hymns & Songs: A Supplement to the Methodist Hymn-Book.*

RATISBON appears to have been derived from *Jesu, meines Zuversicht,* a melody included in C. Runge's *Geistliche Lieder und Psalmen,* 1653. In nearly its present form it was set to the hymn "Jesu, meines Lebens Leben" in Johann G. Werner's *Choralbuch zu den neuen protestantischen Gesangbüchern,* 1815. Since the harmonization is the same as that included in *Hymns Ancient and Modern,* it has been attributed to William H. Monk (1823-1889), its musical editor.

35 The Spacious Firmament on High
Joseph Addison (1672-1719)

This paraphrase of Psalm 19 is one of the five hymns of Addison written within the span of three months and appended to articles printed in *The Spectator*. This one was added to an essay entitled "Faith and Devotion" and was dated August 23, 1712.

An excerpt from the essay shows the setting for the hymn:

> Those who delight in reading books of controversy, which are written on both sides of the question on points of faith, do very seldom arrive at a fixed and settled habit of it. They are one day entirely convinced of its important truths, and the next meet with something that shakes and disturbs them. The doubt which was laid revives again, and shows itself in new difficulties, and that generally for this reason, because the mind, which is perpetually tossed in controversies and disputes, is apt to forget the reasons which had once set it at rest, and to be disquieted with any former perplexities, when it appears in a new shape, or is started by a different hand. As nothing is more laudable than an inquiry after truth, so nothing is more irrational then to pass away our whole lives without determining ourselves one way or other on those points which are of the last importance to us.

This hymn has been included in all Free Methodist hymnals, always to the tune *Creation*. There are no alterations except to change "nor" in 3:3 to "no."

One phrase of this hymn was turned into a delightful pun by Sir William Harcourt in chiding a certain gentleman by the name of Knightly for his fondness of boasting about his ancestry.

> And Knightly to the listening earth
> Repeats the story of his birth.

(Recounted in Percy Dearmer and Archibald Jacob, *Songs of Praise Discussed.*)

CREATION, or HAYDN, is an adaptation of the chorus, "The Heavens Are Telling," from *The Creation* by Franz Joseph Haydn (1732-1809). He declared that: "Never was I so pious, as when composing *The Creation*. I knelt down every day and prayed God to strengthen me for my work." He was undoubtedly sincere when he wrote the words *Laus Deo* (Praise God!) at the end of each of his compositions.

Sir Donald Francis Tovey in *Essays in Musical Analysis*, Vol. V, is the source of this account:

> Haydn's last appearance in public was at a performance of *The Creation* in Vienna.... At the outburst "and there was light" he pointed a trembling hand upwards and was heard by those near him to say, "It came from thence." He was evidently much moved, and could not stay after the first part.

Part I of *The Creation* concludes with "The Heavens Are

Telling."

The arranger of the hymn tune version is unknown but may have been Isaac B. Woodbury, since it is found in his *Dulcimer, or New York Collection of Sacred Music,* 1850. Another earlier collection reported to have included it is *The National Psalmist,* 1848, edited by Lowell Mason and George J. Webb.

36 Songs of Praise the Angels Sang
James Montgomery (1771-1854)

This hymn was published in the eighth edition, 1819, of Thomas Cotterill's *Selection of Psalms and Hymns for Public and Private Use,* in six 4-line stanzas. It was headed "God worthy of all Praise." The omitted sixth stanza reads:

> Borne upon their latest breath,
> Songs of praise shall conquer death;
> Then amidst eternal joy
> Songs of praise their powers employ.

Our 1976 hymnal introduced this hymn to Free Methodist and Wesleyan congregations.

MONKLAND seems to have been derived from a tune in *Hymn Tunes of the United Brethren,* 1824, edited by John Lees. The present arrangement of the tune and the harmonization is attributed to John Wilkes (d. 1882) who was organist at the Monkland Church, Herefordshire, where Henry Williams Baker, editor of *Hymns Ancient and Modern,* was vicar. In this form it appeared in the original musical edition of *Hymns Ancient and Modern,* 1861.

37 O Lord, Our Lord, in All the Earth
Version of Psalm 8 in *The Psalter,* 1912

In *The Psalter,* 1912, of the United Presbyterian Church, this psalm appears in seven 4-line stanzas. Stanzas 2 and 6 are omitted in *HFL*. The omitted stanzas read:

> 2. From lips of children, Thou, O Lord,
>   Hast mighty strength ordained,
>   That adversaries should be stilled
>   And vengeful foes restrained.
> 6. Thou hast subjected all to him,
>   And Lord of all is he,
>   Of flocks and herds, and beasts and birds,
>   And all within the sea.

CHRISTUS DER IST MEIN LEBEN, also known as *VULPIUS* and *BREMEN*, may be found in *Ein schön geistlich Gesangbuch*, 1609, compiled by Melchior Vulpius. Bach's harmonization is from his *Vierstimmige Choralgesänge*, 1769.

38 God, that Madest Earth and Heaven
Stanza 1 by Reginald Heber (1783-1826)
Stanza 2 by Richard Whately (1787-1863)

The original hymn, in one stanza, was first published in Bishop Heber's posthumous *Hymns Written and Adapted to the Weekly Church Service of the Year,* 1827, one of two "Evening" hymns. Heber's hymn seems to have been written about 1822.

The second stanza was written by Richard Whately, Archbishop of Dublin, as a free translation of the ancient Compline Antiphon, "Salve nos, Domine, vigilantes, custodi nos dormientes, ut vigilemus in Christo, et requiescamus in pace." It appeared first in *Sacred Poetry Adapted to the Understanding of Children and Youth. For the Use of Schools,* Dublin, 1838.

This is the first appearance in Free Methodist-Wesleyan hymnody.

AR HYD Y NOS is a traditional Welsh melody commonly used with the words "All through the night." It probably dates from the eighteenth century and may be found in Edward Jones's *Musical Relicks of the Welsh Bards,* 1784. Heber's hymn was likely written for this tune. His sister Mary included both text and tune in the choir book she prepared for use at Hodnet Church.

The text associated with AR HYD Y NOS in Jones's *Musical Relicks* is in both Welsh and English. The English text reads:

> Fain would some with vows persuade me,
>   Ar hyd y nos
> That my faithful swain has fled me;
>   Ar hyd y nos
> But my beating heart will falter,
> Ere it thinks his heart can alter,
>   Ar hyd y nos.

39 He's Everything to Me
Words and Music by Ralph Carmichael (b. 1927)

This song was written in 1964 by Ralph Carmichael as a part of the musical score for the Billy Graham film, *The Restless Ones*.

40 The Man Who Once Has Found Abode
Metrical Version of Psalm 91 from *The Book of Psalms,* 1871

This is the first appearance in a Free Methodist-Wesleyan hymnal of this metrical version of Psalm 91, taken from *The Book of Psalms* of the United Presbyterian Church. There are eleven stanzas in the original.

TALLIS' CANON was one of nine tunes contributed by Thomas Tallis to the psalter written by Matthew Parker, Archbishop of Canterbury, in about 1557 and printed about 1560. *(The whole Psalter, translated into English metre, with an argument and collect to each Psalm:* John Daye, London, n.d.) There was one tune in each of the eight modes and one set to the hymn "Veni Creator."

TALLIS' CANON is the tune in the eighth mode (Mixolydian, plagal), that in Tallis' words "goeth mild; in modest pace." It was set to Parker's Psalm 67. It is in the form of a canon, or round, with each part entering after the first four notes of the tune. It will be observed that in this harmonization the tenor part carries the complete melody beginning with the fifth note and concluding with the opening four notes.

41 Sing Praise to God Who Reigns Above
Johann Jakob Schütz (1640-1690)
Translated by Frances Elizabeth Cox (1812-1897)

This is a translation of "Sei Lob und Ehr dem höchsten Gut" by Schütz, one of five hymns appended to his tract *Christliches Gedenckbüchlein, . . .* 1675. Miss Cox's translation was included in Orby Shipley's *Lyra Eucharistica,* 1864. There were nine stanzas in the German hymn and eight in the translation by Miss Cox.

Our 1951 hymnal was the first Free Methodist-Wesleyan hymnal to include this hymn. We use stanzas 1, 3, 5, and 7.

MIT FREUDEN ZART is taken from the Bohemian Brethren's *Kirchengesänge,* 1566.

Lightwood in *The Music of the Methodist Hymn-Book* quotes a most interesting commentary contained in a letter from two Bohemian Brethren bishops to Emperor Frederick III, and dated October 12, 1574:

> Our ancestors, living among the Papists, . . . adopted, as an attraction for persons of that description, the practice still continued by us, of singing many of our hymns to the old Gregorian tunes. And as others have borrowed our tunes, so

we have borrowed many from others, especially the Germans, some of which we hear are in other languages sung to worldly songs. . . .

Sections of *Mit Freuden Zart* resemble parts of a number of other tunes including a French secular chanson.

42 To God Be the Glory

Fanny Jane Crosby (1820-1915)

This song appeared first in a Sunday school collection *Brightest and Best,* 1875, compiled by William Howard Doane and Robert Lowry. For some reason it was not included in the six volumes of the popular *Gospel Hymns* compiled by Ira D. Shankey, James McGranahan, and George C. Stebbins. As a consequence it was not well known in this country. Sankey did include it in his *Sacred Songs and Solos,* published in Great Britain. Its present popularity can be attributed to its use in the Billy Graham Crusade in 1954 in England where it was printed in the *Greater London Crusade Song Book.* Because of its effective use in the ministry of the Billy Graham team it has now become one of the most popular gospel songs in this country.

Fanny Crosby (Frances Jane Van Alstyne), blind Methodist hymnwriter, produced songs and hymns numbering in the thousands. For a period of time she supplied three texts weekly for the music publishers Bigelow and Main, totaling at one time 5,400 with another 1,000 or so written for William J. Kirkpatrick and others. She is listed in the *Guinness Book of Records* as our most prolific hymnist.

Even after her marriage to Alexander Van Alstyne, blind musician and teacher, she seems to have been known as Mrs. Fanny Crosby.

On the eighty-eighth anniversary of her birth (March 24, 1908) she sent this birthday message to her friends: "Never cross a bridge until you come to it. Never be discouraged. Never look for evil, but have faith and hope — and love."

Fanny Crosby is buried at Bridgeport, Connecticut. On her tombstone are these words: "She hath done what she could."

TO GOD BE THE GLORY was written by William Howard Doane (1832-1915) for this text. Beyond a doubt this tune contributed greatly to the popularity of the song.

43 Great Is Thy Faithfulness
                    Thomas Obediah Chisholm (1866-1960)

The author was born in Kentucky. At sixteen he became a rural school teacher and then coeditor of a weekly newspaper. He was converted under the ministry of Dr. H. C. Morrison, editor of the *Pentecostal Herald*. For two years Chisholm served as office editor of the periodical and then entered the ministry.

Chisholm began writing poetry at an early age. During his long career he wrote more than a thousand Christian songs. Fanny Crosby lent encouragement to his early work. According to the late Phil Kerr, *Music in Evangelism*, 1939, he was quoted as saying:

> I have sought to be true to the Word, and to avoid flippant and catchy titles and treatment. I have greatly desired that each hymn or poem might have some definite message to the hearts for whom it was written....

This song was written in about 1923 and first published along with the music in *Songs of Salvation*, 1923, compiled by William M. Runyan.

FAITHFULNESS is the title assigned by William M. Runyan (1870-1957), its composer.

44 We Lift Our Voice Rejoicing
                    Words and Music by Jack W. Hayford (b. 1934)

This hymn was chosen from more than nine hundred entries as the winner in a "new hymn contest" conducted by the Billy Graham Evangelistic Association in 1961. It was written by the Reverend Jack W. Hayford, at that time a church youth leader and later, senior pastor of First Foursquare Church of Van Nuys and president of L.I.F.E. Bible College.

The story of the origin of the song is given in Hayford's own words:

> We had just concluded a conference held in the splendor of the autumn-spangled hills near Estes Park, Colorado, in 1960. The grand old hymn "To God Be the Glory" had themed the series there, and returning to Los Angeles I would hum that melody and nostalgically meditate on the beauty and blessing found during those days in the Rockies. Yet as excellent as that praiseful song is, something within me yearned to give vent to a *personal* expression of worship.

One evening, as I left the office for home, the song came to me. Completely, without labored premeditation, sparked by a glimpse of the clear, wind-driven sky which served as a backdrop to a single tree being stripped of its leaves, the words poured forth, together with the melody of the first two lines.... I turned the corner, and was confronted by the mountains north of the city. Walking briskly I added the next words: "Let every hill reecho to this the song we raise." Then, the words of the ransomed multitude in Revelation, chapter five, came to mind — "To Him whose blood hath bought us be glory, power and praise."

It was as though the autumn atmosphere had served as a catalyst to unleash the joy of the Lord in my soul.... Arriving home I went immediately to my study, and within minutes the hymn was completed....

45 I Love to Tell the Story
Arabella Catherine Hankey (1834-1911)

This gospel hymn is taken from the second part of a lengthy poem on "The Life of Jesus in Verse," written in two parts. Part I, entitled "The Story Wanted," was begun in January, 1866. The second part, "The Story Told," was completed in November of the same year. The cento which includes, "I Love to Tell the Story," was included in the author's collection entitled *Heart to Heart,* 1870. The text for the refrain was written in 1869 by William G. Fischer when he composed the original melody.

HANKEY was composed by William Gustavus Fischer (1835-1912), a Methodist musician and choral director in Philadelphia. Perhaps the first appearance of the song in Fischer's setting was in *Joyful Songs,* Nos. 1 to 3, 1869. A second appearance was probably in *Music for Campmeetings,* 1872, but its inclusion in Philip P. Bliss and Ira D. Sankey's *Gospel Hymns and Sacred Songs,* 1875, in its present form did most to draw attention to it.

46 Rejoice, the Lord Is King
Charles Wesley (1707-1788)

This hymn, based on Philippians 4:4, was first published in Wesley's *Hymns for Our Lord's Resurrection,* 1746, in six 6-line stanzas. The omitted stanzas in *HFL* are:

4. He sits at God's right hand,
    Till all His foes submit,
 And bow to His command,
    And fall beneath His feet:
 Lift up your heart, etc.

5. He all His foes shall quell,
    Shall all our sins destroy,
 And every bosom swell
    With pure seraphic joy:
 Lift up your heart, etc.

The only alteration is in 6:2, "Jesus the Judge shall come."
The hymn entered Free Methodist hymnody in 1883 in its complete form. It was reduced to three stanzas in 1951 and increased to four in 1976.

DARWALL'S 148th appeared first in Aaron Williams's *New Universal Psalmodist,* 1770. The tune originally began on the fifth note of the scale. The composer John Darwall (1731-1789) wrote a tune for each of the Psalms. Only that for the 148th has survived. It is in a meter called "Hallelujah Meter" in early American hymnals.

George Frederick Handel wrote three tunes for Charles Wesley hymns, one of which was *Gopsal,* to the text "Rejoice, the Lord is King." (See comments at No. 532.)

47   The King of Love My Shepherd Is
Paraphrase of Psalm 23 by Henry Williams Baker (1821- 1877)

This hymn was first published in the 1868 Appendix to *Hymns Ancient and Modern* in six 4-line stanzas. John Ellerton in his *Notes and Illustrations of Church Hymns,* 1881, wrote:

> It may interest many to know that the third verse of this lovely hymn, perhaps the most beautiful of all the countless versions of Psalm XXIII, was the last audible sentence upon the dying lips of the lamented author on February 12, 1877.

Henry W. Baker was the editor of *Hymns Ancient & Modern.* The first edition was published in 1861 and the Appendix in 1868. The revised edition was issued in 1875, to which he contributed thirty-three metrical litanies and translations and four tunes, harmonized by William Henry Monk.

An earlier paraphrase of Psalm 23 by George Herbert must have provided some of Baker's inspiration. The first stanza reads as follows:

> The God of love my shepherd is
>   And he that doth me feed;
> While he is mine, and I am his,
>   What can I want or need?

Baker's hymn was included in our 1951 hymnal in five stanzas. Stanza 5 was omitted.

DOMINUS REGIT ME was composed in 1868 by John Bacchus Dykes (1823-1876) for this text and included in the Appendix of the first edition of *Hymns Ancient & Modern*. The tune title is the opening phrase of Psalm 23 in the Latin Vulgate.

48 O Thou in Whose Presence

Joseph Swain (1761-1796), stanzas 1, 2, and 4
Anonymous, stanzas 3 and 5

The author of this hymn was a convert of John Rippon, Baptist minister and hymnal compiler in England. Subsequently he became minister of a Baptist congregation. His untimely death interrupted a "popular and useful ministry." He wrote a number of hymns, of which "O Thou in whose presence" entered Free Methodist hymnody in 1883 in six 4-line stanzas.

This hymn was first printed in Swain's *Experimental Essays on Divine Subjects in Verse,* 1791, in nine 8-line stanzas. The authorship of stanzas 3 and 5 cannot be determined but were appropriated from nineteenth-century hymnals. Stanza 3 appears in *Songs of Zion,* 1851. Stanza 5 appears in Beecher's *Plymouth Collection,* 1855.

The two stanzas from the 1883 Free Methodist hymnal, not reprinted in 1976, were apparently by Swain and read:

> 3. O why should I wander an alien from Thee,
>   Or cry in the desert for bread?
>   Thy foes will rejoice when my sorrows they see,
>   And smile at the tears I have shed.

> 4. Ye daughters of Zion, declare, have you seen
>   The star that on Israel shone?
>   Say, if in your tents my Beloved has been,
>   And where with his flocks he is gone.

DAVIS, also called SOUL'S DELIGHT, MEDITATION, and BELOVED, was attributed to Freeman Lewis in *The Methodist Hymnal,* 1878, with the arrangement by Hubert P. Main. It may be found in John Wyeth's *A Repository of Sacred Music,* Part II, 1813, where it is unsigned.

49 Children of the Heavenly Father
Caroline V. Sandell Berg (1832-1903)
Translated by Ernst William Olson (1870-1958)

Lina Sandell, sometimes called the Fanny Crosby of Sweden, wrote 650 hymns. Many of them became popular because of their association with attractive tunes. Jenny Lind, the "Swedish Nightingale," herself a devout Pietist, personally provided funds to print the first edition of Oskar Ahnfelt's *Songs* which contained many of Lina Sandell's hymns.

According to J. Irving Erickson, *Twice-Born Hymns,* 1976, "Children of the Heavenly Father" first appeared in Lina Sandell's *Andeliga daggdroppar* (Spiritual Dewdrops) in 1855. The text and the familiar tune were included by Fredrik Engelke in his *Lofsånger och andeliga wisor,* 1873.

The hymn entered Free Methodist-Wesleyan hymnody in the 1976 hymnal.

TRYGGARE KAN INGEN VARA is said to have been printed anonymously in *Song Book for Sunday Schools,* 1871, in a four-part arrangement by Theodore Söderberg. The tune title is the opening line of the original text which translates "No one can be safer."

50 Come, Ye That Love the Lord
Isaac Watts (1674-1748)
Altered by John Wesley (1703-1791)

This hymn was first published in Watts's *Hymns and Spiritual Songs,* 1707, in ten 4-line stanzas. Its title was "Heavenly Joy on Earth." It has been reprinted in many hymnals with different arrangements of stanzas and numerous alterations. Even Watts himself made changes in later editions.

Evidently John Wesley regarded this hymn highly for he printed it in his *Charles-Town Collection,* 1737, in *A Collection of Psalms and Hymns,* third edition, 1744, and again in the "Large Hymnbook," 1780. Wesley altered a number of lines and it is in this form that Methodists generally sing it.

This hymn entered Free Methodist hymnody in 1883 in nine 4-line stanzas using all except stanza 2 but with a number of alterations. The 1976 hymnal uses stanzas 1, 3, 9, and 10.

The omitted stanzas as they appear in later editions of Watts's are interesting, particularly stanza 2.

2. The Sorrows of the Mind
      Be banisht from the Place!
   Religion never was designed
      To make our Pleasures less.

4. The God that rules on high,
      And thunders when he please,
   That rides upon the stormy Sky,
      And manages the Seas.

5. This awful God is ours,
      Our Father and our Love.
   He shall send down his heavenly Powers.
      To carry us above.

6. There we shall see his Face,
      And never, never sin;
   There, from the Rivers of his Grace,
      Drink endless pleasures in.

7. Yes, and before we rise
      To that immortal State,
   The thoughts of such amazing Bliss.
      Should constant Joys create.

8. The Men of Grace have found
      Glory begun below;
   Celestial Fruits on Earthly Ground
      From Faith and Hope may grow.

Watts is buried in the Bunhill Fields Burying Ground where Susannah Wesley is also interred, across the street from City Road Chapel. (See also comments at No. 6.)

ST. THOMAS, one of two tunes with this name, is found in Aaron Williams's *The New Universal Psalmodist,* 1770. It is derived from a longer tune named *Holborn* found in an earlier edition of the *Universal Psalmodist.* It was included in the *Metrical Tune Book* to accompany "Arise, and Bless the Lord" and incorrectly assigned to William Tans'ur, 1768.

51   O Lord of Heaven and Earth and Sea
Christopher Wordsworth (1807-1885)

This hymn was first published in the third edition of the author's *Holy Year,* 1863, in nine 4-line stanzas under the title "Charitable Collections." The author himself revised the text and it is in this form that the hymn is generally sung. *HFL,* 1976, is the first Free Methodist-Wesleyan hymnal to include it, using stanzas 1, 2, 3, 6, and 9.

Stanza 7 carries a fine stewardship message:

> We lose what on ourselves we spend,
> We have as treasure without end
> Whatever, Lord, to thee we lend,
> Who givest all.

Christopher Wordsworth was the nephew of William Wordsworth whom he frequently visited and with whom he carried on a lengthy correspondence. Julian says that Wordsworth, like the Wesleys, "looked upon hymns as a valuable means of stamping permanently upon the memory the great doctrines of the Christian church. He held it to be 'the first duty of a hymnwriter to teach sound doctrine, and thus to save souls.' "

OLDBRIDGE was written in 1903 by Robert Newton Quaile (1867-1927) and was first published in *The English Hymnal,* 1906.

52 How Are Thy Servants Blest

Joseph Addison (1672-1719)

This is one of five hymns written by Addison within the space of three months during 1712 and appended to essays in *The Spectator*. This hymn, sometimes called a hymn for travelers entitled "On The Wonders of the Deep," followed an essay on "Greatness," dated September 20, 1712. The inspiration for the poem evidently was a trip to the Continent in about 1700 which included a near disastrous voyage on the Mediterranean.

The essay is in the form of a letter which begins:

> Sir,
> Upon reading your essay concerning the pleasure of the imagination, I find, among the three sources of those pleasures which you have discovered, that greatness is one. This has suggested to me the reason why, of all objects that I have ever seen, there is none which affects my imagination so much as the sea, or ocean. . . .

Then the poem follows in ten 4-line stanzas.

This hymn appears in the 1910 and 1976 Free Methodist-Wesleyan hymnals. In 1910 six stanzas were included. In the present hymnal, stanzas 1, 6, 9, and 10 are used with the following alterations:

```
2:1 "Yet then from all my griefs, O Lord,"
 :2 "set me"
 :3 "Whilst"
 :4 "My soul took"
```

3:2 "I'll" instead of "we"
:3 "And" instead of "we"
4:1 "My life, if Thou preservs't my life"
:2 "Thy" instead of "A"
:3 "And death, if death must be my doom"
:4 "my soul" instead of "our souls"

CAITHNESS is from the *Scottish Psalter,* 1635, where it is one of the "common tunes", i.e., tunes which could be used interchangeably for any psalm in common meter. There it is called CATHNES TUNE. The melody (i.e., the tenor) in modern notation is as follows:

53 Before the Great Jehovah's Throne

Isaac Watts (1674-1748)
Altered by John Wesley (1703-1791)

This is a paraphrase of Psalm 100 published in Watts's *Psalms of David,* 1719, in six 4-line stanzas. It is best known in the altered form by John Wesley and published in his *Charles-Town Collection,* 1737, and repeated in the Wesleys' *Psalms and Hymns,* 1741, and consisting of Watts's stanza 2 (altered) and stanzas 3, 5, and 6 (essentially unaltered). Wesley's alteration caused him to be charged by the grand jury at Savannah and accused of "making alterations to the metrical psalms."

> original stanza 1)
>> Sing to the Lord with joyful Voice:
>> Let every Land his Name adore;
>> The British Isles shall send the Noise
>> A-cross the Ocean to the Shore.
>
> (original stanza 2)
>> Nations attend before his Throne
>> With solemn Fear, with sacred Joy.
>> Know that the Lord, . . .
>
> (original stanza 4)
>> We are his People, we his Care,

> Our Souls and all our Mortal Frame:
> What lasting Honours shall we rear
> Almighty Maker, to thy Name?

(original 6:3)
> ...*must* stand

In order to convey the intended meaning of "awful" a number of hymnals have altered the line to read, "Before the Lord Jehovah's Throne," "Before Jehovah's *aweful* Throne," and "Before the great Jehovah's Throne." We have chosen the latter.

This hymn has been included in all Free Methodist hymnals since 1883. (See also comments at No. 6.)

ANGELS' SONG (Song 34) was composed by Orlando Gibbons (1583-1625) and included in George Wither's *Hymnes and Songs of the Church,* 1623, where it is set to Luke 2:13.

54 Holy, Holy, Holy! Lord God Almighty
Reginald Heber (1783-1826)

This hymn was published in the author's *Selection of Psalms and Hymns for the Parish Church of Banbury,* third edition, 1826, and then posthumously by his widow in *Hymns Written and Adapted to the Weekly Church Service of the Church Year,* 1827.

It was intended to be sung on Trinity Sunday, eight weeks after Easter, between the Nicene Creed and the sermon. It is a free paraphrase of Revelation 4:8-11.

Heber was born at Malpas, Cheshire. He became successively Rector of Hodnet, Prebendary of Asaph, and Bishop of Calcutta.

This hymn entered Free Methodist-Wesleyan hymnody in 1910.

NICAEA was composed by John Bacchus Dykes (1823-1876) to accompany Heber's hymn in *Hymns Ancient and Modern,* 1861. It draws its name from the central theme of the hymn and from the fact that the doctrine of the Trinity was established as accepted dogma at an Ecumenical Council held at Nicaea in Asia Minor in A.D. 325.

55 Come, Thou Almighty King

Anonymous

According to John Julian, the earliest form of this hymn had five 7-line stanzas and bore the title "An Hymn to the Trinity." It was included in a four-page undated tract together with Charles Wesley's hymn "Jesus, Let Thy Pitying Eye." From its appearance in other publications beginning in 1757, it may be dated approximately.

In the 1883 Free Methodist hymnal there are five stanzas. The second stanza, omitted in 1976, reads:

> Jesus, our Lord, arise,
> Scatter our enemies,
>   And make them fall;
> Let thine almighty aid
> Our sure defence be made;
> Our souls on Thee be stayed;
>   Lord hear our call.

The only change in 1976 occurs in 5:4 where "Thy" replaces "His."

Note the titles of deity used in the hymn: King, Father, Ancient of Days, Word, Spirit of holiness, Holy Comforter, Spirit of power, and One in Three.

MOSCOW (ITALIAN HYMN) is by Felice de Giardini (1716-1796). Giardini was born in Turin, Italy, but moved to England in about 1750 where his artistry as a violinist won him great favor. He moved in aristocratic circles and came under the influence of the Countess of Huntingdon. She encouraged him to write some hymn-tunes for Martin Madan's, *A Collection of Psalm and Hymn-Tunes Sung at the Chapel of the Lock Hospital,* 1769. Giardini contributed four tunes to this famous tune book which came to be known as *The Lock Collection,* since Madan was chaplain of the Lock Hospital and the book was sold for the benefit of the hospital.

One of Giardini's four tunes, harmonized in three parts, was headed "Hymn to the Trinity" to accompany the hymn "Come, Thou Almighty King."

The titles usually associated with this tune are derived from the country of the composer's birth and the city in which he died.

Originally the thirteenth measure had three repeated notes instead of the arpeggio found here and in many other hymnals. The original form of the melody, except for the second measure, may be found at No. 495.

56 Glory Be to God the Father
Horatius Bonar (1808-1889)

This hymn was published first in Bonar's *Hymns of Faith and Hope,* Third Series, 1866, in four 6-line stanzas. By combining lines, the four stanzas are expanded to five in *HFL* and other hymnals. Stanza 5 may be used separately as a doxology.

This is the first appearance of this hymn in Free Methodist-Wesleyan hymnody.

FREUEN WIR UNS ALL IN EIN, attributed to Michael Weisse (1488-1539), is taken from the first German hymnbook of the Bohemian Brethren, *Ein Neu Gesangbüchlein,* 1531, edited by Weisse. The tune name is the opening line of Weisse's translation into German of an earlier Bohemian Brethren hymn written in 1457. The tune is in the Aeolian mode.

In addition to editing the first Brethren hymnal to contain music, Weisse was a diplomat, poet, and composer.

57 Come, Ever Blessed Spirit
Christopher Wordsworth (1807-1885)

This hymn is a cento from part II of a three-part confirmation hymn entitled, "Father of all, in Whom we live," and printed in Wordsworth's *The Holy Year; or Hymns for Sundays and Holy-days, And Other Occasions,* 1862.

This is the first appearance in a Free Methodist-Wesleyan hymnal. (See also comments at No. 51.)

TUGWOOD is by Nicholas C. Gatty (1874-1946). We have been unable to trace it further.

58 We All Believe in One True God
Tobias Clausnitzer (c. 1619-1684)
Translated by Catherine Winkworth (1827-1878)

This metrical version of *The Apostles' Creed,* beginning "Wir glauben all' an einen Gott, Vater, Sohn und heilgen Geist," appeared first in the *Culmbach-Bayreuth Gesangbuch,* 1668, in three 6-line stanzas. The translation by Catherine Winkworth is in her *Chorale Book for England,* 1863.

Clausnitzer was chaplain to a Swedish regiment and in that capacity preached the Thanksgiving sermon in St. Thomas's

Church, Leipzig, on the accession of Queen Christina to the Swedish throne, succeeding her father Gustavus Adolphus.

WIR GLAUBEN ALL' AN EINEN GOTT is taken from the *Kirchengesangbuch,* Darmstadt, 1699, where it is set to Clausnitzer's hymn.

59 O God, Our Help in Ages Past

Isaac Watts (1674-1748)
Altered by John Wesley (1703-1791)

This hymn is Watts's common meter rendering of Psalm 90:1-5 in nine 4-line stanzas. It appeared in his *Psalms of David Imitated in the Language of the New Testament,* 1719, under the heading "Man, Frail, and God Eternal." Julian rates this as undoubtedly one of Watts's "finest compositions, and his best paraphrase." Erik Routley calls it "the gravest and the most universal of English hymns" *(Hymns and the Faith).*

According to Julian the altered text by John Wesley appeared first in his *Collection of Psalms and Hymns,* Charles-Town, 1737. However a facsimile edition of this book does not contain the hymn. It does appear in *A Collection of Psalms and Hymns,* 1738, and again in the "Large Hymnbook," 1780.

The stanzas omitted in our present hymnal are 4, 6, 7, and 8. The Watts's text altered by Wesley is indicated below:

    1:1 "Our God"
    2:2 "Thy saints have dwelt secure".
    5:1 "Our God"
      :3 "while troubles last"
      :4 Wesley changed "eternal" to "perpetual" but this change is not now widely accepted.

This hymn has been in all Free Methodist hymnals since 1883. The recommended tunes in the *Metrical Tune Book* were *St. Martin's* by William Tans'ur and in 1910, *Dundee.* (See also comments at No. 6.)

ST. ANNE, from *A Supplement to the New Version of Psalms, by Dr. Brady and Mr. Tate...,* sixth edition, 1708, is the tune now most often associated with Watts's text. It is reliably attributed to Dr. William Croft (1678-1727). The present version differs rhythmically from the Croft original. Dr. Croft was organist of St. Anne's Church, Soho, hence the title assigned to the tune. (See also comments at No. 80.)

The opening phrase of the tune has been used by both Handel

and Bach, the latter in his *Triple Fugue in E Flat,* known as "St. Anne's Fugue."

The original version of *St. Anne* was in two voices set to Psalm 42 and was notated as follows:

60 O Splendor of God's Glory Bright

Ambrose of Milan (340-397)
Translation compiled by Louis F. Benson (1855-1930)

Splendor paternae gloriae is one of fourteen hymns reliably attributed to Bishop Ambrose. It is a morning hymn to the Trinity.

There are two English translations in common use, one by Robert S. Bridges in the *Yattendon Hymnal,* 1899, and the other derived by Louis F. Benson, 1910, from that of John Chandler (1806-1876), fellow of Corpus Christi and curate of Witley, published in his *Hymns of the Primitive Church,* 1837.

Benson includes the hymn in *The Hymnal Revised,* 1911, of which he was editor. Omitted stanzas in *HFL* are 3, 5, and 6:

> 3. And now to Thee our prayers ascend,
> O Father, glorious without end;
> We plead with Sovereign Grace for power
> To conquer in temptation's hour.
>
> 5. O joyful be the passing day
> With thoughts as pure as morning's ray,
> With faith like noontide shining bright,
> Our souls unshadowed by the night.

6. Dawn's glory gilds the earth and skies,
   Let Him, our perfect Morn, arise,
   The Word in God the Father One,
   The Father imaged in the Son.

The doxology, our fourth stanza, is from *Hymns Ancient and Modern,* 1904 edition.

Ambrose, bishop of Milan, scholar, statesman, theologian, brilliant defender of the Catholic faith against the Arians of the West, musician and poet, has been called "the Father of Church song." As Julian affirms, he introduced from the East the practice of antiphonal chanting, and began the systematizing of the music of the Church.

This is the first appearance of this splendid hymn in a Free Methodist-Wesleyan hymnal.

PUER NOBIS NASCITUR may be found in an early form in Theodoricus Petri's *Piae Cantiones,* 1582. The present form of the melody is that in Michael Praetorius's *Musae Sionae,* VI, 1609, where it is set to the words "Geborn ist Gottes Söhnelein."

61 O Mighty God, When I Behold the Wonder
Carl Gustaf Boberg (1859-1940)
Translated by E. Gustav Johnson (1893-1974)

"O store Gud, när jag den värld beskådar" appeared first in *Mönsteras-Tidningen,* in March, 1886, having been written the previous summer. Its nine stanzas were translated by E. Gustav Johnson in 1925 and, according to J. Irving Erickson, were published in *The Children's Friend,* organ of the Cromwell Children's Home. A shortened version in five stanzas was printed in *The Covenant Hymnal,* 1931.

Boberg's text was translated into German as "Wie gross bist Du" and it was the Russian version of this German text that Stuart K. Hine, an English missionary residing in the Ukraine, learned and translated into English. Dr. J. Edwin Orr heard the Hine text sung in India and brought it to this country. Two words in stanza one of the Hine text, "words" and "mighty" were changed by Orr to "worlds" and "rolling" and have become the accepted text.

By courtesy of Covenant Press we are introducing to Free Methodist-Wesleyan hymnody this fine Swedish hymn as it has been known to Evangelical Mission Covenant congregations since 1931.

O STORE GUD is the Swedish folk melody to which Boberg's

text was first sung. The first published arrangement in 1891 was by Erik Adolf Edgren in three-quarter time. The present arrangement is by Norman E. Johnson (b. 1928).

62 The Lord Jehovah Reigns

Isacc Watts (1674-1748)

This version of Psalm 148 appeared in Watts's *Hymns and Spiritual Songs,* Book II, 1709, in four 8-line stanzas.

Stanza 3 as written by Watts:

> Through all his ancient works
>   Surprising wisdom shines,
> Confounds the powers of hell,
>   And breaks their curs'd designs.
> Strong is his arm
>   And shall fulfil
> His great decrees,
>   His soverign will.

4:1 "and can this mighty King"

This hymn does not appear in *A Collection of Hymns for the use of the People called Methodists,* 1780 (the "Large Hymnbook," nor in *A Pocket Hymn Book.* It does appear in the Supplement to the Methodist Episcopal hymnal, 1836, in the form used in Free Methodist hymnals since 1883. (See also comments at No. 6.)

DARWALL's 148th. (See comments at No. 46.)

63 Praise to the Lord, the Almighty

Joachim Neander (1650-1680)
Translated by Catherine Winkworth (1827-1878)

This is a fine translation of Neander's magnificent hymn of praise "Lobe den Herren, den mächtigen König der Ehren," based on Psalms 103:1-6 and 150. It was first published in Neander's *Glaub- und Liebesübung: aufgemuntert durch einfältige Bundes Lieder und Danck-Psalmen,* 1680, in five 5-line stanzas.

The translation, omitting stanza 4 of the German, appeared in Catherine Winkworth's *Chorale Book for England,* 1863.

LOBE DEN HERREN appeared in the *Stralsund Gesangbuch,* second edition, 1665, with the hymn "Hast du denn, Liebster, dein Angesicht Ganzlich verborgen." It was adapted by Neander in 1680 for his hymn and repeated in Freylinghausen's *Gesangbuch,* 1704, and in most later books.

The present form of the melody and the harmonization were made by William Sterndale Bennett and Otto Goldschmidt the musical editors of *The Chorale Book for England.*

64   God Is My Strong Salvation
James Montgomery (1771-1854)

This hymn in two 8-line stanzas is taken from the author's *Songs of Zion, Being Imitations of the Psalms,* 1822. It is based on selected verses of Psalm 27. The only change in the text of this hymn is the alteration of "Thine" to "Thy" in 2:5. It was included first in our 1951 hymnal.

The quality of Montgomery's more than four hundred hymns is attested by the considerable number still in common use.

James Montgomery was born in Scotland to Irish Moravian parents. After a variety of educational and business experiences he went to Sheffield as assistant to the printer of the *Sheffield Register.* In due time he became editor and owner and changed the name to *The Sheffield Iris.* He continued to edit it for thirty-one years.

He was something of a social reformer and was imprisoned twice for publishing articles politically objectionable. He later attained considerable stature because of his writings, his lecturing on poetry, and his vigorous advocacy of foreign missions and of the Bible Society. For the last two decades of his life he received a Royal pension.

In 1807 Montgomery wrote to a friend:

"When I was a boy I wrote a great many hymns; but as I grew up and my heart degenerated, I directed my talents, such as they were, to other services, and seldom indeed since my fourteenth year have they been employed in the delightful duties of the sanctuary. However, I shall lie in wait for my heart, and when I can string it to the pitch of David's lyre, I will set a psalm 'to the Chief Musician.' "

GREENLAND. The origin of this tune is obscure. It is said to have been found in a *Lausanne Psalter* and the date given is 1790. In Christian Ignatius Latrobe's *Selection of Sacred Music,* 1806, it is said to have been derived from a *Mass* by Johann Michael Haydn (1736-1806), younger brother of Franz Joseph Haydn.

65 This Is My Father's World
Maltbie Davenport Babcock (1858-1901)

Babcock was born in Syracuse, New York, educated at Syracuse University, and ordained to the Presbyterian ministry. He served churches in Lockport, New York; Baltimore, Maryland; and New York City. He died in Naples, Italy, en route home from a trip to the Holy Land.

This hymn, which entered Free Methodist-Wesleyan hymnody in 1951, is taken from a collection of sermons and hymns entitled *Thoughts for Everyday Living,* 1901. It is entitled "My Father's World" and is in sixteen 4-line stanzas. The text of the original is altered slightly.

1:2 "E'en yet to"

Another hymn by Babcock, not as well known, is the following:

1. Be strong! We are not here to play, to dream, to drift;
   We have hard work to do, and loads to lift.
   Shun not the struggle, face it, 'tis God's gift.
   Be strong, be strong!
2. Be strong! Say not the days are evil — who's to blame?
   And fold the hands and acquiesce — O shame!
   Stand up, speak out, and bravely, in God's name.
   Be strong, be strong!
3. Be strong! It matters not how deep intrenched the wrong,
   How hard the battle goes, the day, how long;
   Faint not, fight on! Tomorrow comes the song.
   Be strong, be strong!

TERRA PATRIS (the Father's Earth) was composed by Franklin Lawrence Sheppard (1852-1930), a friend of Babcock. It appeared first in his *Alleluia,* 1915, a songbook for Presbyterian Sunday schools. The tune was called *Terra Beata* by Sheppard.

There is an English traditional melody called *Rusper* in *The English Hymnal* to which *Terra Patris* bears a striking resemblance and which may be the English folk tune that Sheppard insisted was the basis for his hymn tune.

66 How Gentle God's Commands
Philip Doddridge (1702-1751)

Doddridge was a nonconformist clergyman at Kibworth and at the Castle Hill Meeting at Northhampton where he headed a seminary. He is buried in Lisbon, where he died October 26, 1751, having gone there because of ill health. He was a respected author and wrote approximately four hundred hymns. His hymns were published after his death by his friend Job Orton in *Hymns founded on Various Texts in the Holy Scriptures. By the late Reverend Philip Doddridge, D.D. Published from the Author's Manuscript...*, 1755.

Our hymn is taken from this collection. It entered Free Methodist-Wesleyan hymnody in 1910.

The original text reads:

    2:1, 2 "While Providence supports / Let Saints securely dwell"
    4:2   "Down to the present day"

DENNIS, also called RIPON, is by Johann Georg Nägeli (1768-1836), a Swiss composer and music publisher. On one of his European trips, Lowell Mason bought a number of Nägeli's manuscripts. Among these he discovered several hymn-tunes of which *Dennis* was one. Mason arranged it and published it in *The Psaltery,* 1845, set to the text "How Gentle God's Commands."

67 God Moves in a Mysterious Way
William Cowper (1731-1800)

James Montgomery rated Cowper as among "the mightiest masters of the lyre," and of this hymn he said, "It is a lyric of high tone and character...." It was written in about 1773 and published first in John Newton's *Twenty-six Letters on Religious Subjects; to Which Are Added Hymns...*, 1774, by Omicron. It is in six 4-line stanzas and headed, "Conflict. Light shining out of Darkness." The scripture reference John 13:7 is written above it.

The omitted second stanza:

    Deep in unfathomable mines
      Of never-failing skill
    He treasures up his bright designs,
    And works his sovereign will.

The date of composition has often been linked to the date of Cowper's attempted suicide in October, 1774. Julian has concluded, from what he regards as sound evidence, that this hymn was written before October, 1773. Most hymnologists concur.

Cowper wrote sixty-eight hymns in all. His often terse, epigrammatic writing produced many expressions that have found their way into common speech. As Erik Routley noted in *Hymns and Human Life* the whole of "God moves in a Mysterious Way," except for two lines, is quoted in the *Oxford Dictionary of Quotations*. In his writing he sometimes "reaches the simplicity of greatness," to use the words of Felix E. Schelling *(The English Lyric,* 1913).

It has been in all Free Methodist hymnals. All six stanzas appear in 1883 and 1910. Stanza 2 is omitted in 1951 and 1976.

DUNDEE, also called FRENCH, is from the Scottish Psalter, *The One Hundred Fifty Psalmes of David in Prose and Meeter with Their Whole Usuall Notes and Tunes,* 1615. Ravenscroft included it in his *Psalter,* 1621, under the title "Dundy Tune" causing confusion since the tune *Windsor* is called *Dundee* in Scotland.

68 Unto the Hills Around Do I Lift Up
John D. S. Campbell, Duke of Argyll (1845-1914)

This hymn, derived from Psalm 121, is found in *Church Hymnal for the Christian Year,* 1877. The author is John Douglas Sutherland Campbell, Ninth Duke of Argyll. He married H. R. H. Princess Louise, daughter of Queen Victoria, in 1871. From 1878-1883, as Marquis of Lorne, he was Governor-General of Canada.

Stanza 1 of this hymn gives a correct rendering of the opening verse of the Psalm. The hills are not the source of our help but our help comes from God.

This hymn was introduced into Free Methodist-Wesleyan hymnody in 1951.

SANDON, also called LANDON, appeared first in *The Church and Home Metrical Psalter and Hymnal,* 1860, of which Charles Henry Purday (1799-1885) was editor. There it was set to the text "Lead, Kindly Light."

69 Guide Me, O Thou Great Jehovah
William Williams (1717-1791)
Stanza 1 translated by Peter Williams (1722-1796)
Stanzas 2, 3, translated by William Williams

This is a translation of the Welsh hymn "Arglwydd, arwain trwy'r anialwch" which was published in the first edition of Williams's *Alleluia,* 1745, in five 6-line stanzas. Williams was known as the "Sweet Singer of Wales." In the opinion of Dr.

Elvet Lewis, "What Paul Gerhardt has been to Germany, what Isaac Watts has been to England, that and more has William Williams, of Pantycelyn, been to Wales."

Peter Williams translated stanzas 1, 3, and 5, and included them in his *Hymns on Various Subjects...*, 1771. William Williams himself accepted the translation of stanza 1, made his own translations of stanzas 3 and 4 of the original hymn, added a new fourth stanza and printed them in a leaflet headed:

> "A Favourite Hymn
> sung by
> Lady Huntingdon's Young Collegians.
> *Printed by the desire of many Christian friends.*
> Lord, give it Thy blessing!"

In our present hymnal we have adopted the first three stanzas of this version except for the change of "Death of deaths" to "Death of death."

The hymnals of 1883, 1910, and 1951 use a form of the text already in use in the early nineteenth century.

CWM RHONDDA. (See notes for No. 25.)

70 God Is Love, His Mercy Brightens
Sir John Bowring (1792-1872)

This hymn appeared in the author's *Hymns*, 1825, in five 4-line stanzas, with stanza 5 being a repetition of stanza 1. In 3:3 "the mist" was changed to "the gloom" in Godfrey Thring's *Collection*, 1880, and it, together with the omission of stanza 5, has become the generally accepted form of the hymn.

Bowring, a Unitarian, was an editor, a member of Parliament, and a British foreign officer. He was knighted in 1854. He had unusual linguistic ability. It is said that he knew two hundred different languages and could speak with some fluency in a hundred of them, although this is likely an exaggeration.

One of Bowring's accomplishments in Parliament was the introduction of the florin into the currency as a first step towards decimal coinage.

The 1910 hymnal introduced this hymn to Free Methodist and Wesleyan congregations.

WILMOT is attributed to Carl Maria von Weber (1786-1826).

71 There's a Wideness in God's Mercy
Frederick William Faber (1814-1863)

This hymn is a cento composed of stanzas 4, 6, 8, 9, and 13 of a hymn entitled, "Come to Jesus," in thirteen 4-line stanzas in Faber's *Hymns,* 1862:
Stanza 1 reads:

> Souls of men! why will ye scatter
>   Like a crowd of frightened sheep?
> Foolish hearts! why will ye wander
>   From a love so true and deep?

The current speculation about human life on other planets may have been anticipated in Faber's fourth stanza:

> There is grace enough for thousands
>   Of new worlds as great as this;
> There is room for fresh creations
>   In that upper room of bliss.

Julian is the source of the information that the hymn appeared earlier in *Oratory Hymns,* 1854, in eight 4-line stanzas. Either he was in error about the number of stanzas or Faber expanded the hymn later to thirteen. Our 1976 hymnal version is taken from my personal copy of *Hymns,* 1862 (Preface dated 1861).

This hymn is included in the 1883, 1910, and 1951 hymnals. The 1976 hymnal is the first to include stanza 4 (Faber's 9th).

Faber took Holy Orders in the Church of England in 1837 but in 1846 he seceded to the Roman Catholic Church. (See notes at No. 32.)

WELLESLEY, according to H. Augustine Smith, was composed by Lizzie Shove Tourjee Estabrook (1858-1913) as the music for her high school graduation song. Her father, Dr. Eben Tourjee, was the founder of the New England Conservatory of Music and the musical editor of the 1878 Methodist hymnal. He named the tune *Wellesley* after the recently founded women's college in a neighboring town and included it in the Methodist hymnal to the text "Mighty God! while angels bless Thee." Faber's hymn is printed on the same page, indicating it is to be sung to the same tune. The music in our present hymnal follows closely the original rhythm and harmonization, except for a change from duple to quadruple meter.

72 O My Soul, Bless Thou Jehovah
The United Presbyterian Book of Psalms, 1871

This is a metrical version of Psalm 103 taken from *The Book of Psalms of the United Presbyterian Church*, 1871.

The 1976 hymnal introduces this hymn to Free Methodist-Wesleyan congregations.

STUTTGART had been attributed to Christian Friedrich Witt (b. 1660) who together with A. C. Ludwig edited the collection *Psalmodia Sacra,* Gotha, 1715, in which the tune is found.

Henry John Gauntlett (1805-1876) is said to have arranged the tune for use in the original edition of *Hymns Ancient and Modern,* 1861.

73 O God of Bethel, by Whose Hand
Philip Doddridge (1702-1751)
John Logan (1748-1788)

This is the first appearance of this hymn in a Free Methodist-Wesleyan hymnal. It is based on Jacob's vow in Genesis 28:20-22.

According to John Julian the hymn was written by Doddridge on January 16, 1736, and published posthumously with some variations in his *Hymns,* 1755, and in *Scottish Translations and Paraphrases,* 1745 and 1781. In 1781 John Logan published the hymn in his *Poems* with some changes and claimed it as his own. Doddridge's original manuscript is extant and attests his authorship. The Doddridge text is quoted by Julian:

1. O God of Bethel, by whose Hand
   Thine Israel still is fed
   Who thro' this weary Pilgrimage
   Hast all our Fathers led

2. To Thee our humble Vows we raise
   To Thee address our Prayer
   And in Thy kind and faithful Breast
   Deposit all our Care

3. If Thou thro' each perplexing Path
   Wilt be our constant Guide
   If Thou wilt daily Bread supply
   And Raiment wilt provide

4. If Thou wilt spread Thy Shield around
   Till these our wandrings cease
   And at our Father's lov'd Abode
   Our Souls arrive in Peace

> 5. To Thee as to our Covenant God
>   We'll our whole selves resign
>   And count that not our tenth alone
>   But all we have is Thine.

It is unfortunate that stanza 5 was dropped in the later forms of the hymns. It might well be quoted in sermons on tithing and stewardship.

Except for changes in the forms of personal pronouns in our hymnal the form used is that found in Logan's *Poems,* 1781, unless noted otherwise.

1:1 Doddridge
5 *Scottish Translations and Paraphrases,* 1781

This is the form used by Montgomery in his *Christian Psalmist,* 1825.

DUNDEE (FRENCH) (See comments at No. 67.)

74 Beautiful Saviour

Münster Gesangbuch, 1677
Translated by Joseph Augustus Seiss (1823-1904)

The first appearance of the German hymn "Schönster Herr Jesu" seems to have been in *Münster Gesangbuch,* 1677, in five stanzas, the opening lines of which are as follows:

1. Schönster Herr Jesu, Herrscher aller Erden
2. Alle die Schönheit Himmels und der Erden
3. Schamedich Sonne
4. Schön seindt die Beumen
5. Er ist wahrhaftig

In *Schlesische Volkslieder,* 1842, it appears in altered form with stanza 4, our second, considerably changed and beginning with the words "Schön sind die Wälder, noch schöner sind die Felder."

Stanzas 1, 3, and the new stanza were translated anonymously as "Fairest Lord Jesus" and in this form entered Free Methodist-Wesleyan hymnody in 1951.

The translation beginning "Beautiful Saviour" was made by Dr. Joseph Augustus Seiss in the *Sunday School Book,* 1873, of the American Lutheran General Council.

ST. ELIZABETH, also known as CRUSADER'S HYMN and SCHÖNSTER HERR JESU, first appeared in a collection of Silesian folk songs *Schlesische Volkslieder,* 1842, with the

German text of this hymn. Richard Storrs Willis (1819-1900) introduced it in this country in his four-part harmonization in *Church Chorals and Choir Studies,* 1850.

The tune title comes from the use of the tune by Franz Liszt in his oratorio *The Legend of St. Elizabeth,* composed between the years 1857 and 1862.

75, 76, 77   All Hail the Power of Jesus' Name
Edward Perronet (1726-1792)
Altered by John Rippon (1751-1836) and others

The authorship of this hymn was in doubt for a number of years. In the first edition of Oliver Holden's *Union Harmony,* 1793, published in New England, it is attributed to the Reverend Mr. Medley. In Dr. Rippon's *Selection of Hymns,* 1787, he gave no indication of the author. In the early nineteenth century, in England, it was ascribed to the Reverend John Duncan.

By the time John Julian edited his *Dictionary of Hymnology* in 1892 he was able to ascribe the authorship to Perronet quite conclusively. Final confirmation came in about 1911 when Louis F. Benson was preparing his *Studies of Familiar Hymns,* Second Series, 1923. In examining a copy of *Occasional Verses, Moral and Sacred,* 1785, which contained "All Hail the Power," Benson discovered that three poems were written in the form of acrostics, those in memory of Charles Perronet and Damaria Perronet, brother and sister of Edward, and one revealing the name of Edward Perronet himself. This latter one reads:

On Sleep
Emblem of death! as is its couch the *Grave,*
Doom'd to contain the *Coward* and the *Brave;*
Where sleep reclin'd, the *guilty* and the *pure,*
Alike intomb'd — *sequester'd* and *secure;*
Reserv'd alike in that dread hour to wake,
Destin'd to stand — and each their *destine* take.

Peace to the last — while judgment marks the first,
Ere yet arraign'd — accursing, and accurst.
Rais'd from their bed, to wrap in sleep no more,
Reviv'd they gaze, and *horribly* adore.
Oh, fatal sleep! that thus awak'd to woe,
No longer ease — no longer rest shall know!
E'en *here* a foretaste of that keener *steel,*
That *fools* have mock'd — and dying fools must feel.

CORONATION was composed in 1792 by Oliver Holden (1765-1844) for this text. It was first printed in his *Union Harmony,* 1793. A facsimile of a page shows the tune name and ascribes the text incorrectly to "Rev. Mr. Medley." The word "Original" indicates that Holden composed the music.

This piece of music has the distinction of being the oldest American music in continuous use up to the present time. Holden was a self-taught musician, a shopkeeper, a part-time preacher, a real estate dealer, a member of the Massachusetts legislature, a book editor and publisher. According to H. Augustine Smith (*Lyric Religion*) his last words, as he lay dying, were: "I have some beautiful airs running through my head, if I only had strength to note them down."

A stanza of "All Hail the Power" is inscribed on Holden's tomb together with the statement that he was the composer of CORONATION.

MILES LANE has been a popular setting for this hymn since it was composed in about 1779 by William Shrubsole (1759-1806), this in spite of its melodic range of an octave and a fifth. In our version, we have narrowed the range by having the soprano sing a "C sharp" instead of the original "A" at the end of the first line. As published anonymously in the *Gospel Magazine* for November, 1779, the music is written for three parts: alto, tenor, and bass, with the melody in the middle voice. The words "crown Him" are sung successively by each voice, beginning with the bass. The concluding phrase is in four parts.

Shrubsole was born in Canterbury and as a youth he became a chorister in the Cathedral. It was in Canterbury that he became acquainted with Perronet. *Miles Lane* is a corruption of St. Michael's Lane near London Bridge. A meeting house located here had as its pastor Stephen Addington. He published text and tune in his *Collection of Psalm Tunes,* 1780, and there gave the tune its name and identified the composer as Shrubsole.

DIADEM was composed in 1838 by James Ellor, a young self-taught musician in Droylsden, near Manchester. Ellor was a hatmaker by trade but on Sundays he led the choir in the Wesleyan Chapel. The tune was printed in leaflet form and sung at a Sunday school anniversary in Ellor's church. It is reported that it became customary to sing it at other anniversary occasions throughout the area.

Ellor came to the United States in about 1843 and is said to have plied his trade as a hatmaker here.

78 There Is a Name I Love to Hear
Frederick Whitfield (1829-1904)

The author of these stanzas wrote the words while a student at Trinity College, Dublin. They were printed in leaflet form in 1855 and then in his collection *Sacred Poems and Prose,* 1861. Whitfield was a minister in the Church of England. Presumably the present arrangement was made for use in the Salvation Army, which holds the copyright.

THE SAVIOUR'S NAME was composed by William H. Rudd concerning whom no information is available. The melody was submitted to the Music Editorial Department of the Salvation Army (England) written in simple fashion on ordinary paper. The head of that department, Colonel Bramwell Coles, made the harmonization.

79 All Praise to Him Who Reigns Above
William H. Clark

Beyond the fact that Clark lived during the nineteenth century and wrote this text sometime prior to 1887, nothing else has been discovered about him.

This song is found in *The Finest of the Wheat,* 1890, edited by George D. Elderkin. William J. Kirkpatrick is given as the copyright owner and the date is given as 1888.

BLESSED BE THE NAME, or BLESSED NAME, is the title given to the tune Ralph E. Hudson (1843-1901) wrote for this hymn. The music and the refrain are associated with other texts as well, including Charles Wesley's "O for a Thousand Tongues." The arrangement of the music is by William J. Kirkpatrick (1838-1921).

80 Ye Servants of God, Your Master Proclaim
Charles Wesley (1707-1788)

This hymn, based on Malachi 4:2, is to be found in Charles Wesley's *Hymns for Times of Touble and Persecution,* 1744, in six 4-line stanzas. The heading for this and the three hymns which follow it in Wesley's collection is "Hymns to be Sung in a Tumult." The lines altered are these:

3:3 "Our Jesus's Praises"
4:2 "All wisdom"

The omitted second and third stanzas are:

2. The Waves of the Sea
      Have lift up their Voice,
   Sore troubled that we
      In Jesus rejoice:
   The floods they are roaring,
      But Jesus is here:
   While we are adoring,
      He always is near.   (Matthew 18:20)

3. Men, Devils engage,
      The Billows arise,
   And horribly rage,
      And threaten the Skies:
   Their Fury shall never
      Our Steadfastness shock,
   The weakest Believer
      Is built on a Rock.

The hymn has been in Free Methodist hymnals since 1883.

HANOVER by William Croft (c. 1678-1727) appeared first in the sixth edition of *A Supplement to the New Version of the Psalms,* 1708, by Nahum Tate and Nicholas Brady, along with a number of other tunes including *St. Anne's*. It is headed "A New Tune to the 149th Psalm of the New Version, and the 104th of the Old."

John Wesley included the tune in his *Foundery Tune-Book,* 1742, but under another title. One interesting theory about the tune is that it was named *Hanover* at the time Handel was thought to be the composer. Handel had been court-conductor in Hanover just prior to coming to England in 1710.

Croft held a number of important positions in church music: Chorister in the Chapel Royal, St. James, under Dr. John Blow; Organist at St. Anne's, Soho; Organist at the Chapel Royal, St. James; and Organist at Westminster Abbey from 1708 to 1727.

81   When Morning Gilds the Skies
German, Anonymous (c. 1828)
Translated by Edward Caswall (1814-1878)

This is a translation of the German hymn beginning "Beim frühen Morgenlicht," found in Canon Sebastian Portner's *Katholisches Gesangbuch,* 1828, for the use of the Diocese of Würzburg, in fourteen 4-line stanzas with refrain. Another form is found in F. W. Ditfurth's *Fränkische Volkslieder,* 1855, in thirteen 4-line stanzas with refrain. Caswall's translation seems to have been made from still a third version, still unknown. His translation is in Henry Formby's *Catholic Hymns,* 1854, in six 4-line stanzas with refrain.

Stanza 3 is taken from Robert Bridge's (1844-1930) translation for the *Yattendon Hymnal,* 1899.

The 1951 hymnal introduced this hymn to Free Methodist and Wesleyan congregations in the form used in the present hymnal.

LAUDES DOMINI was written for this text by Sir Joseph Barnby (1838-1896) for the 1868 edition of *Hymns Ancient & Modern.*

82   Take the Name of Jesus with You
Lydia Baxter (1809-1874)

This hymn was written by Mrs. Lydia Baxter in 1870 for William Howard Doane. It was published in *Pure Gold for the Sunday School,* 1871, edited by Doane and Robert Lowry. Mrs. Baxter wrote a number of religious poems which were published by her in *Gems by the Wayside,* 1855.

The 1951 hymnal was our first hymnal to include this song although it had appeared in such Free Methodist Gospel song books as: *Light and Life Songs,* No. 2, 1914; *Inspirational Songs,* 1924; *Choice Light & Life Songs,* 1950.

PRECIOUS NAME is the tune written by William Howard

Doane (1832-1915) for this hymn and published with the text in *Pure Gold*.

83 Praise Him! Praise Him!
Fanny Jane Crosby (1820-1915)

Methodist songwriter, Fanny J. Crosby, became blind as an infant, but with indomitable courage, ignored her handicap and became herself a teacher of the blind. Her poems, hymns, and gospel songs are estimated to number more than eight thousand and earned for her an appreciative following throughout the English-speaking world.

In 1858 she married Alexander Van Alstyne, a musician who was also blind.

This particular song was first published in *Bright Jewels*, 1869, published by Bigelow and Main.

The 1951 hymnal was the first Free Methodist-Wesleyan hymnal to include this song, although it had appeared as early as 1918 in the gospel songbook *Light and Life Songs*, No. 3. (See also comments at No. 42.)

ALLEN is the name assigned to this tune composed by Chester G. Allen (1838-1878) for Fanny Crosby's song.

84 All Glory to Jesus, Begotten of God
John W. Peterson (b. 1921)

This is the first appearance of a John W. Peterson song in a Free Methodist-Wesleyan songbook or hymnal. According to Donald Hustad this song was first published in *Chorister* magazine, Vol. 2 (Singspiration), in September, 1957.

PETERSON is the title chosen by the editors of this hymnal. RIDGEMOOR is the title chosen by the composer from the name of the area in Michigan in which his family lived while in Grand Rapids, Michigan.

85 Blessing and Honor and Glory and Power
Horatius Bonar (1808-1889)

This is a cento taken from the poem "Into the heav'n of the

heav'ns hath He gone'' in *Hymns of Faith and Hope,* Third Series, 1866, in eight 4-line stanzas. "Blessing and Honor" seems to have been printed first in *Laude Domini,* 1884, in three stanzas, and later in the fourth edition, 1890, in five 4-line stanzas, headed "Glory to the Lamb."

Our 1951 hymnal was the first Free Methodist-Wesleyan hymnal to include it.

O QUANTA QUALIA is taken from the Paris *Antiphoner,* 1681. The harmonization is derived from that made by John Bacchus Dykes for the 1868 edition of *Hymns Ancient and Modern.*

86 My Jesus, I Love Thee
William Ralph Featherstone (1846-1873)

This hymn was printed anonymously in *The London Hymn Book,* 1864. It is now confidently believed to have been written by Featherstone, a resident of Montreal and member of the Wesleyan Methodist Church in Montreal. According to William J. Reynolds, this church is now the St. James United Church.

The hymn entered Free Methodist-Wesleyan hymnody in 1910.

GORDON was composed for this text by Adoniram Judson Gordon (1836-1895). It first appeared in *The Service of Song for Baptist Churches,* 1876, compiled by Gordon and S. L. Caldwell.

87 Ask Ye What Great Thing I Know
Johann Christoph Schwedler (1672-1730)
Translated by Benjamin Hall Kennedy (1804-1889)

According to John Julian:

> Schwedler was a powerful and popular preacher, and peculiarly gifted in prayer. It is said that sometimes, beginning service at 5 or 6 a.m., he would continue the service to relays who in succession filled the church, till 2 or 3 p.m.

Schwedler was a good friend of Count Zinzendorf. He was a popular hymn writer, basing many of his hymns on ''the Grace of God through Christ, and the joyful confidence imparted to the soul that experienced it.''

Of Schwedler's many hymns, apparently only one was

translated into English. It began "Wollt ihr wissen was mein Preis?" based on I Corinthians 2:2 and Galatians 6:14, and published posthumously in the *Hirschberger Gesangbuch,* 1741, in six 4-line stanzas with the refrain, "Jesu, der Gekreuzigte." It was often used as a funeral hymn in Silesia.

Our translation is by Benjamin Hall Kennedy, English scholar and Anglican clergyman, in his *Hymnologia Christiana, or Psalms and Hymns Selected and Arranged in the Order of the Christian Seasons,* 1863. Its first American appearance was in Schaff's *Christ in Song,* 1869 and 1870, in six 4-line stanzas with refrain.

The omitted second stanza reads:

> What is faith's foundation strong?
> What awakes my lips to song?
> He who bore my sinful load
> Purchased for me peace with God,
>   Jesus Christ, the Crucified.

The late Robert Guy McCutchan, editor of the 1935 *Methodist Hymnal,* used to accompany one of the Methodist bishops on evangelistic tours and lead the congregational singing. This great hymn of affirmation was one of his favorites on such occasions.

Hymns of the Living Faith, 1951, was the first Free Methodist-Wesleyan hymnal to include this hymn.

HENDON was composed by Henri Abraham César Malan (1787-1864) of Geneva, judged by Julian to be the greatest name in the history of French hymns. Malan was known for his evangelistic zeal and conducted lengthy tours of evangelism both on the Continent and in Britain. Although he frequently preached to large congregations, he also used every available opportunity to deal with individuals. He was a man of many interests: artist, mechanic, carpenter, printer, poet. He wrote a number of melodies for his own hymns. Lowell Mason brought this particular tune to America and included it in his *Carmina Sacra,* 1841.

88 Up Calvary's Mountain

Avis M. Burgeson Christiansen (b. 1895)

William J. Reynolds in *Hymns of Our Faith,* gives the information that it was while listening to a sermon on the subject, "Our Blessed Redeemer," that Harry Dixon Loes (1892-1965) was inspired to write this music. Loes, a longtime teacher at Moody Bible Institute, sent the music and the suggested title to his friend, Mrs. Christiansen. She wrote the three stanzas and the refrain as they now appear.

The song appeared first in *Songs of Redemption,* 1921.

89 A Wonderful Saviour Is Jesus My Lord
Fanny Jane Crosby (1820-1915)

This song appeared first in *The Finest of the Wheat,* 1890, edited by George D. Elderkin and published by R. R. McCabe and Co., Chicago. The music was composed by William James Kirkpatrick (1838-1921), who copyrighted text and music in 1890. It has been in Free Methodist-Wesleyan hymnals since 1910.

William W. Tromble (b. 1932) arranged the music for this hymnal.

See notations under hymns 42 and 83 for further information on Fanny Crosby (Fanny Jane Van Alstyne).

90 O the Unsearchable Riches of Christ
Attributed to Fanny Jane Crosby (1820-1915)

The music for this song was written by John R. Sweney and copyrighted in 1882 by John J. Hood. The text cannot be definitely traced to Fanny Jane Crosby.

The 1976 hymnal is the first Free Methodist-Wesleyan hymnal to include it although it was included in *Inspirational Songs,* 1924.

91 I Will Sing of My Redeemer
Philip Paul Bliss (1838-1876)

This gospel song was written in 1876 or earlier since it was found in Bliss's trunk, undamaged in the train wreck at Ashtabula, Ohio, that claimed the lives of Bliss and his wife. It is said that Bliss could have escaped but chose to remain with his wife and both died in the flaming wreckage.

The song seems to have been published first in *Welcome Tidings, A New Collection for Sunday Schools,* 1877. In 1878 it was included in *Gospel Hymns,* No. 3. It entered Free Methodist-Wesleyan Hymnody in 1951.

MY REDEEMER was composed in 1877 by James McGranahan (1840-1907) for this text.

92 Christ, Whose Glory Fills the Skies
Charles Wesley (1707-1788)

This is the first appearance of this hymn in a Free Methodist hymnal. It was published in John and Charles Wesley's *Hymns and Sacred Poems,* 1740, in three 6-line stanzas and entitled "A Morning Hymn." It is based on Malachi 4:2. Some hymnals contain an altered version, but the form used in our hymnal is as the hymn was published by Wesley.

For some strange reason John Wesley took a stanza from another hymn in *Hymns and Sacred Poems,* 1740 (the hymn which begins "Lord, how long, how long shall I / Lift my weary eyes in pain?") and combined it with stanzas 2 and 3 of "Christ, Whose glory fills the skies" for inclusion in the "Large Hymnbook." The stanza reads as follows:

> O disclose thy lovely face,
>   Quicken all my drooping powers!
> Gasps my fainting soul for grace,
>   As a thirsty land for showers:
> Haste, my Lord, no longer stay,
> Come, my Jesus, come away.

In this form the hymn remained in the "Large Hymnbook" until the 1875 revision.

Some scholars regard the hymn as one of Charles Wesley's best. This is the first Free Methodist-Wesleyan hymnal to include it.

RATISBON comes from Johann G. Werner's *Choralbuch zu den neuen protestantischen Gesangbüchern,* 1815, published in Leipzig where it is set to the text beginning "Jesu, meines Lebens Leben." The tune title may be derived from the city of Ratisbon, now called Regensburg.

93 Who Can Cheer the Heart Like Jesus?
Thoro Harris (1874-1955)

Words and music for this song were composed by Thoro Harris about 1931 and published in *Revival Echoes,* 1931. Mr. Harris, musical editor of the *Free Methodist-Wesleyan Hymnal,* 1910, was born in Washington, D.C., March 31, 1874. According to Haldor Lillenas, he wrote his first songs at age five. At eleven he invented a system of musical shorthand. In 1903 he moved to Chicago where he became active in church publishing. In 1932 he moved to Eureka Springs, Arkansas, where he continued to be active as a songwriter and publisher.

HFL is the first Free Methodist-Wesleyan hymnal to include this song although it had been included earlier in the gospel song book, *Choice Light and Life Songs,* 1950. It is probably Harris's best known composition.

94 Come, Christians, Join to Sing
Christian Henry Bateman (1813-1889)

This is probably the best-known hymn of Bateman. It was published first in the author's *Sacred Melodies for Children,* 1843, in five 5-line stanzas, with the opening line of stanza 1 reading, "Come, Children, Join to Sing."

Bateman was successively a Moravian and then a Congregationalist before being ordained in the Church of England.

This is the first inclusion in a Free Methodist-Wesleyan hymnal.

SPANISH HYMN, also known as SPANISH CHANT and MADRID was composed at least as early as 1824. The composer is unknown. Benjamin Carr copyrighted variations on the melody for piano in 1825. In 1826 he published it under the title *Spanish Hymn Arranged and Composed for the Concerts of the Musical Fund Society of Philadelphia by Benjamin Carr, The Air From an Ancient Spanish Melody.* The arrangement was for solo voice, quartet, full chorus, and accompaniment.

In England the tune was found first in *A Collection of Psalms and Hymns,* 1827, by Montagu Burgoyne.

95 Majestic Sweetness Sits Enthroned
Samuel Stennett (c. 1727-1795)

This hymn was written by Samuel Stennett, a prominent dissenting minister in London. It was one of thirty-eight hymns he contributed to the collection of his friend, Dr. John Rippon, *Selection of Hymns from the Best Authors,* 1787, and was headed "Chief among ten thousand, or the excellencies of Christ."

There were nine 4-line stanzas in the original. *HFL* uses stanzas 3, 4, 5, 7, and 9. The omitted stanzas are:

> 1. To Christ, the Lord let every tongue
>   Its noblest tribute bring;
>   When he's the subject of the song,
>   Who can refuse to sing?

2. Survey the beauties of his face,
   And on his glories dwell;
   Think of the wonders of his grace
   And all his triumphs tell.

6. His hand a thousand blessings pours
   Upon my guilty head:
   His presence gilds my darkest hours,
   And guards my sleeping bed.

8. To heav'n, the place of his abode,
   He brings my weary feet,
   Shows me the glories of my God,
   And makes my joys complete.

The second line of stanza 3, our first, originally read: "Upon his awful brow."

The 1951 hymnal was the first Free Methodist-Wesleyan hymnal to include this hymn.

ORTONVILLE was composed in 1837 for this text by Thomas Hastings (1784-1872) and first appeared in his *Manhattan Collection,* 1837, in the key of C. A member of our Joint Hymnal Commission suggested the rhythmic pattern used in *HFL.*

96 Awake, My Soul, in Joyful Lays
Samuel Medley (1738-1799)

Most of Medley's hymns were first printed in leaflets or in magazines. This one seems to have been printed first in J. H. Meyer's *Collection of Hymns for Lady Huntingdon's Chapel,* 1782, in eight 4-line stanzas. Then it was reprinted in Rippon's *Selection of Hymns from the best Authors,* 1787, with one stanza omitted.

This hymn entered Free Methodist hymnody in 1883 in six stanzas, our four and two others. The omitted stanzas read:

5. Soon shall I pass the gloomy vale,
   Soon all my mortal powers must fail;
   O may my last expiring breath
   His loving kindness sing in death.

6. Then let me mount and soar away
   To the bright world of endless day;
   And sing, with rapture and surprise,
   His loving kindness in the skies.

WAREHAM was discussed at No. 14.

97 Jesus! What a Friend for Sinners
J. Wilbur Chapman (1859-1918)

The author of this fine hymn was a Presbyterian minister serving churches in Albany, New York; Philadelphia, Pennsylvania; and New York City. He became widely known through his evangelistic tours, many of them in association with Charles M. Alexander, noted gospel singer. He was the first director of the Winona Lake Bible Conference.

The hymn with its tune was published first in *Alexander's Gospel Songs, No. 2,* 1910. *HFL* is the first Free Methodist-Wesleyan hymnal to include it.

HYFRYDOL was composed by Rowland Hugh Pritchard (1811-1887) when he was about twenty years old. It seems to have been published first in *Halelwiah Drachefn,* 1855, edited by Griffith Roberts. This harmonization was made by Robert Harkness (1887-1961), brilliant evangelistic pianist. Born in Australia, he was led to Christ by Charles M. Alexander and later became pianist for the Torrey-Alexander campaigns. Still later he became associated with J. Wilbur Chapman.

98 At the Name of Jesus
Caroline Maria Noel (1817-1877)

This is the best known hymn of Caroline Noel and was written in 1870 as a Processional for *Ascension Day.* It is based on Philippians 2 and was published in the enlarged edition of her *Name of Jesus and Other Verses for the Sick and Lonely,* 1870, in seven 8-line stanzas.

Like Charlotte Elliott, Miss Noel suffered a great deal and her verses, primarily written for private meditation, reflect something of her own suffering.

Originally, the first line read "In the Name of Jesus" but "At the Name of Jesus" seems to have become the generally accepted form.

The stanzas omitted in *HFL* are the fourth and fifth:

> 4. Bore it up triumphant
>   With its human light,
>   Through all ranks of creatures
>   To the central height,
>   To the throne of Godhead,
>   To the Father's breast;
>   Filled it with the glory
>   Of that perfect rest.

5. Name him, brothers, name him,
   With love as strong as death,
   But with awe and wonder
   And with bated breath:
   He is God the Savior,
   He is Christ the Lord,
   Ever to be worshipped,
   Trusted and adored.

This is the first appearance in Free Methodist-Wesleyan hymnody.

KING'S WESTON was composed for this text by Ralph Vaughan Williams (1872-1958) in *Songs of Praise,* 1925, of which he and Martin Shaw were music editors. The tune is named after a country house located on the Avon River near Bristol, England.

99 There's Within My Heart a Melody
Luther Burgess Bridgers (1884-1948)

Bridgers, sometime student at Asbury College, wrote both text and music. It is presumed that he was prompted to write the song after suffering the loss of his wife and three sons in the fire that destroyed his father-in-law's home in Harrodsburg, Kentucky, in 1910.

He served as pastor in a number of Methodist churches. In 1914 he became a general evangelist in the Methodist Episcopal Church, South, but returned to the pastorate in the later years of his life.

This song appeared first in *The Revival No. 6,* 1910, compiled by Charlie D. Tillman.

100 Jesus, Thou Joy of Loving Hearts
Attributed to Bernard of Clairvaux (c. 1090-1153)
Translated by Ray Palmer (1808-1887)

This hymn is a translation of a cento from the Latin hymn *Jesu dulcis memoria,* described by Dr. Schaff in *Christ in Song* as "the sweetest and most evangelical ... hymn of the Middle Ages." From the thirteenth century on, the Latin hymn was attributed to St. Bernard. Scholarly research in recent decades has cast serious doubts upon Bernard's authorship. Dr. F. J. E. Raby, writing in *The Hymn Society of Great Britain and Ireland Bulletin* (October, 1945), seems reasonably certain that the poem was the work of an Englishman living about the end of the twelfth century.

Whether author of this poem or not, Bernard was a remarkable person. Although of high birth, he chose to become a monk. Accompanied by an uncle and two brothers and others whom he had recruited, he entered the monastery of Citeaux. When this monastery became overcrowded, Bernard founded a sister abbey at Clairvaux in the Valley of Wormwood. He remained as abbot until his death.

In influence he was probably the greatest religious personality of his age.

Ray Palmer was a prominent Congregational minister in Bath, Maine, and later in Albany, New York. In 1865 he became Secretary of the American Congregational Union, New York. This translation appeared first in *Sabbath Day Hymn Book,* 1858, where it was entitled "Delight in Christ." The five stanzas in *HFL* are 4, 3, 16, 24, and 10 of the Latin.

The 1951 hymnal introduced this hymn to Free Methodist and Wesleyan congregations.

HESPERUS, also known as QUEBEC and ELIM, was written in 1854 by Henry Williams Baker (1835-1910), by his own account, when he was a student at Exeter College, Oxford. According to Lightwood it was inserted anonymously in the *Penny Post* (April, 1862) as a suitable tune for Keble's "Sun of My Soul." Later it was published in John Grey's *Hymnal for Use in the English Church,* 1866, with the composer's permission.

101   Jesus, the Very Thought of Thee
Attributed to Bernard of Clairvaux (c. 1090-1153)
Translated by Edward Caswall (1814-1849)

This hymn like the preceding one is taken from the Latin hymn *Jesu dulcis memoria.* Edward Caswall's translation appeared in *Lyra Catholica,* 1849. Originally in ten stanzas, our hymnal uses the first five. (See also comments at No. 100.)

All Free Methodist-Wesleyan hymnals since 1910 have included this hymn.

ST. AGNES was composed for this hymn by John Bacchus Dykes (1823-1876) and first appeared in John Grey's *Hymnal for Use in the English Church,* 1866.

102 Jesus My King, My Wonderful Saviour
John M. Harris

Mr. and Mrs. John M. Harris were active in the Holiness Association Camp Meeting movement during the early years of this century. Among the songbooks compiled by Mr. Harris are *Inspiring Songs, Glorious Gospel Songs,* and *Waves of Glory* No. 1.

103 I Will Sing the Wondrous Story
Francis Harold Rowley (1854-1952)
Altered by Ira David Sankey (1840-1908)

The circumstances surrounding the writing of this hymn as told by Rowley are given by Armin Haeussler in *The Story of Our Hymns*. A revival was being held in 1886 at the First Baptist Church of North Adams, Massachusetts, of which Rowley was the pastor. Peter P. Bilhorn was assisting with the music and suggested that Rowley write a hymn for which he, Bilhorn, would compose the music. This song is the result of that collaboration.

George C. Stebbins harmonized the melody. Presumably Bilhorn added the popular refrain. Together they showed the song to Ira D. Sankey who accepted it as a gift. He made a number of alterations in the text and copyrighted it in 1887. It was published first in *Gospel Hymns No. 5,* 1887, and then in Sankey's *Sacred Songs and Solos,* also in 1887.

The 1910 Free Methodist-Wesleyan hymnal introduced this song to their respective communions.

HYFRYDOL. (See comments at No. 97.)

104 Jesus, the Name High over All
Charles Wesley (1707-1788)

This hymn appeared first in Charles Wesley's *Sacred Poems,* Vol. I, Part II, 1749, under the heading "After Preaching (in a Church)." It consisted of twenty-two 4-line stanzas, of which we print stanzas 9, 10, 13, 18, and 22. The original hymn began with this stanza:

> Jesu, accept the grateful song,
>   My Wisdom and my Might,
> 'Tis Thou hast loosed the stammering tongue,
>   And taught my hands to fight.

When John Wesley included a cento in his *Collection of Hymns for the Use of the People Called Methodists,* 1780, he used stanzas 9, 10, 12, 13, 18, and 22. Stanza 12 reads:

> Jesus the prisoner's fetters breaks
> And bruises Satan's head,
> Power into strenghtless souls it speaks,
> And life into the dead.

G. J. Stevenson in his notes on *The Methodist Hymn Book,* 1883, mentions that this hymn "...has long been a great favourite with the Methodist people generally, and several well-authenticated instances are known of its having been used by godly persons to exorcise the devil."

Stevenson gives a number of instances where the closing stanza was quoted by people on their deathbeds.

The circumstances which are believed to have suggested the writing of the hymn are given by Charles Wesley in his *Journal* for August 6, 1744.

This hymn has been a part of Free Methodist hymnody since 1883 when it included the original twelfth stanza in addition to the five in our present hymnal.

GRÄFENBERG is new to our hymnody and was chosen because its character was more in keeping with that of the text. It appeared first in the second edition of Johann Crüger's *Praxis Pietatis Melica,* 1647, and is thought to have been written by Crüger. (See also comments at No. 200.)

105 Lord of All Being! Throned Afar
Oliver Wendell Holmes (1809-1894)

This hymn is dated 1848 by Julian, but it is believed that the first appearance was in the *Atlantic Monthly* (December, 1859) at the conclusion of the final essay in the series, *The Professor at the Breakfast Table.* It is entitled "Sun-Day Hymn."

Holmes was educated as a physician and practiced in Boston until he was elected to the Chair of Anatomy at Harvard in 1847. He was a Unitarian.

This hymn was included in our 1883 hymnal in five stanzas. Stanza 4, omitted in 1976, is also an excellent one:

> Lord of all life, below, above,
> Whose light is truth, whose warmth is love,
> Before thy ever-blazing throne
> We ask no lustre of our own.

MENDON is the name assigned to this tune by Lowell Mason

in the 1833 edition of *The Choir.* Its first published appearance is believed to have been in the revised edition of Ephraim Reed's *Musical Monitor,* 1824.

106 Wonderful Grace of Jesus
Haldor Lillenas (1885-1959)

This song was written in 1917 or 1918 while Lillenas resided in Olivet, Illinois. He died in Aspen, Colorado, August 18, 1959. He had been an evangelist, pastor, and music editor. He wrote more than three thousand songs during his long career.

This is the first appearance in a Free Methodist-Wesleyan hymnal.

107 Of the Father's Love Begotten
Aurelius Clemens Prudentius (348-413)
Translated by John Mason Neale (1818-1866)
and Henry Williams Baker (1821-1877)

The lengthy Latin poem from which this hymn is taken was written at the beginning of the fifth century. The poem begins with the words "Da puer plectrum, choreis ut canam fidelibus" in Prudentius's *Hymnus omnis horae.* The refrain and the doxology did not appear in the original but were added at a later time using the last words of the complete poem.

Our hymn is a translation of the cento beginning "Corde natus ex Parentis, ante mundi exordium," made by John Mason Neale and included in *The Hymnal Noted,* 1854 (Thomas Helmore, editor), revised by Henry W. Baker for *Hymns Ancient and Modern,* 1861. Stanzas 1-3 are by Neale (altered). Stanza 4 is by Baker.

In speaking of Prudentius's poetry, Canon C. Winfred Douglas in *Church Music in History and Practice* calls attention to "a lovely human tenderness, an emotional warmth, a wealth of symbolism, and a free use of Old Testament types...." Although his poems were not meant for singing, parts of them soon became a part of the *Mozarabic Breviary,* and the section from which "Of the Father's Love" is drawn was taken into English breviaries in the eleventh century.

This hymn entered Free Methodist-Wesleyan hymnody in 1951.

DIVINUM MYSTERIUM is a thirteenth-century plainsong

melody (Mode V) which was published in *Piae Cantiones Ecclesiastical et Scholasticae...*, 1582, by Didrik Pedersen. Thomas Helmore took the tune from *Piae Cantiones* and set it to Neale's translation. Canon C. Winfred Douglas (1887-1944) restored much of the original rhythm and harmonized the melody for use in *The Hymnal,* 1916.

108   Lift up Your Heads, Ye Mighty Gates
Georg Weissel (1590-1635)
Translated by Catherine Winkworth (1829-1878)

This paraphrase of Psalm 24 is an Advent hymn beginning with the words: "Macht hoch die Tür, die Tor', macht weit." It was published first in *Preussische Fest-lieder,* 1642, in five 8-line stanzas.

Our translation by Catherine Winkworth was published in her *Lyra Germanica,* First Series, 1855, in five 8-line stanzas. In *HFL* the hymn is abbreviated to fit the long-meter tune *Truro* as follows:

Stanzas 1 (lines 1-4); 3 (lines 1-4); 4 (lines 1-4); 5 (lines 1-4); 4 (lines 5-6); 5 (lines 5-6).

Stanza 2 reads:

> The Lord is just, a helper tried,
> Mercy is ever at His side,
> His kingly crown is holiness,
> His sceptre, pity in distress,
> The end of all our woe He brings;
> Wherefore the earth is glad and sings
>   Praise, O my God, to Thee!
>   O Savior, great Thy deeds shall be!

This is the first appearance in a Free Methodist-Wesleyan hymnal.

TRURO seems to have appeared first in Thomas Williams's *Psalmodia Evangelica,* Vol. II, c. 1789. There it is set to the text: "Now to the Lord a noble song." Although sometimes attributed to Charles Burney, there is no firm evidence to support the claim.

109   Come, Thou Long Expected Jesus
Charles Wesley (1707-1788)

This hymn appeared first in Charles Wesley's tract, *Hymns for the Nativity of Our Lord,* 1744. The tract was the first of those called the "Festival Hymns." Interestingly, this hymn was not included in Wesleyan hymnals until 1875 although it was used by both Rippon, Madan, and Toplady in their respective collections.

The last of the *Hymns for the Nativity of Our Lord* beginning with the words, "All glory to God in the sky," was judged by John Wesley to be "The very best hymn in the whole Collection." Although posterity would hardly agree, it is of special interest to students of Wesley because he attempted to sing it on his deathbed.

The *Free Methodist Hymn-Book*, 1883, and the succeeding ones have all included this Advent hymn.

HYFRYDOL. (See notes at No. 97.)

110 Hail to the Lord's Anointed
James Montgomery (1771-1854)

This hymn was written for and included in a Christmas Ode sung at a Moravian Settlement in the United Kingdom, Christmas, 1821. It is a paraphrase of Psalm 72. In Julian's opinion, "Of all Montgomery's renderings and imitations of the Psalms this is the finest. It forms a rich and splendid Messianic hymn."

The hymn in its entirety is quoted by Dr. Adam Clarke in his *Commentary on the Bible*, 1822, as part of his commentary on Psalm 72. He had heard Montgomery recite the hymn at the close of an address and requested the manuscript.

The first printed version had eight 8-line stanzas. Our hymnal uses three of the eight stanzas as Montgomery wrote them, stanzas 1, 2, 4, and a stanza consisting of the first half of the original seventh and the last half of the original eighth.

Montgomery himself made only slight alterations in succeeding printed versions. HFL follows the revised text of 1828 as did earlier Free Methodist hymnals.

Line 8 in our fourth stanza was originally "His Name — what is it? *Love*."

Montgomery's rendering of Psalm 72 should be compared with Watts's version of the same psalm, "Jesus shall reign where'er the sun."

MENDEBRAS is a traditional German melody brought back to this country from Europe by Lowell Mason (1792-1872). It appeared first in his *Modern Psalmist*, 1839, set to "I Love Thy Kingdom, Lord."

111 Wake, Awake, for Night Is Flying

Philip Nicolai (1556-1608)
Translated by Catherine Winkworth (1827-1878)

This hymn, called "the King of Chorales," is an excellent translation of Nicolai's beautiful "Wachet auf! ruft uns die Stimme," based on Matthew 25:1-13; Revelation 19:6-2; 21:21; I Corinthians 2:9; Ezekiel 3:17; and Isaiah 52:8.

Its first appearance was in his *Frewden-Spiegel des ewigen Lebens,* 1599, in three 10-line stanzas. It seems to have been written in Westphalia in 1597 at the time a terrible plague was raging. No doubt Pastor Nicolai was called on to conduct many funerals, said to number as many as thirty a day. In the preface of *Frewden-Spiegel* he wrote in part:

> ... then day by day I wrote out my meditations, found myself, thank God! wonderfully well, comforted in heart, joyful in spirit, and truly content; gave to my manuscript the name and title of a *Mirror of Joy,* ... to leave behind me (if God should call me from this world) as the token of my peaceful, joyful, Christian departure, or (if God should spare me in health) to comfort other sufferers whom He should also visit with the pestilence. ...

There have been several translations of which perhaps two are best known. "Sleepers wake, a voice is calling" by William Ball and used by Felix Mendelssohn in his oratorio *St. Paul.* The other is by Catherine Winkworth in her *Lyra Germanica,* Second Series, 1858, and revised in her *Chorale Book for England,* 1863.

The original German hymn is full of scriptural images. Some of the color of this imagery is lost in the Winkworth translation. More literal are those made by Francis C. Burkitt (1864-1935) in *The English Hymnal,* 1933, and Frances E. Cox, in *Lyra Messianica,* 1864. Erik Routley in *Hymns Today and Tomorrow* suggests a composite of these two translations to bring out the full force of the imagery.

1. (Burkitt)
   Wake, O wake! with tidings thrilling
   The watchmen all the air are filling,
      Arise, Jerusalem, arise!
   Midnight strikes! no more delaying,
   "The hour has come!" we hear them saying.
      Where are ye all, ye virgins wise?
   The Bridegroom comes in sight,
   Raise high your torches bright!
        Alleluya!
   The wedding song
   Swells loud and strong:
   Go forth and join the festal throng.

2. (Burkitt)
   Sion hears the watchmen shouting,
   Her heart leaps up with joy undoubting
     She stands and waits with eager eyes;
   See her Friend from heaven descending,
   Adorned with truth and grace unending!
     Her light burns clear, her star doth rise.
   Now come, thou precious Crown,
   Lord Jesu, God's own Son!
       Hosanna!
     Let us prepare
     To follow there,
     Where in thy Supper we may share.

3. (Cox)
   Praise to Him who goes before us!
   Let men and angels join in chorus,
     Let harp and cymbal add their sound.
   Twelve the gates, a pearl each portal —
   We haste to join the choir immortal.
     Within the Holy City's bound.
   Ear ne'er heard aught like this,
   Nor heart conceived such bliss,
       Alleluia!
     We raise the song,
     We swell the throng,
     To praise thee ages all along.

There are three stanzas in the Burkitt translation in *The English Hymnal*. The first two are reprinted here by permission of Oxford University Press.

In the original German the concluding two lines break into what Routley calls "merry Latin," which cannot really be captured in English:

> Dess sind wir froh, i-o, i-o!
> Ewig in dulci iubilo.

This is the first appearance of this hymn in a Free Methodist-Wesleyan hymnal.

WACHET AUF, the melody which was associated with the hymn from the beginning, is also believed to be the work of Nicolai. It was used by Mendelssohn in his *St. Paul* and by J. S. Bach in his Cantata No. 140, 1731.

112   Let all Together Praise Our God

Nicolaus Hermann (c. 1485-1561)
Translated by Arthur Tozer Russell (1806-1874)

This Christmas hymn, "Lobt Gott, ihr Christen allzuglisch," was written c. 1554 and published in 1560, as the first of "Three Spiritual Christmas Songs of the New-born Child Jesus, for the Children in Joachimsthal" in Bohemia.

Russell translated stanzas 1, 3, 6, and 8 of the German hymn and published them in his *Psalms and Hymns Partly Original, Partly Selected, for the Use of the Church of England,* 1851.

This is the first appearance of this hymn in a Free Methodist-Wesleyan hymnal.

LOBT GOTT, IHR CHRISTEN is also by Hermann. It was written in 1554, set to another text, but was set to our text when it was published in 1560.

113   The Coming of Our King

Anonymous translation based on Charles Coffin (1676-1749)

This is a translation of the Latin hymn "Instantis adventum Dei" by Charles Coffin given in the *Paris Breviary,* 1736, and also in the author's *Hymni Sacri,* 1736. It appears that this translation may be derived from that made by John Chandler and included in his *Hymns of the Primitive Church,* 1837.

Six stanzas of the Latin text are given in the *Historical Edition to Hymns Ancient & Modern,* 1862, No. 48. Our text is formed from stanzas 1, 3, and 6.

The fifth stanza as altered by the editors of the 1875 edition of *Hymns Ancient & Modern* is interesting:

> Before the dawning day
>   Let sin's dark deeds be gone;
> The old man all be put away,
>   The new man all put on.

This is the first appearance of this hymn in Free Methodist-Wesleyan hymnody.

COFFIN appeared anonymously in the form of melody only. William W. Tromble (b. 1932), a member of the Joint Hymnal Commission, prepared this harmonization.

114 Saviour of the Nations, Come

Ambrose of Milan (340-397)
German version by Martin Luther (1483-1546)
Translated by William M. Reynolds (1812-1876)

"Veni Redemptor gentium" is one of the hymns credited to St. Ambrose by the Benedictine editors. Other early writers confirm that this Christmas hymn is indeed a hymn by Ambrose. Originally there were seven stanzas in the Latin. The eighth stanza, our fifth, is a doxology.

This hymn is new to Free Methodist-Wesleyan hymnody.

NUN KOMM, DER HEIDEN HEILAND is the opening line of Luther's translation of the Ambrose hymn. The melody is anonymous. Johann Sebastian Bach harmonized it and included it along with one stanza of Luther's translation in Cantata No. 36 (c. 1730) and again with another harmonization in Cantata No. 62 (c. 1740). Our setting is a composite of these two arrangements.

115 Joy to the World! The Lord Is Come

Paraphrase of Psalm 98 by Isaac Watts (1674-1748)

This hymn appeared first in Watts's, *The Psalms of David Imitated in the Language of the New Testament,* 1719, in four 4-line stanzas, as Part II of his version of Psalm 98. There it is entitled "The Messiah's Coming and Kingdom." It has been included in all Free Methodist hymnals since 1883. Watts's original text is restored in 1976. (See also comments at No. 6).

ANTIOCH appeared first in Lowell Mason's *Modern Psalmist,* 1839, with the notation "from Handel." Lightwood says that the tune is not Handel and not Mason but there are echoes of "Lift up your heads" and "Comfort ye" from the *Messiah*. In *The Modern Psalmist* Mason appears to make a general claim as composer or arranger.

Note that the melody in the first four measures is a descending major scale.

116 O Come, O Come, Emmanuel

Latin hymn translated by John Mason Neale (1818-1866)
and Henry Sloan Coffin (1877-1954)

"Veni, veni Emmanuel" is the metrical form of five of the

seven great Antiphons for the Advent season dating from about the ninth century. Each of the Antiphons addressed the Saviour by one of the titles ascribed to Him in Scripture: "Emmanuel," "Dayspring," "Rod of Jesse," "Key of David," "Lord of Might," and so forth. The metrical version has been traced to *Psalteriolum Cantionum Catholicarum,* Cologne, 1710.

Our stanzas 1 and 2 follow the form used in the first edition of *Hymns Ancient & Modern,* 1861. Stanzas 3 and 4 are paraphrases of the first and sixth antiphons: *O Sapienta, quae ex ore altissimi* and *O Rex gentium et disideratus,* neither of which had been translated by Neale. Coffin's translation was made in 1916 and included in his *Hymns of the Kingdom of God.*

This is the first appearance in a Free Methodist-Wesleyan hymnal.

VENI EMMANUEL in its present form comes from *Hymnal Noted,* 1854, edited by Thomas Helmore. According to Helmore, in an article on Plainsong in *Dictionary of Musical Terms,* 1881, the tune was "copied by the late J. M. Neale from a French Missal."

A Catholic music researcher may have discovered the source of the tune by chance. In doing research in the Bibliothèque Nationale, Paris, she examined a small fifteenth-century Processional which belonged to a community of French Franciscan nuns. It accompanies a text beginning with the words "Bone Jesu, dulcis cunctis aeterni patris filius." The resemblance to VENI EMMANUEL is unmistakable. (See *The Musical Times,* 1966, and *The Hymn,* April, 1967.)

117 Hark! the Herald Angels Sing

Charles Wesley (1707-1788)
Altered by George Whitefield (1714-1770),
Martin Madan (1776-1790)
and *Hymns Ancient and Modern,* 1861,
Refrain added in the *New Version,* 1782.

This hymn, originally in ten 4-line stanzas, was entitled "Hymn for Christmas Day." It was published first in *Hymns and Sacred Poems,* Part II, 1739, and in revised form in the fourth edition (1743) of the same work.

As Charles Wesley wrote the hymn his first four stanzas read as follows:

> 1. Hark how all the welkin rings,
>   "Glory to the King of Kings
>   Peace on earth and mercy mild,
>   God and sinners reconciled!"

2. Joyful, all ye nations rise,
   Join the triumph of the skies;
   Universal Nature, say,
   "Christ the Lord is born to-day!"

3. Christ, by highest heaven adored,
   Christ, the everlasting Lord,
   Late in time behold Him come,
   Offspring of a virgin's womb.

4. Veiled in flesh, the Godhead see,
   Hail th'incarnate Deity!
   Pleased as man with men t'appear
   Jesus, our Immanuel here!

The form used in our hymnal is close to the 1743 revision with some stanzas omitted and with the following changes:

1:1 "the herald angels sing (Whitefield)
1:2 "the new-born King" (Whitefield)
1:7, 8 "With th'angelic host proclaim,
   Christ is born in Bethlehem" (Madan)
Refrain "Hark! the herald angels sing, etc." *(New Version)*
2:7 "to dwell" *(Hymns Ancient & Modern,* 1861)
2:8 omitting the word "here" at the end of the line
   (HA & M)
3:1 "heaven-born" (Whitefield)

Robert Bridges, in the *Yattendon Hymnal,* 1899, objects to the alteration of the first line of the hymn. His argument is that the angels are not heralds, nor do they sing "Glory to the new-born King."

All Free Methodist hymnals since 1883 have included this hymn.

MENDELSSOHN, also called BERLIN, is derived from the second chorus, "Vaterland in deinen Gauen," in Mendelssohn's *Festgesang,* Op. 68, No. 7, 1840, written for male voices and brass instruments. Mendelssohn later made an arrangement for mixed voices and William H. Cummings, organist at Waltham Abbey, adapted it to Wesley's hymn in about 1856.

118 Lo, How a Rose E'er Blooming

Anonymous, Cologne (1599)
Stanzas 1 and 2 translated by Theodore Baker (1851-1934)
Stanza 3 translated by Harriet R. Spaeth (1845-1925)

This Rhineland carol was first published in the *Catholische*

Geistliche Kirchengesang, Cologne, 1599, in twenty-three 7-line stanzas. The German text for stanzas 1 and 2 is as follows:

> Es ist ein' Ros' entsprungen
> > Aus einer Wurzel zart,
>
> Als uns die Alten sungen:
> > Aus Jesse kam die Art;
> > Und hat ein Blümlein bracht,
> > Mitten in kalten Winter,
>
> Wohl zu der halben Nacht.
>
> Das Röslein, das ich meine,
> > Davon Jesaias sagt,
>
> Ist Maria die reine,
> > Die uns dies Blümlein bracht,
> > Aus Gottes ew'gem Rat
> > Hat sie ein Kindlein g'boren,
>
> Ist bleib'n ein' reine Magd.

This is the first appearance in a Free Methodist-Wesleyan hymnal.

ES IST EIN' ROS' is Michael Praetorius's harmonization of the carol melody in his *Musae Sionae,* VI, 1609.

119 Angels from the Realms of Glory
James Montgomery (1771-1854)

This hymn first appeared in *The Sheffield Iris,* December 24, 1816, the newspaper edited by Montgomery for thirty-one years. It was in five 6-line stanzas and entitled "Nativity." Montgomery republished it in his *Christian Psalmist,* 1825, with minor changes. This is the form used in *HFL.* It was also included among "Three New Carols" in *The Christmas Box,* 1825.

The omitted fifth stanza:

> Sinners, wrung with true repentance,
> > Doomed for guilt to endless pains;
>
> Justice now revokes the sentence,
> > Mercy calls you — break your chains;
>
> Come and worship, etc.

All Free Methodist hymnals since 1883 have included this fine Christian hymn.

REGENT SQUARE was written by Henry Thomas Smart (1813-1879) for *Psalms and Hymns for Divine Worship,* 1867, where it was used with Horatius Bonar's "Glory be to God the Father." The editor of the book was Dr. James Hamilton, minister of Regent Square Presbyterian Church, hence the title given to Smart's tune. Robert Guy McCutchan in his *Hymn Tune Names* reports an interesting sidelight that it was in Regent Square Church, prior to Hamilton's pastorate, that the "speaking with unknown tongues," described by Thomas Carlyle, frequently took place.

120 A Virgin Unspotted
Traditional. Adapted by Lawrence R. Schoenhals (b. 1912)

The origin of this English Christmas Carol is uncertain. There is a printed version dated 1734. The text varies considerably and many tunes have been used. *The Oxford Book of Carols* prints five tunes.

One version of the text from a collection of carols made by William Sandys in 1833 is as follows:

> A virgin most pure, as the prophets do tell,
> Hath brought forth a baby, as it hath befel,
> To be our Redeemer from death, hell, and sin,
> Which Adam's transgression hath wrapped us in.
> Refrain:
> Aye and therefore be merry, rejoice and be you merry,
> Set sorrows aside, Christ Jesus our Saviour was born on this tide.

Our version is that printed in *The Singing Master's Assistant,* 1778, by William Billings.

121 O Come, All Ye Faithful
Attributed to John Francis Wade (1710-1786)
Translated by Frederick Oakeley (1802-1880)

The seven extant manuscripts of *Adeste Fideles* are written, signed and dated by Wade, a music copyist and teacher of Latin. All have four stanzas. The second, omitted in *HFL,* together with Oakeley's translation, is as follows:

> Deum de Deo
> lumen de lumine,
> gestant puellae viscera,
> Deum verum, genitum, non
>   factum.
>   venite, adoremus
>   Dominum.
> God of God,

>Light of Light,
>Lo, he abhors not
>The virgin's womb,
>Very God,
>Begotten, but not
>   created:
>O Come, let us adore
>   him, etc.

Oakeley's translation was made for All Saints, Margaret Street, in London, in 1841. It was first printed in Murray's *Hymnal,* 1852, with slight modifications.

Another translation of this hymn from the Latin was made by John Ellerton in 1871. It appeared in his *Hymns Original and Translated,* 1888.

The 1910 hymnal was the first to introduce this hymn into Free Methodist-Wesleyan hymnody.

ADESTE FIDELES may also be the work of Wade since it is found in all seven extant manuscripts signed and dated by Wade. Samuel Webbe, Sr., included the arrangement of the tune in common use in his *Essay on the Church Plain Chant,* 1782.

122 Angels We Have Heard on High

Traditional French Carol, 1855
Translated in *Crown of Jesus,* 1862

The old French carol, "Les anges dans nos campagnes," was first published in the *Nouveau recueil de cantiques,* 1855. The translation used here is that found in *Crown of Jesus,* 1862, with the following alterations:

>1:4 "Echo still"
>2:2 "rapturous strain"
>3:1 "Come to Bethlehem, come and see"
>3:4 "The Infant Christ, the newborn King"
>4:1 "See within a manger laid"
>4:4 "To celebrate our Savior's birth"

This is the first Free Methodist-Wesleyan hymnal to include this carol.

GLORIA, called IRIS in Britain, is the tune associated with the French carol in *Nouveau recueil de cantiques,* 1855.

123 Silent Night! Holy Night!

Joseph Mohr (1792-1848)
Translated by John Freeman Young (1820-1885)

"Stille Nacht! heilige Nacht!" was written in 1818 by Mohr in a little Alpine village near Salzburg, Austria. The story of its composition is well known. When it was discovered that the organ to be used for the Christmas Eve service was broken and the music planned for the service could not be used, Mohr hurriedly wrote this charming little carol. He gave the text to Franz Grüber and asked him to compose a tune. The resulting composition was sung that evening.

There are six 5-line stanzas in the German text. English versions commonly use three or four stanzas.

The translation by John Freeman Young appeared first in John Clark Hollister's *Sunday-School Service and Tune Book*, 1863, and is the one most frequently used in this country with additional stanzas sometimes derived from other sources.

The first stanza of the German text is as follows:

> Stille Nacht, heilige Nacht!
> Alles schläft, einsam wacht
> Nur das traute, heilige Paar.
> Holder Knab in lockigen Haar:
> Schlafe in Himmlischer Ruh!

This song did not enter Free Methodist-Wesleyan hymnody until 1951.

STILLE NACHT was composed by Franz Grüber (1787-1863), acting organist of the church of which Mohr was assistant priest. He wrote the tune for two voices, choir, and guitar.

124 Love Came Down at Christmas

Christina Georgina Rossetti (1830-1894)

This text is taken from the author's *Time Flies, a Reading Diary*, 1885. This is the first appearance in a Free Methodist-Wesleyan hymnal.

HERMITAGE was written for the 1925 edition of *Songs of Praise* by Reginald Owen Morris (1886-1948), a professor in The Royal College of Music and brother-in-law of Ralph Vaughan Williams.

125 Away in a Manger

Anonymous (late nineteenth century)

The origin of this carol still remains in doubt although it is quite certainly of American origin. An article by Richard S. Hill in *Music Library Association Notes* (December, 1945) proves quite conclusively that Martin Luther had no part in writing this children's hymn. The first appearance of the text that Hill was able to locate is in *Little Children's Book,* 1885, by J. C. File, two stanzas only. Slight modifications of the text were made soon thereafter and have become accepted generally.

Stanza 3 was added later, about 1892. The last line read originally: "And take us to heaven to live with Thee there." Hill first located this stanza in *Gabriel's Vineyard Songs,* 1892.

This carol entered Free Methodist-Wesleyan hymnody in 1951.

AWAY IN A MANGER seems to have been written by James R. Murray. It appears with his initials in his *Dainty Songs for Little Lads and Lasses,* 1887. A number of songbooks still list this tune title as *Mueller* and suggest that the composer is Carl Mueller. The American composer Carl Mueller in conversation one day assured me he had not written the melody.

126 Break Forth, O Beauteous Heavenly Light

Johann Rist (1607-1667)
Stanza 1 translated by John Troutbeck (1832-1899)
Stanza 2 translated by Arthur Tozer Russell (1806-1874)

Stanza 1 is based on Isaiah 9:2-7 and is a translation of the ninth stanza of Johann Rist's Christmas hymn "Ermuntre dich, mein schwacher Geist" beginning with the line "Brich an du schones Morgenlicht." Rist's hymn, one of approximately six hundred eighty that he wrote, was published first in his *Himlischer Lieder,* 1641, in twelve 8-line stanzas and headed "A hymn of praise on the joyful Birth and Incarnation of our Lord and Savior Jesus Christ."

This stanza was used by Johann Sebastian Bach in his *Christmas Oratorio,* 1734. The Reverend John Troutbeck translated and adapted the German text for the English version of the oratorio. The G. Schirmer edition is followed in our hymnal except for line 5 which reads: "This child now weak in infancy."

Stanza 2 is taken from a translation made by Arthur Tozer Russell of "Ermuntre dich." Stanzas 2, 6, and 12 are included in his *Psalms and Hymns,* 1851.

This hymn entered Free Methodist-Wesleyan hymnody in 1951.

ERMUNTRE DICH or SCHOP was written for this text by Johann Schop (c. 1590-1664), music editor of Rist's *Himmlischer Lieder,* 1641. The form of the melody and the harmonization used in *HFL* is by Johann Sebastian Bach and taken from Part II of his *Christmas Oratorio.*

127 While Shepherds Watched Their Flocks
Nahum Tate (1652-1715)

This hymn based on Luke 2:8-15 is found in the *Supplement to a New Version of the Psalms of David, Fitted to the Tunes Used in Churches* by N. Tate and N. Brady, London: 1699. There it is entitled "Song of the Angels at the Nativity of our Blessed Savior."

The text is printed in our hymnal without alteration. The hymn entered Free Methodist-Wesleyan hymnody in 1951.

CHRISTMAS is the hymn tune version of the soprano aria, "Non vi piacque ingiusti Dei" in *Siroe,* 1728, an opera by George Frederick Handel. It appeared as a hymn tune in James Hewitt's *Harmonia Sacra,* 1812, and later in David Weyman's *Melodia Sacra,* 1815. This tune derives its name from association with "While Shepherds Watched." Interestingly enough, it now seems to be more often used with Doddridge's "Awake, My Soul, Stretch Every Nerve" and *Winchester Old* is used with the Christmas hymn instead.

128 All My Heart this Night Rejoices
Paul Gerhardt (1607-1676)
Translated by Catherine Winkworth (1827-1878)

"Fröhlich soll mein Herze springen," in fifteen 8-line stanzas, was written by Paul Gerhardt and included in Johann Crüger's *Praxis pietatis melica,* 1653.

Catherine Winkworth translated rather freely ten of the fifteen stanzas and included them in her *Lyra Germanica,* Second Series, 1858. In abbreviated form she included it in her *Chorale Book for England,* 1863.

Stanzas used in our hymnal are 1, 7, and 8 of Gerhardt's hymn.

This nativity hymn entered Free Methodist-Wesleyan hymnody in 1951 set to another variation of Ebeling's tune.

WARUM SOLLT ICH, also called EBELING and BONN, was written by Johann Georg Ebeling (1637-1676), Cantor of St. Nicholas Church, Berlin, and included in his *Das ander Dutzet Geistlicher Andacht-Lieder Herrn Paul Gerhards,* 1666.

The harmonization of Ebeling's tune used here is by Johann Sebastian Bach from Part III of his *Christmas Oratorio,* 1734, where it is set to the fifteenth stanza of Gerhardt's hymn.

129 Who Is He in Yonder Stall?
Benjamin Russell Hanby (1833-1867)

This Christmas song appeared first in *The Dove: A Collection of Music for Day and Sunday Schools,* 1866. Hanby also wrote a tune for the text which included this 4-line refrain:

> 'Tis the Lord! O wondrous story!
> 'Tis the Lord, the King of Glory!
> At His feet we humbly fall —
> Crown Him, crown Him Lord of All!

Hanby's hymn in ten stanzas together with his tune may be found in *Sacred Songs and Solos* compiled by Ira D. Sankey, n.d.

This is the first inclusion in a Free Methodist-Wesleyan hymnal.

RESONET IN LAUDIBUS is a German carol melody from the fourteenth century, found in *Piae Cantiones,* Griefswald, Finland, 1582. The tune has been abbreviated to accommodate the shortened refrain.

130 From Heaven Above to Earth I Come
Martin Luther (1483-1546)
Translated by Catherine Winkworth (1827-1878)

This hymn is thought to have been written by Martin Luther for his children. It appeared first in Klug's *Geistliche Lieder,* 1535, in fifteen 4-line stanzas. The first stanza was taken by Luther almost entirely from a popular sacred song which began "Ich komm aus fremden Landen komm' ich her." The remainder is original.

According to Luther's instructions, the first seven stanzas

were to be sung by a man dressed as an angel. He was then greeted by the children singing the remaining eight stanzas.

Catherine Winkworth's excellent translation was published in her *Lyra Germanica*, First Series, 1855. She adds the notation that Luther wrote the hymn for his little son, Hans.

Our hymnal uses stanzas 1, 2, 13, 14, and 15 without alteration.

HFL is the first Free Methodist-Wesleyan hymnal to include this hymn.

VON HIMMEL HOCH, also called ERFURT, is sometimes credited to Luther but without proof. It is found in Valten Schumann's *Geistliche Lieder*, 1539, where it is set to "From Heaven Above to Earth I Come." The tune in various forms was used by Bach five times in his *Christmas Oratorio*. The harmonization used here accompanies the choral "Ah! Dearest Jesus, Holy Child" which concludes Part I.

131 There's a Song in the Air
Josiah Gilbert Holland (1819-1881)

The author was at one time editor of *Scribner's* magazine. His Christian songs appeared first in W. T. Griffe's *The Brilliant*, 1874, a Sunday school collection, and later in the author's *Complete Poetical Writings*, 1879, where it was copyrighted by Charles Scribner's Sons.

The first inclusion of Holland's hymn in a Free Methodist-Wesleyan hymnal was in 1910 set to a tune written by Thoro Harris, for the hymnal. The 1951 hymnal omitted it.

CHRISTMAS SONG was written by Karl Pomeroy Harrington (1861-1953) in July, 1904. He was a prominent university professor and a competent musician. He was one of the musical editors of the *Methodist Hymnal*, 1905.

132 Sleep Sweetly, Wee Jesus
Brazilian Folk Carol
Translated by Lois Kempton (b. 1930)

Mrs. Kempton heard this song in Londrina, state of Parana, in interior Brazil. It was sung by two young ladies, members of a touring choir. One member of the duet accompanied the singing on a guitar. It was so hauntingly beautiful that Mrs. Kempton sought out the singers to obtain a copy of the song. She was informed that they had never seen it in print. They told her it was something that all Brazilians knew and sang at Christmas time.

Mrs. Kempton committed the music to memory and added her own translation of the text. She submitted it to the editors of *Hymns of Faith and Life* who accepted it and printed it with the Brazilian tune title REPOUSO TRANQUILO.

Mrs. Kempton, a native of Ohio and a graduate of Taylor University, is married to the Reverend Charles Kempton. Together they served as missionaries in Brazil under the Oriental Missionary Society. Since returning to the United States they have served at Oakdale Christian High School, in Free Methodist pastorates in Ohio and Kentucky, and at present are in charge of Logan Christian Academy, in Ohio, which they founded in 1977.

This is a part of Mrs. Kempton's response to our inquiry:

> Who wrote the song? Perhaps an illiterate laborer, accustomed to long hours on a plantation, with precious few moments to spend with a battered guitar? a gaucho? a pioneer? a priest or a nun? No one knows; it will probably always remain a mystery.
>
> All we can say is that it came from a heart that felt the mystery and beauty of that first Christmas, keenly, and that it adds a distinctively Brazilian touch to the rich mosaic of Christmas music of the world.

133 Unto Us a Boy Is Born

Latin, fifteenth century
Translated by Percy Dearmer (1867-1936)

The text and original melody are in a fifteenth-century manuscript discovered in the ancient city of Trier in Germany. The Latin text begins:

> Puer nobis nascitur
>   Rector angelorum
> In hoc mundo pascitur
>   Dominus Dominorum.

A German translation ("Uns ist geboren ein kindelein") was printed in 1544. The English translation used here is by Percy Dearmer in the *Oxford Book of Carols,* 1928, published by Oxford University Press, in five stanzas, where stanza 5 reads:

> Omega and Alpha he!
>   Let the organ thunder,
> While the choir with peals of glee
>   Doth rend the air asunder.

Our version of the fifth stanza is taken from *Songs of Praise* (Oxford University Press) of which Percy Dearmer was words editor, hence, it, too, may be considered an authorized translation.

PUER NOBIS, also named PUER NOBIS NASCITUR and OMEGA AND ALPHA is said to have been found in the Trier manuscript and also in *Piae Cantiones,* 1582. The harmonization is by Geoffrey Shaw (1879-1943) in the *Oxford Book of Carols,* 1928, where each stanza is given different harmonic treatment.

134 Cradled in a Manger
                          Frances Martha Hubbert

The text of this Christmas hymn is taken from *Hymns for Children* published in 1965 by the Hymn Society of America. Miss Hubbert lives in Toronto, Canada, and is a graduate of Hamilton Teachers' College and the Anglican Women's Training College. She has served the Anglican Church in a number of positions.

This is the first appearance of either text or tune in a Free Methodist-Wesleyan hymnal.

GLENFINLAS is a simple pentatonic (5-note) tune written by Kenneth George Finlay (b. 1882) for the *Church and School Hymnal* (S.P.C.K.), 1926. Because that publication was delayed, the tune actually appeared first in print in *Songs of Praise,* 1925, set to the Jan Struther hymn beginning "Daisies are our silver."

135 Sing, O Sing, This Blessed Morn
                          Christopher Wordsworth (1807-1885)

This Christmas hymn was written by the nephew of the poet laureate, William Wordsworth, whom he visited regularly at Rydal and with whom he carried on a lengthy correspondence. The hymn appeared first in the author's *Holy Year,* 1862. In the third edition, 1863, the hymn was divided into two parts and a doxology was added.

Our present hymn uses stanzas 1, 3, 4, 6, and 10. The omitted doxology reads:

> Glory to the Father give,
> And to Son in whom we live;
> Glory to the Spirit be,
> Godhead one, and Persons three.
> *Refrain*

Stanza 3 contains one of the rare references to Adam in hymns.

This is the first appearance of this hymn in Free Methodist-Wesleyan hymnody. (See also comments at No. 51.)

ENGLAND'S LANE was adapted from an old English melody by Geoffrey Shaw (1879-1943) for the *Public School Hymn Book,* 1919.

136 O Little Town of Bethlehem
Phillips Brooks (1835-1893)

The author of this Christmas hymn, following his graduation from Harvard College in 1855, was successively Rector of Holy Trinity Episcopal Church in Philadelphia, Rector of Trinity Church in Boston, and Bishop of Massachusetts.

In 1865 Brooks visited the Holy Land, journeying from Jerusalem to Bethlehem on horseback during the Christmas week. The experiences made a deep impression on him and he recaptured some of them in this beautiful carol written for a Sunday school Christmas festival in his church in 1868. It was published in *The Church Porch, a Service Book and Hymnal for Sunday Schools,* 1874. Free Methodist-Wesleyan hymnals have included it since 1910.

ST. LOUIS is the original tune associated with this text and was written by Lewis Henry Redner (1831-1908), Brooks's organist. The name has no connection with a saint or a city. It was assigned to the tune in William Reed Huntington's *The Church Porch.*

137 Go, Tell It on the Mountain
American Folk Hymn
Adapted and arranged by John Wesley Work III (1901-1967)

The text and possibly the tune of this spiritual have been attributed to Frederick J. Work. The song was used by the Fisk Jubilee Singers early in the twentieth century. The present adaptation and arrangement were made by John Wesley Work III, himself director of the Fisk Men's Glee Club and later of the famous Fisk Jubilee Singers.

Spirituals such as "Go Tell It on the Mountain" are included in Free Methodist-Wesleyan hymnody for the first time in *Hymns of Faith and Life.*

GO TELL IT ON THE MOUNTAIN uses a pentatonic (5-tone) scale, characteristic of many folk melodies, except for the half-note "C" just before the D.C.

138　In the Bleak Midwinter
Christina Georgina Rossetti (1830-1894)

This is one of four Christmas poems written by Christina Rossetti.

W. Garrett Horder, writing in *A Dictionary of Hymnology* (ed. John Julian), said, "Miss Rossetti's verses are profoundly suggestive and lyrical, and deserve a larger place than they occupy in the hymnody of the church. Her sonnets are amongst the finest in the English language."

Nearly a century has elapsed since he wrote those words. Time has confirmed his judgment in that most hymnals now include one or more of her poems.

"In the Bleak Midwinter" was written sometime before 1872 and first printed in *Scribner's Monthly,* January, 1872. It was published later in the author's *Poems.* The first hymnal to include it was *The English Hymnal,* 1906.

There are five stanzas in the original poem. The omitted stanza 3 reads:

> Enough for Him, whom Cherubim
> >Worship night and day,
> A breastful of milk,
> >And a manger full of hay;
> Enough for Him, whom angels
> >Fall down before,
> The ox and ass and camel
> >Which adore.

Originally 4:5 (our 3:5) read "But only His mother."

This is the first appearance in a Free Methodist-Wesleyan hymnal.

CRANHAM was written by Gustav Theodore Holst (1874-1934) for this text for inclusion in *The English Hymnal,* 1906.

139 Once in Royal David's City
Cecil Frances Alexander (1818-1895)

This children's Christmas hymn is a commentary on the article of "The Apostle's Creed" which reads: "Who was conceived by the Holy Ghost, born of the Virgin Mary." Mrs. Alexander (nee Humphreys), an Irish poet, wrote the hymn in six 6-line stanzas and published it in her *Hymns for Little Children,* 1848. The omitted sixth stanza reads:

> Not in that poor lowly stable,
>   With the oxen standing by,
> We shall see Him; but in Heaven,
>   Set at God's right Hand on high,
> When like stars His children crowned,
>   All in white, shall wait around.

The hymn entered Free Methodist-Wesleyan hymnody in 1951. Mrs. Alexander also wrote the lovely children's hymn, "All Things Bright and Beautiful," which has gained new visibility through three contemporary novels which took their titles from the first three phrases of the refrain. (See also comments at No. 215 and No. 303.)

IRBY by Dr. Henry John Gauntlett (1805-1876) was composed for this text and printed in his *Christmas Carols,* 1849, for voice and piano. Later in the same form he included it in his musical edition of Mrs. Alexander's book, *Hymns for Little Children,* 1858. When the hymn was used in the first edition of *Hymns Ancient and Modern,* 1861, he prepared a four-part setting.

140 Thou Didst Leave Thy Throne
Emily Elizabeth Steele Elliott (1836-1897)

This hymn was first printed privately in 1864 for use in St. Mark's Church, Brighton, England, of which Miss Elliott's father was rector. Later it was published in the *Church Missionary Juvenile Instructor,* 1870, of which Miss Elliott was the editor. Originally the refrain was the same for each stanza. It was in this form when the hymn was introduced into Free Methodist-Wesleyan hymnody in 1910, set to a tune by Ira D. Sankey.

MARGARET was written for these words by the Reverend Timothy Richard Matthews (1826-1910) and included in *Children's Hymns and Tunes,* 1876.

141 O Master Workman of the Race
Jay Thomas Stocking (1870-1936)

This hymn was written at the request of the editors of *The Pilgrim Hymnal*, 1912. They wanted a hymn that would dignify labor. While Stocking was watching carpenters at work at his summer camp in the Adirondacks, he said later on, that "the figure of the carpenter, as applied to Jesus, flashed on me as never before, and I sat down and wrote the hymn, almost, if not quite, in the exact form in which it now appears."

This is the first inclusion in a Free Methodist-Wesleyan hymnal.

ST. MICHEL'S, also known as BEULAH and WOOLWICH COMMON, is taken from William Gawler's *Hymns and Psalms Used at the Asylum for Female Orphans*, c. 1788, the second of three books of tunes for the use of the children. In the original form it was a long-meter tune in the key of B flat, set to the text "Creator Spirit by Whose Aid."

At a later time the tune was extended to accommodate an 8-line text.

142 O Love Divine, by Christ Revealed
Wilson T. Hogue (1852-1920)

This hymn by a bishop of the Free Methodist Church was included in the *Free Methodist-Wesleyan Hymnal*, 1910, and in each of the succeeding hymnals. The third stanza, omitted in 1976, reads:

> O Cross divine, by Christ endured,
>   Thou cross on which He groaned and died,
> And man's redemption thus secured,
>   In Thy blest shadow let me hide.

ANGELUS is derived from a melody set to a hymn by Johann Scheffler in *Heilige Seelen-Lust...*, 1657. When Scheffler joined the Roman Catholic Church he took the name "Angelus," hence the name assigned to this tune. It is possible that the tune was composed by Georg Joseph.

The tune was modified in *Cantica Spiritualia*, 1847, and again in the first edition of *Hymns Ancient and Modern*. In the 1875 edition the present rhythm was adopted.

143 How Sweet the Name of Jesus Sounds
John Newton (1725-1807)

This hymn in seven 4-line stanzas was first published in Newton's *Olney Hymns,* 1779, with the title, "The Name of Jesus," and the Scripture reference Song of Solomon 1:3. John Wesley gave it prominence by printing it in the *Arminian* magazine in 1781. Strangely enough, the "Large Hymnbook," 1780, did not include it until the revised edition of 1875. Newton's text has been restored in *HFL* except for the substitution of "Guardian" for "Husband" in the original stanza 5 and the omission of stanzas 4 and 6:

> 4. By Thee my pray'rs acceptance gain,
>   Altho' with sin defil'd;
>   Satan accuses me in vain,
>   And I am own'd a child.
> 6. Weak is the effort of my heart,
>   And cold my warmest thought;
>   But when I see Thee as Thou art,
>   I'll praise Thee as I ought.

All Free Methodist hymnals since 1883 have included the hymn.

ST. PETER, also called CHRIST CHURCH, was composed by Alexander Robert Reinagle (1799-1877) and first published in his *Psalm-Tunes for the Voice and Pianoforte,* c. 1830, where it was set to Psalm 118. In the composer's *Collection of Psalm and Hymn-Tunes,* 1840, it was assigned the name St. Peter. The reason is obvious for Reinagle served as organist of St. Peter-in-East, Oxford, from c. 1821 to 1853.

144 O Love, How Deep, How Broad, How High
Latin, fifteenth century
Translated by Benjamin Webb (1819-1885) and revised by the editors of *Hymns Ancient and Modern,* 1861.

This is a translation of a portion of the Latin Christmas hymn which begins "Apparuit benignitas" found in a fifteenth-century manuscript. The Reverend Benjamin Webb's translation begins with line 5 "O amor quam exstaticus" and consists of eight 4-line stanzas. There are twenty-three stanzas (92 lines) in the original, of which 2, 9, 10, 11, 12, and the doxology which was added by the editors of the first edition of *Hymns Ancient and Modern* are used here.

In Webb's translation, stanza 3 began:

> For us He preaches and He prays,
> Would do all things, would try all ways;

and stanza 4 read:

> For us to wicked men betrayed,
> Scourged, mocked, in crown of thorns arrayed;
> For us He bore the cross's death,
> For us at length gave up His breath.

DEO GRACIAS, or DEO GRACIAS ANGLIA, or AGINCOURT, is a fifteenth-century melody apparently improvised on the battlefield by King Henry V and his poorly equipped army as a song of thanksgiving for victory on October 25, 1415.

> Deo gracias Anglia redde pro victoria.
> Owre Kynge went forthe to Normandy
> With grace and might of chyvalry.
> Ther God for hym wrought mervelusly,
> Wherefore Englonde may calle and cry:
> Deo gracias!

145 One Day When Heaven Was Filled
J. Wilbur Chapman (1859-1918)

The words of this gospel hymn were written sometime prior to 1910, according to the composer of the music, Charles Howard Marsh. Marsh was associated with Chapman at the Winona Lake Bible Conference. When Dr. Chapman was asked to conduct a Bible Conference at Stony Brook, Long Island, New York, he took Marsh with him. It was here that he gave the words of "One Day" to Marsh and it was here during that summer that the music was written. The year was about 1908 or 1909 as Marsh recalled in a letter to William J. Reynolds.

This is the first appearance of the song in a Free Methodist-Wesleyan hymnal. (See also comments at No. 97.)

CHAPMAN was composed by Charles Howard Marsh (1886-1956) probably during the summer of 1908 or 1909.

146 All Glory, Laud, and Honor
St. Theodulph of Orleans (c. 750-821)
Translated by John Mason Neale (1818-1866) and others

Theodulph of Orleans, author of "Gloria laus et honor" seems to have been a native of either Italy or Spain. He was brought to

France by Charlemagne about 781. He became Bishop of Orleans about 785. The full text in seventy-eight lines is based on Psalm 24:7-10; Psalm 118:25, 26; Matthew 21:1-17; and Luke 19:37, 38. According to legend, the hymn was connected with the Palm Sunday procession from the time of its composition.

Dr. John Mason Neale made two translations of the hymn, the second was made for and published in the *Hymnal Noted,* 1854, in eight 4-line stanzas. The compilers of *Hymns Ancient and Modern* took this latter version, made some alterations with Dr. Neale's approval, and printed it in six 4-line stanzas, later increased to eight.

One stanza of the Latin text usually sung until the seventeenth century, as translated read:

> Be Thou, O Lord, the Rider,
>   And we the little ass;
> That to God's holy city
>   Together we may pass.

As altered in a later edition of *Hymns Ancient and Modern,* this became:

> Thy sorrow and Thy triumph
>   Grant us, O Christ, to share,
> That to the holy city
>   Together we may fare.

In traditional usage, stanza one (lines 1-4 of the poem) is sung as a refrain after each stanza, that is, after each four lines of the poem which would then always use the third and fourth lines of the music.

The hymn entered Free Methodist-Wesleyan hymnody in 1951.

ST. THEODULPH was composed about 1614 by Melchior Teschner (d. 1635), precentor of a Bavarian church. It is the second of two five-part settings of the funeral hymn "Valet will ich dir geben," by Teschner's pastor Herberger. It was published in *Ein Andächtiges Gebet...,* 1615.

J. S. Bach uses the chorale melody in his *St. John Passion.*

147 Hosanna, Loud Hosanna

Jennette Threlfall (1821-1880)

This Palm Sunday hymn, probably the most widely used of Miss Threlfall's, was published in her *Sunshine and Shadow,* 1873. Miss Threlfall, a helpless invalid as a result of two tragic accidents, nevertheless exerted a powerful influence throughout her parish by her loving and cheerful spirit and by her generosity.

Upon her death, beautiful tributes were given by Dean Stanley of Westminster Abbey and by Canon Farrar.

The hymn entered Free Methodist-Wesleyan hymnody in 1951.

ELLACOMBE appears in two metrical versions, C.M.D. and 7.6.7.6.D. (See notes at No. 16.)

148 'Tis Midnight, and On Olive's Brow
William Bingham Tappan (1794-1849)

After a period spent in business, Tappan became active in Sunday school work in Massachusetts. Under the title of "Gethsemane" the hymn was printed in his *Poems,* 1822. In the original, Tappan wrote:

    2:2 *Immanuel* wrestles
    4:1 from *ether* plains

All Free Methodist hymnals have included this hymn. Those of 1883 and 1910 changed "Immanuel" to "The Savior" (2:2) but retained "ether plains." The editions of 1951 and 1976 are the same.

OLIVE'S BROW was written by William Batchelder Bradbury (1816-1868) for this text and published in *The Shawm,* 1853, compiled by Bradbury and George Frederick Root.

149 O Perfect Life of Love
Henry Williams Baker (1821-1877)

This hymn was written by Sir H. W. Baker for the 1875 edition of *Hymns Ancient and Modern.* Baker was one of the members of the original committee in 1859 (and the first secretary) which produced *Hymns Ancient and Modern.* (See notes on No. 47, also.)

There were seven stanzas originally of which we print 1, 2, 3, 5, and 7. The changes made in the text are these:

    2:3 His toil, His sorrows, one by one,
    2:4 Scripture

The omitted stanzas are:

    4. And on His thorn-crowned Head,
       And on His sinless Soul,

> Our sins in all their guilt were laid,
>> That He might make us whole.
> 6. In every time of need,
>> Before the judgment-throne
> Thy work, O Lamb of God, I'll plead,
>> Thy merits, not my own.

This is the first appearance in a Free Methodist-Wesleyan hymnal.

SOUTHWELL first appeared in *Psalmes of David in English Meter, with Notes of foure parts set unto them...*, 1579, with the melody in the tenor part. The publication was issued by John Bull without the consent of William Damon who had provided the harmonizations. In 1591 Damon (c. 1540-1591) issued a corrected edition and in the same year another edition in which the soprano part carried the melody. The two prior editions had the psalm tune in the tenor part.

150 Go to Dark Gethsemane
James Montgomery (1771-1854)

The author made two versions of this hymn. The first appeared in Cotterill's *Selection of Psalms and Hymns,* ninth edition, 1820, and the second in 1822 in the *Selection of Hymns, Compiled and Original,* the so-called *Leeds Selection.* Montgomery included this latter version with minor changes in his *Christian Psalmist,* 1825. This is the form used in our hymnal except that stanza 4 is omitted.

> Early hasten to the tomb,
>> Where they laid His breathless clay;
> All is solitude and gloom,
>> — Who hath taken Him away?
> Christ is risen; — He meets our eyes;
> Savior, teach us how to rise.

The hymn entered Free Methodist-Wesleyan hymnody in 1951. (See also comments at No. 64.)

REDHEAD NO. 76, also known as PETRA and GETHSEMANE, was written by Richard Redhead (1820-1901) and published in his *Church Hymn Tunes, Ancient and Modern,* 1853, to the text "Rock of Ages." Redhead did not give names to his tunes but only numbers. From 1864 for the next thirty years he presided over the music at St. Mary Magdalene, Paddington. He was skilled as a trainer of boys' voices and as an organist. It is said he was "an accompanist of devotional spirit, whose extemporizing seemed inspired by his faith."

151 Behold the Saviour of Mankind
Samuel Wesley, Sr. (1662-1735)

This hymn was written by the father of John and Charles Wesley sometime before the fire which burned down the Epworth Rectory in 1709. It is said that the manuscript was found in the Rectory garden after the fire. It was published by John in the *Charles-Town Collection,* 1736/37, and again in *Hymns and Sacred Poems,* Pt. II, 1739, under the title "On the Crucifixion," in four 4-line stanzas. In the original there were six 4-line stanzas.

After Charles Wesley's conversion he found great satisfaction in ministering to the prisoners at Newgate prison. Among the hymns sung on such occasions, and also at Tyburn prior to the executions, was "Behold the Savior of Mankind." He recorded in his *Journal* for July 19, 1738, that after the executions "I spoke a few suitable words to the crowd. . . . That hour under the gallows was the most blessed hour of my life."

All Free Methodist hymnals have included the hymn.

WINDSOR, known in Scotland as DUNDEE, is found in William Damon's *Booke of Musicke,* 1591. It seems to have been derived from the tune Christopher Tye used in his *Actes of the Apostles,* 1553, Chapter 3.

There is a reference to *Windsor* in Addison's *Spectator* recounting the troubles of the precentor with a lady in the congregation:

> As to herself, I had one day set the Hundredth Psalm and was singing the first line in order to put the congregation into the tune; she was all the while courtseying to Sir Anthony in so affected and indecent manner, that the indignation I conceived at it made me forget myself so far, as from the tune of that psalm to wander into SOUTHWELL tune, and from thence into WINDSOR tune, still unable to recover myself till I had with the utmost confusion set a new one.

152 O Love Divine, What Hast Thou Done
Charles Wesley (1707-1788)

This is the third of three hymns under the general heading "Desiring to Love" in *Hymns and Sacred Poems, Pt. I,* 1742. There are four 6-line stanzas. The changes from the original are these:

    1:2 *Th'immortal* God *hast*
    1:5 The *Immortal God* for me
    2:2 To bring us rebels *near*
    2:4 *We* all are brought
    3:3 Come *see, ye worms, your maker* die

Stanzas 2 and 3 in the original have been interchanged, following the lead of *The Methodist Hymnal,* 1935.

The refrain "My Lord, my Love, is crucified" has an interesting history. It was used by Ignatius in his *Epistle to the Romans,* "Amor meus crucifixus est." John Mason in his *Songs of Praise,* 1683, used it as the opening line of a hymn. Frederick Faber used a variant as a refrain in his hymn, "O Come, and Mourn with Me Awhile":

> Come, take Thy stand beneath the cross
>   And let the blood from out that side
> Fall gently on thee, drop by drop!
>   Jesus, our Love, is crucified!

The hymn entered Free Methodist hymnody in 1883 in the form printed here except for the reversal of stanzas 2 and 3.

The preface to *Hymns and Sacred Poems,* 1742, hymn No. 152, published jointly by John and Charles Wesley, is devoted to an exposition of the doctrine of Christian Perfection. After declaring what perfection is *not* and then what it *is,* the Wesleys conclude in this manner:

> This it is to be *a perfect man,* to be *sanctified throughout, created anew in Jesus Christ.* Even "to have a heart so all-flaming with the love of God," (to use Archbishop Usher's words) "as continually to offer up every thought, word, and work, as a spiritual sacrifice, acceptable unto God through Christ." In every thought of our hearts, in every word of our tongues, in every work of our hands, *to show forth His praise who hath called us out of darkness into His marvellous light!* O that both we, and all who seek the Lord Jesus in sincerity may thus be *made perfect in One!*

SELENA by Isaac Baker Woodbury (1819-1858) appeared first in his *Anthem Dulcimer,* 1850, where it was set to "Asleep in Jesus."

153 I Stand All Amazed
Words and music by Charles Hutchison Gabriel (1856-1932)

This hymn written about 1898 was copyrighted in that year by E. O. Excell. The author and composer was associated with the Rodeheaver Company from 1912 until his death. He occasionally wrote songs using the pseudonym Charlotte G. Homer.
This is the first Free Methodist-Wesleyan hymnal to include this hymn.

154 I Stand Amazed in the Presence
Words and music by Charles Hutchison Gabriel (1856-1932)

This song was written about 1905 and published in that year in *Praises,* a publication of E. O. Excell.

155 Beneath the Cross of Jesus
Elizabeth Cecilia Clephane (1830-1869)

Since the author died in 1869 it is thought this hymn was written about 1868. Ernest K. Emurian in his book *Famous Stories of Inspiring Hymns,* 1956, confirms the date as the summer of 1868. It was published posthumously in *The Family Treasury,* 1872, a popular Scottish Presbyterian magazine, under the caption "Breathings from the Border."
In introducing that volume, the editor, the Reverend W. Arnot, wrote:
"These lines express the experiences, the hopes, and the longings of a young Christian lately released. Written on the very edge of this life, with the better land fully in the view of faith, they seem to us footsteps printed on the sands of Time, where these sands touch the ocean of Eternity...."
There are five stanzas in the poem of which we print 1, 4, and 5. Variations in the text include these changes:

    2:2 Mine eye *at times* can see
    2:7 The wonder of *His glorious love,*
    3:1, 2 *I take, O Christ, Thy* shadow
          For my abiding place
    3:4 The sunshine of *His* face:
    3:6 *To know no* gain *nor* loss—
    3:8 My *glory all the* Cross.

The alterations in stanza 3 seem to have been made by the editors of the *Anglican Hymn Book,* 1965.

The omitted stanzas are:

2. O safe and happy shelter,
  O refuge tried and sweet,
 O trysting-place where heaven's love
  And heaven's justice meet!
 As to the holy patriarch
  That wondrous dream was given,
 So seems my Savior's Cross to me,
  A ladder up to heaven.

3. There lies beneath its shadow,
  But on the farther side,
 The darkness of an awful grave
  That gapes both deep and wide;
 And there between us stands the Cross,
  Two arms outstretched to save,
 Like a watchman set to guard the way
  From that eternal grave.

The hymn is full of biblical symbolism and imagery. See particularly Isaiah 4:6; 28:12; 32:2; Psalm 63:1; Jeremiah 9:2; and Matthew 11:30.

The 1951 hymnal was the first Free Methodist-Wesleyan hymnal to include this hymn.

ST. CHRISTOPHER was composed by Frederick Charles Maker (1844-1927) for this text and included in the Supplement to *The Bristol Tune Book,* 1881.

156 O Sacred Head, Now Wounded

From the Latin, twelfth century
Translated from the Latin by Paul Gerhardt (1607-1676)
Translated from the German by James Waddell Alexander (1804-1859)

The original Latin text, sometimes attributed to Bernard of Clairvaux, is a poem 350 lines in length with 50 lines devoted to each of the several members of the body of Christ. The seven parts are:

1. Salve Mundi Salutare   (To the feet)
2. Salve Jesu, Rex sanctorum   (To the knees)
3. Salve Jesu, pastor bone   (To the hands)
4. Salve Jesu, summe bonus   (To the side)
5. Salve salus mea, Deus   (To the breast)
6. Summi Regis cor aveto   (To the heart)
7. Salve Caput cruentatum   (To the face)

The entire Latin poem has been translated a number of times into German. The best is a free version by Paul Gerhardt. Translations have also been made from the Latin directly into English.

Of all the translations, only those of the seventh hymn (Salve caput cruentatum) seem to have survived in common use. In this country James Waddell Alexander's translation of Paul Gerhardt's translation, "O Haupt voll Blut und Wunden," is the most popular. It appeared in Joshua Leavitt's *Christian Lyre,* 1830. In Britain the translations directly from Latin to English by Sir Henry W. Baker for *Hymns Ancient and Modern,* 1860, and by Robert Bridges for the *Yattendon Hymnal,* 1899, are most often used.

Gerhardt's translation in ten 8-line stanzas entitled, "To the Suffering Face of Jesus" (O Haupt voll Blut and Wunden), was published in Johann Crüger's *Praxis Pietatis Melica,* 1656. Alexander translated stanzas 1, 2, 4, 5, and 7-10 and published them in *The Christian Lyre,* 1830. Later he revised these and added translations of stanzas 3 and 6 for Schaff's *Deutsche Kirchen Freund,* 1849.

This hymn entered Free Methodist-Wesleyan hymnody in 1910.

PASSION CHORALE first appeared in Hans Leo Hassler's *Lustgärten neuer teutscher Gesäng,* 1601, where it was set to a trivial love song beginning "Mein G'müth ist mir verwirret / Das Macht ein Jungfrau zart / Bin gan z und gar verwirret, / Mein Hertz das Kränckt sich hart." This might be translated:

> Confused are all my feelings,
> A tender maid's the cause.

In *Harmoniae Sacrae,* third edition, 1613, it was set to the hymn "Herzlich thut mir Verlangen" by Christoph Knoll and then to Paul Gerhardt's text in 1656.

Johann Sebastian Bach was especially fond of the tune for he used it in various forms and keys and harmonic settings in the *St. Matthew's Passion* and in the *Christmas Oratorio.* Our setting is a composite from these two sources and makes use of a beautiful Phrygian cadence.

The melody as it appeared in Hassler's *Lustgarten* is as follows:

157 Hail, Thou Once Despised Jesus

Attributed to John Bakewell (1721-1819)
Altered by Martin Madan (1726-1790) and
Augustus Toplady (1740-1778)

The original hymn, sixteen lines in length, is found in a small pamphlet entitled *A Collection of Hymns addressed to the Holy, Holy, Holy, Triune God* ... MDCCLVII. On somewhat uncertain grounds the authorship is assigned to John Bakewell, an evangelist and class leader associated with the Methodists. It is claimed that Thomas Olivers wrote "The God of Abraham Praise" in Bakewell's home.

Bakewell's grave is near that of John Wesley at City Road Chapel burying ground. On his tombstone are inscribed these words: "adorned the doctrine of God our Savior 80 years, and preached His glorious gospel about 70 years."

Bakewell's text:

    1:3 *Who* didst ...
    1:4 *Who* didst ...
    1:5 ... *universal* Savior
    1:6 *Who has* borne ...
    1:7 By *whose* merits ...

Toplady was responsible for the changes in stanza 1. Stanza 2 is taken from Martin Madan's *Collection of Psalms and Hymns*, 1760 with alterations from Toplady.

2:3 ... *appointed*
2:5 *Ev'ry Sin may be forgiv'n*
3:1-4 is from Bakewell
3:5 is from Madan
3:6 is from Toplady
3:7, 8 is from Madan and Toplady
4:1-4 completes Bakewell's text
4:5-8 is from Madan except for a change by Toplady in 4:7. Madan wrote: 'Help to sing our Jesu's merits.

This hymn has appeared in all Free Methodist hymnals except for 1951.

IN BABILONE is a traditional Dutch melody found in *Oude en nieuwe Hollantse Boerenlities en Contradanseu,* c. 1710. The arrangement is by Julius Röntgen (1855-1932).

158 Ah, Holy Jesus, How Hast Thou Offended?

Johann Heermann (1585-1647)
Translated by Robert Seymour Bridges (1844-1930)

"Herzliebster Jesu, was hast du verbrochen" was written by Johann Heermann during the period of The Thirty Years' War in fifteen 4-line stanzas and first published in his *Devoti Musica Cordis,* 1630. The title was "The Cause of the bitter sufferings of Jesus Christ, and consolation from His love and grace." It was based on No. VII of the *Meditationes* often attributed to St. Augustine.

The translation by Bridges is taken from his *Yattendon Hymnal,* 1899, where it is marked as a retranslation from St. Augustine. At another place he attributes it more accurately to St. Anselm. The *Meditationes* is a compilation of the works of several writers and No. VII is by Anselm.

This is the first appearance in a Free Methodist-Wesleyan hymnal.

HERZLIEBSTER JESU is a melody of Johann Crüger found in his *Neues vollkömmlisches Gesangbuch,* 1640. The harmonization used here is a composite harmonization derived from settings in *St. John Passion* and *St. Matthew Passion* by Johann Sebastian Bach (1685-1750).

159 Deep Were His Wounds, and Red
William Johnson (b. 1906)

The text of this moving hymn was written by William Johnson, a Minnesota farmer. According to Dr. William R. Seaman, author of the *Companion to the Service Book and Hymnal,* Johnson had little formal education but was an avid reader of the Bible, Shakespeare, Dickens, and so forth. A number of his poems have appeared in *The Lutheran Companion* of the Augustana Synod. He is said to have written many of his poems in the quiet of the milk house or barn. Ninety of his poems were published in *Wild Flowers,* 1948.

MARLEE was written for this text by Leland Bernhard Sateren (b. 1913) and published in the Lutheran *Service Book and Hymnal,* 1958. Sateren is a native of Everett, Washington. Since 1946 he has served as a music professor at Augsburg College. He is the composer of 300 choral works and was a member of the hymnal commission which prepared the *Service Book and Hymnal,* 1958.

160 Alone Thou Goest Forth
Peter Abelard (1079-1142)
Translated by Francis Bland Tucker (b. 1895)

This hymn, based on Lamentations 1:12, is found in the reedited edition of Abelard's hymns under the title *Hymnarius Paraclitensis.* His hymns seemed to have been written for his wife Heloise's Convent of the Paraclete.

The free translation by Francis Bland Tucker was made in 1938 for *The Hymnal 1940.* Tucker was Rector of Christ Church, Savannah, Georgia.

BANGOR is taken from *A Complete Melody or Harmony of Zion,* 1734, by William Tans'ur (1706-1783), where it is set to Psalm 11. (See also comments at No. 10.)

161 Cross of Jesus, Cross of Sorrows
William John Sparrow-Simpson (1860-1952)

This hymn is part of the book of words compiled by Simpson for John Stainer's *Crucifixion,* 1887. There are ten 4-line stanzas in the original. (Stanza 10 is the same as stanza 1.) Our hymnal uses stanzas 1, 2, 3, 4, 10.

This is the first inclusion in a Free Methodist-Wesleyan hymnal.

CROSS OF JESUS is John Stainer's (1840-1901) tune and harmonization for this text in his *Crucifixion*. The first performance of the oratorio was in Marylebone Parish Church in London, the parish church of Charles Wesley.

Stainer was an organist, composer, and choral conductor of considerable stature. His choir at St. Paul's Cathedral was said to be the best in all of England. Queen Victoria knighted him in 1888.

162-168 The Words from the Cross
Thomas Benson Pollock (1836-1896)

This is a series of seven hymns comprising a metrical litany entitled, "The Seven Words on the Cross," included in the author's *Metrical Litanies for Special Services and General Use*, 1870.

Part V, stanza 2, read originally:

> Pant for us in mercy still;
> May we Thy desires fulfil, —

This is the first inclusion in a Free Methodist-Wesleyan hymnal.

The tunes in this section are interchangeable. SONG 13, also known as CANTERBURY, was written by Dr. Orlando Gibbons (1583-1625) for George Wither's *Hymnes and Songs of the Church*, 1623, and set to "Oh, my love, how comely now" based on the Song of Solomon, chapter 1.

SWEDISH LITANY, according to *The Hymnal 1940 Companion*, is taken from the *Hemmets Koralbok*, 1697.

LITANY OF THE PASSION was written for the "Litany of the Passion" in the 1875 edition of *Hymns Ancient and Modern* by John Bacchus Dykes (1823-1876).

LEBBAEUS is taken from *St. Alban's Tune Book*, 1866, *Music of the Appendix to the Hymnal Noted)*. The arrangement is by Arthur Seymour Sullivan (1842-1900) in his *Church Hymns with Tunes*, 1874.

HERVEY'S LITANY was composed for Thomas Benson

Pollock's *Litany of the Incarnate Word* by Frederick Alfred John Hervey (1846-1910). It appears in the 1875 edition of *Hymns Ancient and Modern.*

169   On the Cross of Calvary
David Livingstone Ives (b. 1921)

The author of this text was a student at Fort Wayne Bible College in the 1940s. He then established the Ives Music Press in Archbold, Ohio. He wrote both words and music for numerous gospel songs.

This is the first inclusion in a Free Methodist-Wesleyan hymnal.

GERIG was composed for this text in about 1942 by Richard E. Gerig (b. 1922). Gerig was at one time director of music at First Missionary Church in Fort Wayne, Indiana. He now occupies the same position at Wheaton Bible Church and is Director of Public Relations at Wheaton College.

170   Were You There?
Traditional Spiritual

The text and tune of this folk song are anonymous. The earliest known printed source is *Old Plantation Melodies,* 1899. The melody is evidently much older.

The hymnal arrangement is an adaptation from an anthem prepared for the use of the Seattle Pacific College a Cappella Choir by Lawrence R. Schoenhals.

The effect of this spiritual sung unaccompanied by the late negro tenor Roland Hayes many years ago is still vivid in my memory.

171   The Day of Resurrection
St. John of Damascus (d. 780).
Translated by John Mason Neale (1818-1866)

This hymn is derived from the first Ode of the Golden Canon for Easter Day by St. John of Damascus, c. 750. There are eight Odes in a Festival Canon. The translation is a free one by John Mason Neale and appeared first in his *Hymns of the Eastern*

Church, 1862. It entered Free Methodist-Wesleyan hymnody in 1951.

LANCASHIRE was composed by Henry Thomas Smart (1813-1879) for a music festival in Blackburn, England, in 1835. It was written for, and associated with, the hymn "From Greenland's Icy Mountains." Its first inclusion in a hymnal was in the composer's *Psalms and Hymns for Divine Worship,* 1867.

172   Christ the Lord Is Risen Today
Charles Wesley (1707-1788)

This hymn in eleven 4-line stanzas without alleluias appeared in The Wesleys' *Hymns and Sacred Poems,* Pt. II, 1739, under the title "Hymn for Easter-Day." The alleluias at the end of each line were not in the original but were added when the hymn was adapted to the tune EASTER HYMN. *HFL* uses stanzas 1, 2*a* and 3*b*, 4, and 5.

The omitted couplets from stanzas 2 and 3 are:

(2*b*) Lo! our Sun's eclipse is o'er;
Lo! He sets in blood no more.
(3*a*) Vain the stone, the watch, the seal;
Christ has burst the gates of hell!

The omitted stanzas are not generally included in present-day hymnals.

All Free Methodist hymnals since 1883 include this hymn. In 1883 stanzas 1, 2, 3, 4, and 5 are used with textual modifications derived, apparently, from John Rippon, *A Selection of Hymns from the Best Authors,* 1787.

EASTER HYMN also called WORGAN is an anonymous tune which appeared first in *Lyra Davidica,* 1708, in somewhat different form. The present form was published in John Wesley's *Foundery Collection,* 1742. It had been printed a year earlier in John Arnold's *The Complete Psalmodist,* 1741.

173   Come, Ye Faithful, Raise the Strain
St. John of Damascus (eighth century)
Translated by John Mason Neale (1818-1866)

This is the first Ode of the Canon for St. Thomas's Sunday. It is based on "Song of Moses" in Exodus 15. The translation by

Neale is of the first half only of the canon and appears in his *Hymns of the Eastern Church*, 1862.

This hymn was included in *Hymns of the Living Faith*, 1951, in three stanzas. An additional stanza from the original was added in 1976.

ST. KEVIN was composed by Arthur Seymour Sullivan (1842-1900) for this text in the *Hymnary*, 1872, edited by Joseph Barnby, but without title. The tune name was given in Sullivan's *Church Hymns with Tunes*, 1874. Coemgen or St. Kevin, a name that means "fair begotten," was a hermit who is supposed to have established a monastery in Ireland. He died c. 618 at the age of 120 years. (For comments on Sir Arthur Sullivan see No. 411.)

174 Our Blessed Lord Was Slain
Oswald Jeffray Smith (b. 1890)

This is another fine example of the productive collaboration of Dr. Smith and B. D. Ackley. The text was written originally in 1938 while Dr. Smith was recovering from an attack of malaria. In 1944 Ackley asked him to write something on the theme of the Resurrection but without reference to Easter. He said that his brother, A. H., had long contended that since Christ's Resurrection is central to our salvation, songs on this theme ought not to be restricted to the Easter season exclusively.

Dr. Smith, remembering his poem of 1938, revised it and removed all references to Easter Sunday, and mailed it off to Mr. Ackley. The resulting song was an immediate success and has retained its popularity through the years since.

The gospel song book *Choice Light and Life Songs*, 1950, introduced the song to Free Methodist congregations. The following year it was included in *Hymns of the Living Faith*, produced cooperatively by the Wesleyan and Free Methodist denominations.

HE ROSE TRIUMPHANTLY was composed for this text in 1944 by Bentley DeForest Ackley (1872-1958).

175 Low in the Grave He Lay
Robert Lowry (1826-1899)

This Easter song was written by a Baptist hymn writer in

1874 and first published in a Sunday school songbook *Brightest and Best,* 1875.

Lowry served a number of Baptist churches and was for many years connected with the University of Lewisburg, now Bucknell University, both as student and as Crozer Professor of Rhetoric.

This song entered Free Methodist-Wesleyan hymnody in 1910.

CHRIST AROSE is the tune Robert Lowry wrote as a setting for "Low in the Grave He Lay."

176 That Easter Day with Joy Was Bright
Latin, fourth or fifth century
Translated by John Mason Neale (1818-1866)

The Latin hymn, "Aurora lucis rutilat," from which this translation is taken has been attributed to St. Ambrose but may have been of a later origin. The stanzas selected here are from Part III beginning with the words "Claro paschali gaudio."

The English translation is based on that of John Mason Neale in the *Hymnal Noted,* 1851. Stanzas 3 and 4 are in the form of a double Eastertide doxology.

The hymn entered Free Methodist-Wesleyan hymnody in 1951.

PUER NOBIS NASCITUR was discussed at No. 60.

177 I Know that My Redeemer Lives
Charles Wesley (1707-1788)

This hymn in twenty-three 4-line stanzas is taken from *Hymns and Sacred Poems,* Pt. II, 1742, and is entitled "Rejoicing in Hope." Our hymnal uses stanzas 1, 2, 10, 15, and 19. It has been a part of Free Methodist hymnody since 1883, using the same selection of stanzas.

BRADFORD is derived from the soprano aria "I Know that My Redeemer Liveth" from the *Messiah* by George Frederick Handel (1685-1759).

178 Thine Is the Glory

Edmond Louis Budry (1854-1932)
Translated by Richard Birch Hoyle (1875-1939)

The French text dates from 1884. The translation is dated 1923 and appeared in *Cantate Domino,* the hymnal of the World Student Christian Federation.

JUDAS MACCABEUS, or MACCABEUS, is derived from the chorus "See the Conquering Hero Comes," from the oratorio *Judas Maccabeus* by George Frederick Handel (1685-1759). The tune was originally intended to be included in *Joshua,* first performed in London in 1748. It was transferred to *Judas Maccabeus* about 1751.

Handel professed not to like the tune as well as some other things he had written, but prophesied to a friend ". . . you will live to see it a greater favourite with the people than my other finer things." It soon became very popular and John Wesley mentions hearing it on at least two occasions.

Handel was said to have been ungodly and profane. When angry he would swear in three languages. During the last few years of his life it is said he had a marked change of heart and became a regular church attendant.

Although there is no firm evidence it seems reasonable that Charles Wesley would have met Handel at the home of a mutual friend, a Mrs. Rich, in Chelsea. Handel set three of Wesley's hymns to music and these tunes still exist in manuscript form. They were published by Samuel Wesley who discovered them. GOPSAL, our number *532,* is one of these tunes.

179 Christ Is Risen, Raise Your Voices

Frank von Christierson (b. 1900)

The author of this fine contemporary hymn is minister of the First Presbyterian Church, Roseville, California. A native of Finland, he came to the United States at the age of five. He is a graduate of Stanford University and San Francisco Theological Seminary. Prior to his present assignment he served a number of Presbyterian churches in California and also served as moderator of the San Francisco and Los Angeles presbyteries.

HYMN TO JOY (See notes on hymn No. 5.)

180 The Strife Is O'er, the Battle Done

From the Latin, 1695
Translated by Francis Pott (1832-1909)

The Latin text beginning "Finita iam sunt praelia" of which this hymn is a translation is found in the *Symphonia Sirenum...*, Cologne, 1695. According to Julian the translation by Francis Pott was made about 1859 and first published in his *Hymns Fitted to the Order of Common Prayer,* 1861.

Originally an Easter hymn it is appropriately used as a funeral hymn.

This is the first appearance in a Free Methodist-Wesleyan hymnal.

VICTORY is a very much altered form of *Gloria Patri et Filio* from the *Magnificat Tertii Toni,* 1591, by Giovanni Pierluigi da Palestrina (1525-1594). The arrangement was made by William Henry Monk for *Hymns Ancient & Modern,* 1861. Monk added original alleluias and changed the tonality.

181 Praise the Saviour, Now and Ever

Venantius Fortunatus (c. 535-600)

This is an English translation of the Swedish version of the fine Latin medieval hymn, *Pange lingua, gloriosi proelium certaminis*. It should be compared with the Neale translation "Sing, my tongue, the glorious battle" (No. 514).

It is included in a Free Methodist-Wesleyan hymnal for the first time.

RIDDARHOLM (UPP, MIN TUNGA) is an anonymous tune taken from the Swedish *Koralbok* of 1697. It, too, appears for the first time in a Free Methodist hymnal.

182 Hail the Day that Sees Him Rise

Charles Wesley (1707-1788)

This hymn is taken from Wesley's *Hymns and Sacred Poems,* Part II, 1739, where it appears in ten 4-line stanzas and is entitled "Hymn for Ascension Day." It was reprinted in at least two of the later Wesley hymnbooks (1747 and 1765) but not in the "Large Hymnbook" of 1780. *Hymns of Faith and Life* uses stanzas 1, 2, 5, 8, and 10, with these alterations:

1:2 Ravished from our wishful eyes!
1:4 Reascends His native heaven!
2:1 There the *pompous* . . .

This is the first Free Methodist-Wesleyan hymnal to include this fine Wesley hymn.

LLANFAIR or BETHEL with alleluias is ascribed to a blind basket maker named Robert Williams. It is asserted that it was found in his music manuscript book where it is dated July 14, 1817. There is sufficient uncertainty about its authorship so that many authorities simply call it *Alaw Gymreig* (Welsh Air).

Robert Guy McCutchan in *Hymn Tune Names,* 1957, gives the meaning of the tune name as follows:

Llan means "saint" or "holy" or "church."

Fair means "Mary," therefore "Church of St. Mary." Llan is a common prefix to Welsh town names. A few years ago I visited a town in Montgomery County, Wales, that had the longest name of any town in the world, having 58 letters in it: Llanfairpwllgwyngyllgogerychwyrndrobwllllantysiliogogogoch. Understandably, local residents abbreiviate it as Llanfair P.G. or simply, Llanfair. The translation according to McCutchan is "Church of St. Mary in a hollow of white hazel near the rapid whirlpool of the Church of St. Tysillio by the red cave."

183 Crown Him with Many Crowns
Matthew Bridges (1800-1894) and Godfrey Thring (1823-1903)

Matthew Bridges's hymn beginning with this opening line appeared in his *Hymns of the Heart,* second edition, 1851 in six 8-line stanzas. Godfrey Thring composed at least two hymns using parts of Bridges's hymn. Our second stanza is taken from Thring's *Hymns and Sacred Lyrics,* 1874.

Stanzas 1 and 3 are substantially the same as written by Bridges. Stanza 2 is Thring's stanza 4, and stanza 4 is a combination of Bridges's stanzas 3 and 6.

The changes are as follows:

3:4 *Absorbed in . . .*
4:3 *Rich* wounds . . .
4:7 Thy praise *shall never, never* fail

Thring's hymn was written at the request of the Reverend H. W. Hutton to replace some of the stanzas of Bridges's hymn which he and others thought objectionable. Later it was thought better to rewrite the whole hymn so that the two hymns might be distinct. They were not kept distinct and most hymnals use a combination of the two.

"Crown Him with Many Crowns" entered Free Methodist-Wesleyan hymnody in 1910 in four stanzas as follows:

      Stanza 1 Bridges Stanza 1
      Stanza 2 Bridges Stanza 3
      Stanza 3 Bridges Stanza 4 altered
      Stanza 4 Bridges Stanza 5a and Stanza 6b

The 1976 hymnal uses the form adopted in the 1951 hymnal.

DIADEMATA was written by Sir George Job Elvey (1816-1893) for the 1868 Appendix to the first edition of *Hymns Ancient and Modern*. The name is derived from the Greek word for "crowns" as used in the New Testament. Elvey was a long time organist at St. George's Chapel, Windsor, having been chosen for that position at age eighteen over the more experienced and better known Samuel Sebastian Wesley.

184 God Is Gone up on High

Charles Wesley (1707-1788)

This is from Charles Wesley's *Hymns for Ascension Day* published in Bristol in 1746 in six 6-line stanzas.

DARWELL'S 148TH. (See notes for hymn No. 46.)

185 Once Our Blessed Christ of Beauty

N. B. Herrell (1879-1954)

The author, a minister in the Church of the Nazarene, was residing in Olivet, Illinois, when this song was written. He wrote to Haldor Lillenas:

> I was pastoring a church at Georgetown, a nearby village. It was the year 1916. Those were difficult and heartbreaking days. We had just suffered the loss of our five-year-old son, William. While traversing this valley of sorrow the song was born *(Modern Gospel Song Stories,* 1952).

Evidently the scriptural image is taken from Matthew 27:51.

This is the first Free Methodist-Wesleyan hymnal to include this song although it had appeared earlier in *Choice Light and Life Songs,* a gospel songbook.

THE UNVEILED CHRIST was written by Herrell for the text and is the title by which the song is generally known.

186 Lo, He Comes, with Clouds Descending
Charles Wesley (1707-1788)
Based on a hymn by John Cennick (1718-1755)
Altered by Martin Madan (1726-1790)

This hymn is one of forty appearing in Wesley's *Hymns of Intercession for All Mankind,* 1758, in four 6-line stanzas.

In about 1750 John Cennick had written a hymn beginning with the words "Lo! He cometh, countless trumpets blow before his bloody sign!" Charles Wesley would have been familiar with Cennick's hymn and may have taken his inspiration from it.

Martin Madan, in his *Collection of Psalms and Hymns,* 1760, took parts of Cennick and Wesley and produced the form generally followed since that time. He titled the hymn "The Second Advent."

Stanzas 1 and 2 are as Wesley wrote them.

Stanza 3 is Cennick as altered by Madan.

Stanza 4 is as Wesley wrote it except *Jah Jehovah* is replaced by "O come quickly" from Cennick.

John Cennick was engaged by John Wesley to assist at Kingswood School. He was a native of Reading and has been described as a person of "sincere piety and zeal" and "of respectable education." He disassociated himself from the Wesley's over a point of doctrine and became a follower of George Whitefield. Within three years he had left Whitefield and became affiliated with the Moravians. He was something of a hymnwriter. Charles Wesley is known to have corrected some of his hymns for publication.

HYFRYDOL was discussed at No. 97.

187 Marvelous Message We Bring
Words and music by John Peterson (b. 1921)

This is the first appearance in a Free Methodist-Wesleyan hymnal.

188 Wounded for Me
W. G. Ovens (1870-1945) and Gladys Wescott Roberts (b. 1888)

OVENS was written by the Reverend W. G. Ovens who also wrote the opening stanza of the text. This is the first appearance in a Free Methodist-Wesleyan hymnal.

189 Look, Ye Saints! The Sight Is Glorious
Thomas Kelly, (1769-1854)

Thomas Kelly, a lawyer by training, underwent a spiritual change, and took Holy Orders instead of practicing law. Because of his strong* evangelical preaching in Dublin, he and his companion Rowland Hill were prevented from preaching in the established church in that city. He then became an independent minister and erected a number of independent churches in which he ministered.

Kelly was talented musically, something of a linguist, and a skilled poet. His hymns number 765, written over a period of fifty-one years.

This hymn was first published in the author's *Hymns on Various Passages of Scripture,* third edition, 1809, in four 6-line stanzas. It entered Free Methodist-Wesleyan hymnody in 1910.

CORONAE was composed in 1871 by William Henry Monk (1823-1889) for Kelly's text. A distinguished church musician, he arranged more than sixty of the tunes in the 1861 edition of *Hymns Ancient & Modern,* to which he also contributed fifteen original tunes.

190 Christ Is Coming! Let Creation
John Ross MacDuff (1818-1895)

MacDuff, a minister in the Established Church in Scotland, wrote approximately thirty-one hymns. Only one remains in general usage. "Christ Is Coming" was published in the author's *The Gates of Praise,* 1875. Evidently, MacDuff's literary efforts brought him considerable renown during his lifetime for he was awarded doctoral degrees by the University of Glasgow and by New York University.

This hymn entered Free Methodist-Wesleyan hymnody in 1910.

UNSER HERRSCHER or NEANDER is probably the work of Joachim Neander (1650-1680) for it appeared in his collection *Alpha und Omega,* published in Bremen in 1680, and set to the words of his hymn "Unser Herrscher, unser König." Originally the last two lines were in 6/4 time, a form preferable to the present modern arrangement.

191   Rejoice, Rejoice, Believers!
Laurentius Laurenti (1660-1722)
Translated by Sarah Borthwick Findlater (1823-1886)

Laurenti was born in Husum in northern Germany and died in Bremen where he was cantor and director of the music in the cathedral church. He was considered one of the best hymnwriters of the Pietistic school.

"Ermuntert euch, ihr Frommen," Laurenti's advent hymn, is probably his finest and appeared in his *Evangelica Melodica,* 1700, in ten 8-line stanzas. It is based on Matthew 25:1-13 and Revelation 20 and 21.

Mrs. Findlater translated stanzas 1-3, 7, 8, and 10, beginning with the words "Rejoice, all ye believers." The first publication was in *Hymns from the Land of Luther,* First Series, 1854. A number of American hymnals, beginning as early as 1867, included varying centos with stanza 1 altered as we have it in *Hymns of Faith and Life. Laudes Domini* (1890 edition), is the immediate source of our text.

This hymn entered Free Methodist-Wesleyan hymnody in 1910.

GREENLAND was discussed at No. 64.

192   When He Shall Come
Words and music by Almeda J. Pearce (b. 1893)

Almeda J. Pearce (Mrs. Rowan C.) was born in Carlisle, Pennsylvania, and was married there in 1919. In a personal letter to the author she described the background of this beautiful song:

"It was in the awful days of the 'great depression' . . . that I remembered as the hardest days of my whole life. But oh were the *most blessed,* because my husband and I learned then to really pray and know our God. Living in Collingswood, New Jersey, we were given the responsibility of Bible Study and leadership of eager young people . . . after a great awakening and revival in the

Methodist Church. The 'Class' as it became known ... met in our home weekly.... It was there that the first knowledge of the Second Coming of the Lord was being brought out in messages of visiting Bible teachers. We were thrilled with the prophetic truth of the 'Rapture of the Church' promised in I Thessalonians 4:16, 17, of the 'blessed hope.' What it meant to be an 'overcomer' in that glorious day of His coming....

"It was during prayer one night when heaven came close, and the words of Revelation 7:9, 10 ... began to sing in my heart and Revelation 3:4 spoke down deep of the 'overcomers walking with Him in white' that the melody of the song, with the words, was formed in my heart.... I had a slight knowledge of composition in New York at the Institute of Musical Art ... majoring in voice....

"Our son Bill Pearce was at Moody radio station WMBI then and I visited Moody and heard my song sung by the Moody Chorale. A joy to my heart, that the Lord used His Spirit in the blessing of hearts even in far away places."

193   Sing of Our God

Words and music by Ronald Meyer
Music arranged for this hymnal by William W. Tromble (b. 1932).

194   Jesus Shall Reign Where'er the Sun

Isaac Watts (1674-1748)

This metric version of the second part of Psalm 72 in eight 4-line stanzas is taken from Watts's *The Psalm of David Imitated* ..., 1719. Included here are stanzas 1, 4-6, 8. Stanzas 2, 3, 7, and 8 in Watts were bracketed, indicating he would approve their omission. Rowland Hill was among the first to adopt the hymn for congregational use and he included it in his *Psalms and Hymns, First Edition*, 1783. Its popularity increased in the nineteenth century as interest in foreign missions grew. Today it is probably one of the few hymns included in every hymnal of merit. It has been in every Free Methodist hymnal since 1883. (See also comments at No. 6.)

DUKE STREET was composed by John Hatton (c. 1710-1793) of whom very little is known. The tune appeared anonymously in Henry Boyd's *Select Collection of Psalm and Hymn Tunes,* 1793, where it was called *Addison's 19th Psalm* (The Spacious Firmament). Hatton was assigned as the composer by William

Dixon in his *Euphonia,* 1805. He was supposed to have lived on Duke Street in the town of St. Helens in Lancaster, England.

195 Lord God, the Holy Ghost
James Montgomery (1771-1854)

This hymn was first published in Thomas Cotterill's *Selection of Psalms and Hymns for Public and Private Use,* eighth edition, 1819, in three 8-line stanzas. Montgomery altered it slightly when he included it in his own *Christian Psalmist,* 1825.

The omitted quatrain (first four lines of stanza 3) reads:

>Spirit of light, explore
>and chase our gloom away,
>With lustre shining more and more
>unto the perfect day.

The hymn entered Free Methodist hymnody in 1883 without omissions.

ST. MICHAEL (OLD 134th) is the shortened form of a tune found in the *Genevan Psalter,* 1551, where it was set to Psalm 101. It was used with Psalm 134 in considerably altered form in the Anglo-Genevan *Four Score and Seven Psalms,* 1561. After a period of disuse it was revived by Dr. William Crotch in his *Psalm Tunes,* 1836, where it was assigned its present title, after St. Michael's College, Tenbury, England.

196 Holy Ghost, with Light Divine
Andrew Reed (1787-1862)

This hymn in four 8-line stanzas is found in the author's *The Hymn Book,* 1842. It seems to have been published first in 1817 in Reed's *Supplement* to Watts under the title "Prayer to the Holy Spirit." *Hymns of Faith and Life* uses the first half of each stanza. The omitted lines are as follows:

>1:5-8
>>Let me see my Saviour's face,
>>Let me all his beauties trace.
>>Show those glorious truths to me,
>>Which are only known by thee.
>
>2:5-8
>>Oft I of its power complain,
>>Yet I live beneath its reign:

> In thy mercy pity me,
> From this bondage set me free.
> 3:5-8
> Yield a sacred, settled peace,
> Bid it grow and still increase;
> Till each anxious thought expires,
> Till my joy to heaven aspires.
> 4:5-8
> See, to thee I yield my heart,
> Shed thy life through every part;
> A pure temple I would be,
> Wholly dedicate to thee.

Andrew Reed wrote approximately twenty-one hymns of which perhaps two remain in current use. He was a Congregational minister in England but was best known as the founder of social service institutions. A doctor of divinity degree was conferred on him by Yale College.

All Free Methodist hymnals since 1883 have included this hymn.

MERCY (LAST HOPE) was arranged by Edwin Paul Parker (1836-1925), a Congregational minister in Hartford, Connecticut, from the piano composition "The Last Hope" by Louis Moreau Gottschalk (1829-1869).

197 Spirit of God, Descend upon My Heart

George Croly (1780-1860)

This fine hymn is the work of Dr. George Croly, an Anglican minister in Ireland and later in London. It appeared first, according to Julian, in his *Psalms and Hymns for Public Worship*, 1854, to which he contributed ten psalms, twelve hymns, and six poems. It was headed "Holiness Desired."

The 1951 Free Methodist-Wesleyan hymnal introduced this hymn to the two denominations.

MORECAMBE by Frederick Cook Atkinson (1841-1897) was written in 1870 originally as a setting for Lyte's "Abide with Me." The name derives from Morecambe, a town and a bay in West England, near which Atkinson served as a church organist.

198 Gracious Spirit, Dwell with Me
Thomas Toke Lynch (1818-1871)
Stanza 3 altered by Evan K. Gibson (b. 1909)

This hymn in six 6-line stanzas was first published in the author's *The Rivulet, a Contribution to Sacred Song*, 1855. There it was entitled "Holy Spirit's Presence Desired." The publication of *The Rivulet* provoked a bitter hymnological controversy. Dr. Binney, among others, came to the defense of Lynch's book. As John Telford wrote years later ". . . it is difficult in our day to understand how such a storm arose over so inoffensive a volume." The original lines changed by Dr. Gibson are:

> 3:5-4 And whatever I can be
> Give to Him who gave me Thee!

His comment is that the above lines are "vague and confusing" and do not "carry out the theme of the stanza (holiness) as do the other two (graciousness and truthfulness)."

Dr. Gibson, until his retirement in 1975, was Professor of English at Seattle Pacific University.

Hymns of the Living Faith introduced this hymn to Free Methodist-Wesleyan congregations.

REDHEAD NO. 76 is discussed at No. 150.

199 Come, Holy Spirit, Heart's Desire
George E. Failing (b. 1912)

This hymn was submitted anonymously to the Joint Hymnal Commission by a member of the Commission, the present editor of *The Wesleyan Methodist*. As originally written the first stanza read:

> Come, come Holy Spirit heart's desire
> Cast down on me celestial fire,
> Come now to comfort, teach and heal,
> Come now our God the Son reveal.

ANGELUS had its origin in a tune composed by Georg Joseph to a hymn by Johann Scheffler (1624-1677) (Angelus Silesius) and published in *Heilige Seelenlust, oder geistliche Hirtenlieder der in ihren Jesu verliebten Psyche*, 1657. The hymn began:

> Du meiner seelen güldne ziehr
> Du Freude die dein Vater mir

In much altered form the tune appeared in *Cantica Spiritualia*,

Part II, 1847. This is the form adopted in our hymnal except for the rhythm in measures 7 and 15. (See also comments at No. 142.)

200 Come, Holy Spirit, Heavenly Dove
Isaac Watts (1674-1748)
Altered by Charles Wesley (1707-1788)

This hymn appeared first in Watts's *Hymns and Spiritual Songs,* Book II, 1707, in five 4-line stanzas, and entitled "Breathing After the Holy Spirit: or, Fervency of Devotion Desir'd."

There have been many alterations to the original. Stanzas 2 and 4 seemed most troublesome. John (or Charles) Wesley omitted stanza 2 entirely in his *Collection of Psalms and Hymns,* 1743, and altered stanza 4 to read: "And shall we then for ever live."

The original unaltered lines are:

    2:2 . . . of these *trifling* toys
    2:3 Our souls *can neither fly nor go*
    4:1 *Dear Lord,* . . .

Hymns of Faith and Life is the first Free Methodist-Wesleyan hymnal to include this hymn. (See also comments at No. 6.)

GRAFENBERG appeared first in Johann Crüger's (1598-1662) *Praxis Pietatis Melica,* second edition, 1647, where it was set to Paul Gerhardt's "Nun danket all." Some writers have noted a similarity to tunes in the *Genevan Psalter,* 1562.

201 Holy Spirit, Faithful Guide
Words and music by Marcus M. Wells (1815-1895)

According to Wells he wrote the text and the tune on an October Sunday in 1858. It was published first in Isaac B. Woodbury's monthly musical periodical, the *New York Musical Pioneer,* for November, 1858. Later it was included in *The Sacred Lute,* 1864, edited by T. E. Perkins.

The 1910 Free Methodist-Wesleyan hymnal introduced this hymn to the congregations of the two denominations.

202 Hover O'er Me, Holy Spirit

Elwood Haines Stokes (1815-1895)
Altered by Evan K. Gibson (b. 1909)

Dr. Stokes was one of the founders of the Ocean Grove religious community in New Jersey and president of the Ocean Grove Campmeeting Association. According to Phil Kerr *(Music in Evangelism),* Stokes felt a need for more hymns emphasizing the work of the Holy Spirit and wrote this song to help meet this need. It was copyrighted in 1879.

The alteration by Dr. Gibson changes the following words:

1:4 *Come, O come and fill me now.*

By this change he avoided a "meaningless figure" and made "the prayer specific."

This song entered Free Methodist-Wesleyan hymnody in 1910.

FILL ME NOW was written by John R. Sweney (1837-1899) for this text in 1879. He wrote it while on his knees in prayer. At the time he was serving as musical director at the famous Ocean Grove Campmeeting.

Sweney, along with R. Kelso Carter, taught music for a number of years in the Pennsylvania Military Academy. A profound spiritual crisis in 1871 caused him to turn his attention to religious work. He was much in demand as a song leader at conventions and camp meetings. In association with William J. Kirkpatrick he published more than sixty gospel songbooks.

Perhaps Sweney's best-known tune was written for the text "Beulah Land." Ira D. Sankey sang this song at Sweney's funeral.

203 Spirit of Faith, Come Down

Charles Wesley (1707-1788)

This text was first published in John and Charles Wesley's small volume of thirty-two hymns entitled *Hymns of Petition and Thanksgiving for the Promise of the Father,* 1746, in five 8-line stanzas.

Stanza 2 is omitted here and there is one small alteration:

3:2 The *great* atoning ...

This hymn appears in all Free Methodist hymnals except 1951.

NEARER HOME, by Isaac Baker Woodbury (1819-1858), is

taken from *The Choral Advocate,* 1852, an American musical journal. Originally there was a refrain which has now dropped out of use. The title derives from the James Montgomery hymn for which it was written, "Forever with the Lord."

The arrangement by Sir Arthur Seymour Sullivan (1842-1900) was made c. 1874.

204 Creator Spirit! by Whose Aid

Latin (ninth century)
Translated by John Dryden (1631-1700)
Adapted by John Wesley (1703-1791)

This hymn is a translation of "Veni Creator Spiritus," one of the seven great hymns of the Medieval Church, made by John Dryden, and it appeared in his *Miscellaneous Poems,* Part III, 1693, in seven stanzas of unequal length. There are thirty-nine lines in all. John Wesley recognized its suitability for congregational purposes and included it in his *Collection of Psalms and Hymns,* Part I, 1741, in four 6-line stanzas. Note that the final stanza is in the form of a doxology.

The omitted fourth stanza reads as follows:

> Create all new; our wills control;
> Subdue the rebel in our soul;
> Chase from our minds th'infernal foe,
> And peace, the fruit of faith, bestow:
> And lest again we go astray,
> Protect and guide us in Thy way.

In Dryden's version it reads:

> 1:3 ... every *pious* mind, 2:1 ... uncreated *light.*
> 4:1-2 (omitted)
> *Our frailties help, our vice control,*
> *Submit the senses to the soul.*

Dryden was Poet Laureate and Historiographer Royal, 1670-1689. He is buried in Westminster Abbey.

This hymn appeared in the 1883 and 1910 hymnals but was omitted in 1951.

ATTWOOD (VENI CREATOR) is derived from an anthem "Come, Holy Ghost" by Thomas Attwood (1765-1838), organist at St. Paul's Cathedral in London, beginning in 1796. The anthem was composed on two days' notice from Bishop Blomfield of London for an ordination service on Trinity Sunday. It is said that Attwood was still writing out the vocal parts while riding in his carriage to the Cathedral.

Attwood studied in Vienna under Mozart, the only English pupil the great composer ever accepted. Attwood wrote on one of his exercises, "Thomas Attwood presents his compliments to Mr. Mozart, and hopes he will find the exercise satisfactory, as he has left no possible room for correction!" Mozart returned one exercise with this notation, "You are an ass." (Quoted in James T. Lightwood, *The Music of the Methodist Hymn-Book.*)

Mendelssohn was Attwood's house guest on occasion and sometimes accompanied him to St. Paul's. At times he would take Attwood's place at the organ and play the voluntary.

205 Awake, My Soul, and with the Sun
Thomas Ken (1637-1710)

This hymn is ranked by John Julian as "one of the four which stand at the head of all hymns in the English language." The others are: "When I Survey," "Hark, the Herald Angels Sing," and "Rock of Ages."

Ken, left an orphan at an early age, went to live with his stepbrother-in-law, Izaak Walton, the famous authority on fishing and author of *The Compleat Angler*.

Ken's eloquent preaching, his piety, and his forthright moral stands brought him recognition in the Anglican Church. He stoutly opposed immorality even in the royal court. However, Charles II respected his honesty and said at one time he would go and hear Ken "tell him of his faults." Later he appointed him Bishop of Bath and Wells. Subsequently, unwilling to compromise his conscience, Ken was deposed from his bishopric by a later king, James II, and was imprisoned for a time in the Tower of London. Macaulay judged his character to be "as near as human infirmity permits to the ideal perfection of Christian virtue."

Today Ken is probably best known as the author of "Praise God from Whom All Blessings Flow," the doxology appended to his *Morning, Evening,* and *Midnight* hymns. These hymns were included in the 1695 edition of his *Manual of Prayers For the Use of the Scholars of Winchester College.* . . . Opposite the title page is a coat of arms with the words, "Manners make the man." The first edition (1674) contained no hymns but reference to the *Morning* and *Evening* hymns suggests that they had already been circulated among the students.

"Awake, My Soul, and with The Sun," entitled "A Morning Hymn," is in fourteen 4-line stanzas of which stanza 14 is the familiar doxology. *Hymns of Faith and Life* uses stanzas 1, 12, 13, and 14.

Spurious editions of Ken's hymns seem to have prompted the

issuance in 1709 of what has come to be regarded as the authentic text. A number of alterations to the 1695 text appear in the 1709 version and are thought to have been made by Ken.

All Free Methodist hymnals since 1883 have included this hymn.

MORNING HYMN was written for Ken's hymn by François Hippolyte Barthélémon (1741-1808) and included in a collection *Hymns and Psalms Used at the Asylum for Female Orphans,* 1785.

206 Come, O Lord, Like Morning Sunlight
Milton Smith Littlefield (1864-1934)

This hymn appeared in *The Hymnal for Young People,* 1928, edited by Milton S. Littlefield and Margaret Slattery, and published by A. S. Barnes and Company. It was said to have been written in 1927.

Littlefield was a Presbyterian minister originally in the New York area, but a Congregationalist for the last twenty-three years of his life. He edited three hymnbooks.

This hymn entered Free Methodist-Wesleyan hymnody in 1951.

TRUST or CONTEMPLATION is from "An Anthem for a Mezzo Soprano Solo...," written in 1840 by Mendelssohn (1809-1847) as a setting for Psalm 13. It was first performed in 1848 in London. The hymn tune comes from the second of the three movements.

The circumstances surrounding the writing of the anthem were included in a letter written by Ignace Moscheles (1794-1870) to his wife. Moscheles, one of the leading pianists of his time, was a frequent visitor in the Mendelssohn home. He wrote that one of his pupils, the Reverend Charles Bayles Broadley, had come to him with the request that Mendelssohn, Spohr, and he compose musical settings with orchestral accompaniments for some psalms. Each was to receive £20. Moscheles chose Psalm 93 and Mendelssohn, Psalm 13.

207 Still, Still with Thee
Harriet Beecher Stowe (1812-1896)

Mrs. Stowe, daughter of the Reverend Lyman Beecher and

sister of Henry Ward Beecher, is probably best known as the author of *Uncle Tom's Cabin,* 1852. She contributed three hymns to the *Plymouth Collection of Hymns and Tunes,* 1855, edited by her brother. "Still, Still with Thee" is one of these. It was written two years earlier, in 1853, and originally had six stanzas. Stanza 3 is omitted here.

Our 1951 hymnal was the first to include this hymn.

MORNING STAR was written in 1892 by James Procktor Harding (1850-1911) as part of an anthem to be sung at a mission in a London slum district. The title derives from the association of the tune with Bishop Heber's "Brightest and Best of the Sons of the Morning." The first American hymnal to have used the tune was *The Church Hymnal,* 1894, of the Protestant Episcopal Church.

Hymns of Faith and Life is the first Free Methodist-Wesleyan hymnal to use this tune.

208 Morning Has Broken

Eleanor Farjeon (1881-1965)

This popular song, used currently as a theme song of a religious TV program, was published first in *Songs of Praise,* 1931.

This is the first Free Methodist-Wesleyan hymnal to include either the text or the tune.

BUNESSAN, a traditional Gaelic melody, was arranged by David Evans (1874-1948) for the *Revised Church Hymnary,* 1927.

209 Softly Now the Light of Day

George Washington Doane (1799-1859)

This hymn in two 8-line stanzas by George W. Doane, Episcopalian clergyman and Bishop of New Jersey, was included in his *Songs by the Way,* 1824, under the title of "Evening."

The concluding four lines of the original are generally omitted as in our 1883 and 1976 hymnals, the only two Free Methodist hymnals to include the hymn. The alterations include the changing of "my" to "our" and "I" to "we" in Stanza 1 and "Soon, for me" to "when for us" in stanza 3.

The omitted quatrain reads:

> Thou Who, sinless, yet hast known
>   All of man's infirmity;
> Then, from Thine eternal throne,
>   Jesus, look with pitying eye.

Doane was born in the year George Washington died and was named for him.

SEYMOUR is derived from the opening chorus of the opera *Oberon* composed by Carl Maria von Weber, 1825/26. It was arranged as a hymn tune by Henry Wellington Greatorex (1813-1858) and first appeared in his *Collection of Psalm and Hymn Tunes, Chants, Anthems, and Sentences for the Use of the Protestant Episcopal Church in America*, 1851.

210 All Praise to Thee, My God, This Night
Thomas Ken (1637-1710)

This is the "Evening" hymn of Bishop Ken referred to in the notes on No. 205. There are twelve stanzas in the original of which the twelfth is the doxology "Praise God from Whom All Blessings Flow." *Hymns of Faith and Life* uses stanzas 1, 2, 4, 5, and 12. Note that stanza 4 is for insomniacs!

This hymn was included in the 1883 and 1910 hymnals with the opening line "Glory to Thee, my God, this night," taken from the 1695 edition of Ken's *Manual of Prayers*.... The 1709 revision of the *Manual* with the opening lines "All praise to Thee, my God, this night" was adopted in the 1951 hymnal.

TALLIS' CANNON (See notes at No. 40.)

211 Day Is Dying in the West
Mary Artemisia Lathbury (1841-1913)

This vesper hymn was written at the request of Methodist Bishop John H. Vincent, founder of the Chautauqua Assembly, for the vesper services held on the shores of beautiful Lake Chautauqua near Jamestown, New York. The Chautauqua movement began in 1873. Mary Lathbury became secretary to Dr. Vincent about a year later.

The date of the writing of the hymn is variously reported as 1877 and 1880. The earlier date seems more probable since early songbooks indicate that it was copyrighted in that year by J. H. Vincent. The hymn enjoyed immediate popularity and continued to be sung regularly for years as the opening hymn at the Sunday evening services at Chautauqua. H. Augustine Smith called it the "vesper hymn of a nation."

Originally there were two stanzas only. The author added two more in 1890. Our 1910 and 1951 hymnals print all four. Note that the refrain is a form of the *Ter Sanctus*.

Mary Lathbury was much loved by her associates at Chautauqua. France E. Willard said that a "high courageous faith, a loyalty to the best ideals, and a devotion to the truth that gave inspiration to all with whom she came in contact, characterized 'our Mary'." She became known as "Poet Laureate and Saint of Chautauqua."

This hymn entered Free Methodist-Wesleyan hymnody in 1910.

CHAUTAUQUA or EVENING PRAISE was composed in the summer of 1877 for this hymn by William Fisk Sherwin (1826-1888) who was the music director of the Assembly.

212, 213 Now the Day Is Over
Sabine Baring-Gould (1834-1924)

This hymn was written for the children at Horbury Bridge near Sheffield where Sabine Baring-Gould was vicar at the time. It seems to have been written in 1865 and then printed for the first time in *The Church Times*, 1867. Originally there were eight 4-line stanzas. Our hymnal uses stanzas 1, 3, 7, and 8. Note that stanza 8 is in the form of a doxology.

The second stanza, now generally omitted, reads:

> Now the darkness gathers,
>   Stars begin to peep.
> Birds and beasts and flowers
>   Soon will be asleep.

The author composed the tune EUDOXIA for this text for the 1868 Appendix to *Hymns Ancient and Modern*.

Our 1951 hymnal was the first Free Methodist-Wesleyan hymnal to include the hymn.

GLENFINLAS was written by Kenneth George Finlay (b. 1882) for the *Church and School Hymnal*, 1926, but actually appeared in print first in *Songs of Praise*, 1925. This gentle tune written in the pentatonic scale was undoubtedly composed with children in mind. There is a four-part setting at No. 134.

MERRIAL was written by Joseph Barnby (1838-1896) in 1868 and included in his *Original Tunes to Popular Hymns,* 1869. Its first publication in America seems to have been in Charles S. Robinson's *Spiritual Songs for Social Worship,* 1878. There is a story, apparently without basis in fact, that Robinson derived the title from his daughter's name, Mary L.

214 Sun of My Soul, Thou Saviour Dear
John Keble (1792-1866)

This hymn was written in 1820 (dated November 25, 1820) and first published in *The Christian Year: Thoughts in Verse for the Sundays and Holydays Throughout the Year,* 1827, under the title "Evening." There are fourteen 4-line stanzas, of which *Hymns of Faith and Life* uses stanzas 3, 7, 8, 13, and 14.

The original first stanza reads:

> 'Tis gone, that bright and orbèd blaze,
> Fast fading from our wistful gaze;
> Yon mantling cloud has hid from sight
> The last faint pulse of quivering light.

All Free Methodist hymnals since 1883 have included "Sun of My Soul."

HURSLEY is the name of the town where parts of *The Christian Year* were written, and where Keble is buried. The earliest form of the melody is found in *Katholische Gesangbuch,* Vienna, where it is dated 1774. There it was associated with the German hymn "Grosser Gott, wir loben dich."

Routley *(Hymns and Human Life)* relates a story told him by a German theologian. Hitler sent one of his aides to harangue the people of Berlin on the virtues of Nazism. Although he tried valiantly for some three hours, his words were effectively drowned out by the singing of "Grosser Gott, wir loben dich," the original form of *Hursley,* sung by German Catholics.

The first association of *Hursley* with the Keble text seems to have been in W. J. Irons and Henry Lahee, *Metrical Psalter,* 1855. (See also notes on No. 463.)

215 There Is a Green Hill Far Away
Cecil Frances Alexander (1818-1895)

This hymn, based on the fourth article of "The Apostles'

Creed" (suffered under Pontius Pilate ...) was published in the author's small booklet of seventy-two pages, *Hymns for Little Children,* 1848, but written a year earlier.

The only change from the original is in the first stanza:

> 1:2 *"Beside a ruined* city wall,"

(See also comments at No. 139 and No. 303.)

MEDITATION was written in 1890 by John Henry Gower (1855-1922) for Isaac Watts's text "There is a land of pure delight" and published first in the composer's *Service Book and Hymnal,* 1891.

216 I Hear the Saviour Say
Elvina Mabel Hall (1820-1889)

The text was written in 1865 by Mrs. Hall during a service in the Methodist Episcopal Church of Baltimore. She is said to have scribbled it on the flyleaf of the hymnal *New Lute of Zion* during a lengthy pastoral prayer.

There have been many alterations and additions to the original five stanzas. As printed in Philip Phillips's *Hallowed Songs,* 1871, the following changes may be noted:

> 2:2 Thy *faith* and ...
> 3:3 ... my *garment* ...
> 4:3 I'll *lay my trophies down,*
> 4:4 *All down, at Jesus' feet.*

An omitted stanza following stanza 3 reads:

> When from my dying bed
>   My ransomed soul shall rise,
> Then "Jesus paid it all"
>   Shall rend the vaulted skies.

Hymns of the Living Faith, 1951, was the first Free Methodist-Wesleyan hymnal to include this song.

JESUS PAID IT ALL was written by John Thomas Grape (1835-1915) in about 1865. It was published in *Sabbath Chords,* 1868.

Ira D. Sankey, in *My Life and the Story of the Gospel Hymns,* quotes John Grape as follows:

> Our church was undergoing some alterations and the cabinet organ was placed in my care. Thus afforded a pleasure not before enjoyed, I delighted myself in playing

over our Sunday school hymns. I determined to give tangible shape to a theme that had been running in my mind for some time — to write ... an answer to Mr. Bradbury's beautiful piece, "Jesus paid it all." I made it a matter of prayer and study, and gave to the public the music, now known as the tune to "All to Christ I owe." It was pronounced very poor by my choir and my friends but my dear wife persistently declared that it was a good piece of music and would live. Time has proved the correctness of her judgment....

A Reverend M. Schrick told Grape that Mrs. Hall had written some words that he thought would fit the music. Thus it was that text and tune, composed separately, were joined and have been inseparable ever since.

217 There Is a Fountain Filled with Blood
William Cowper (1731-1800)

This hymn was written about 1771 and published in Conyer's *Collection of Psalms and Hymns,* 1772, in seven 4-line stanzas. In *Olney Hymns,* Book I, 1779, it was headed "Praise for the Fountain Opened."

The text has been altered in a number of collections. James Montgomery objected to the first stanza's representation of a fountain being *filled,* instead of *springing up.* His version, dated 1819, reads:

> From Calvary's cross, a Fountain flows
>   Of water and of blood,
> More healing than Bethesda's pool,
>   Or famed Siloam's flood.

The textual changes in *Hymns of Faith and Life* are noted below:

1:4 *Lose* all ...
2:3 And there *have* I, *as* vile as he,
2:4 *Wash'd* all ...

Stanzas 6 and 7 as they appear in *Olney Hymns* read:

> 6. Lord, I believe Thou hast prepar'd
>   (Unworthy tho' I be)
>   For me a blood-bought free reward,
>   A golden harp for me!

> 7. 'Tis strung, and tun'd, for endless years,
>   And form'd by pow'r divine;
>   To sound, in God the Father's ears,
>   No other name but Thine.

It has been a part of Free Methodist hymnody since 1883.

CLEANSING FOUNTAIN is designated as a "Western Melody" in a number of nineteenth-century gospel songbooks. Lowell Mason's tune "Cowper" bears some similarity to it. The one may have inspired the other.

218 The Whole World Was Lost in the Darkness
Philip Paul Bliss (1838-1876)

This song, of special interest to Free Methodists through its adoption as theme song for the "Light and Life Hour" in 1944, was printed first in *The International Lessons Monthly,* 1875, under the title "Light of the World" and in the same year in *Gospel Hymns and Sacred Songs.* Subsequently it became widely known in both Great Britain and America.

Both words and music came to Bliss during the summer of 1875 quite spontaneously while at his home in Chicago.

Hymns of the Living Faith, 1951, was the first Free Methodist-Wesleyan hymnal to include this song although it had been popularized in the denominations through publication in some of their gospel songbooks.

219 O Boundless Salvation!
William Booth (1829-1912)

According to Salvation Army sources, this song is known throughout the world as the Founder's Song. It found its inspiration in a Boundless Salvation campaign held in Great Britain in the fall of 1893. The climax of the campaign came in Boundless Salvation meetings in London's Exeter Hall, conducted by William Booth the founder of the Salvation Army. It was during the Exeter Hall meetings that Booth composed the song and for the occasion he added a refrain also:

> The heavenly gales are blowing,
> The cleansing stream is flowing,
> Beneath its waves I'm going,
> Hallelujah! Praise the Lord!

Two of the songs used in the meetings were "Boundless the Salvation Jesus Offers at the Cross" and "Boundless as the Mighty Ocean." These are thought to have been Booth's inspiration for writing his song.

"O Boundless Salvation" was the last song Booth sang publicly, according to his diary. The occasion was his eighty-third birthday celebration in Royal Albert Hall on May 9, 1912.

The song was published first in *The War Cry* for December 23, 1893.

MY JESUS, I LOVE THEE was written in 1887 by one J. Ellis, according to the notation in *Hymns and Songs for Mission Services* published by Charles H. Kelly in 1887. There the title is given as *Callestr,* according to Major D. Steadman-Allen, head of the Music Editorial Department of Salvationist Publishing and Supplies, Ltd., in London. Slight variations in the melody occur in older hymnals.

220 Wonderful Story of Love
J. M. Driver (nineteenth century)

The author of words and music is reported to have been an American minister.

221 'Tis the Grandest Theme
William Augustus Ogden (1841-1897)

Ogden wrote both words and music for this gospel song which appeared first in E. O. Excell's *Triumphant Songs for Sunday Schools and Gospel Meetings,* 1887. According to William J. Reynolds *(Companion to Baptist Hymnal,* 1976), Ogden studied music under Lowell Mason and Thomas Hastings, among others. From 1887 until his death he was supervisor of music for the Toledo, Ohio, public schools.

Hymns of the Living Faith, 1951, was the first Free Methodist-Wesleyan hymnal to include this song.

222 Sometimes a Light Surprises
William Cowper (1731-1800)

This cheerful hymn appears in *Olney Hymns,* Book III, 1779, under the heading "Joy and Peace in Believing," in four 8-line stanzas.

The only changes from the original text are

2:7 *E'en* let *the'unknown* ...

4:1 *The* vine . . .
4:3 . . . should *whither,* (perhaps a misprint)

It is considered by some to be the greatest of the Cowper hymns.

This marks its first appearance in a Free Methodist-Wesleyan hymnal.

BENTLEY was written by John Pyke Hullah (1812-1884) and contributed by him, according to Lightwood, to *Psalms and Hymns for Divine Worship,* 1867.

223 Sing Them Over Again to Me
Philip Paul Bliss (1838-1876)

Both words and music were written by Bliss and appeared in the first issue of a Sunday school paper entitled *Words of Life,* 1874. Its first hymnal inclusion was in *Gospel Hymns No. 3,* 1878.

Hymns of the Living Faith, 1951, was the first Free Methodist-Wesleyan hymnal to include this song. In our present hymnal the refrain is abbreviated by the omission of the repeat.

224 O Love Divine, How Sweet Thou Art
Charles Wesley (1707-1788)

This hymn in seven 6-line stanzas appeared in Wesley's *Hymns and Sacred Poems,* Vol. I, 1749. It is one of six hymns on "Desiring to Love." In common with many hymnals, we use stanzas 1-4. This is one of three Wesley hymns set to music by Handel. The Handel tune is known as "Wentworth."

Except for 1951 this hymn has appeared in all Free Methodist hymnals.

RAVENDALE by Walter Stokes (1847-1916) is not to be confused with another tune by the same name written by John Wilson.

225 All Ye that Pass By
Charles Wesley (1707-1788)

This hymn is from Wesley's *Hymns and Sacred Poems,* Vol. I, 1749, in seven 6-line stanzas and is headed "Invitation to

Sinners." *Hymns of Faith and Life* uses stanzas 1, 4, 5, and 6. It was not included in the "Large Hymnbook" until the *Supplement to the Wesleyan Hymn Book,* 1830.

Hymns of Faith and Life is the first Free Methodist-Wesleyan hymnal to include this fine invitation hymn.

DARLINGTON is the work of an unknown composer. The English *Methodist Hymn-Book* lists the source as *The Hallelujah,* 1849, of the Rev. J.J. Waite, but Lightwood claims it is not found therein. Waite conducted Psalmody classes during the middle-nineteenth century.

226   Immortal Love, Forever Full
John Greenleaf Whittier (1807-1892)

This hymn, written in 1866 by the Quaker poet Whittier, is a cento from a poem in thirty-five 4-line stanzas entitled "Our Master" included in *The Tent on the Beach, and Other Poems,* 1867. The stanzas included in our hymnal are 1, 5, 13, 14, and 16.

Note omitted stanzas 15, 16, 20, and 30.

15. Through Him the first fond prayers are said
      Our lips of childhood frame;
    The last low whispers of our dead
      Are burdened with His name.

16. O Lord, and Master of us all,
      Whate'er our name or sign,
    We own Thy sway, we hear Thy call,
      We test our lives by Thine.

20. Yet weak and blinded though we be,
      Thou dost our service own;
    We bring our varying gifts to Thee,
      And Thou rejectest none.

30. Apart from Thee all gain is loss,
      All labor vainly done;
    The solemn shadow of the cross
      Is better than the sun.

Whittier did not intentionally write hymns but those extracted from his poems have been so widely accepted that Routley speaks of him as "perhaps the most influential of American hymn-writers...."

This hymn entered Free Methodist-Wesleyan hymnody in 1951.

page 173

DUNFERMLINE is one of the "Common" tunes (8.6.8.6.) in *The Scottish Psalter,* 1615, published by Andro Hart. It is said to have been composed by Dean John Angus who was connected with the "Abbacie of Dunfermling," an old spelling for Dunfermline. Dunfermline is a community in Scotland and the early home of Andrew Carnegie.

227 Come unto Me When Shadows Darkly Gather
Catherine Watterman Esling (1812-1897)

This hymn is new to Free Methodism, entering our hymnody in the 1976 hymnal. Catherine Watterman wrote it prior to her marriage to Captain George J. Esling. It is the only hymn by which she is remembered. It appeared in *The Christian Keepsake,* an annual, 1839, in nine 4-line stanzas. *Hymns of Faith and Life* uses stanzas 3, 8, and 9. Mrs. Watterman's poems were published in *The Broken Bracelet and Other Poems,* 1850.

HENLEY was composed by Lowell Mason (1792-1872) and first published in *The Hallelujah,* 1854, a compilation by Mason.

228 Not What These Hands Have Done
Horatius Bonar (1808-1889)

This hymn appears in Bonar's *Hymns of Faith and Hope,* Second Series, 1861, in twelve 4-line stanzas under the title "Salvation Through Christ Alone." Our hymnal uses stanzas 1, 2, 3, 5, and 7.

Dr. Bonar was educated in the University of Edinburgh and served for a time in the Established Church. In May, 1843, he joined the Free Church of Scotland. In 1883 he was chosen Moderator.

Dr. John Brownlie, in his article on Bonar in Julian's *Dictionary of Hymnology,* summed up Bonar's contribution to hymnody:

> His hymns satisfy the fastidious by their instinctive good taste; they mirror the life of Christ in the soul, partially, perhaps, but with vivid accuracy; they win the heart by their tone of tender sympathy; they sing the truth of God in ringing notes....

ST. AUGUSTINE is found, according to Lightwood, in Michael Weisse's *Ein neu Gesangbuchlein,* 1531, the first hymnbook of the

Bohemian Brethren. Later on it appeared in Johann Sebastian Bach's *Choralgesänge,* 1769, where it is associated with the Michael Weisse text "Als der gütige Gott." The hymn tune melody ST. AUGUSTINE omits two measures from the chorale melody.

229 Walk in the Light

Bernard Barton (1784-1849)

This hymn appeared in Barton's *Devotional Verses,* 1826, in six 4-line stanzas. Barton was known as the "Quaker Poet." He was a friend of Charles Lamb, Boswell, Sir Walter Scott, and Lord Byron. Of his numerous poetical works about twenty came into common use as hymns, but only "Walk in the Light" seems to be in general use today.

This hymn has been in Free Methodist hymnals since 1883. Omitted stanzas are:

> 2. Walk in the light, and sin, abhorred,
>   Shall ne'er defile again;
> The blood of Jesus Christ thy Lord
>   Shall cleanse from every stain.
>
> 4. Walk in the light, and thou shalt own
>   Thy darkness passed away,
> Because that light hath on thee shown,
>   In which is perfect day.   (In *FMHB,* 1883)

Alterations in *HFL* are the following:

> 4:1, 2 (original 6:1, 2)
>   Walk in the light! *Thy path shall be*
>   *Peaceful, serene, and bright:*

OAKSVILLE is attributed to Heinrich Christoph Zeuner (1795-1857), sometimes listed as Charles Zeuner. He chose the simpler name "Charles" when he left Germany to settle in America. He was a composer of some competence but of more renown as an organist in Boston and Philadelphia. His hymn tunes are found in the *American Harp,* 1832. A second collection was entitled *The Ancient Lyre.*

230 Sinners Jesus Will Receive

Erdmann Neumeister (1671-1756)
Translated by Emma Frances Bevan (1827-1909)

Perhaps the best hymn written by Neumeister was "Jesus nimmt die Sünder an! Saget doch dies Trostwort allen," a hymn for Lent, published in his *Evangelischer Nachklang,* 1718, in eight 6-line stanzas. The excellent translation by Mrs. Bevan was published in her *Songs of Eternal Life,* 1858, a series of translations from the German.

Stanza 1 reads as follows in her translation:

> Sinners Jesus will receive;
> Tell this word of grace to all
> Who the heavenly pathway leave,
> All who linger, all who fall;
> This can bring them back again:
> "Christ receiveth sinful men."

This text entered our hymnody in the 1951 hymnal.

WILSON was written by Dr. James E. Wilson, chairman of the music department at Greenville College, for the use of his college choir. He was born in Ottawa, Ontario. He is a graduate of Marion College and has earned master's and doctor's degrees from Indiana University.

231 Standing on the Promises

Words and music by Russell Kelso Carter (1849-1926)

The text and tune were first published in *Songs of Perfect Love,* 1886 (Copyright 1886 by John J. Hood), in five 4-line stanzas with refrain. Stanza 3 is now generally omitted. It reads:

> Standing on the promises I now can see
> Perfect, present cleansing in the blood for me;
> Standing in the liberty where Christ makes free,
> Standing on the promises of God.

The song is included in a Free Methodist-Wesleyan hymnal for the first time.

PROMISES is the tune title assigned by the editors of the *Baptist Hymnal,* 1956.

232 Under His Wings I Am Safely Abiding
William Orcutt Cushing (1823-1902)

This was one of the popular hymns sung by the young women at the seminary in Northfield, Massachusetts. When Dwight L. Moody would arrive there to conduct morning worship he would be greeted by it.

Hymns of the Living Faith, 1951, was the first Free Methodist-Wesleyan hymnal to include it.

CUSHING was one of the later tunes written by Ira David Sankey (1840-1908) and was composed for this text. It appeared in his *Sacred Songs No. 1,* 1896. This title was chosen by the editor of *HFL.*

233 There Shall Be Showers of Blessing
Daniel Webster Whittle (1840-1901)

Whittle served in the Union army during the Civil War and advanced to the rank of major, a title he used throughout the remainder of his life. He became treasurer of the Elgin Watch Company but resigned in 1873 to become an evangelist. He was assisted as song leader by Philip B. Bliss until Bliss's tragic death and then by James McGranahan and George C. Stebbins.

Major Whittle wrote most of his songs under the pseudonym "El Nathan."

SHOWERS OF BLESSING was composed by James McGranahan (1840-1907). Phil Kerr *(Music in Evangelism)* writes that when Philip Bliss was killed in a train wreck at Ashtabula, Ohio, McGranahan hurried to the scene of the accident:

> There he met for the first time Major Whittle, the evangelist for whom Bliss had been working. He recognized the major and introduced himself. The evangelist recalled that Bliss had often spoken of this man and then and there beside the wrecked train which was Bliss's funeral pyre, McGranahan and Whittle formed a friendship which was to continue through eleven successful years of joint evangelistic activity.

234 He Who Would Valiant Be

John Bunyan (1628-1688)
Adapted by Percy Dearmer (1867-1936)

Although John Bunyan was not a hymn writer by design, he did write poetry which has been adapted as hymns. Two lyrics from the 1684 edition of *Pilgrim's Progress* are included in this hymnal.

Valiant's song from part 2 occurs in this context. He is recounting the obstacles and the discouraging warning he received on his pilgrimage to the Celestial City.

> *Great-Heart:* "Then this was your victory even your faith."
> *Valiant-For-Truth:* "It was so. I believed and therefore came out, got into the way, fought all that set themselves against me, and, by believing, am come to this place."

Then these three stanzas follow:

> Who would true valour see,
>   Let him come hither;
> One here will constant be,
>   Come wind, come weather;
> There's no discouragement
> Shall make him once relent
> His first avow'd intent
>   To be a pilgrim.
>
> Whoso beset him round
>   With dismal stories,
> Do but themselves confound;
>   His strength the more is.
> No lion can him fright,
>   He'll with a giant fight,
> But he will have a right
>   To be a pilgrim.
>
> Hobgoblin nor foul friend
>   Can daunt his spirit;
> He knows he at the end
>   Shall life inherit.
> Then fancies fly away,
>   He'll not fear what men say;
> He'll labour night and day
>   To be a pilgrim.

Percy Dearmer, general editor of *The English Hymnal,* 1906, seems to have been among the first to see hymnic possibilities in the lyric. He felt that it was necessary to alter the vivid imagery of the original and produced the form used in our hymnals beginning in 1951. Because of the changes in stanza 3, particularly, the hymn becomes one of personal expression.

Baptist John Bunyan's forthrightness as a preacher and as a writer strikes a welcome and much needed note even 300 years after his death. He said, "I preached what I felt and what I smartingly did feel, even under that which my poor soul did groan and tremble to astonishment."

Bunyan is buried in Bunhill Fields, the Puritan burying ground across the street from John Wesley's City Road Chapel in London.

ST. DUNSTAN'S was written on December 15, 1917, by C. Winfred Douglas (1867-1944) on a train returning from New York City to their home, St. Dunstan's Cottage in Peekskill, New York, according to a personal letter to the author from his widow.

235 Would You Be Free from the Burden of Sin?
Lewis Edgar Jones (1865-1936)

Words and music of this song were written by Lewis E. Jones (1865-1936) and published for the first time in *Songs of Praise and Victory,* 1899. This is the first appearance in an official Free Methodist-Wesleyan hymnal.

Gospel songs such as this one have been used unwittingly as a means of evangelism. Aminidab Torres, Free Methodist missionary in Mexico, tells how God transformed his life through the singing of this particular song:

> Born in Mexico, he went to California as a young man. Riding in a car in Placentia with three of his friends, all of whom had been drinking, he heard a hymn from a church. The song was, "There is power, power, / Wonder-working power, / In the blood of the Lamb."
>
> He persuaded his friends to stop the car and go into the church. He said, "I was drunk, and I don't know who preached, but I heard the Word of the Lord clearly. That night I came to the Lord and I told Jesus Christ three things: 'If You really forgive a sinner, here I am. If You can transform a sinner, here I am. And if You can use a sinner, here I am.' My heart received a great blessing. A year later I received a call to the ministry and a call to go back home to Mexico."
>
> — From "Love Breaks Down Walls,"
> *The Missionary Tidings* (July-August, 1978).
> An interview with Marian W. Groesbeck.

236 God Has Spoken by His Prophets
George Wallace Briggs (1875-1959)

The author of this text was canon and vice-dean of Worcester Cathedral from 1934-56. He wrote a number of hymns and a few tunes. This hymn was written in 1952 and published by the Hymn Society of America in *Ten New Hymns on the Bible,* 1953, celebrating the publication of the *Revised Standard Version of the Bible,* 1952. (See also comments at No. 490.)

AUSTRIAN HYMN or AUSTRIA is derived from the "Hymn to the Emperor" by Franz Joseph Haydn (1732-1809), composed as a setting for a patriotic hymn beginning with the words "Gott erhalte Franz, den Kaiser," written by the Austrian poet Lorenz Hauschka. It was sung throughout Austria on the Emperor's birthday, February 12, 1797. The tune was a favorite of Haydn and he used it as the theme of the slow movement of his Quartet in C (Op. 76, No. 5) around which he skillfully wove a set of variations.

237 That Day of Wrath, That Dreadful Day
Thomas of Celano (thirteenth century)
Translated by Sir Walter Scott (1771-1832)

The medieval Latin hymn *Dies Irae* from "Mass for the Dead," translated by Sir Walter Scott and included in his *Lay of the Last Minstrel,* is generally credited to Thomas of Celano, a Franciscan friar and friend and biographer of St. Francis of Assisi.

In the Roman Rite it is used as the Sequence in the *Mass for the Dead.* Julian attests the hold the text has had "upon the minds of men of various nations and creeds" by noting that by the beginning of the twentieth century there were approximately ninety translations into German and more than one hundred fifty into English. This statistic is remarkable in view of the fact that at the same point in time there were only thirty-eight translations of *Adeste Fideles* and sixty-three translations of *Ein' feste Burg* into English.

The opening line of the sequence, "Dies irae, dies illa," is taken verbatim from Zephaniah 1:15 (Vulgate version). Scott's version is introduced at the close of *The Lay of the Last Minstrel,* 1805, in three 4-line stanzas, preceded by these lines:

> The mass was sung, and prayers were said,
> And solemn requiem for the dead;
> And bells toll'd out their mighty peal,

    For the departed spirit's weal;
    And ever in the office close
    The hymn of intercession rose;
    And far the echoing aisles prolong
    The awful burden of the song —
        DIES IRAE, DIES ILLA!
        SOLVET SAECLUM IN FAVILLA;
    While the pealing organ rung;
        Were it meet with sacred strain
        To close my lay so light and vain,
    Thus the holy Fathers sung:

And then follow the three stanzas of Scott's translation.

Soon after the publication of *The Lay of the Last Minstrel,* the three-stanza poem was introduced as a hymn for public worship in a number of hymn collections.

The Right Honorable William E. Gladstone, in a speech at Hawarden in 1866, praised the hymn with these words:

> I know nothing more sublime in the writings of Sir Walter Scott — certainly I know nothing so sublime in any portion of the sacred poetry of modern times, I mean of the present century — as the "Hymn for the Dead" ... embodied in *The Lay of the Last Minstrel.*

Among the many worthy translations into English was one made in 1864 by Arthur P. Stanley (1815-1881). In modified and abbreviated form this translation was used in the *Free Methodist-Wesleyan Hymnal,* 1910, and in *Hymns of the Living Faith,* 1951. The Scott translation is introduced into Free Methodist-Wesleyan hymnody for the first time in 1976.

WINDHAM was composed by Daniel Read (1757-1836) and published in his *American Singing Book,* 1785, where it is associated with Isaac Watts's "Broad Is the Road that Leads to Death." Originally the melody was in the tenor voice in the natural minor key. In our version the harmonic form of the minor scale is used and a number of rhythmic and harmonic changes are made including a lowering of pitch from F minor to D minor.

There is a much older tune than WINDHAM almost universally associated with the Latin text and also known as *Dies Irae.* A portion of the tune in medieval style notation and in modern notation is as follows:

Composers have frequently incorporated this melody into their compositions when they wished to convey the idea of death. Many examples could be cited, but the following are illustrative:

>Saint Saens, *Danse Macabre* (1874)
>Berlioz, *Symphonie Fantastique* (Fifth movement, "Dream of a Witch's Sabbath," played by two tubas and later parodied by pizzicato strings)
>Rachmaninoff, *Rhapsody on a Theme of Paganini* (1934)
>Rachmaninoff, *Isle of the Dead* (1907)
>Liszt, *Totentanz* (1859) (a series of variations on *Dies irae*, inspired by the fourteenth-century fresco, *The Triumph of Death*, on one of the walls of the Campo Santo in Pisa)
>Khachaturian, *Second Symphony* (Third Movement: *Andante Sostenuto*), composed 1943-44.

238 Thou Judge of Quick and Dead
Charles Wesley (1707-1788)

This is one of a series of "Hymns for the Watchnight" in Wesley's *Hymns and Sacred Poems*, 1749. It is in four 8-line stanzas of which we print stanzas 1, 2, and 4.

The complete hymn was included in the *Free Methodist Hymn-Book*, 1883, and in abbreviated form in 1910. It was omitted in 1951.

ICH HALTE TREULICH STILL is taken from *Musicalisches Gesang-Buch heraus gegeben von Georg Christian Schemelli*, 1736. There is speculation that it might have been composed by J. S. Bach.

239 Jesus Is Tenderly Calling Thee Home
Fanny Jane Crosby (1820-1915)

Frances Crosby, blind since the age of six weeks, was one of America's most prolific song writers. Since she often used a pseudonym, the exact number of her songs and hymns may never be known, but is almost certainly more than two thousand. Some estimate it as high as eight thousand. Her first songs were secular. It was not until age forty-one that she wrote her first hymn.

In 1858 she was married to Alexander Van Alstyne who was a blind musician.

"Jesus Is Tenderly Calling" was published first in *Gospel Hymns No. 4,* 1883.

Hymns of the Living Faith, 1951, was the first Free Methodist-Wesleyan hymnal to include it. (See also comments at No. 42).

JESUS IS CALLING was written for this text by George Coles Stebbins (1846-1945) and published with it in *Gospel Hymns No. 4.*

240 Softly and Tenderly Jesus Is Calling
Will Lamartine Thompson (1847-1909)

Both words and music were composed by Thompson and copyrighted in 1880.

The story is told that shortly before Dwight L. Moody's death Thompson called on him. The evangelist reached out his hand and said, "Will, I would rather have written 'Softly and Tenderly' than anything I have been able to do in my whole life."

Thompson was a resident of East Liverpool, Ohio, where he operated a music publishing firm, the Will L. Thompson and Company.

241 Sinners, Turn; Why Will You Die?
Charles Wesley (1707-1788)

This hymn with the heading "Why Will Ye Die, O House of Israel?" (Ezekiel 18:31) is found in Wesley's *Hymns on God's Everlasting Love* (Second Series), 1741, in sixteen 8-line stanzas, of which we print stanzas 1, 2, and 3. In John Wesley's hymnals only stanzas 1-4 were used. The omitted fourth stanza reads:

>Dead, already dead within,
>Spiritually dead in sin,
>Dead to God, while here you breathe,
>Pant ye after second death?
>While ye still in sun remain,
>Greedy of eternal pain?
>O ye dying sinners, why,
>Why will you for ever die?

In the three-stanza form this hymn was included in the 1883 and 1910 hymnals. Omitted in 1951 it is restored in 1976 with a new tune.

ARFON is a melody popular in Wales, but its origin is uncertain. It is set to a Christmas text in a book of French Christmas Carols, 1875.

242 In Times Like These You Need a Saviour
Ruth Caye Jones (1902-1972)

Words and music were composed by Ruth Caye Jones in 1943 and copyrighted in 1944. It was in the dark days of World War II when the words of II Timothy 3:1 came with special meaning to Mrs. Jones as she was about her housework in the family home in the Dormont area of Pittsburgh. Words and music came spontaneously to her. She took a pad of paper from her apron pocket, jotted down the words, melody, and harmony almost exactly as they are found today.

According to the Reverend Bert L. Jones, son of the hymnwriter, in a letter to the author, one of the first places where the song was sung, other than in the family's home church in Pittsburgh, was in the Houghton College Church, Houghton, New York, on a wintry Sunday night in 1944. Bert was living at the time in the home of Professor Alfred Kreckman and had asked him, as a music teacher, to go over the manuscript for Mrs. Jones before they had the song printed. Professor Kreckman liked it and he and his wife sang it at the church just before the pastor Dr. C. I. Armstrong preached.

Mrs. Jones was born in 1902 in Wilmerding, Pennsylvania, near Pittsburgh. She was converted at age twelve in a Methodist revival meeting. In 1926 she was married to Bert Jones, a YMCA secretary. Later he became a Methodist minister and evangelist. In 1948 they founded the family devotional broadcast "A Visit with the Joneses," a ministry that continues today under the leadership of the family members. Her husband died in 1961.

243 Come, Ye Sinners, Poor and Wretched

Joseph Hart (1712-1768)
Altered by Augustus M. Toplady (1740-1778)

This hymn was first published in Hart's *Hymns Composed on Various Subjects,* 1759, in seven 6-line stanzas. It was headed "Come, and Welcome, to Jesus Christ." The form used in *Hymns of Faith and Life* is that found in Toplady's *Psalms and Hymns for Public and Private Worship,* 1776, using stanzas 1-4.

The omitted stanzas read:

> 5. View Him prostrate in the garden;
>   On the ground your Maker lies!
>   On the bloody tree behold Him;
>   Hear Him cry, before He dyes,
>   "It is finished:"
>   Sinner, will not this suffice?
>
> 6. Lo th'incarnate God, ascended,
>   Pleads the merit of His Blood:
>   Venture on Him, venture wholly,
>   Let no other trust intrude;
>   None but Jesus
>   Can do helpless sinners good.
>
> 7. Saints and Angels, joined in concert,
>   Sing the praises of the Lamb;
>   While the blissful seats of heaven
>   Sweetly echo with His name.
>   Hallelujah!
>   Sinners, here, may sing the same.

The hymn was included in the *Free Methodist Hymn-Book,* 1883, in seven stanzas and in 1910 in five stanzas, using the form in general use in American Methodist hymnals. The 1951 hymnal omitted it.

PLEADING SAVIOUR is a pentatonic melody found in Joshua Leavitt's *Christian Lyre,* 1830, where it appears with the hymn, "Now the Saviour Stands A-pleading," by John Leland (1754-1841).

244 Come, Every Soul, by Sin Oppressed

John Hart Stockton (1813-1877)

This invitation song was written by Stockton, a Methodist pastor and evangelist, about 1873. It was at this time that Sankey began to use it in meetings with D. L. Moody. It was published first, along with the music, in the author's *Salvation Melodies, No. 1,* 1874, in five stanzas with refrain.

Sankey altered the song to its present form and published it in 1875. The fifth stanza and the refrain as written by Stockton read:

> O Jesus, blessed Jesus, dear,
>   I'm coming now to Thee
> Since thou hast made the way so clear
>   And full salvation free.
> Come to Jesus, come to Jesus, come to Jesus now, . . .

The *Free Methodist Hymn-Book,* 1883, includes the Sankey version in the section at the back of the book headed "Social Worship." It has been included in each succeeding hymnal.

STOCKTON is an appropriate title for the tune, since John H. Stockton wrote both words and music of this song.

245 Give Me Thy Heart
Eliza Edmunds Hewitt (1851-1920)

Miss Hewitt was a gifted writer of gospel song lyrics which were set to music by the principal gospel song composers of her day: John R. Sweney, William J. Kirkpatrick, B. D. Ackley, P. P. Bilhorn, Charles H. Gabriel, E. S. Lorenz, and Homer Rodeheaver. Her songs are said to number more than two thousand. She was a personal friend of Fanny Crosby. No doubt their physical afflictions brought them close together.

This song was copyrighted in 1898. Note the trinitarian ascription in the three stanzas. It entered Free Methodist-Wesleyan hymnody in 1951. (See also comments at Nos. 330 and 427.)

BOURNE was written for this text by William James Kirkpatrick (1838-1921). It derives from the *nom de plume* (Annie F. Bourne) used on occasion by Kirkpatrick.

246 O Soul, Are You Weary and Troubled?
Helen Howarth Lemmel (1863-1961)

Words and music of this gospel song were written in 1918 although they appear not to have been copyrighted until 1922 under the title "The Heavenly Vision."

As a young woman Mrs. Lemmel traveled extensively in the

United States and Europe as a concert singer. For much of her life she lived in Seattle. In later years she lived in the home of Mr. and Mrs. Jesse K. Leise and then in the King's Garden Retirement Home. Although blind and confined to a wheel chair toward the end, her spirit was undiminished.

I recall her attendance at a performance of Handel's *Messiah* I conducted. Because of frail health she had to leave during an intermission and the choir broke out spontaneously in singing the refrain "Turn Your Eyes upon Jesus," an emotional experience still vivid years later.

This is the first inclusion in an official Free Methodist-Wesleyan hymnal.

247 The Saviour Is Waiting
Ralph Richard Carmichael (b. 1927)

Both words and music of this invitation song were written in 1958 by Ralph Carmichael for evangelistic services in Temple Baptist Church, Los Angeles, conducted by the pastor, Dr. Lester Harnish. Carmichael was minister of music there at the time. The harmonization appearing in our hymnal was made by Don Hustad in 1966 and first published in *Favorite Hymns of Praise,* 1967.

CARMICHAEL was chosen as the tune title by the editors of *Hymns for the Living Church,* 1974.

248 God Calling Yet! Shall I Not Hear?
Gerhard Tersteegen (1697-1769)
Translated by Sarah Borthwick Findlater (1823-1907)
Altered by Edward Amasa Park (b. 1808)

"Gott rufet noch, sollt' ich nicht endlich hören," based on Psalm 95:7, was first published in Tersteegen's *Geistliches Blumengärtlein,* Book III, second edition, 1735, in eight 4-line stanzas. Mrs. Findlater's translation which omitted stanzas 7 and 8 was published in *Hymns from the Land of Luther, Second Series,* 1855. It was in 11.11.11.11. meter with the opening line, "God calling yet! — and shall I never hearken?"

Most American hymnals follow the long-meter form given in the Andover *Sabbath Hymn Book,* 1858, edited by Edward A. Park. In this form Findlater's translation of Tersteegen's stanza 5 is omitted.

Hymns of the Living Faith, 1951, was the first Free Methodist-Wesleyan hymnal to include this hymn.

FEDERAL STREET was composed by Henry Kemble Oliver in 1832, apparently for Anne Steele's "So fades the lovely blooming flower," and published in Lowell Mason's *Boston Academy Collection of Church Music,* 1836. Federal Street is the name of the street in Salem, Massachusetts, where the composer's wife was reared and also the name of a street in Boston where a church stood which Oliver attended as a child.

249 Depth of Mercy! Can There Be?
Charles Wesley (1707-1788)

This hymn appeared in the Wesleys' *Hymns and Sacred Poems,* Pt. II, 1740, in thirteen 4-line stanzas. It was headed "After a Relapse into Sin." *Hymns of Faith and Life* uses stanzas 1, 2, 13, and 9.

Five stanzas were used in our hymnals of 1883, 1910, and 1951. In 1910 a curious refrain was added:

> God is love, I do believe;
> He is waiting to forgive,
> He is waiting, waiting to forgive.

The stanza omitted in 1976 reads:

> 7. Kindled His relentings are;
> Me He now delights to spare;
> Cries, "How shall I give thee up?"
> Lets the lifted thunder drop.

SEYMOUR is discussed at No. 209.

250 Years I Spent in Vanity and Pride
William Reed Newell (1868-1956)

The author, a faculty member at Moody Bible Institute, wrote this text on the back of an envelope. He gave the verses to Daniel B. Towner, the director of music at the Institute, and asked him to compose music for them. The result is the song as we have it today. It was published in *Famous Hymns,* 1895.

AT CALVARY is the title associated with both words and

music. The music was composed by Daniel Brink Towner (1850-1919).

251 Out of the Depths I Cry to Thee
Metrical version of Psalm 130 by Martin Luther (1483-1546)
English translation by Benjamin Latrobe (1725-1786).

Psalm 130 *(De Profundis)* was freely rendered into German beginning with the words "Aus tiefer Not schrei ich zu dir" by Martin Luther in four 7-line stanzas. It appeared in *Etlicher christlicher Lieder Lobgesänge,* 1524. It was sung at Halle on February 20, 1546, when Luther's body was being taken to its last resting place at Wittenberg.

There have been many translations into English. Perhaps one of the best is the one by Catherine Winkworth, included in her *Chorale Book for England,* 1863.

One of the earliest translations was included by Bishop Miles Coverdale in his *Goostly Psalmes and Spiritualle Songes,* 1539, beginning "Out of the depe crye I to the."

Benjamin Latrobe, for whom Charles wrote an epitaph, was a prominent Moravian minister.

Despite the influence of this text upon John Wesley, this is the first appearance of the hymn in a Free Methodist-Wesleyan hymnal. John Wesley records in his *Journal* for May 13, 1738, that in the afternoon he went to St. Paul's. The anthem sung on this occasion was *De Profundis.* The musical setting may have been composed either by Henry Purcell, a former organist of Westminister Abbey, or by William Croft, also organist at Westminster.

Charles Wesley has a hymn based on Psalm 130 in his *Hymns for Those That Seek...,* 1747. It is headed "Savior, the World's and Mine." The opening line reads: "Out of the deep I cry."

AUS TIEFER NOT, also called COBURG, was composed by either Luther or Johann Walther. It was published with the Luther text in *Enchiridion geistlicher Gesänge und Psalmen für die Laien* (Erfurt, 1524) and in Johann Walther's *Geistliches Gesangbüchlwen* (Wittenberg, 1524). The tune, in the Phrygian mode, was used by Johann Sebastian Bach in his Cantata No. 38, (c. 1740).

252 Out of My Bondage, Sorrow, and Night
William True Sleeper (1819-1904)

The author of this hymn was a pastor in Massachusetts about 1880 when George C. Stebbins asked him to write a hymn poem on the text, "Ye must be born again." Thus began a long friendship between the two men and a collaboration on at least one other hymn, "Out of My Bondage, Sorrow, and Night," copyrighted in 1887 by Ira D. Sankey and published in *Gospel Hymns No. 5*, 1887, compiled by Ira D. Sankey, James McGranahan, and George C. Stebbins. It carried the scripture heading: "Deliver me, O my God" (Psalm 71:4).

The text remains unchanged in our 1951 and 1976 hymnals, the only two Free Methodist-Wesleyan hymnals to include it.

A poignant story regarding the use of this hymn was related to the author some years ago by Dr. Robert Hess of Malone College. The substance of the story is as follows:

In one of the African countries in which the Friends have a work, the builder and principal of a Girls School, Abeli Benyoni, was known for his leadership ability and for his radiant testimony. He possessed also a beautiful singing voice and loved to sing even when engaged in physical labor connected with the erection of the school.

During a period of political turmoil involving guerilla activity he was accused unjustly of being a revolutionary. In due time he, along with others, was seized and led away to be executed. The soldiers inquired of their prisoners, "Is there a last request you wish to make?" Standing in a line with the condemned men the educator requested permission to sing. Granted permission he changed the whole atmosphere of the place by singing all stanzas of "Jesus, I come," as translated into his own language.

The hushed soldiers refused to shoot either the singer or the others. Thereupon the angry commander completed the execution himself.

JESUS, I COME was written for this text by George Coles Stebbins (1846-1945).

253 Just As I Am, Without One Plea
Charlotte Elliott (1789-1871)

This hymn was written in 1834 and first published in *The Invalid's Hymn Book,* 1836, in six 4-line stanzas. It was headed with the text, "Him that cometh unto Me, I will in no wise cast out." In the same year it was included in the author's *Hours of*

Sorrow Cheered and Comforted, 1836, with an additional stanza:

> Just as I am, of that free love
> "The breadth, length, depth, and height" to prove,
> Here for a season, then above,
> O Lamb of God, I come.

A few years ago on a quiet, misty Sunday morning Mrs. Schoenhals and I visited Dove Cottage, the home of the English poet William Wordsworth, at Grassmere in the lake district of England. It was too early for the typical tourist and we could study the home and its contents at leisure.

On the wall of one of the side rooms was a framed letter written by the husband of Wordsworth's only daughter, Dora, to Charlotte Elliott. It was introduced by a covering letter as follows:

> The following letter from Edward Quillinan to Charlotte Elliott, of Brighton ... serves to explain with moral certainty, two features of Dora Quillinan's head-stone in Grassmere churchyard — the Sculptured Lamb, and the Text, *Him that cometh unto me I will in no wise cast out.*
>
> As Miss Elliott's nephew by marriage, I venture to offer this reprint from *Poems by Charlotte Elliott* ... to the treasury at Dove Cottage.
>
> Handley Dunelm
Auckland Castle, January 1908

Loughrigg Holme
Ambleside
July 28, 1849

Dear Miss Elliott:

The day I received your very kind and welcome note, with music of the hymn, I was moving from home, and I did not return till last night. I need not say how much I am obliged to you. That hymn was originally sent to us, for my dying wife, by a relation of ours, a clergyman's wife in Kent; and it is rather remarkable that *her* daughter, who is on a visit to us, was the first person (as yet the only one) from whom I heard the music, which is exactly what it should be. This young lady was in the room when I received it, and she immediately, at my request, sang it without difficulty, to her own accompaniment....

When I first got the letter enclosing them, from Kent, I said to the beloved sufferer, who knew she was soon to leave us, "Here is a hymn from your friend Charlotte.... Shall I read it to you?" She answered hesitatingly, "Yes, I *must* hear it since it comes from *her.* She is so good, and it ought to be worth hearing." I read it; and had no sooner finished than she said very earnestly, "That is the very thing for me." At least ten times that day she asked me to repeat it to her; she desired me to write it in "Horne's Manual for the Afflicted." ... and every morning from that day till her decease two months later, the first thing she asked me for, was her hymn....

Mrs. Wordsworth has told me that your hymn forms part of her daily solitary prayers. I do not think that Mr. W_____ could bear to have it repeated aloud in his presence, but he is not the less sensible of the solace it gave his one and matchless daughter.

Believe me, dear Miss Elliott, with true sympathy

Your obliged and
faithful friend,
Edward Quillinan

Miss Elliott is buried in the churchyard of St. Andrew's Church, Hove, adjacent to Brighton, England.

This moving hymn has been in all Free Methodist hymnals since 1883.

WOODWORTH was composed by William Batchelder Bradbury (1816-1868) for the text "The God of love will sure indulge." It was included first in the *Mendelssohn Collection,* 1849, jointly edited by Bradbury and Thomas Hastings.

254 To Thee, O Lord, the God of All

Magnus Brostrup Landstad (1802-1880)
Translated by Carl Doving (1867-1937)

This penetential hymn was written by Magnus B. Landstad, a native of Norway. While attending the university in Norway, he came into possession of a volume by Philipp Nicolai entitled *Freuden-Spiegel des ewigen Lebens.* It contained four of Nicolai's hymns. These made a deep impression on him and he set about translating them. As he later wrote, he received "the first impetus in the direction of hymnwriting. Furthermore, it gave me a deeper insight into the life and spirit of the old church hymns."

Landstad's hymns were subsequently published in his *Kirke-Salmebog* which he edited and which was published in 1869 and adapted for use in The Church of Norway.

Carl Doving was also a Norwegian. He came to the United States in about 1890 and after attending college and seminary served a number of Norwegian Lutheran congregations. He was a gifted linguist, able to converse in at least six languages. He was a member of the committee which prepared the *Lutheran Hymnary* in 1913. It contained thirty-two of Doving's translations of German and Scandinavian hymns.

EISENACH was written by Johann Hermann Schein (1586-1630) for the hymn "Machs mit mir, Gott, nach deiner Güt" and published first in 1628 in a leaflet. Schein, one of the most distinguished musicians of his time, wrote the text, the melody, and five-part setting for "Machs mit mir" for the funeral of Margarita, wife of Caspar Werner, a town councillor at Leipzig and a church warden of St. Thomas Church.

Johann Sebastian Bach used the chorale melody in his *St. John Passion*.

The harmonization used in our hymnal is a composite of Bach's setting of Schein's hymn and of his setting in his *St. John Passion* to another hymn text. The melody we use is the form used in the *Passion*.

255 All My Life Long I Had Panted
Clara Tear Williams (1858-1937)

This text, often printed with the title "Satisfied," was written by Miss Clara Tear, later Mrs. W. H. Williams, in about 1875 according to a manuscript *Autobiography* in the Clark Hymnological Library in Houghton, New York.

I am indebted to Keith C. Clark for the following quotation from Clara Tear Williams's *Autobiography:*

> [I] was helping in meetings in Troy, Ohio, where Prof. R. E. Hudson conducted the singing, when just before retiring one night he asked me to write a song for a book he was preparing to publish. Before sleeping I wrote "Satisfied." In the morning he composed the music.

The song was published in 1881 in *Gems of Gospel Song,* compiled by E. A. Hoffman, J. H. Tenney, and Ralph E. Hudson. All Free Methodist-Wesleyan hymnals have included it.

SATISFIED was composed by Ralph E. Hudson (1843-1901). (See comments at No. 400.)

256 I Hear Thy Welcome Voice
Words and music by Lewis Hartsough (1828-1919)

The author and composer of this hymn was born in Ithaca, New York, August 31, 1828, and died in Mt. Vernon, Iowa, January 1, 1919. He was a Methodist minister and presiding elder in New York State, Wyoming, and Iowa from 1851 until his retirement in 1895. He served as musical editor of J. Hillman's

Revivalist in which this hymn was printed in the 1872 edition. Later it was included in Sankey's *Gospel Hymns and Sacred Poems,* 1875.

Of this hymn Ira D. Sankey in *My Life and Sacred Songs,* 1906, wrote, "The words and music of this beautiful hymn were first published in a monthly entitled 'Guide to Holiness,' a copy of which was sent to me in England in 1873. I immediately adopted it and had it published. . . . It proved to be one of the most helpful of the revival hymns. . . ."

Free Methodist-Wesleyan hymnals have included "I Hear Thy Welcome Voice" since 1951.

257 How Oft Have I the Spirit Grieved
Attributed to Charles Wesley (1707-1788)

Although attributed to Charles Wesley, it cannot be found in the Osborn edition of *The Poetical Works of John and Charles Wesley.* It is included in the 1849 edition of *Hymns for the Use of the Methodist Episcopal Church,* attributed there to Charles Wesley, and in the 1867 edition edited by Philip Phillips *(New Hymn and Tune Book: An Offering of Praise for the Methodist Episcopal Church).*

It has been included in all Free Methodist hymnals since 1883.

GERALD was written in 1834 by Louis Spohr (1784-1859) as a solo with chorus in his oratorio *Das Heiland's letzte Stunden.* It was adapted as a hymn tune by J. Stimpson to accompany the text "As pants the hart."

Robert McCutchan in his *Hymn Tune Names* describes the origin of the title *Gerald.* It was selected for use in *The Methodist Hymnal* of 1935 by the editorial committee as a composite from the names of Dr. Fitz*gerald* Sale Parker and Miss *Gerald*ine Reid Sherrill, the former a valued member of the Hymnal Commission and the latter the faithful secretary to the editor.

258 Blessed Be the Fountain of Blood
Eden Reeder Latta (b. 1839)

Information on the date and origin of this song is lacking. It was included in Sankey's *Sacred Songs and Solos* in an edition prior to 1890. *The Finest of the Wheat,* copyrighted 1890, prints it (No. 9) with the notation "Used by permission of Oliver Ditson and Company." Latta is known to have attended the Winona Lake Bible Conference in 1913.

This is the first Free Methodist-Wesleyan hymnal to include this song although it has appeared in two or three Free Methodist gospel songbooks.

FOUNTAIN is the tune title assigned by the editor of *HFL*. No information is available on the composer other than that the tune was arranged from Henry S. Perkins.

259 I Can Hear My Saviour Calling

E. W. Blandy

No information has been located about the author of this text. It is printed anonymously in some early books and also under the name of E. W. Blandy, e.g., *Make His Praise Glorious,* 1900 (E. O. Excell) and *Pentecostal Hymns,* No. 4, 1907 (Henry Date).

The 1951 hymnal was the first Free Methodist-Wesleyan hymnal to include it.

WHERE HE LEADS ME was written and copyrighted in 1890 by John Samuel Norris (1844-1907), a Congregational pastor in Iowa. The music, in a trio arrangement, appears in *Pentecostal Hymns,* 1894, (No. 190) with the notation "Arr. by Ira Orwig Hoffman" and accompanying a text by the Reverend Elisha A. Hoffman. *Light and Life Songs, No. 3,* 1918, and others print the music essentially as we have it, with the notation "Arr. from P. P. Bliss."

260 I Was Once a Sinner, but I Came

Words and music by C. Austin Miles (1868-1946)

Miles was a pharmacist by profession, but abandoned his career and became involved in the field of gospel music as both a writer and composer and also as an editor and manager for the Rodeheaver-Hall-Mack Company.

At the age of twelve he began his music career by playing the organ for a funeral service in a small Methodist church. The reed organ was one of those early editions with only four of the twenty stops serviceable. In his own words he reported, "As the funeral procession entered, I began to play the one march I knew. . . . The preacher commended me, mother was most proud." It was not until five years later that he discovered his "funeral march" was really the "wedding march" from *Lohengrin*. *(Music in Evangelism)*.

This is the first inclusion of this song in a Free Methodist hymnal.

261 Lord, I Hear of Showers of Blessing
Elizabeth Harris Codner (1824-1919)

This song was written in the summer of 1860 by Mrs. Codner at Weston-super-Mare, England. Originally, it had seven 4-line stanzas with refrain and was headed "Bless Me, Even Me Also, O My Father." The inspiration for writing the song came from news of a religious revival in Ireland. The author published it in leaflet form in 1861. The omitted final stanza reads:

> Pass me not! Thy lost one bringing,
>   Bind my heart, O Lord, to Thee;
> While the streams of life are springing,
>   Blessing others, O bless me.

In Ira D. Sankey's *Sacred Songs and Solos*, Part I, six stanzas are printed with some alterations of the text and the omission of the original stanza 5.

EVEN ME was written by William Batchelder Bradbury (1816-1868). It appeared first in *The Golden Shower*, 1862.

262 I Have Decided to Follow Jesus
Folk Melody from India

This song is said to have originated in India. It gained some popularity in the late 1940s in the United States. An arrangement was copyrighted in 1950 by the Young Peoples Missionary Society of the Free Methodist Church and published in *Choice Light and Life Songs*, 1950.

In a personal letter to the author, veteran missionary to India, Loretta P. Root, stated that the song was well known there in both Hindi and in English in the 1930s. She herself learned it from an Indian lady evangelist from Agra in late 1937 or in 1938.

ASSAM is the tune title adopted by William J. Reynolds when the song was included in *Christian Praise*, 1964.

263 Jesus, the Sinner's Friend, to Thee

Charles Wesley (1707-1788)

This hymn in thirteen 4-line stanzas is found in the **Wesleys'** *Hymns and Sacred Poems*, Part I, 1739. Our hymnal uses stanzas 1, 2, 6, and 10. The 1883 hymnal included this hymn, using stanzas 1, 2, and 10, and concluded with stanza 12:

> What shall I say Thy grace to move?
> Lord, I am sin, but Thou art love:
> I give up every plea beside,
> Lord, I am damned, but Thou hast died!

"Damned" was changed to "lost."
This form was repeated in 1910. The hymn was omitted in 1951.

DEUS TUORUM MILITUM (GRENOBLE) derives its name from the opening words of a Latin hymn in the *Grenoble Antiphoner*, 1753.

264 Art Thou Weary, Art Thou Troubled?

John Mason Neale (1818-1866)
Altered by Edward Henry Bickersteth (1825-1906)

This hymn mistakenly attributed to St. Stephen (725-794), a resident of the monastery at Mar Saba southeast of Jerusalem, must be regarded as an original composition of Neale rather than a translation. He himself wrote that there was very little from the Greek contained in the hymn. The text appeared first in Neale's *Hymns of the Eastern Church*, 1862, in seven 4-line stanzas.

Some of the commonly accepted alterations in the text were made by Bishop Edward H. Bickersteth for *Hymnal Companion to the Book of Common Prayer*, 1870.

Textual changes are the following:

> 1:1 ... art thou *languid*
> 7:3 *Angels, Martyrs,* prophets, *virgins*

The hymn is so structured that it may be sung antiphonally with good effect.

This hymn entered Free Methodist-Wesleyan hymnody in 1910.

STEPHANOS was composed by Henry Williams Baker (1821-1877) and harmonized by William Henry Monk (1823-1889) for this text in the appendix to the first edition of *Hymns Ancient and Modern*, 1868.

Benson, from his reading of the novel *Cape Cod Folks,* seems confident that it was *Stephanos* to which George Olver and Luke Cradlebow sang "Art Thou Weary."

265 I Am Coming to the Cross
William McDonald (1820-1901)

This text was written in 1870 by McDonald, a Methodist minister in the city of Brooklyn, New York. It was sung first at a campmeeting in Hamilton, Massachusetts, on June 22, 1870, according to Robert G. McCutchan. It was printed first in *The Baptist Praise Book,* 1871.

The principal change made in our hymnal is the use of the refrain as the fourth stanza.

TRUSTING was written by William Gustavus Fischer (1835-1912) apparently prior to the writing of the text and McDonald wrote his hymn to fit the tune.

266 Father, I Stretch My Hands to Thee
Charles Wesley (1707-1788)
Stanza 5 by Edwin Othello Excell (1851-1921)

This hymn appeared in the Wesleys' *Collection of Psalms and Hymns,* 1741, in six 4-line stanzas. It is headed "A Prayer of Faith." Charles Wesley cannot conclusively be shown to be the author, but the hymn is quite likely his. Stanzas used here are 1, 2, 5, and 4 of the original.

Our stanza 5 appears to have been added as a refrain, probably by E. O. Excell. In the songbook, *Make His Praise Glorious,* 1900, edited by Excell, it is added as a refrain to another text "Come, humble sinner, in whose breast" with the notation, "Arranged by E. O. E."

Our 1883 hymnal prints all six stanzas as do those of 1910 and 1951. The present hymnal is the first to add the stanza "I do believe."

The omitted stanzas read:

> 3. O Jesus, could I this believe
>   I now should feel Thy power,
>   And all my wants Thou wouldst relieve,
>   In this accepted hour.

6. How would my fainting soul rejoice,
    Could I but see Thy face;
  Now let me hear Thy quickening voice,
    And taste Thy pardoning grace.

I DO BELIEVE, also called CONFIDENCE, is evidently an American melody dating from the nineteenth century. It is associated with this text in Sankey's *Sacred Songs and Solos* where the refrain "I do believe" is also used.

The tune I DO BELIEVE is associated elsewhere with "There Is a Fountain" to which the refrain "I Do Believe" is added with these textual changes:

  I do believe, I now believe
    I will hold out no more;
  I sink, by dying love compelled,
    I own the conqueror.

The music in two parts is credited to "Golden Censer" in *The Old Paths: or Ancient Sacred Harmonies,* 1869, compiled by the Reverend William James Selby.

267 Jesus, My Strength, My Hope
Charles Wesley (1707-1788)

This hymn is found in the Wesleys' *Hymns and Sacred Poems,* Part 2, 1742, in seven 8-line stanzas. It is entitled "A Poor Sinner." In the so-called "Large Hymnbook," John Wesley placed stanza 2 as the last.

Our 1883 and 1910 hymnals included this text using three stanzas only: 1, 3, and 4. The hymn was omitted in 1951.

LEOMINSTER is adapted as a hymn tune from an anthem entitled "The Pilgrim Song" by George William Martin (1828-1881), which was published in *The Journal of Part Music,* 1862.

268 My Faith Looks Up to Thee
Ray Palmer (1808-1887)

This hymn was written in 1830 by Ray Palmer, a Congregational minister. It seems to have been the first of thirty-eight hymns written by Palmer and is today his best-known lyric. The inspiration for writing it came from reading a short German poem. Of the experience, he said,

I gave form to what I felt by writing, with little effort, these stanzas. I recollect I wrote them with very tender emotion, and ended the last line with tears.

Palmer wrote the poem in a notebook and frequently read it during his private devotions. He did not think of it as a hymn for public use.

All Free Methodist hymnals have included this hymn.

OLIVET was composed in 1830 or 1831 for this text by Lowell Mason (1792-1872) and for inclusion in *Spiritual Songs for Social Worship: Adapted to the Use of Families . . .*, 1831, compiled by Mason and Thomas Hastings.

Mason knew something of Palmer's reputation as a poet. One day, meeting him by chance on a street in Boston, he asked whether Palmer had any verses that might be set to music. Palmer remembered the poem in his notebook and made a copy for Mason on the spot.

A few days later the two men met again and Mason is reported to have said, "Dr. Palmer, you may live many years and do many good things, but I think you will be best known to posterity as the author of 'My Faith Looks Up to Thee.'"

Mason came from hardy New England stock. An ancestor Robert Mason had come from England along with John Winthrop in 1630. He showed an early aptitude for music but was discouraged from following music as a career. At age twenty he went to Savannah, Georgia, to accept a position in a bank. While there he studied music, wrote a number of compositions, directed church choirs, and served as a church organist.

While in Savannah, Mason began to compile a hymn collection which was subsequently published in Boston. This proved to be a profitable venture and resulted in an invitation to return to Boston where, before long, he championed the teaching of music in the public schools. He was a pioneer in organizing music conventions. In the opinion of John Tasker Howard in *Our American Music,* "few single American musicians have ever exerted so wide an influence in the improvement of musical taste and standards as did Lowell Mason over a period of forty years." In recognition of his work he was awarded the first honorary doctor of music degree ever granted in America. New York University conferred the degree in 1855.

269 Amazing Grace! How Sweet the Sound

John Newton (1725-1807)
Stanza 5, anonymous (c. 1829)

It is interesting that this hymn which is so widely sung in the United States is not included in most contemporary British collections. Of those consulted it appeared only in *Hymns of Faith,* 1964, published by Scripture Union. It was published first in *Olney Hymns, Book I,* 1779, in six 4-line stanzas under the title "Faith's Review and Expectation." It is based on I Chronicles 17:16-17.

The omitted stanza 6 reads:

> The earth shall soon dissolve like snow,
>   The sun forbear to shine;
> But God, who call'd me here below,
>   Will be for ever mine.

Our present stanza 6, according to William J. Reynolds, was associated with "Jerusalem, My Happy Home" in early nineteenth-century collections. Early in the twentieth century it was added as a final stanza to "Amazing Grace," possibly by E. O. Excell in about 1910, e.g., in *Make Christ King,* 1912 (No. 251), edited by E. O. Excell and William Edward Biederwolf.

The immense popularity of this hymn is something of a modern-day miracle. No doubt John Newton, were he alive today, would be pleased to have his poetic personal testimony sung both in churches and concert halls, and on radio and TV. Not long ago at a Boston Pops concert the soloist led the audience in singing several stanzas, a moving and surprisingly reverent experience.

John Newton was buried in the crypt beneath St. Mary Woolnoth in the City of London. An Underground station now occupies the crypt, and Newton's body has been removed to Olney. His epitaph which he wrote himself is inscribed on a marble tablet and mounted on a wall of the sanctuary of St. Mary Woolnoth. It reads:

> JOHN NEWTON
> CLERK
> ONCE AN INFIDEL AND LIBERTINE
> A SERVANT OF SLAVES IN AFRICA
> WAS
> BY THE RICH MERCY
> OF OUR LORD AND SAVIOR
> JESUS CHRIST
> PRESERVED, RESTORED, PARDONED
> AND APPOINTED TO PREACH THE FAITH
> HE HAD LONG LABOURED TO DESTROY.

HE MINISTERED
NEAR XVI YEARS AS CURATE AND VICAR
OF OLNEY IN BUCKS
AND XXVIII YEARS AS RECTOR
OF THESE UNITED PARISHES

ON FEB^Y THE FIRST MDCCL HE MARRIED
MARY
DAUGHTER OF THE LATE GEORGE CATLETT
OF CHATHAM KENT
WHOM HE RESIGNED
TO THE LORD WHO GAVE HER
ON DEC^R THE XVTH MDCCXC.

The above Epitaph was written by the Deceased who directed it to be inscribed on a plain Marble Tablet.

He died on Dec^R the 21TH, 1807. Aged 82 years.
and his mortal remains
are deposited in the Vault
beneath this Church.

Newton is said to have remarked not long before his death, "My memory is nearly gone, but I remember two things, that I am a great sinner, and that Christ is a great Savior." (See comment at No. 143 also.)

AMAZING GRACE is an American folk melody which appeared anonymously in *Virginia Harmony,* 1831. It is included also in William Walker's *Southern Harmony,* 1835, under the title *New Britain* and associated with the text "Amazing Grace." The arrangement is in three parts with the melody in the tenor.

E. O. Excell is generally credited with arranging the music as widely adopted in twentieth-century song books, although usually somewhat simplified melodically.

In Excell's *Make His Praise Glorious,* 1900, it is No. 235, and carries this notation: E.O.E. Arr.

270 Jesus, Thy Blood and Righteousness
Nicholaus L. von Zinzendorf (1700-1760)
Translated by John Wesley (1703-1791)

The hymn "Christe Blut und Gerechtigkeit" was written by Count von Zinzendorf in 1739, basing a part of the first stanza on a hymn by Paul Eber. It was first published in Herrnhut *Gesangbuch, Appendix VIII,* 1739, in thirty-three 4-line stanzas.

John Wesley's excellent but rather free translation in twenty-four 4-line stanzas (omitting Zinzendorf's stanzas 6, 11, 13, 22, 23, and 25-28) was printed in *Hymns and Sacred Poems,* Part II, 1740, under the title, "The Believer's Triumph." Our hymnal uses stanzas 1, 2, 7, 8, 12, and 19.

Telford records that this hymn was a great favorite of Rowland Hill and that it was sung at his funeral.

All Free Methodist hymnals since 1883 have included it.

Shortly after Wesley's conversion in 1738 he went to Germany to acquaint himself with the Moravians there. Just as their singing had impressed him on shipboard en route to Georgia he found the Pietistic movement in Germany to be a singing movement. In Wesley's home on City Road in London there is a copy of the Herrnhut *Gesangbuch* signed by John and dated 1739. Perhaps it was brought back from Germany by him on this trip.

HESPERUS or QUEBEC (See comments at No. 100.)

271 Saved by the Blood of the Crucified One
S. J. Henderson (nineteenth century)

This gospel song was copyrighted in 1903 by the composer of the music, Daniel Brink Towner (1850-1919). No biographical data is available on Henderson. For information on Towner, see comments at No. 250 and No. 368.

272 Where Shall My Wondering Soul Begin?
Charles Wesley (1707-1788)

This hymn was written in Little Britain near St. Paul's Cathedral, London, in May, 1738. On the Tuesday following Charles Wesley's conversion (Sunday, May 21, 1738) he wrote in his diary:

> I waked under the protection of Christ, and gave myself up, soul and body, to Him. At nine I began a hymn upon my

conversion, but was persuaded to break off, for fear of pride. Mr. Bray coming, encouraged me to proceed in spite of Satan. I prayed Christ to stand by me, and finished the hymn. Upon my afterwards showing it to Mr. Bray, the devil threw in a fiery dart, suggesting that it was wrong, and I had displeased God. My heart sunk within me; when, casting my eye upon a Prayer book, I met with an answer for him. "Why boastest thou thyself, thou tyrant, that thou canst do mischief?" Upon this, I clearly discerned it was a device of the enemy to keep back glory from God. . . .

On the following day the hymn was sung in Charles's room when "towards ten," Charles wrote, "my brother was brought in triumph by a troop of our friends, and declared, 'I believe.' We sang the hymn with great joy, and parted with prayer."

It cannot be determined with certainty whether the hymn mentioned was this one or "And Can It Be?" Tradition seems to favor "Where Shall My Wondering Soul Begin?"

The hymn was published first in *Hymns and Sacred Poems,* Part II, 1739, in eight 6-line stanzas, under the title "Christ the Friend of Sinners." Stanza 6 was omitted by John in the "Large Hymnbook", 1780. Stanzas used in *Hymns of Faith and Life* are 1, 2, 3, and 7 without alteration. It is included in the Free Methodist hymnals of 1883, 1951, and 1976.

FILLMORE is attributed to Jeremiah Ingalls (1764-1828) and arranged by William Gustavus Fischer (1835-1912). It is thought that the tune was named for Millard Fillmore, thirteenth president of the United States, from 1850-53. Ingalls has been described as a "tavern-keeper, farmer, cooper, singing-school teacher, composer, compiler, and choirmaster." Whether Ingalls wrote *Fillmore* or not we do not know, but we are indebted to him for this bit of poetry on music:

> Enlisted in the cause of sin,
>   Why should a good be evil?
> Music, alas, too long has been
>   Press'd to obey the devil.

According to the *Companion to the Hymnal* (Abingdon) this tune is found in *Joyful Songs Nos. 1-3 Combined,* 1869, compiled by William G. Fischer and published by the Methodist Episcopal Book Rooms.

A copy of *The Revivalist,* dated 1868, is owned by the Free Methodist Historical Center. In it the tune, unnamed, is printed with the text "And Can It Be?" The arrangement of the music is credited to William G. Fischer.

273 And Can It Be?

Charles Wesley (1707-1788)

This hymn, written in 1738 soon after Charles Wesley's conversion experience, was published in *A Collection of Psalms and Hymns,* 1738, and again in *Hymns and Sacred Poems,* Part II, 1739, under the title "Free Grace." Originally, there were six 6-line stanzas. In *Hymns and Sacred Poems,* 1747, it is the concluding hymn.

Our hymnal uses stanzas 1, 3, 4, and 6. The original second and fifth stanzas read:

> 2. 'Tis mystery all! The Immortal dies!
>   Who can explore His strange design?
> In vain the first-born seraph tries
>   To sound the depths of Love Divine.
> 'Tis mercy all! Let earth adore;
> Let angel minds inquire no more.

> 5. Still the small inward voice I hear,
>   That whispers all my Sin forgiv'n:
> Still th'atoning Blood is near,
>   That quenched the wrath of hostile Heav'n:
> I feel the Life His wounds impart,
> I feel my Savior in my Heart.

This latter stanza was omitted by John Wesley in his 1780 "Large Hymnbook."

The hymns of Wesley often contain allusions to other literary works indicating his acquaintance with a broad range of writing. For instance, "Thine eye diffused a quickening ray" echoes two lines from *Eloisa to Abelard* by Alexander Pope:

> Thy eyes diffused a reconciling ray,
> And gleams of glory brightened all the day.

"And Can It Be?" was printed in the five-stanza form in our 1883 and 1910 hymnals. Omitted in 1951 it captured the attention of Free Methodists in the late 1950s when it was widely sung to the tune *Sagina.*

The General Conference of 1960 declared the hymn together with this tune to be the "denominational hymn of the church."

SAGINA is attributed to one Thomas Campbell or T. Campbell. Julian gives brief biographical information about Thomas Campbell the poet (1777-1844), who is buried in Westminster Abbey. No reference is made to his music.

Lightwood says that SAGINA was published in Thomas Campbell's *Boquet,* 1825, containing twenty-three original tunes. He was said to be a native of Sheffield. Julian's Campbell was born in Glasgow. In the absence of better information the assumption must be made that these are two different people. To complicate matters further, at least one hymnal, *Hymns of Faith* (Scripture Union, London, 1964), gives the dates of the composer of SAGINA as 1825-76.

274 Lord of Mercy, God of Might
Wilson T. Hogue (1852-1920)

This hymn, written by a bishop of the Free Methodist church, has appeared in all Free Methodist-Wesleyan hymnals since 1910. There is no record of the date of its composition nor of the circumstances of its writing.

SEYMOUR is discussed at No. 209.

275 For God So Loved This Sinful World
Lelia Naylor Morris (1862-1929)

Words and music of this song were written about 1899 by Mrs. Charles H. Morris, a lifelong Methodist and resident of Ohio. It was copyrighted in that year by Dr. Henry Lake Gilmour, a dentist by profession but also an active church worker in the Methodist church. He was a gifted soloist and choir director and gave a great deal of musical encouragement and assistance to Mrs. Morris.

It entered Free Methodist-Wesleyan hymnody in 1951.

276 Down at the Cross Where My Saviour Died
Elisha Albright Hoffman (1839-1929)

Hoffman was born at Orwigsburg, Pennsylvania, May 7, 1839. He was a minister most of his active life but also wrote, it is said, more than two thousand gospel songs. For many of these he wrote the music also. This particular song appeared first in *Joy to the World,* 1878, compiled by T. C. O'Kane, C. C. McCabe, and John R. Sweney, but was written in 1877 or earlier. It seems to have become popular quickly for it appears in a number of books published in the late 1800s.

GLORY TO HIS NAME is the title usually assigned to the

tune. It was written by John Hart Stockton (1813-1877) for this text.

277, 278 Jesus, Lover of My Soul
Charles Wesley (1707-1788)

Under the title "In Temptation," this hymn was printed in the Wesleys' *Hymns and Sacred Poems, Part I,* 1740, in five 8-line stanzas. *Hymns of Faith and Life* uses stanzas 1, 2, 4, and 5.

The omitted stanza reads:

> Wilt thou not regard my call?
> > Wilt thou not accept my prayer?
>
> Lo! I sink, I faint, I fall —
> > Lo, on Thee I cast my care:
>
> Reach me out Thy gracious hand!
> > While I of Thy strength receive,
>
> Hoping against hope I stand,
> > Dying, and behold, I live!

At the beginning of the twentieth century, John Julian placed this hymn along with "Hark! The Herald Angels Sing" and "Hail the Day that Sees Him Rise" as the three hymns of Charles Wesley that had attained greatest popularity.

It was included in the Wesleys' hymnals of 1753 (reduced to four stanzas), 1765, and in the *Pocket Hymn-Book* of 1785. Strangely omitted by John Wesley in the "Large Hymnbook" of 1780, it was included by Toplady, his theological antagonist, in 1776. Martin Madan included it in his *Psalms and Hymns,* 1760, as did Conyers in his hymnbook of 1774.

Some lines have caused hymnal editors difficulty and have invited experimental changes. The intimacy of the term "lover" as applied to Christ is one of them. None of the changes has been widely accepted. The basis for the term is the *Wisdom of Solomon* 11:26: "But Thou sparest all: for they are Thine, O Lord, Thou Lover of souls."

Approximately one-hundred fifty-four attempts at revision of the first four lines have been noted.

Henry Ward Beecher said:

> I would rather have written that hymn of Wesley's "Jesus, Lover of my Soul," than to have the fame of all the kings that ever sat on the earth. It is more glorious. It has more power in it.... That hymn will go on singing until the last trump brings forth the angel band; and then, I think, it will mount up on some lips to the very presence of God.

Erik Routley calls this "a hymn for the crises of life."

All Free Methodist hymnals have included "Jesus, Lover of My Soul."

ABERYSTWYTH was written by Joseph Parry (1841-1903) in the seaside Welsh town of Aberystwyth where he was a music professor at the University College of Wales. It was printed first in E. Stephen and Joseph D. Jones's *Ail Llyfr Tonau ac Emynau,* 1879 (Second book of Hymns and Tunes), where it is set to the Welsh hymn, "Beth sydd i mi yn y byd." Later the composer used the tune together with the text "Jesus Lover of My Soul" as the concluding number of his cantata *Ceridwen,* perhaps the first use with this hymn.

REFUGE was written about 1862 by Joseph Perry Holbrook (1822-1888) and printed in Charles H. Robinson's *Songs of the Church,* or *Hymns and Tunes for Christian Worship,* 1862, of which he was music editor.

279   In Tenderness He Sought Me
W. Spencer Walton (1850-1906)

According to Donald P. Hustad this hymn was first published in *The Coronation Hymnal,* 1894, edited by A. J. Gordon and A. T. Pierson. Walton is thought to have been an associate of Gordon.
This is the first inclusion of this song in a Free Methodist-Wesleyan hymnal.

CLARENDON was composed by Adoniram Judson Gordon (1836-1895), pastor of the Clarendon Street Baptist Church in Boston. The change of 6/8 meter to 2/2 meter was made by Hustad in *Worship and Service Hymnal,* 1957.

280   O How Happy Are They
Charles Wesley (1707-1788)

This exuberant text is one of a series of thirty-seven hymns under the general title "For One Fallen from Grace." It appeared in two parts first in Charles Wesley's *Hymns and Sacred Poems, Vol. I,* 1749, in sixteen 6-line stanzas (seven stanzas in Part I and nine stanzas in Part II). Our hymnal uses stanzas 1, 2, 3, 4, and 7.
The poet took rhythmic liberties which require some editorial

adjustments. For example stanza 1 as written by Charles Wesley was 5.6.9.D.

> How happy are they,
> Who the Savior obey
>   And have laid up their treasure above,
> Tongue cannot express
> The sweet comfort, and peace
>   Of a soul in its earliest love.

Similarly stanza 2 was 569.669 and stanza 3 was 658.569.

The hymn was not included in the "Large Hymnbook" during John Wesley's lifetime but it was included in the *Pocket Hymn Book*.

The original stanza 6 was printed in Free Methodist hymnals of 1883, 1910, and 1951:

> I rode on the sky,
> (Freely justified I!)
>   Nor envied *Elijah* his seat;
> My soul mounted higher
> In a chariot of fire,
>   And the moon it was under my feet.

In 1883 the hymn had already been changed rhythmically to 6.6.9.D and stanza 1 changed to "O how happy are they,..." Stanza 5 (original 6) became:

> I then rode on the sky,
> Freely justified I,
>   Nor did envy Elijah his seat:
> My glad soul mounted higher
> In a chariot of fire,
>   And the moon it was under my feet.

DAVIS also called BELOVED and MEDITATION is attributed to Freeman Lewis (1780-1859), a surveyor by profession in Uniontown, Pennsylvania.

McCutchan in *Our Hymnody* believes the tune dates from its inclusion in *The Beauties of Harmony*, 1813, of which Lewis was the compiler. It is also reported to have been included in Wyeth's *Repository of Sacred Music, Part II*, 1813.

The harmonization is essentially that made in 1869 by Hubert Platt Main (1839-1926).

281 I Heard the Voice of Jesus Say

Horatius Bonar (1808-1889)

This hymn was written by Horatius Bonar, a minister of the Free Church of Scotland, while serving at Kelso. It was published in his *Hymns, Original and Selected,* 1846, in three-line stanzas, under the heading "The Voice from Galilee."

According to the Reverend John Brownlie *(The Hymns and Hymn Writers of the Church Hymnary,* 1899), the qualities that placed Bonar as the principal hymnwriter of Scotland are these: "his hymns are poetic," "they are childlike," "they are manly," "they are hopeful," and finally "they are sympathetic." Louis F. Benson said of him, "He lived with God, the humblest of His children, and had only one great aim in his life — to bring men to Christ."

Bonar was interested in prophecy and considered himself an ardent premillenarian. For twenty-five years he edited *The Quarterly Journal of Prophecy.*

A penciled draft of the hymn is reproduced in *Studies of Familiar Hymns* (Second Series), 1923, by Louis F. Benson. It is taken from a notebook Bonar always kept handy and shows "doodling" in the margins.

The text in *Hymns of Faith and Life* follows that of the facsimile. Changes, presumably made by Bonar, for his *Hymns of Faith and Hope* (First Series), 1857, are these:

    2:3   The living water; *thirsty one,*
    3:3-4 Look unto me, thy *morn shall rise*
            And all thy *day* be bright.

Erik Routley in *Hymns and Human Life* calls this "a classic of personal devotion" that "will live many generations yet."

It has been in all Free Methodist hymnals since 1883.

VOX DILECTI was written by John Bacchus Dykes (1823-1876) for this text for the supplement to the 1875 edition of *Hymns Ancient and Modern.* The first half of the tune is in minor and the last half in major, a device the composer also used in his ST. ANDREW OF CRETE. (See No. 412.)

282 I Was a Wandering Sheep

                              Horatius Bonar (1808-1889)

Under the heading "Lost but Found, 'Ye were as sheep going astray; but are now returned unto the Shepherd and Bishop of your souls, I Peter 2:25,'" this hymn was published in the author's *Songs in the Wilderness, First Series,* 1843, in five 8-line stanzas. It was one of his early hymns.

The omitted third stanza reads:

    They spoke in tender love,
    They raised my drooping head,

> They gently closed my bleeding wounds.
> My fainting soul they fed;
> They wash'd my filth away,
> They made me clean and fair;
> They brought me to my home in peace,
> The long-sought wanderer.

The "they" refers to the "Shepherd" and the "Father" in stanza 2.

All Free Methodist hymnals since 1883 have printed this hymn in the same altered form.

LEBANON was written by John Zundel (1815-1882) and published in 1855 in the *Plymouth Collection*. It is not to be confused with a tune by the same name derived from a composition of Spohr. Zundel was organist at Henry Ward Beecher's *Plymouth Congregational Church* in Brooklyn, New York, where his organ playing so complemented Beecher's preaching that people were often heard to say, "We will go hear Beecher and Zundel."

283 I Have a Song I Love to Sing
Edwin Othello Excell (1851-1921)

Excell wrote both words and music for this song. It appeared first in one of the fifty or so songbooks he published, *Echoes of Eden for the Sunday School,* 1884.

The omitted fourth stanza reads:

> I have a joy I can't express,
>   Since I have been redeemed,
> All thro' his blood and righteousness,
>   Since I have been redeemed.

This song entered Free Methodist-Wesleyan hymnody in 1951.

The tune title OTHELLO has been adopted in a number of contemporary hymnals. It is derived from the composer's middle name.

284 Redeemed, How I Love to Proclaim It
Fanny Jane Crosby (1820-1915)

This song was written in 1882 or earlier and became popular

almost immediately. It entered Free Methodist-Wesleyan hymnody in 1951. A fifth stanza, omitted in our hymnal, reads:

>I know there's a crown that is waiting
>In yonder bright mansion for me,
>And soon, with the spirits made perfect,
>At home with the Lord I shall be.
>   Refrain

(See notes at No. 42.)

REDEEMED was written for this text by William J. Kirkpatrick (1838-1921) and copyrighted by him in 1882. It was published in *Songs of Redeeming Love*, 1882.

285 I Sought a Flag to Follow
John W. Peterson (b. 1921)

This song dates from about 1956, the year it was copyrighted. (See comments at No. 84.)

286 I Sought the Lord
Anonymous (c. 1880)

All efforts to identify the author of this hymn have failed. According to *The Hymnal 1940 Companion* it was printed first in the Roberts Brothers' *Holy Songs, Carols, and Sacred Ballads*, 1880.

Hymns of the Living Faith, 1951, is the first Free Methodist-Wesleyan hymnal to include this hymn.

PEACE was composed by George Whitefield Chadwick (1854-1931), composer, teacher, church organist, and director of the New England Conservatory of Music for thirty-three years. It is dated 1890 by McCutchan. The tune has been rhythmically altered in this hymnal in order to make the accents fit the text better.

287 Blessed Assurance, Jesus Is Mine!
Fanny Jane Crosby (1820-1915)

Called by John Telford one of Fanny Crosby's "most

impressive hymns," this text was written to fit a tune composed by Phoebe Palmer Knapp. Mrs. Knapp, visiting Fanny Crosby one day, said, "Here is a new hymn tune I have written. What does it suggest to you?"

After Mrs. Knapp had played her new tune over several times, the blind hymnwriter's face brightened and she exclaimed, "Why, the music says, 'Blessed Assurance, Jesus is mine.'"

Will Carleton, writing during Fanny Crosby's lifetime, gave this evaluation of her songs:

> All over this country, and, one might say, the world, Fanny Crosby's hymns are singing themselves into the hearts and souls of the people. They have been doing this for many years, and will continue to do so as long as civilization lasts.... She is easily the greatest living writer of hymns.
> (Introduction to *Fanny Crosby's Life Story, by Herself*, Everywhere Publishing Co., N.Y., 1905).

Perhaps this prophecy is too extravagant but, about seventy years later, this hymn and others by Fanny Crosby continue to enjoy almost unabated popularity. Free Methodist-Wesleyan hymnals have been printing "Blessed Assurance" since 1910. (See also comments at No. 42.)

ASSURANCE was written in 1873 by Phoebe Palmer Kmapp and copyrighted in that year by her husband, Joseph F. Knapp, founder of the Metropolitan Life Insurance Company. It, together with Fanny Crosby's text, was included in the same year in John R. Sweney's *Gems of Praise*. Mrs. Knapp is well known to church musicians as the composer of "Open the Gates of the Temple."

288 Arise, My Soul, Arise

Charles Wesley (1707-1788)

This hymn appears under the title "Behold the Man" in the Wesleys' *Hymns and Sacred Poems, Part II,* 1742, in five 6-line stanzas.

The hymns of Charles Wesley are not the exclusive property of Methodist bodies. Ernest Edwin Ryden, Lutheran hymnologist, in his *Story of Christian Hymnody* wrote:

> While hymns of many other writers gradually disappear from modern hymnals, those of Charles Wesley continue to reveal a remarkable hold on the worship life of the church, and a new appreciation is sometimes shown for lyrics once forgotten but again recovered.

Then he mentions Wesley's communion hymn "Victim Divine, Thy Grace We Claim," as an example which was included in the Lutheran *Service Book and Hymnal*. This same hymnal contains nineteen hymns by Charles Wesley, more than by any other writer.

All Free Methodist hymnals have included this hymn.

LENOX, also called TRUMPET because it is in the trumpet meter (6666.88) used by Charles Wesley for the hymn "Blow Ye the Trumpet, Blow," was composed by Lewis Edson, Sr. (1748-1820), and first printed in *The Chorister's Companion,* 1782, and in William Law's *The Rudiments of Music,* 1783. LENOX in its original form was a "fuguing" tune. This feature has been eliminated in the harmonic version printed in our 1976 hymnal. Both versions were used in the 1910 hymnal.

Edson was a blacksmith by trade but was also an amateur musician of note. He was highly regarded as a singer in Massachusetts, New York, and Connecticut. Edson did not edit any tune books nor did he compose much music but three of his tunes attained considerable popularity: LENOX, GREENFIELD, and BRIDGEWATER, which were named after Massachusetts towns. All are examples of "fuguing" tunes.

289 Saved! Saved! Saved!
Oswald Jeffray Smith (b. 1889)

The text of this song was written in 1917 by the longtime pastor of Peoples Church in Toronto. It was his first gospel song to achieve popularity.

According to Dr. Smith's own account he was selling hymn books in the aisles of Massey Hall, Toronto, during an evangelistic campaign held there in 1919 by Paul Rader and Arthur W. McKee. Without Smith's prior knowledge, Mr. McKee announced that the congregation would sing a brand new song entitled "Saved" and then pointed to Smith as the author. As the 3,400 people sang it under McKee's inspired direction, Dr. Smith was hearing it for the first time.

The text with its tune was copyrighted in 1918 by Arthur W. McKee, long associated with the Winona Lake Bible Conference as Executive Manager. Bob Jones University conferred an honorary doctor of sacred music degree upon McKee in 1952.

This is the first Free Methodist-Wesleyan hymnal to include the song.

HICKMAN is the title assigned to this tune. It was composed for this text by Roger M. Hickman (1888-1968).

290 O Happy Day, that Fixed My Choice
Philip Doddridge (1702-1751)

The author of this hymn was a nonconformist minister, friend of Lady Huntingdon and of the venerable Isaac Watts. It was at the latter's insistence that Doddridge wrote *The Rise and Progress of Religion in the Soul* which became influential throughout Christendom.

Although a nonconformist, Doddridge cordially supported Whitefield and Wesley for which he was angrily condemned by his brethren and even by Dr. Watts at first. It was Doddridge's prayer that there would be harmony among Protestant Christians. He wrote:

> O for that happy time when the question shall be, not how much we may lawfully dispute, but on the one side, what may we *waive,* and on the other, what may we *acquiesce in,* from a principle of mutual tenderness and respect, without displeasing our common Lord, and injuring that great cause of original Christianity which He hath appointed us to guard.

The dates of Dr. Doddridge's various hymns cannot be determined. He distributed them widely in manuscript form but did not publish them. His untimely death at age fifty prevented his doing so. Most of them were used to reinforce his sermons and were probably lined out from the pulpit.

After his death, his friend and pupil, Job Orton, published *Hymns Founded on Various Texts in the Holy Scripture, by the Late Reverend Philip Doddridge, D.D., Published from the Author's Manuscript...,* 1755.

Orton, in his Preface, mentioned the difficulty in deciphering some of the manuscripts, hence our uncertainty about Doddridge's exact wording. A later collection, *Scriptural Hymns by the Reverend Philip Doddridge, D.D., New and Corrected Edition...,* 1839, contains additional hymns and textual changes from Orton. This collection was taken from original manuscripts by John Doddridge Humphreys, the author's great-grandson,

In December, 1850, while Doddridge was en route to St. Albans' to officiate at the funeral of a good friend and benefactor, he caught a severe cold. This in time developed into tuberculosis. His health continued to decline during the winter and into the following summer. A sea voyage was prescribed and through the generosity of Lady Huntingdon and others, he embarked for Lisbon.

Among Doddridge's last words to Lady Huntingdon were these: "I can as well go to heaven from Lisbon, as from my own study at Northhampton." Then he said:

> I see indeed no prospect of recovery yet my heart rejoiceth in my God and my Savior, and I can call him, under this failure of everything else, its strength and everlasting portion. God hath indeed been wonderfully good to me, but I am less than the least of his mercies, less than the least hope of his children. Adored be his grace for whatever it hath wrought by me.

Shortly after arriving in Lisbon his condition worsened and he died on October 26, 1851. His grave is in the English cemetery there, near that of the English novelist Henry Fielding.

"O Happy Day" was written in five 4-line stanzas without refrain under the title "Rejoicing in Our Covenant Engagements to God."

The Orton text and the Humphrey text agree except in the fourth stanza:

> Now rest my long divided heart,
>   Fix'd on this blissful centre, rest;
> With ashes who would grudge to part
>   When call'd on Angels' bread to feast?"
>   (Orton)

> "Now rest my long-divided heart,
>   Fix'd on this blissful centre, rest;
> O who with earth would grudge to part
>   When call'd with angels to be bless'd!
>   (Humphrey)

Our hymnal uses another form of stanza 4. Upon the recommendation of the text committee, lines 3 and 4 follow that of *The Methodist Hymnal,* 1935.

James Montgomery said, "Blessed is the man that can take the words of this hymn and make them his own from similar experience."

The hymn has appeared in all Free Methodist hymnals since 1883.

The refrain often used with this hymn was added when the Edward F. Rimbault tune was adapted for use with this text. The refrain seems to have been printed first in *The Wesleyan Sacred Harp,* Boston, 1854, with John Cennick's "Jesus, My All, to Heaven Is Gone."

Our 1976 hymnal drops the refrain and uses ST. PETERSBURG which in the opinion of the Hymnal Commission complements the text more satisfactorily. The tune is attributed to Dimitri Stepanovich Bortniansky (1752-1825), director of the

Russian Imperial Choir at St. Petersburg, now Leningrad. It was published in *Choralbuch,* 1825, edited by Johann Heinrich Tscherlitzky. Since the tune was included in an edition of Bortniansky's sacred works compiled by Tchaikovsky in 1884, it seems to establish his authorship.

291 That God Should Love a Sinner Such as I
C. Bishop (unknown)

Haldor Lillenas recounts that he was given the manuscript by Robert Harkness, evidently about 1929, the year the song was copyrighted by Lillenas. We have no identification of Bishop except as the author of these words. Lillenas edited the text considerably.

The music was composed by Robert Harkness (1880-1961), well-known pianist for the Torrey-Alexander evangelistic campaigns.

292 Once I Was Bound by Sin's Galling Fetters
Haldor Lillenas (1885-1959)

Lillenas presumably wrote this song in about 1917. It was copyrighted May 25, 1917, by Hall-Mack Company and first printed in *New Songs of Pentecost #2.*

GLORIOUS FREEDOM was composed by Alfred Judson. I have been unable to learn anything about the composer.

293 There Is a Balm in Gilead
American Folk Hymn

This traditional folk hymn is based on Jeremiah 8:22 and 46:11.

HFL is the first Free Methodist-Wesleyan hymnal to include it.

294 Take My Life and Let It Be
Frances Ridley Havergal (1836-1879)

This hymn was written on February 4, 1874, in twelve 2-line stanzas by Frances Ridley Havergal, one of the most cultured women of her time and possessing a deeply religious nature. It was published first in the appendix of Snepp's *Songs of Grace and Glory,* 1874, and later in the author's *Loyal Responses,* 1878. She described the origin of the hymn as follows:

> I went for a little visit of five days [to Areley House in December, 1873]. There were ten persons in the house, some unconverted and long prayed for, some converted but not rejoicing Christians. He gave me the prayer: "Lord, give me *all* in this house!" And He just *did!* Before I left the house everyone had got a blessing. The last night of my visit ... I was too happy to sleep, and passed most of the night in praise, and renewal of my own consecration, and these little couplets formed themselves, and chimed in my heart, one after another till they finished with "Ever, only, ALL for Thee!"

In a letter to a friend, written in August, 1878, she revealed the extent of her consecration:

> The Lord has shown me another little step, and of course I have taken it with extreme delight. "Take my silver and my gold" now means shipping off all my ornaments ... to the Church Missionary House.... Nearly fifty articles are being packed up. I don't think ... I ever packed a box with such pleasure.

Miss Havergal retained only a brooch or two for daily wear and an additional item or two for which she had a sentimental attachment.

All Free Methodist hymnals since 1883 have included this hymn.

The music to which Miss Havergal always sang this hymn was PATMOS or CONSECRATION, written by her father, the Reverend William Henry Havergal. NOTTINGHAM, attributed erroneously to Wolfgang Amadeus Mozart (1756-1791), was chosen by the Hymnal Commission to replace the more familiar HENDON in order to bring new interest and vitality to the text. It is taken from the Kyrie of the *Twelfth Mass,* which is now generally believed to be the work of an anonymous eighteenth-century composer. This tune is not to be confused with another tune sometimes called NOTTINGHAM or ST. MAGNUS.

295 My Life, My Love I Give to Thee
Ralph E. Hudson (1843-1901)

The author of this text was well known as a gospel singer and composer. He was also active in the Prohibition movement. The song appeared first in his *Salvation Echoes,* 1882.

This is the first Free Methodist-Wesleyan hymnal to include the song. The refrain is printed here as an optional fourth stanza.

DUNBAR was probably written by Charles R. Dunbar about 1882, the year of the copyright. Nothing has been discovered about the composer.

296 My God and Father, While I Stray
Charlotte Elliott (1789-1871)

This hymn was first published in the appendix to the first edition of Miss Elliott's *Invalid's Hymn-Book,* 1834, in eight 4-line stanzas. She revised it in 1835, 1836, and 1839. Our hymnal uses stanzas 1, 6, 7, and 8 of the 1834 version. The omitted stanzas are:

> 2. Though dark my path, and sad my lot,
>   Let me "be still," and murmur not,
>   Or breathe the prayer divinely taught,
>   "Thy will be done!"
>
> 3. What though in lonely grief I sigh
>   For friends beloved, no longer nigh,
>   Submissive still would I reply,
>   "Thy will be done!"
>
> 4. If thou shouldst call me to resign
>   What most I prize, it ne'er was mine;
>   I only yield thee what is thine;
>   "Thy will be done!"
>
> 5. Should pining sickness waste away,
>   My life in premature decay,
>   My father! still I strive to say,
>   "Thy will be done!"

Miss Elliott seemed to have a preference for meters which have a short last line. In this hymn it is 8.8.8.4. In "Just As I Am" it is 8.8.8.6. In "O Holy Saviour, Friend Unseen" it is also 8.8.8.6. In all she wrote approximately one hundred fifty hymns.

The Free Methodist hymnals of 1883 and 1910 also include this hymn. In 1883 the stanzas used were 1, 2, 4, 5, 6, and 7. In

1910 all were printed except stanza 5. (See also comments at No. 253.)

ALMSGIVING was written by John Bacchus Dykes (1823-1876) for Bishop Christopher Wordsworth's hymn, "O Lord of Heaven and Earth and Sea," and included in the musical edition of *The Holy Year,* 1865.

297 Lord, We Have Come to Thee
Edward Hewlett Gladstone Sargent (b. 1887)

Words and music for this hymn were written in 1913 by Edward Hewlett Gladstone Sargent.

298 Have Thine Own Way, Lord
Adelaide Addison Pollard (1862-1934)

Adelaide Addison Pollard was a native of Iowa. She was a Bible teacher and writer, spending about eight years as a staff member of the Missionary Training School at Nyack-on-the-Hudson. In a prayer meeting she heard an elderly woman pray, "But it's all right, Lord; it doesn't matter what you bring into our lives; *just have your own way with us!*" That night Miss Pollard wrote this hymn. The date cannot be assigned definitely. It has been given as 1902 and also more indefinitely as in the late 1890s.

Originally Miss Pollard's first name was Sarah but disliking this she chose the name Adelaide.

POLLARD was written in 1907 for this text by George Coles Stebbins (1846-1945) and printed in his *Northfield Hymnal with Alexander's Supplement,* 1907.

299 My Jesus, As Thou Wilt
Benjamin Schmolck (1672-1737)
Translated by Jane Laurie Borthwick (1813-1897)

The German hymn "Mein Jesu, wie du willt" was first published in Schmolck's *Heilige Flammen der himmlisch gesinnten Seele,* 1704, in eleven 8-line stanzas. Miss Borthwick's translation, omitting stanzas 2, 6, 7, and 9, was printed in her *Hymns from the Land of Luther,* First Series, 1854.

This hymn, based on Mark 14:36, entered Free Methodist hymnody in 1910 in abridged form using stanzas 1, 4, and 7 of Borthwick's translation.

JEWETT is derived from the passage for horns in the overture to *Der Freischütz* by Carl Maria von Weber written in 1820.

Robert Guy McCutchan relates a little-known fact in *Our Hymnody* — that Weber's favorite motto was "As God wills." Weber is reported to have said as he lay dying in London, "Let me go back to my own home and then 'God's will be done.' " This phraseology and that of the key phrase of the hymn are in curious agreement.

The adaptation of Weber's music as a hymn tune seems to have been made by Joseph Perry Holbrook (1822-1888), music editor of Charles S. Robinson's hymnals. The tune with the Borthwick text appeared in Robinson's *Songs of the Church, or Hymns and Tunes for the Christian Worship, 1862.*

300 All for Jesus, All for Jesus

Mary D. James (1810-1883)

It was impossible to learn anything about the author of this song. It is believed that she was active in the camp meeting movement. The song was written about 1873 and was published in *Redemption Songs,* 1889, edited by John R. Sweney, William J. Kirkpatrick, and John J. Lowe, where it was set to a tune by Kirkpatrick.

An omitted third stanza reads:

> Worldlings prize their gems of beauty,
> Cling to gilded toys of dust,
> Boast of wealth, and fame, and pleasure.
> Only Jesus will I trust.
> Only Jesus! only Jesus!
> Only Jesus will I trust.

The song entered Free Methodist-Wesleyan hymnody in 1910.

DULCE CARMEN also known as ALLELUIA DULCE CARMEN was published anonymously in plainsong notation in *An Essay on the Church Plain Chant,* 1782, set to the text "Tantum ergo."

The Hymnal Commission ordered that this strong tune be substituted for the traditional one in the belief that the text would be strengthened thereby.

301 O to Be Like Thee! Blessed Redeemer
Thomas Obediah Chisholm (1866-1960)

This was Chisholm's first successful hymn. He went on to write texts for most of the prominent gospel music composers of his day. Regarding his style he wrote:

> I have sought to be true to the Word, and to avoid flippant and catchy titles and treatment. I have greatly desired that each hymn or poem might have some definite message to the hearts for whom it was written. . . .

From about 1904 to 1916 Chisholm lived in the vicinity of Winona Lake, Indiana, and for seven of those years he served as a life insurance agent.

This is the first Free Methodist-Wesleyan hymnal to include the song. (See comments at No. 43.)

RONDINELLA was composed for this text by William James Kirkpatrick (1838-1921). One of his music teachers was Pasquale Rondinella, whose last name has been chosen as the title of this tune in some contemporary hymnals.

302 O Jesus, I Have Promised
John Ernest Bode (1816-1874)

This hymn was written in 1866 for the confirmation of Bode's two sons and a daughter. It was published in leaflet form in 1868 by the Society for the Promotion of Christian Knowledge (S.P.C.K.) and then in the 1869 *Appendix* to the S.P.C.K. *Psalms and Hymns for Public Worship* in six 8-line stanzas.

Originally the opening line read "O Jesus, we have promised," but this was changed to the first person singular form in the hymnal version. The hymn was entitled "A Hymn for the Newly Confirmed" and Luke 9:57 was quoted.

The omitted stanzas are the fourth and sixth.

> 4. O let me see Thy features,
>   The look that once could make
> So many a true disciple
>   Leave all things for Thy sake;
> The look that beam'd on Peter
>   When he Thy Name denied;
> The look that draws Thy loved ones
>   Close to Thy pierced side.
> 6. O let me see Thy foot-marks,
>   And in them plant mine own;

>   My hope to follow duly
>   Is in Thy strength alone:
>   O guide me, call me, draw me,
>   Uphold me to the end;
>   And then in heaven receive me,
>   My Savior and my Friend.

Our 1951 hymnal was the first Free Methodist-Wesleyan hymnal to include it.

ANGEL'S STORY, also called WATERMOUTH, was composed by Arthur Henry Mann (1850-1929) and contributed by him to the *Methodist Sunday-School Tune Book,* 1881. It was written for Emily H. Miller's hymn, "I Love to Hear the Story Which Angel Voices Tell," hence the title of the tune.

303 Jesus Calls Us O'er the Tumult
Cecil Frances Alexander (1818-1895)

This hymn was contributed by the author to the S.P.C.K. *Hymns for Public Worship,* 1852, in five 4-line stanzas and entitled "St. Andrew's Day." It is based on Matthew 4:18-20.

A number of changes in the text have come to be accepted over the years. Mrs. Alexander herself revised it drastically in 1881.

Our only alteration from the 1852 text is:

3:4 *That we* love *Him* more than these.

The omitted stanza is the second:

>   As, of old, Saint Andrew heard it
>   By the Galilean lake,
>   Turned from home and toil and kindred,
>   Leaving all for His dear sake.

John Brownlie's estimate of Mrs. Alexander's work is probably shared by most hymnologists when he wrote that her "best hymns are for children, in which department she excelled."

This hymn entered Free Methodist-Wesleyan hymnody in 1951. (See also comments at No. 139 and No. 215.)

GALILEE is one of two tunes assigned this name. This one was composed in 1874 for this text by William Herbert Jude (1851-1922) and first printed in *The Congregational Church Hymnal,* 1887 (London).

304 O Thou Who Camest from Above

Charles Wesley (1707-1788)
Altered by Edward Henry Bickersteth (1825-1906)

This hymn, based on Leviticus 6:13, was printed in Charles Wesley's *Short Hymns on Select Passages of the Holy Scriptures,* 1762, in two 8-line stanzas. The two stanzas are often expanded to four in order to fit 4-line tunes.

The second stanza read originally:

> There let it for Thy glory burn
> With inextinguishable blaze.

The long word "inextinguishable" has presented difficulties for hymnal editors. Some books simply delete this stanza. Bishop Bickersteth changed line 2 to "unquenched, undimmed in darkest days," a change we have accepted in our 1976 hymnal. He believed "that this admirable hymn would have been far more popular had it not been for the very long word "inextinguishable." He continued, "Words of *five* syllables must be admitted into hymns sparingly; but for a whole congregation to be poised on *six,* practically leads to a hymn being passed by."

Robert Bridges in his *Yattendon Hymnal,* 1899, objected to the long word on other grounds. He believed that:

> the accents of a melody have too much meaning to allow of such a distribution over one word, the parts of which are not in English of sufficient importance so that the expression of the musical phrase is ridiculously superabundant.

The writers of the Methodist *Companion to the Hymnal* took an opposing view. They wrote "There is something grandly extravagant about the polysyllable here which makes its point by its very awkwardness."

The Free Methodist hymnal, 1883, used Charles Wesley's second stanza as he wrote it except for line 4 where "love" was substituted for "prayer," an editorial change made by John Wesley in the "Large Hymnbook" of 1780. The 1910 Free Methodist-Wesleyan hymnal followed John Wesley's lead. The 1951 hymnal omitted the entire hymn.

MORNING HYMN. (See comments at No. 205.)

305 Make Me a Captive, Lord

George Matheson (1842-1906)

This hymn by the blind Scottish minister and poet, George

Matheson, was published in four 8-line stanzas in his *Sacred Songs,* 1890, under the title "Christian Freedom." According to Dr. Matheson it was written in 1890 at Row, Dumbartonshire, Scotland. The biblical text printed with the hymn was Ephesians 3:1.

Note the effective use of paradox in this hymn.

This hymn entered Free Methodist-Wesleyan hymnody in 1951.

LEOMINSTER (See comments at No. 267.)

306 Lord, Possess Me Now, I Pray
Oswald Jeffray Smith (b. 1889)

Dr. Smith sent the text of this song to B. D. Ackley in 1940. Ackley wrote the music for it immediately. Shortly afterward he wrote to Dr. Smith: "I believe you and I have collaborated on something in this song that will carry along many years after we have both passed over to the other side."

A few years later, on March 16, 1944, Ackley wrote again that this song "is worth all the effort you and I have put on the many hundreds we have written."

(See comments at No. 289.)

WITH THY SPIRIT FILL ME was composed by Bentley DeForest Ackley (1872-1958). Ackley was a longtime composer and editor for The Rodeheaver Company, residing in Winona Lake until his death. In 1952 Bob Jones University conferred on him the doctor of sacred music degree on the occasion of their twenty-fifth anniversary commencement.

307 Just as I Am, Thine Own to Be
Marianne Hearne (1834-1909)

The author of this text, a member of the Baptist denomination in England, wrote under the nom de plume Marianne Farningham, after her birthplace Farningham, in Kent. Of her several hymns this one was probably inspired by Charlotte Elliott's earlier hymn. Miss Hearne's hymn was printed in *The Voice of Praise,* 1887, in six 4-line stanzas.

The omitted stanza 5 reads:

> With many dreams of fame and gold,
> Success and joy to make me bold,

>But dearer still my faith to hold,
>For my whole life, I come.

This is the first Free Methodist-Wesleyan hymnal to include it.

JUST AS I AM was composed originally by Joseph Barnby (1838-1896) for Charlotte Elliott's hymn. It was printed in *Home and School Hymnal,* 1892.

308 I Gave My Life for Thee
Frances Ridley Havergal (1836-1879)

It is said that the inspiration for this hymn was Sternberg's painting *Ecce Homo* with its inscription:

>This I have done for thee;
>What hast thou done for me?

This was the same painting, hanging in the art gallery of Dusseldorf, that earlier had impressed the young Count Zinzendorf. It was on January 10, 1858, that Miss Havergal read the motto and wrote the words of this hymn on a scrap of paper. Reading them over she thought them so poor that she later threw the paper in the fire but it fell out unburned and she retrieved it.

Some months later she showed the text to her father, who wrote the tune *Baca* for it. The hymn was printed in leaflet form in 1859 and in *The Ministry of Song,* 1869.

This hymn was printed in the 1883 Free Methodist hymnal in the section entitled "Social Worship." Our present stanza 2 was omitted there and this stanza was given in its place:

>I spent long years for thee
>>In weariness and woe,
>
>That an eternity
>>Of joy thou mightest know.
>
>I spent long years for thee.
>Hast thou spent one for me?

This same form was followed in 1910. The 1976 hymnal follows the form used in 1951.

BLISS, also known as KENOSIS, was composed for this text by Philip Paul Bliss (1838-1876) and published in his *Sunshine for Sunday Schools,* 1873.

309 Jesus, I My Cross Have Taken
Henry Francis Lyte (1793-1847)

This hymn appeared anonymously in Lyte's *Sacred Poetry*, third edition, 1824, in six 8-line stanzas, where it was headed "Lo, We Have Left All, and Followed Thee." (See Mark 10:28.) In Lyte's *Poems Chiefly Religious*, 1833, it was printed in slightly different form. Ernest Ryden calls this "a noble lyric" and describes Lyte's hymns as "scriptural in language, rich in imagery, and exalted in poetic conception."

All six stanzas were included in the 1883 and 1910 hymnals. In 1951 and 1976 the hymn was reduced to four stanzas.

The omitted stanzas, 3 and 5, read:

> 3. Go, then, early fame and treasure!
>   Come, disaster, scorn, and pain!
> In thy service, pain is pleasure;
>   With Thy favor, loss is gain.
> I have called thee, "Abba Father,"
>   I have set my heart on Thee:
> Storms may howl, and clouds may gather,
>   All must work for good to me.

> 5. Know, my soul, thy full salvation;
>   Rise o'er sin, and fear, and care;
> Joy to find in every station
>   Something still to do or bear,
> Think what spirit dwells within Thee;
>   What a Father's smile is Thine;
> What a Savior died to win Thee:
>   Child of heaven, shouldst thou repine?

ELLESDIE is the work of an anonymous composer. Although sometimes attributed to Mozart it has never been traced to a Mozart source. The title seems to be derived from the initials L.S.D., according to McCutchan, giving a possible clue to the composer. The tune, also called *Disciple*, was printed in *The Christian Lyre*, 1830. Hubert Platt Main (1839-1925) arranged it and included it in *Winnowed Hymns*, 1873.

310 All to Jesus I Surrender
Judson W. Van DeVenter (1855-1939)

This hymn is something of a personal testimony of the author. It was written while he was conducting a meeting in East Palestine, Ohio, and while he was in the home of George Sebring, founder of the Sebring Camp Meeting in Ohio and the city of Sebring, Florida.

Evidently the first publication was in *Gospel Songs of Grace and Glory,* 1896, issued by Hall-Mack Co.

SURRENDER was composed in 1896 for this text by Winfield Scott Weeden (1847-1908). Weeden was often in demand as a song leader and soloist in conventions. He also engaged in evangelistic work in association with Van DeVenter. During the latter part of his life he owned a small hotel in lower Manhattan. Inscribed on his tombstone is the title of the hymn, "I Surrender All," for which he had provided the music.

The arrangement by Charles H. Finney (b. 1911) was made for inclusion in *Hymns of the Living Faith,* 1951, the first Free Methodist-Wesleyan hymnal to include this hymn.

311 I Am Thine, O Lord
Fanny Jane Crosby (1823-1915)

Under the title "Holiness Desired" this hymn was published in *Brightest and Best,* 1875, compiled by William H. Doane and Robert Lowry. The author wrote the hymn in Cincinnati, Ohio, while visiting in the home of William H. Doane. It is based on Hebrews 10:22.

DRAW ME NEARER was composed for this text by Dr. William Howard Doane (1832-1915).

312 Jesus, Thy Boundless Love to Me
Paul Gerhardt (1607-1676)
Translated by John Wesley (1703-1791)

"O Jesu Christ, mein schönstes Licht" was written by Paul Gerhardt and published in Johann Crüger's *Praxis pietatis melica,* fifth edition, Berlin, 1653, in sixteen 9-line stanzas. His inspiration was a prayer in a volume of devotions published in 1612 by Joseph Arndt under the title *Paradiesgärtlein.* The subjective note is prominent in Gerhardt's hymns. Sixteen of them are said to begin with the pronoun "I," yet they are not objectionably sentimental.

There have been a number of fine translations into English. One of the best is that of John Wesley in sixteen 6-line stanzas and published in his *Hymns and Sacred Poems,* 1739, but written a year or more earlier.

In John Wesley's, *A Plain Account of Christian Perfection,* he says that in Savannah in 1736 he wrote:

> Is there a thing beneath the sun
>   That strives with thee my heart to share?
> Ah, tear it thence, and reign alone,
>   The Lord of every motion there!

Then he writes that in the beginning of 1738, returning from Georgia, the cry of his heart was:

> O, grant that nothing in my soul
> May swell but Thy pure love alone!
> O, may Thy love possess me whole,
> My joy, my treasure, and my crown!
> Strange fires far from my heart remove:
> My every act, word, thought, be love!

He continues, "I never heard that anyone objected to this, and indeed who can object? Is not this the language, not only of every believer, but of every one that is truly awakened? But what have I wrote, to this day, which is either stronger or plainer?"

John Wesley uses the metaphor of "fire" four times in his translation. In stanza 1 he speaks of "my constant flame." In stanza 2 the phrase "strange fires" (altered in most Methodist hymnals as early as 1821 to read "strange flames") possibly alludes to Leviticus 10:2. In stanza 4 (not included in our hymnal) Wesley writes, "Hourly within my breast renew / This holy flame, this heavenly fire;" and in stanza 11 he writes further: "Be thou my flame; within me burn."

Both John and Charles Wesley were impressive scholars and they did not use terms carelessly. They were able to draw upon imagery and expressions from the Bible and from contemporary literature. For example, in Matthew Prior's *Henry and Emma* there are these lines:

> If love, alas! be pain, the pain I bear
> No thought can figure and no tongue declare.

It is easy to recognize the same idea, much improved, in Wesley's opening lines. It is obvious that his translation of Gerhardt's hymn is not literal at all points.

Some hymnal editors have taken great liberties with this hymn. For instance, *The Baptist Hymn Book,* 1871, reduces Wesley's sixteen 6-line stanzas to four 4-line stanzas. One of the four has no relationship to the Wesley hymn and of the remaining twelve lines, eight are substantially altered.

ST. PETERSBURG (See comments at No. 290.)

313 Spirit of the Living God
Daniel Iverson (b. 1890)

The author of this song was a Presbyterian minister in North Carolina at the time of its composition in 1926. It was composed in Orlando, Florida, and first used in a citywide revival there, conducted by the George T. Stephans Evangelistic Party. At last report, Iverson was retired and living in Asheville, North Carolina.

314 O for a Closer Walk with God
William Cowper (1731-1769)

This hymn, written on December 9, 1769, was published first in Richard Conyer's *Collection of Psalms and Hymns, from Various Authors,* second edition, 1772, in six 4-line stanzas. Later it was published in Toplady's *Psalms and Hymns,* 1776, in eight stanzas. In *Olney Hymns,* Book I, 1779, it is entitled "Walking with God." There are six stanzas.

The hymn was written during the serious illness of Cowper's friend Mrs. Mary Unwin. In a letter Cowper said that he began to compose the lines "before daybreak, but fell asleep at the end of the first two lines; when I awakened again, the third and fourth were whispered to my heart in a way which I have often experienced...." Then followed the six stanzas of the hymn.

In Toplady's hymnbook, two additional stanzas are printed. Their origin is in doubt.

> Jesus, my Lord, my life, my light,
>   O come with blissful ray:
> Break radiant through the shades of night,
>   And chase my clouds away.
>
> Then shall my soul with rapture trace
>   The token of thy love:
> But the full glorys of thy face
>   Are only known above.

Toplady's version introduces a number of textual alterations in the other stanzas also.

All Free Methodist hymnals since 1883 have included this hymn.

BEATITUDO was composed by John Bacchus Dykes (1823-1876) for the revised edition of *Hymns Ancient and Modern,* 1875. There it was associated with the hymn "How Bright Those Glorious Spirits Shine."

315 Come, Holy Spirit, God and Lord!

Martin Luther (1483-1546)
Translated by Catherine Winkworth (1827-1878)

The pre-Reformation German hymn, "Komm heiliger Geist, Herre Gott," based on an early Latin antiphon, "Veni Sancte Spiritus, *reple tuorum corda fidelium,*" was modified by Martin Luther and with the addition of two original stanzas was published in *Ein Enchiridion oder Handbuchlein,* 1524, in three 8-line stanzas.

A number of translations were made from the German into English, including one by Miles Coverdale ("Come Holy Spirite, most blessed Lorde") and included in his *Goostly Psalmes and Spiritualle Songes* (c. 1539). Our translation is by Catherine Winkworth and published in her *Lyra Germanica,* First Series, 1855, in three 8-line stanzas.

Our hymnal uses 1*a,* 2*a,* 2*b,* and 3*b.*
The omitted portions read as follows:

> 1*b.* Thy light this day shone forth so clear,
> All tongues and nations gather'd near,
> To learn that faith, for which we bring
> Glad praise to Thee, and loudly sing,
>   Hallelujah, Hallelujah!

> 3*a.* Thou sacred Ardour, Comfort Sweet,
> Help us to wait with ready feet
> And willing heart at Thy command,
> Nor trial fright us from Thy band.

This is the first Free Methodist-Wesleyan hymnal to include this hymn.

WAREHAM (See comments at No. 14.)

316 I Hear My Blessed Saviour Say

George D. Watson (dates unknown)
Stanza 4 altered by Evan K. Gibson (b. 1909)

This text is found in *Songs of Joy and Gladness,* 1885, (No. 29), compiled by W. McDonald, Joshua Gill, John R. Sweney, and W. J. Kirkpatrick, in five 8-line stanzas. There it is attributed to the Rev. G. D. Watson, D.D. Alterations in the text have been numerous. The changes are these:

> 1:1 I hear my *dying* Savior say,
> 1:2, 3:8 Follow me, *come,* follow me;
> 1:4 ... *tread* ...

1:5 ... *give* ...
1:6 ... *drink* ...

The omitted stanza 2 reads:

> I know thy life of guilt and pain,
> Follow me, come, follow me;
> I know each ache of heart and brain,
> Follow me, ...
> For Thee I left my heavn'ly train,
> For thee I've open'd ev'ry vein,
> And now I plead yet once again,
> Follow me, ...

Changes included:

> 3:6 Thy God, *and* guide ...
> 4:2, 4 *I'll follow thee, yes, follow thee;*
> 4:8 *I'll follow thee, yes, follow thee.*

TUCKER. I have been unable to locate the source of this tune. It appears in *The Salvation Army Tune Book* set to "Thou Christ of Burning, Cleansing Flame," a hymn written by William Booth (1829-1912), founder of the Salvation Army.

317 Come, O Thou Traveler Unknown
Charles Wesley (1707-1788)

This hymn is regarded as one of the greatest of the Wesley hymns although, strictly speaking, it is not a hymn at all. H. A. L. Jefferson *(Hymns in Christian Worship,* 1950) describes it as "a passionate devotional poem ... intimate and mystical, and ... intensely personal...." Because of this and because of its length, it has been ruled out of many hymnbooks. Even though some of the language would be unfamiliar to many in the congregation, Erik Routley would accept this as a hymn because it is scriptural — "since we may require of our congregations education in the scriptures but not in any other field" *(Hymns and Human Life).*

This text was first published in *Hymns and Sacred Poems,* 1742, in fourteen 6-line stanzas under the title of "Wrestling Jacob." It is based on the incident in Jacob's life recorded in Genesis 32:24-31. Stanzas used in our hymnal are 1, 3, 8, and 9.

Some of the omitted stanzas are:

> 2. I need not tell Thee who I am,
>   My misery and sin declare;
> Thyself hast called me by my name;
>   Look on Thy hands, and read it there.

> But who, I ask Thee, who art Thou?
> Tell me Thy name, and tell me now.

> 6. What tho' my shrinking flesh complain,
>   And murmur to contend so long?
>   I rise superior to my pain:
>   When I am weak, then am I strong,
>   And when my all of strength shall fail,
>   I shall with the God-man prevail.

(Note the paradox in line 4, which is taken from I Corinthians 12:10*b*.)

> 7. My strength is gone, my nature dies;
>   I sink beneath Thy weighty hand;
>   Faint to revive, and fall to rise:
>   I fall, and yet by faith I stand,
>   I stand, and will not let Thee go,
>   Till I Thy name, Thy nature know.

> 10. My prayer hath power with God; the grace
>   Unspeakable, I now receive;
>   Through faith I see Thee face to face;
>   I see Thee face to face and live,
>   In vain I have not wept and strove;
>   Thy nature and Thy name is Love.

> 14. Lame as I am, I take the prey;
>   Hell, earth, and sin, with ease o'ercome;
>   I leap for joy, pursue my way,
>   And as a bounding hart fly home,
>   Through all eternity to prove,
>   Thy nature and Thy name is Love.

Our text is printed without alteration except 4:5 which read originally "... thy *bowels* move."

Charles Wesley preached on this episode in Jacob's life on at least eight occasions; in Bristol, May 24, 1741; in Cardiff, July 16, 1741; at the Foundery in London, October 6, 1743, and so forth. When John Wesley was told of his brother's death he was in a service at Bolton. As he tried to give out the lines,

> My company before is gone,
> And I am left alone with Thee,

it is reported that he burst into tears, sat down in the pulpit and buried his face in his hands.

Dean Stanley quoted this same verse at the unveiling of the Wesley memorial plaque in Westminster Abbey in 1876.

In the *Minutes of the Methodist Conference,* 1788, John Wesley gave a brief obituary of his brother and said,

> His least praise was his talent for poetry, although Dr. Watts did not scruple to say that that single poem,

Wrestling Jacob, was worth all the verses he himself had written.

James Montgomery, in the preface to *The Christian Psalmist,* 1825, wrote:

> Among Charles Wesley's highest achievements may be recorded, "Come, O Thou Traveler Unknown," ... in which, with consummate art, he has carried on the action of a lyrical drama; every turn in the conflict with the mysterious being against whom he wrestles all night, being marked with precision by the varying language of the speaker, accompanied by intense increasing interest, till the rapturous moment of discovery, when he prevails, and exclaims, "I know Thee, Savior, Who Thou art."

This is high praise indeed and it should cause us to look upon this hymn with renewed interest. The selection of stanzas printed in our hymnal is excellent, but, of necessity, omits some of the narrative. It would be well to introduce the hymn with appropriate comments and quotations from the Genesis account.

The *Free Methodist Hymn-Book,* 1883, attempted to solve the problem of length by making three hymns out of the fourteen stanzas: 1-4, 6; 8-11, 12-14. The hymnal of 1910 followed the same pattern. In 1951 one 6-stanza hymn was printed using stanzas 1, 2, 3, 8, 9, and 14.

WRESTLING JACOB. The origin of this tune is unknown. It appears anonymously in The Free Methodist-Wesleyan hymnal, 1910, set to this text.

318   Search Me, O God

J. Edwin Orr (b. 1912)

According to Orr, a well-known evangelist, this song was composed in 1936 in New Zealand. He wrote the text to fit a Maori tune he had heard. The hymn was published first by Marshall, Morgan and Scott, *All Your Need,* 1936.

The tune MAORI became popular in the United States set to a text beginning "Now is the hour."

319   Jesus, Thy All-Victorious Love

Charles Wesley (1707-1788)

This is a cento from the hymn "My God, I Know, I Feel Thee Mine," published in the Wesleys' *Hymns and Sacred Poems* Part

II, 1740, in twelve 4-line stanzas under the title "Against Hope, Believing in Hope." Stanzas used in *Hymns of Faith and Life* are 4, 7, 8, 9, 11, and 12. Wesley's original text has been restored.

"No verse of the Wesleys," wrote J. Ernest Rattenbury, referring to our fourth stanza, "has been sung with deeper fervour or with richer and more abiding results than their passionate prayer to God the Holy Ghost" *(The Evangelical Doctrines of Charles Wesley's Hymns,* p. 187).

Two omitted stanzas are of special interest:

> 1. My God! I know, I feel Thee mine,
>   And will not quit my claim,
> Till all I have be lost in Thine,
>   And all renew'd I am.

> 5. Love only can the conquest win,
>   The strength of sin subdue,
> (Mine own unconquerable sin,
>   And form my soul anew.

MARTYRDOM or AVON was composed by Hugh Wilson (1764-1824) and appeared first in Robert Archibald Smith's *Sacred Music Sung in St. George's Church, Edinburgh,* 1825. There it was in triple time and called an "Old Scotch Melody," but Wilson's authorship was established after his death by a lawsuit over the copyright. The tune was written some years earlier since it had been distributed in leaflet form during the late eighteenth century. Originally it was in quadruple time. We assume that the change from quadruple to triple time was made by Smith whose dates are 1780-1829. Except for the soprano note C, the melody is pentatonic.

320 Come, Holy Ghost, All-Quickened Fire!

Charles Wesley (1707-1788)

This hymn in eight 6-line stanzas was printed in *Hymns and Sacred Poems,* 1740, under the title "Hymn to God the Sanctifier." Stanzas included in *Hymns of Faith and Life* are 1, 4, 5, and 7.

Note the omitted stanza 8:

> Come, Holy Ghost, all-quickening fire,
> My consecrated heart inspire.
>   Sprinkled with the atoning blood:
> Still to my soul Thyself reveal;
> Thy mighty working may I feel,
>   And know that I am one with God!

Among the papers of the late Commissioner Brengle of the Salvation Army was found this note: "Years ago the cadets at Clapton were singing —

My will be swallowed up in Thee...
Called the full strength of trust to prove...

and there my heart cried out, 'Yes, Lord, let me prove the full strength of trust!'"

The 1883 Free Methodist hymnal used a different cento beginning with stanza 4, and including 5, 7, and 8, a practice followed in the hymnals of 1910 and 1951.

HOLY FAITH was composed by Sir George Clement Martin (1844-1916) for Faber's hymn "Faith of Our Fathers." It appeared in *Additional Hymns,* 1894. Martin became chief organist at St. Paul's Cathedral in London upon the resignation of Sir John Stainer in 1888. He is buried in the crypt of the cathedral.

321 Called unto Holiness, Church of Our God
Lelia Naylor Morris (1862-1929)

Words and music of this song were written by Mrs. C. H. Morris and copyrighted in 1900 by H. L. Gilmour. The omitted fourth stanza reads:

"Called unto holiness," glorious thought!
Up from the wilderness wanderings brought,
Out from the shadows and darkness of night,
Into the Canaan of perfect delight.
Refrain

(See also comments at No. 275.)
This is the first appearance in a Free Methodist-Wesleyan hymnal.

322 Thou Hidden Love of God
Gerhard Tersteegen (1697-1769)
Translated by John Wesley (1703-1791)

The original German hymn "Verborgne Gottesliebe du" appeared first in Tersteegen's *Geistliches Blumengärtlein innigen Seelen,* 1729, in ten 7-line stanzas. It was entitled "The Longing of the Soul Quietly to Maintain the Secret Drawings of the Love of God." In abbreviated form it was printed in the *Herrnhut Gesangbuch,* 1735.

John Wesley's excellent translation, omitting stanzas 4 and 5, was made in 1736 while he was in Savannah. He revised the text once or twice and made a final revision for the "Large Hymnbook," 1780. As printed in *Psalms and Hymns,* 1738, a portion of our second stanza read:

> Ah, tear it thence, that thou alone
> May'st reign unrivall'd Monarch there;
> From earthly loves I must be free
> Ere I can find repose in Thee.

1:5, 6 seems to have no parallel passage in the original German. Wesley must have drawn on his knowledge of Augustine's *Confessions* (I, i) where we find this:

> Thou movest us to delight in praising Thee; for Thou hast formed us for Thyself, and our hearts are restless till they find rest in Thee.

A modern echo of this same passage may be found in the writings of Howard Thurman *(Deep River,* 1955): "[The river] is restless till it finds its rest in the sea."

Both Oliver Wendell Holmes and Emerson regarded "Thou Hidden Love of God" as the one "supreme hymn."

Our 1951 and 1976 hymnals print stanzas 1, 4, 5, and 8. In 1883 and 1910 stanza 6 was included also. It read:

> O love! thy sovereign aid impart,
>   To save me from low-thoughted care:
> Chase this Self-will through all my Heart,
>   Through all its latent Mazes there.
> Make me thy duteous child, that I
> Ceaseless may Abba Father cry.

The other omitted stanzas, as included in the "Large Hymnbook," 1780, read as follows:

> 2. Thy secret voice invites me still
>   The sweetness of thy yoke to prove;
>   And fain I would: but though my will
>   Seem fixt, yet wide my passions rove:
>   Yet hindrances strew all the way;
>   I aim at thee, yet from thee stray.

> 3. 'Tis mercy all, that thou hast brought
>   My mind to seek her peace in thee!
>   Yet while I seek, but find thee not,
>   No peace my wand'ring soul shall see:
>   O when shall all my wanderings end,
>   And all my steps to thee-ward tend?

7. Ah, no! Ne'er will I backward turn:
   Thine wholly, thine alone I am!
   Thrice-happy he, who views with scorn
   Earth's toys for thee his constant flame!
   Oh! help, that I may never move
   From the blest footsteps of thy love!

ST. CHRYSOSTOM was composed by Sir Joseph Barnby (1838-1896) and printed in the *Musical Times* (December, 1871). In 1872 it appeared in Novello's *Hymnary,* of which Barnby was the editor. It was written for the Henry Collins hymn, "Jesus, my Lord, my God, my all."

323 I Thirst, Thou Wounded Lamb of God
Stanzas 1 and 2 by Nicolaus Ludwig von Zinzendorf (1700-1760)
Stanzas 3-5 by Johann Nitschmann (1712-1783)
Translated by John Wesley (1703-1791)

This hymn is a composite translation from two German hymns: "Ach! mein verwund'ter Fürste!" by Zinzendorf and "Du blutiger Versühner!" by Nitschmann, both found in the *Herrnhut Gesangbuch,* 1735. Wesley's translation, in eight 4-line stanzas, appeared first in *Hymns and Sacred Poems,* Part I, 1740. Our hymnal uses stanzas 1-4 and 6.

All Free Methodist hymnals since 1883 have included this hymn. A stanza (5) included in 1883 and 1910 reads:

How can it be, Thou heavenly King,
That thou shouldst us to glory bring?
Make slaves the partners of Thy throne,
Decked with a never-fading crown?

ROCKINGHAM OLD may be traced to a tune named TUNBRIDGE (10.11.10.11.) in Aaron Williams's *Supplement to Psalmody in Miniature* (c. 1780). Dr. Edward Miller (1735-1807) arranged it as a long-meter tune and harmonized it in its present form and included it in his *Psalms of David,* 1790. He assigned the name ROCKINGHAM to it. It is now generally called ROCKINGHAM OLD to distinguish it from Lowell Mason's later tune by the same name. It honors the name of the Marquis of Rockingham, friend and patron of Miller and twice prime minister of England. The tune has had a long association with Watts's "When I Survey the Wondrous Cross," particularly in England.

324 What Is Our Calling's Glorious Hope?
Charles Wesley (1707-1788)

This is a cento composed of stanzas 9-14 from a fourteen-stanza hymn beginning "Jesu, Redeemer of Mankind" in the Wesley's *Hymns and Sacred Poems*, 1742. It is based on Titus 2:14.

The original first stanza reads:

> Jesu, Redeemer of Mankind,
>   How little art Thou known
> By sinners of a carnal mind,
>   Who claim thee for their own.

Only minor textual changes are made in our hymnal:

> 2:3 ... a faith that *roots* out sin
> 2:4 ... purifies *my heart*
> 5:4 *To cleanse* and *fill* thy heart

All Free Methodist hymnals since 1883 have included this hymn.

WINCHESTER OLD appears to be based on the second half of Christopher Tye's (c. 1500-c. 1572) melody for Chapter VIII of his *Actes of the Apostles*, 1553. Tye chose George Kirbye (c. 1560-1634) whom he knew to be "experte in the Arte," to arrange some of his tunes, including this one. WINCHESTER OLD appeared in Thomas Este's (c. 1540-1608) *Whole Book of Psalmes with Their Wonted Tunes*, 1592, set to Psalm 84. It was unnamed in Este's book. The name comes from the historic cathedral town of Winchester in Hampshire, England. The present form of the tune is found in *Hymns Ancient and Modern*, 1861, where it is set to "While shepherds watched their flocks by night."

325 Cleanse Me from My Sin, Lord
Richard Hudson Pope (1879-1967)

326 Blest Are the Pure in Heart
John Keble (1792-1866)

This hymn in seventeen 4-line stanzas is dated 1819 and was published first in John Keble's *Christian Year*, 1827. It is entitled "The Purification."

In his *Mitre Hymn Book*, 1836, William John Hall (1793-1861), published a cento composed of two stanzas from *The Christian Year* (1 and 17) and two that were new. There is some evidence that the alterations had the approval of Keble. Hall was Prebendary of St. Paul's Cathedral beginning in 1826 and later became Vicar of Tottenham.

The stanza omitted in Hall's version reads:

> The Lord, who left the sky,
>   Our life and peace to bring,
> And dwelt in lowliness with men,
>   Their pattern, and their King.

In our hymnal there are slight alterations:

1:1 *Bless'd* are the ...
2:3 And for His *cradle* ...
3:2 *May ours* this blessing be:
3:3 *O give the* pure and lowly heart,

The Free Methodist Hymnal of 1883 printed two stanzas only (our 1 and 2). Omitted in 1910, the hymn was restored in 1951, using the three-stanza cento similar to 1976. Keble's poem is a paean of praise to the new-born King. Note these selected stanzas:

> 3. Such the triumphed hymns
>   On Sion's Prince that wait
>   In high procession passing on
>   Towards His Temple gate.
>
> 4. Give ear, ye kings — bow down
>   Ye rulers of the earth —
>   This, this is He; your Priest by grace,
>   Your God and King by birth.
>
> 5. No pomp of earthly guards
>   Attends with sword and spear,
>   And all-defying, dauntless look,
>   Their Monarch's way to clear:
>
> 6. Yet are there more with Him
>   Than all that are with you —
>   The armies of the highest heaven,
>   All righteous, good, and true.

GREENWOOD was composed by Joseph Emerson Sweetser (1825-1873).

327 O for a Heart to Praise My God
                              Charles Wesley (1707-1788)

This hymn in eight 4-line stanzas was printed in the Wesley's *Hymns and Sacred Poems,* Part I, 1742, and is based on the

Prayer Book version of Psalm 51:10. Our hymnal uses stanzas 1-4 and 8, with Wesley's original text restored.

John Wesley wrote in his journal: "I find scarcely any temptation from anything in the world: My danger is from persons." Then he quotes:

> O for a heart to praise my God,
> A heart from sin set free!

Of this hymn John Fletcher said, "Here is undoubtedly an evangelical prayer for the love which restores the soul to a state of sinless rest and scriptural perfection."

BEATITUDO was composed for the 1875 edition of *Hymns Ancient and Modern,* by John Bacchus Dykes (1823-1876). It has always seemed curious that a child would be given the name of Bacchus, a name associated with drunkenness and revelry. The explanation is simple. It was an old family name.

328 The Thing My God Doth Hate
Charles Wesley (1707-1788)

This hymn is made from the union of two Charles Wesley hymns from the volume *Short Hymns on Selected Passages of Holy Scripture,* 1762. Our stanza 1 is the hymn in two 4-line stanzas based on Jeremiah 44:4 and our stanzas 2 and 3 are the hymn in two 8-line stanzas based on Jeremiah 31:33.

This hymn has been in all Free Methodist hymnals since 1883.

DINBYCH was composed by Dr. Joseph Parry (1841-1903) and is from the enlarged (1870) edition of *Llyfr Tonau Cynulleidfaol,* published originally in 1859. (See also comments at No. 277.)

329 Lord, Jesus, I Long to Be Perfectly Whole
James L. Nicholson (1828-1876)

This song, said originally to have begun "Dear Jesus, I long," was written by an American Methodist minister. It was published in *Joyful Songs No. 4,* 1872, a pamphlet containing twelve songs. There have been a number of alterations in the text. Our version is taken from Sankey's *Sacred Songs and Solos,* 1878. The omitted second stanza reads:

> Lord Jesus, let nothing unholy remain,

Apply Thine own blood and extract every stain;
To get this blest cleansing I all things forego —
Now wash me, and I shall be whiter than snow.
                              Refrain

Our 1951 hymnal was the first Free Methodist-Wesleyan hymnal to include this song although it had appeared in other gospel song collections published by the denominations.

WHITER THAN SNOW was composed for this text by William Gustavus Fischer (1835-1912) and copyrighted by him in either 1871 or 1872. Both dates are given in various collections.

330 O for a Heart that Is Whiter than Snow
                    Eliza Edmunds Hewitt (1851-1920)

This song, one of an estimated two thousand by Miss Hewitt, was presumably written about 1892. (See also comments at Nos. 245 and 427.)

WHITER THAN SNOW (Kirkpatrick) was composed for this text by William James Kirkpatrick (1838-1921) about 1892, the year he copyrighted it.

331 Take Time to Be Holy
                    William Dunn Longstaff (1822-1894)

This song was written about 1882 by Longstaff, according to Ira D. Sankey, after hearing missionary Dr. Griffith John preach from the text "Be ye holy; for I am holy." Subsequently he brought the song to the attention of the Moody-Sankey evangelistic party. He numbered Dwight L. Moody, Ira Sankey, and William Booth as personal friends, all of whom were guests in his home from time to time. Longstaff was treasurer of Bethesda Chapel in Sunderland, England.

Free Methodist-Wesleyan hymnals since 1910 have included this song.

HOLINESS was composed in 1890 for this text by George Coles Stebbins (1846-1945) while he was involved in a series of meetings and conferences in India. He sent the tune to Ira D. Sankey in New York who copyrighted it and included it in his *Winnowed Songs for Sunday School*, 1890.

332 Breathe, O Mighty One from Heaven
George Hall

The opening line originally, "Breathe, O mighty Breath from heaven," was changed in our hymnal with the permission of the owner. The song was first published in 1930, presumably by Herbert G. Tovey, the copyright owner. The music was revised in 1963, perhaps by the composer Gordon E. Hooker.

This is the first appearance of this song in a Free Methodist-Wesleyan hymnal.

333 O Spread the Tidings 'Round
Frank Bottome (1823-1894)

The author of this song was born in Derbyshire, England. He came to the United States in 1850 and entered the ministry of the Methodist Episcopal Church. In 1872 he received the doctor of sacred theology degree from Dickinson College in Carlisle, Pennsylvania.

Dr. Bottome seems to have been an earnest exponent of "The Spirit-filled life." Earlier hymns were entitled: "Come, Holy Ghost, All Sacred Fire," 1872; "Full Salvation, Full Salvation," 1871; and "O Bliss of the Purified, Bliss of the Free," 1869.

An omitted fifth stanza of our hymn reads:

> Sing, till the echoes fly above the vaulted sky,
> And all the saints above to all below reply,
> In strains of endless love, the song that ne'er will die:
> The Comforter has come!
>
> Refrain

All Free Methodist-Wesleyan hymnals since 1910 have included this song.

COMFORTER was composed by William James Kirkpatrick (1838-1921) and copyrighted by him in 1890.

334 I Would Be Thine; O Take My Heart
Eliza Holmes Reed (1794-1867)

Mrs. Reed's hymns were published anonymously along with those of her husband Dr. Andrew Reed (1787-1862) in his *Hymn Book, Prepared from Dr. Watts's Psalms and Hymns and Other Authors, with Some Originals*, 1842. Authorship was established in the *Wycliffe Chapel Supplement*, 1872.

In our hymnal we have restored the text to the 1842 form.
All Free Methodist hymnals since 1883 have included this hymn.

EVAN was arranged by Lowell Mason (1792-1870) from a longer tune which William Henry Havergal (1793-1870) composed and published in 1847 for the Robert Burns poem "O Thou Dread Pow'r, Who Reign'st Above." Mason called the tune *Eva* originally when he included it in his *New Carmina Sacra* (Copyright, July 18, 1850) but changed it to *Evan* in his *Cantica Laudis* (copyright, August 10, 1850).

Havergal was not pleased with Mason's arrangement and called it "a sad estrangement." He wrote, "I do not approve the tune."

335 Love Divine, All Loves Excelling
Charles Wesley (1707-1788)

The British hymnologist Erik Routley in *Hymns and the Faith* says that "there is nobody like Charles Wesley for packing a volume of pregnant thought into a short hymn." This hymn supports that judgment. Charles Wesley published it in *Hymns for Those that Seek and Those that have Redemption in the Blood of Jesus Christ*, 1747, in four 8-line stanzas. John Wesley made some editorial changes when he included it in his "Large Hymnbook" of 1780. He omitted stanza 2 entirely, presumably on doctrinal grounds. The original text reads:

> 2:5 ... our *power of* sinning;
> 4:2 Pure and *sinless* let us be;

John Wesley's alterations are these:

> 3:2 ... all thy grace receive;
> 4:2 Pure and *spotless* ...

Stanza 1 seems obviously patterned after the secular poem "Fairest Isle" in Dryden's *King Arthur*, which Purcell set to music. The opening lines are:

> Fairest isle, all Isles excelling
>   Seat of Pleasures and of Loves;
> Venus here will choose her dwelling
>   And forsake her Cyprian Groves.

The expression "second rest" in 2:4 has been altered to "promised rest" in many hymnals, beginning with those by Martin Madan (1760), Toplady (1776), Countess of Huntingdon (1786), and R. Conyers (1767).

John Fletcher also objected to the term "second rest." "Mr. Wesley says *second rest,* because an imperfect believer enjoys a first inferior rest; if he did not, he would be no believer." Fletcher continued: "Take away the power of sinning?" He asks, "Is not this expression too strong? Would it not be better to soften it by saying, 'Take away the love of sinning?' (or the bent of the mind towards sin). Can God take away from us our *power of sinning* without taking away our power of free obedience?"

All Free Methodist hymnals since 1883 have included this hymn, using all four stanzas.

BEECHER was composed by John Zundel (1815-1882) for this text and included in his *Christian Heart Songs,* 1870. The tempo marking in the index indicates sixty-five seconds per stanza, much slower than any modern congregation is likely to sing it. The title of the tune honors Henry Ward Beecher with whom Zundel was associated for twenty-eight years.

According to Osborne, in *If Such Holy Song,* John Wesley's choice of tune was one by Henry Purcell which Wesley named WESTMINSTER when he included it in *Sacred Melody,* 1761. HYFRYDOL is the preferred tune in many hymnals.

336 Breathe on Me, Breath of God

Edwin Hatch (1835-1889)

This hymn was published first in 1878 in a small, privately printed collection entitled *Between Doubt and Prayer* and later in Henry Allon's *Congregational Psalmist Hymnal,* 1886. Hatch was an Oxford professor who, although a scholar, was said to have possessed a faith "as simple and unaffected as a child's."

Originally, one line in stanza 3 read:

3:2 Blend all my soul with Thine.

The hymn entered Free Methodist-Wesleyan hymnody in 1951.

TRENTHAM was composed by Robert Jackson (1842-1914) for Henry W. Baker's "O Perfect Life of Love," and included in *Fifty Sacred Leaflets,* 1888 (1894 according to some sources). After a musical education at the Royal Academy of Music, Jackson became organist at St. Mark's Grosvener Square, London. In 1868 he returned to the town of his birth, Oldham, and succeeded his father as organist at St. Peter's. Together father and son held that post for ninety-four years.

Trentham is a village in Staffordshire, England.

337 Gracious Spirit, Holy Ghost
Christopher Wordsworth (1807-1885)

This metrical paraphrase of I Corinthians 13 was written by Bishop Christopher Wordsworth of Lincoln in eight 4-line stanzas and published by him in *The Holy Year,* 1862. (See also comments at Nos. 51, 57, and 135.)

Wordsworth's biographer, the Reverend J. H. Overton, remarks that the poet, "like the Wesleys, looked upon hymns as a valuable means of stamping permanently upon the memory the great doctrines of the Christian church. He held it to be the first duty of a hymnwriter to teach sound doctrine and thus to save souls."

Our hymnal uses stanzas 1, 2, 4, 5, and 7. The omitted stanzas read:

> 3. Though I as a Martyr bleed,
>   Give my goods the poor to feed
>   All is vain, if love I need;
>   Therefore, give me love.
>
> 6. Faith will vanish into sight;
>   Hope be emptied in delight;
>   Love in heaven will shine more bright;
>   Therefore, give us love.
>
> 8. From the overshadowing
>   Of Thy gold and silver wing,
>   Shed on us, who to Thee sing,
>   Holy, heavenly love.

CHARITY was composed by Sir John Stainer (1840-1901) for the 1868 Appendix to the first edition of *Hymns Ancient and Modern.* Stainer, distinguished organist at St. Paul's Cathedral in London, succeeding John Goss, later succeeded Sir F. A. Gore Ouseley as professor of music at Oxford. He composed a number of hymn tunes and anthems, one oratorio, and a number of cantatas, notably, the *Crucifixion, The Daughter of Jairus,* and *St. Mary Magdalen.* It has been said of him that "he was one of the very few touched with the radiance of the inner life of sacred music."

338 I'm Rejoicing Night and Day
Herbert Buffam (1879-1939)

The author of this text was born in Lafayette, Illinois. As a youth he began preaching for the Volunteers of America. Later he spent several years as a pastor in the Nazarene denomination before entering the independent evangelistic field. From about his eighteenth year onward he wrote gospel songs, some of which became well known. It is said that he had more than ten thousand accepted for publication.

HE ABIDES was composed by D. M. Shanks who may have been associated with God's Bible School, since early printings of the song carry the notation "owned by God's Bible School."

339 God of All Power, and Truth, and Grace
Charles Wesley (1707-1788)

After appearing in the 1883 and 1910 Free Methodist hymnals, this hymn was omitted in 1951. It is now restored in more complete form. It was published first in the Wesley's *Hymns and Sacred Poems, Part II,* 1742, in twenty-eight 4-line stanzas, under the title "Pleading the Promise of Sanctification" and based on Ezekiel 36:23-28. Our cento is made up of stanzas 1, 3, 7, 8, and 14.

The alterations are few:

    3:3 ... from every *evil* thought,
    5:2 Thy word *might* to the ...

Note the original stanzas 12 and 13.

12. Cause me to walk in Christ my Way;
    And I Thy statutes shall fulfil,
  In every point Thy law obey,
    And perfectly perform Thy will.

13. Hast Thou not said, who canst not lie,
    That I Thy law shall keep and do?
  Lord, I believe, though men deny;
    They all are false, but Thou art true.

This hymn was appended to John Wesley's Sermon No. 40 on "Christian Perfection" and to John Fletcher's *Last Check to Antinomianism.*

OMBERSLEY was composed by William Henry Gladstone (1840-1891), eldest son of W. E. Gladstone. It is the name of a village near Worcester. This tune appeared originally in *The Hymnary,* 1872, to the text "Sun of my soul."

340 Lord, I Believe a Rest Remains
Charles Wesley (1707-1788)

Like the preceding hymn, this hymn is restored to Free Methodist hymnody after being omitted in 1951. It was published first in *Hymns and Sacred Poems,* Part II, 1740, in seventeen 4-line stanzas, and is based on Hebrews 4:9. Our cento is made up of stanzas 1, 2, 10, 11, and 14. The original fourth and fifth stanzas contained expressions that Wesley found indefensible so he marked them to be omitted in later editions.

> 4. Our life is hid with Christ in God;
>   The agony is o'er;
> We wrestle not with flesh and blood;
>   We *strive* with sin no more
>
> 5. Our spirit is right, our heart is clean,
>   Our nature is renew'd;
> We cannot now, we cannot sin,
>   For we are born of God.

Our stanzas 2 and 3 were altered by Augustus Toplady in his *Psalms and Hymns,* 1776, so as to describe the "rest" as being achieved in heaven.

> Then shall I sing and never tire,
>   In that blest house above,
> Where doubt, and fear, and pain expire,
>   Cast out by perfect love.
> Celestial Spirit, make me know
>   That I shall enter in.
> Now, Savior, now the pow'r bestow,
>   And wash me from my sin.

It was this kind of mutilation of Wesley texts that John Wesley so strongly denounced in the Preface of the "Large Hymnbook."

REDHEAD No. 66, also called METZLER, was composed by Richard Redhead (1820-1901). It is contained in his *Ancient Hymn Melodies and Other Church Tunes,* 1859. Since Redhead did not assign titles to his tunes they are generally known by the number of the tune in his book.

341 O for that Flame of Living Fire
William Hiley Bathurst (1796-1877)

Bathurst, educated at Winchester and at Christ Church, Oxford, served as rector in the Anglican Church for a time. He resigned and retired to private life because he could not reconcile his doctrinal views with those of the *Book of Common Prayer.*

His hymns and psalm paraphrases are included in his *Psalms and Hymns for Public and Private Use,* 1831. (See also comments at No. 374.)

UXBRIDGE was composed by Lowell Mason (1792-1872) and published in 1830 in *The Boston Handel and Haydn Society Collection of Church Music,* ninth edition. It probably derives its name from the village in Massachusetts near the Rhode Island border.

342 In the Hour of Trial

James Montgomery (1771-1854)
Stanzas 3 and 4 altered by Frances A. Hutton (1811-1877)

The original manuscript of this hymn is dated October 13, 1834. Montgomery's opening line read "Jesus, *pray* for me." A later manuscript in the author's handwriting changed "pray" to "stand." In Godfrey Thring's *Church of England Hymn Book,* 1880, "plead" was substituted and is generally used now as the accepted form. Montgomery's second stanza began, "with its witching pleasures...." Mrs. Hutton's revision of stanzas 3 and 4 included in Prebendary H. W. Hutton's *Supplement and Litanies,* n.d., are also widely used in American hymnals. Montgomery's third and fourth stanzas are as follows:

> 3. If, with sore affliction,
>   Thou in love chastise,
>   Pour thy benediction
>   On the sacrifice;
>   Then upon Thine altar
>   Freely offered up,
>   Though the flesh may falter,
>   Faith shall drink the cup.
>
> 4. When in dust and ashes,
>   To the grave I sink,
>   While heaven's glory flashes
>   O'er the shelving brink,
>   On Thy truth relying,
>   Through that mortal strife,
>   Lord, receive me, dying
>   To eternal life.

Although popular in this country, this hymn does not seem to be greatly used in Great Britain and is not included in many of the contemporary British hymnals.

This hymn entered Free Methodist-Wesleyan hymnody in 1951. (See also comments at No. 20.)

PENITENCE was composed in 1875 by Spencer Lane (1843-1903), choirmaster at the time in St. James Episcopal Church, Woonsocket, Rhode Island. It was first published in *The Church Hymnal,* 1879, edited by Dr. Charles L. Hutchins, as one of the tunes for this text.

343 God Be in My Head

From the *Sarum Primer* 1514

This short hymnic prayer appears in a Free Methodist-Wesleyan hymnal for the first time in 1976. It is said to have been taken from a Primer in use at Salisbury Cathedral in the sixteenth century. "The term *Primer,* in its ritual sense, designates a series of devotional books for the laity...." In this sense the term was used as early as the fourteenth century. This particular hymn is found on the title page of the *Sarum Primer* printed by Pynson and printed in London on May 12, 1514. *The Historical Companion to Hymns Ancient and Modern,* 1962, is the source of the following interesting information on the text and its source. "Hore beate marie / virginis ad usum in / signis ac preclare ec / clesie Sarum." The inscription reads: "Impresse in ciuitate / Londini per (Richardum Pynson) / Regium Impressorem.... Anno domini / MCCCCCXiiii...."

Apart from the use of modern spelling, the text is the same as ours except for substitution of "mine" for "my."

The Guinness *Book of Records,* 1977, asserts that the earliest hymn for which an exact date can be given is the French one "Jesus soit en ma teste et mon entendement," 1490, of which "God be in my head" is a translation into English.

GOD BE IN MY HEAD was composed by Sir Henry Walford Davies (1869-1941) and published in 1910 in leaflet form. Lightwood is of the opinion that the British *Methodist Hymn-Book,* 1933, was the first church hymnal to use the melody although it had appeared in songbooks as early as 1912.

344 I Want a Principle Within

Charles Wesley (1707-1788)

Hymns and Sacred Poems, Vols. I and II, 1749, bear the name of Charles Wesley. John Wesley did not see them until after they were published. "I want a principle" is in Vol. II, Part II, in five 8-line stanzas, under the title "For a Tender Conscience." Stanza 1 begins "Almighty God of truth and love."

In the "Large Hymnbook" of 1780 (1781 edition) John Wesley shortened the hymn to five 4-line stanzas, beginning with "I want a principle within," the original second stanza. The order of stanzas related to Charles Wesley's original are: 2a, 3a, 3b, 4a, and 5a.

Our cento is composed of the following sections of Charles Wesley's original text with alterations noted:

    1: (original stanza 2)
    1:7 ... *wanderings* ...
    2: (original stanza 3)
    2:1 From Thee that I no more may part,
    3: (original stanzas 1a and 5a)
    3:2 ... Thy power *exert,*
    3:3 The *mountain* from my soul remove,
    3:6 My *well instructed* soul,

His stanza 4 reads:

    If to the right, or left I stray
    That moment, Lord, reprove,
    And let me weep my life away
    For having grieved Thy love:
    Give me to feel an idle thought
    As actual wickedness,
    And mourn for the minutest fault
    In exquisite distress.

Our 1883 and 1910 hymnals printed this hymn in three 8-line stanzas, following the pattern used in later editions of the "Large Hymnbook" of John Wesley. Stanzas 1 and 2 are like our present hymnal. Stanza 3 was derived from 3a and 5a. Our 1951 hymnal adopted the cento used in our present hymnal but with some variations in the text.

GERALD was discussed at No. 257.

345 We Praise Thee, O God, for the Son
                                William Paton Mackay (1839-1885)

After his education at the University of Edinburgh the author of this hymn followed the medical profession. Then he became a Presbyterian minister. His ministry was cut short by an accident leading to his untimely death.

At least seventeen of his hymns were published of which this one is best known. It was written in 1863 and revised in 1867.

The original fourth stanza, generally omitted, reads:

> All glory and praise to the God of all Grace,
> Who has bought us, and sought us, and guided our ways.

It is conjectured that the refrain was not a part of the original hymn but was added when the hymn became associated with the Husband tune.

This hymn was included in Free Methodist-Wesleyan hymnals beginning in 1951.

PEN Y BRYN appears to have been composed or arranged by J. Lloyd Jones of Johnstown, Pennsylvania. It was chosen by the Hymnal Commission to replace the more familiar tune by John J. Husband because of the secular associations which had grown up around that tune.

The text first associated with the Husband tune seems to have been Horatius Bonar's "Rejoice and Be Glad, the Redeemer has come," written for Sankey's *Sacred Songs and Solos* (c. 1875).

346 A Charge to Keep I Have

Charles Wesley (1707-1788)

This hymn, said by Erik Routley to be an almost literal versification of Matthew Henry's paragraph on Leviticus 8:35, was published in *Short Hymns on Select Passages of Holy Scripture,* Vol. I, 1762, in two 8-line stanzas and entitled "Personal Responsibility." Interestingly enough it was omitted from the second edition of the *Short Hymns,* 1794, but was included in John Wesley's *Collection of Hymns for the Use of the People Called Methodists,* 1780.

All Free Methodist hymnals since 1883 have included "A Charge to Keep," unaltered, except that in the 1883 hymnal the two-stanza arrangement was followed.

BOYLSTON was composed by Lowell Mason (1792-1872) and he included it in *The Choir, or Union Collection of Church Music,* 1832, where it was set to the text "Our days are as grass." It has been associated with other texts in later collections, e.g., "Not all the blood of beasts" (Watts) in Sankey's *Sacred Songs and Solos* and "Now is the accepted time" (Dobell) in *The Epworth Hymnal,* 1885, and to three texts in *Gospel Hymns. Pentecostal Hymns,* No. 2, 1898, may have been one of the first to set the tune to "A charge to keep."

Boylston is a prominent street in Boston and is also the name of a Massachusetts town.

There is a striking resemblance noted by William J. Reynolds between *Boylston* and the tune *Hobart* which was said to have been "arranged from an Ancient Chant."

The tune in *Hymns of Faith and Life* was arranged by the editor.

347 I Need Thee Every Hour
Annie Sherwood Hawks (1835-1918)

This hymn by Baptist hymnwriter Annie Sherwood Hawks, written in June, 1872, in five 4-line stanzas, was published in a small collection compiled for use in the National Baptist Sunday School Convention held in Cincinnati in November, 1872. It was published later in *Royal Diadem for the Sunday School*, 1873, edited by Robert Lowry and William H. Doane. The circumstances surrounding the writing of the song were recounted by Mrs. Hawks. "I remember well the morning," she wrote, "when in the midst of the daily cares of my home ... I was so filled with a sense of the nearness of the Master that, wondering how one could live without Him, either in joy or pain, these words 'I need Thee every hour,' were flashed into my mind.... Seating myself by the open window in the balmy air of the bright June day ... the words were soon committed to paper.... It was not until long years afterward, when the shadow fell over my way — the shadow of a great loss — that I understood something of the comforting power in the words which I had been permitted to give out to others in my hours of sweet security and peace." (Quoted in *Companion to the Song Book of the Salvation Army*, 1961.)

Our hymnal of 1951 was the first Free Methodist-Wesleyan hymnal to include this song. In 1976 the complete five-stanza text is used.

NEED was composed for this text by Mrs. Hawks's pastor, Dr. Robert Lowry (1826-1899), who also added the text for the refrain.

348 Jesus, Keep Me Near the Cross
Fannie Jane Crosby (1820-1915)

This gospel song was published first in *Bright Jewels for the Sunday School*, 1869.

Hymns of the Living Faith, 1951, was the first official Free

Methodist-Wesleyan hymnal to include the song. (See also comments at No. 42.)

NEAR THE CROSS was composed by William Howard Doane (1832-1915). The tune was written first and Fanny Crosby was then asked to provide the text.

349   From Every Stormy Wind that Blows
Hugh Stowell (1799-1865)

This hymn was published in *The Winter's Wreath, A Collection of Original Contributions in Prose and Verse,* 1828 (Preface dated 1827), in six 4-line stanzas. It was rewritten and included in Stowell's *Selection of Psalms and Hymns Suited to the Services of the Church of England,* 1831. The revised form is now generally followed except that stanza 6 is omitted. Of Canon Stowell's many hymns this appears to be the only one in current use.

The omitted stanza 6 reads:

> Oh! may my hand forget her skill,
> My tongue be silent, stiff, and still;
> My bounding heart forget to beat,
> If I forget the mercy seat.

Thomas Alfred Stowell, son of Canon Stowell, wrote concerning his father, "My father's last utterances abundantly showed his love of, and delight in, prayer.... The morning of his death the only articulate words that we could catch . . . were, 'Amen! Amen!' "

Stowell was a powerful evangelical voice in the Church of England. His influential ministry was mainly in the Manchester area of England. He was known for his love of children.

All Free Methodist hymnals since 1883 have included this hymn.

RETREAT was composed for this text by Thomas Hastings (1784-1872) in 1840 and published in his *Sacred Songs for Family and Social Worship,* 1842.

Although largely self-taught, Hastings established a firm reputation as an authority on church music. In recognition of his accomplishments, the University of the City of New York conferred the doctor of music degree on him in 1858.

350 Prayer Is the Soul's Sincere Desire
James Montgomery (1771-1854)

This hymn was written in 1818 in eight 4-line stanzas at the request of Bishop Edward Bickersteth for his *Treatise on Prayer*, 1819. In the same year it was printed along with three other hymns on prayer by Montgomery in a small pamphlet for use in the Sunday schools of Sheffield. It was printed next in Bickersteth's *Treatise* and in Thomas Cotterill's *Selection of Psalms and Hymns...*, eighth edition, 1819, with some textual differences in stanzas 5 and 6. In Montgomery's *Christian Psalmist*, 1825, the Bickersteth form is followed. In his personal copy he noted that stanzas 4 and 5 should be transposed in future reprints. This arrangement is followed in our hymnal.

The omitted stanzas in our 1976 hymnal are:

3. Prayer is the simplest form of speech
     That infant lips can try;
   Prayer the sublimest strains that reach
     The Majesty on high.

7. Nor prayer is made on earth alone;
     The Holy Spirit pleads,
   And Jesus on the eternal throne
     For mourners intercedes

John Julian's estimate of Montgomery would likely be shared by most knowledgeable people:

> The secrets of his power as a writer of hymns were manifold. His poetic genius was of a high order, higher than most who stand with him in the front rank of Christian poets. His ear for rhythm was exceedingly accurate and refined. His knowledge of the Holy Scripture was most extensive. His religious views were broad and charitable. His devotional spirit was of the holiest type. With the faith of a strong man he united the beauty and simplicity of a child. Richly poetic without exuberance, dogmatic without uncharitableness, tender without sentimentality, elaborate without diffusiveness, richly musical without apparent effort, he has bequeathed to the Church of Christ wealth which could only have come from a true genius and a sanctified heart.

This hymn has appeared in all Free Methodist hymnals since 1883, using a cento comprised of stanzas 1-5 and 8.

LAMBETH was composed about 1871 by Wilhelm A. F. Schulthes (1816-1879). Schulthes, son of a German Army officer, was brought up in the Lutheran Church. He became a Roman Catholic through the reading of Frederick W. Faber's books. One of his hymn tunes *Requiem* was published in *Oratory Hymn-Tunes*, 1871, set to a Faber hymn.

351 Sweet Hour of Prayer
Attributed to William W. Walford (1772-1850)

The basis for attributing this hymn to one W. W. Walford is an item by the Reverend Thomas Salmon (1800-1854) in the *New York Observer* for September 13, 1845. Salmon claimed to have made the acquaintance of Walford, a blind preacher, who recited the four stanzas of this hymn. The *Observer* printed the hymn along with the explanation.

Research since has failed to find any information about a blind preacher named Walford in Coleshill, Warwickshire, where Salmon claimed to have met him. There was a Reverend William Walford, a Congregational minister, who was president of Homerton Academy. From a comparison of his writings and the hymn, some striking similarities have been noted. Authorities are divided, however, on whether the Walford of Coleshill and the Walford of Homerton are one and the same person.

The omitted fourth stanza reads:

> Sweet hour of prayer, sweet hour of prayer,
> May I Thy consolation share,
> Till, from Mount Pisgah's lofty height,
> I view my home, and take my flight!
> This robe of flesh I'll drop, and rise,
> To seize the everlasting prize;
> And shout, while passing through the air,
> "Farewell, farewell, sweet hour of prayer!"

This song entered Free Methodist hymnody in 1910.

SWEET HOUR was probably composed about 1859 for this hymn and was copyrighted in that year by William Batchelder Bradbury (1816-1868). According to Charles S. Nutter and Wilbur F. Tillett in *The Hymns and Hymn Writers of the Church*, 1911, the text and tune were first published in *Cottage Melodies*, 1859, but William J. Reynolds affirms that it did not appear in this collection until later editions.

The harmonization was made by the editor for use on broadcasts of the "Light and Life Hour."

352 What a Friend We Have in Jesus
Joseph Medlicott Scriven (1819-1886)

The authorship of this hymn was in doubt for a time. Some early hymnals, e.g., *Gospel Hymns No. I,* 1875, attributed it to Horatius Bonar but Dr. Bonar denied having written it. According to McCutchan it was probably published first, unsigned, in *Social Hymns, Original and Selected,* 1865.

The hymn seems to have been written by Joseph Scriven about 1855 for the comfort of his mother at a time of personal sorrow. He said that "the Lord and I did it between us." Scriven was born at Seapatrick, County Down, Ireland, September 10, 1819, and died by drowning in Rice Lake, near Bewdley, Ontario, August 10, 1886. A small cottage located between the business district of Port Hope and the bay is known locally as the Joseph Scriven home. A monument to Scriven's memory is located at the northeast corner of the Port Hope City Park.

Joseph Scriven served as tutor in the home of Lieutenant Pengelly overlooking Rice Lake. He is buried in the Pengelly family cemetery on the family farm. A monument erected in 1919 marks the grave. The Pengelly farm is best located by turning east at Bailieboro, fourteen miles north of Port Hope and then taking the first road south. A historical marker has been erected at the farm near the entrance to the cemetery.

CONVERSE also called ERIE was composed about 1868 by Charles Crozat Converse (1832-1918), musician, lawyer, philologist, and inventor. It was published first in a small Sunday school book *Silver Wings,* 1870. Text and tune have been in Free Methodist-Wesleyan hymnals since 1910.

353 Our Father, Thou in Heaven Above
Martin Luther (1483-1546)
Translated by Catherine Winkworth (1827-78) and others

This hymn "Vater unser im Himmelreich" by Martin Luther in nine 6-line stanzas was included in Valten Schumann's *Geistliche Lieder,* 1539, under the title "The Lord's Prayer Briefly Expounded and Turned into Metre." Some authorities have rated this as Luther's finest hymn, others as a close second to *Ein' feste Burg.* The first eight stanzas expound one of the clauses of the Lord's Prayer and the ninth amplifies the Amen.

Miss Winkworth's translation appeared in her *Chorale Book for England,* 1863. The text has undergone some changes since.

This is the first appearance in a Free Methodist-Wesleyan

hymnal. Because of its length, imagination must be exercised in using it. Parts of it may be recited antiphonally, alternating with singing. Stanzas may be interspersed in a sermon on the Lord's Prayer.

VATER UNSER is also called *Old Hundred Twelfth* because it was associated with Psalm 112 in some English psalters. It is generally ascribed to Martin Luther and it accompanies his setting of the Lord's Prayer in Schumann's *Geistliche Lieder*. John Wesley regarded it highly and included it in his *Foundery Tune-Book,* 1742.

Johann Sebastian Bach harmonized the tune and used it in Cantatas 101 and 102 and in several organ compositions. Mendelssohn used it in his *Sixth Organ Sonata*. Our harmonization is a composite derived from the settings in the two cantatas.

354 What Various Hindrances We Meet
William Cowper (1731-1800)

This hymn by William Cowper (pronounced "Cooper") is found in *Olney Hymns, Book II,* 1779, in six 4-line stanzas, under the heading "Exhortation to Prayer."

The omitted stanza 4 reads:

> When Moses stood with arms spread wide,
> Success was found on Israel's side;
> But when through weariness they fail'd,
> That moment Amelek prevail'd.

This hymn was included in a four-stanza form in the 1883 and 1910 Free Methodist hymnals. Omitted in 1951 it is restored in 1976 with an additional stanza.

BRESLAU is taken from a collection of "spiritual and pleasing new songs," Christian Gall's *As Hymnodus sacer,* 1625, set to "Herr Jesu Christ Lebens Licht." It is a later form of a German traditional melody found in *Locheimer Gesangbuch* (c. 1452), with a text beginning "Ich fahr dahin."

Felix Mendelssohn adapted and harmonized the melody for the chorale "O Thou, the true and only light" in his oratorio *St. Paul*. This is the form used in our hymnal.

355   Our Father Which Art in Heaven

The Lord's Prayer in modern textual idiom set to a West Indian Folk Tune transcribed in 1945 by Olive Pattison and harmonized in 1972 by Richard D. Wetzel.

356   Jesus, My Lord, My Life, My All
Henry Augustine Collins (1827-1919)

The author of this hymn belonged to the Oxford school. Ordained to the Anglican ministry he became a Roman Catholic in 1857 and entered the Cistercian Order in 1860. His hymns were published by him before leaving the Church of England in his *Hymns for Missions,* 1854.

Originally the first line read: "Jesus, my Lord, my *God,* my all," and the refrain was plural. When the hymn entered Free Methodist-Wesleyan hymnody in 1951 the present arrangement of the text was adopted.

There was a hymn written about five years earlier by Frederick W. Faber with the same opening line as Collins's hymn and with this refrain.

> Sweet Sacrament! We Thee adore!
> O, make us love Thee more and more!

ST. CHRYSOSTOM was composed for this text by Sir Joseph Barnby and published in the *Musical Times* for December, 1871. In 1872 he included it in the *Hymnary* of which he was the editor.

357   Be Thou My Vision
Ancient Irish hymn (c. eighth century)
Prose translation by Mary Elizabeth Byrne (1880-1931)
Versified by Eleanor Henrietta Hull (1860-1935)

The prose text of this ancient poem was published in *Erin,* Vol. II, 1905. The versification of the prose text appeared in Eleanor Hull's *Poem-book of the Gael,* 1912.

Since its first appearance as a hymn in the 1927 edition of *The Church Hymnary* it has attained considerable acceptance and is regarded by some as one of the finest hymns of this century.

This is the first appearance in a Free Methodist-Wesleyan hymnal.

SLANE is a traditional Irish melody from Patrick W. Joyce's *Old Irish Folk Music and Songs,* 1909, set to a secular text. The arrangement of the tune was made by the editor for this hymnal. SLANE derives its name from a hill in the vicinity of Tara, ancient capital of Ireland.

358   Lord, Enthroned in Heavenly Splendor
George Hugh Bourne (1840-1925)

This hymn was published in the author's privately printed *Seven Post-Communion Hymns,* 1874, apparently for use in the Chapel of St. Edmund's College, Salisbury, of which institution he was warden. It was published later in the 1889 Supplement to *Hymns Ancient and Modern* in five stanzas.

In the Westminster Abbey wedding records, it is interesting to note that although this is not a wedding hymn it was chosen on at least one occasion for an Abbey wedding.

Different centos are used in various hymnals and alterations in the text are reported to have been sanctioned by the author.

Stanzas in *Hymns Ancient and Modern* omitted in our hymnal read:

> 3. Though the lowliest form doth veil Thee
>   As of old in Bethlehem,
>   Here as there Thine angels hail Thee,
>   Branch and Flower of Jesse's stem
>   Alleluiah!
>   We in worship join with them.
>
> 4. Paschal Lamb! Thine offering finished,
>   Once for all, when Thou wast slain,
>   In its fulness undiminished
>   Shall for evermore remain,
>   Alleluiah!
>   Cleansing souls from every stain.
>
> 5. Life-imparting heavenly manna,
>   Stricken Rock, with streaming side,
>   Heaven and earth, with loud hosanna,
>   Worship Thee, the Lamb who died;
>   Alleluiah!
>   Risen, ascended, glorified!

Two additional stanzas are printed in the *Anglican Hymn Book.*

This is the first appearance in a Free Methodist-Wesleyan hymnal.

BRYN CALFARIA is a popular Welsh hymn tune arranged

from a melody by William Owen (1813-1893). Born in Bangor he early showed promise as a singer and a composer of melodies. This particular tune was wedded to an evangelistic Welsh hymn "Gwaed y groes sy'n codi fynny." Some of his compositions were published by Owen in his *Y Perl Cerddorol* (The Pearl of Music). *Bryn Calfaria* was included in Volume II of this work. It means "Mount Calvary."

359 Kum Ba Yah, My Lord
African Folk Spiritual (Angola)

360 We Give Thee but Thine Own
William Walsham How (1823-1897)

This hymn was written about 1858 and published first in the enlarged edition of Thomas B. Morrell's and How's *Psalms and Hymns*, 1864, in six 4-line stanzas.

Our 1951 hymnal was the first Free Methodist-Wesleyan hymnal to include this hymn. Stanzas 1, 2, 4, and 6 were used. The omitted stanzas 3 and 5 are:

> 3. Oh, hearts are bruised and dead,
>   And homes are bare and cold,
> And lambs, for whom the Shepherd bled,
>   Are straying from the fold.

> 5. The captive to release,
>   To God the lost to bring,
> To teach the way of life and peace,
>   It is a Christ-like thing.

The 1889 edition of *Hymns Ancient and Modern* added a seventh stanza not in the original as a doxology. It is not used in modern collections.

> All might, all praise be Thine,
>   Father, Co-equal Son,
> And Spirit, bond of love Divine,
>   While endless ages run.

SCHUMANN is found in *Cantica Laudis*, 1850, compiled by Lowell Mason and George J. Webb. The tune, also called BUCER, WHITE, and HEATH, was thought to have been composed by Robert Schumann. Clara Schumann, responding to an inquiry from the Scottish hymnologist, James Love, said she doubted that it had been derived from any of her husband's works.

361 Hark! The Voice of Jesus Crying
Daniel March (1816-1909)

The author, an American Congregational minister, wrote this hymn in 1868, in six 8-line stanzas. According to Dr. March he wrote it "at the impulse of the moment to follow a sermon ... on the text Isaiah VI:8."

The omitted stanzas 4 and 5 as contained in Sankey's *Sacred Songs and Solos* read:

> 4. If you cannot be the watchman,
>   Standing high on Zion's wall,
>   Pointing out the path to heaven,
>   Offering life and peace to all;
>   With your prayers and with your bounties
>   You can do what heaven demands;
>   You can be like faithful Aaron,
>   Holding up the prophet's hands.

> 5. If among the older people
>   You may not be apt to teach,
>   "Feed my lambs," said Christ our Shepherd,
>   "Place the food within their reach."
>   And it may be that the children
>   You have led with trembling hand
>   Will be found among your jewels,
>   When you reach the better land.

ELLESDIE. (See comments at No. 309.)

362 I'd Rather Have Jesus
Rhea Florence Miller

The text was written presumably about 1922, the year it was copyrighted by the author. The music was composed by George Beverly Shea (b. 1909) sometime during the 1930s. Shea, longtime soloist with the Billy Graham organization, is an alumnus of Houghton College from which institution he received an honorary doctorate also. He is the author of *Then Sings My Soul* (1968) and *Songs That Lift the Heart* (1972). Dr. Shea was a member of the Joint Hymnal Commission in both 1951 and 1976.

363 Let My Life Speak for Thee, Dear Lord
Haldor Lillenas (1885-1959)

This song was submitted to the committee preparing the

collection *Choice Light and Life Songs,* 1950, and chosen by the committee for inclusion in the book. The rights were purchased from the late composer and author and the song was copyrighted in 1949 by Light and Life Press.

364 Jesus, And Shall It Ever Be

Joseph Grigg (c. 1720-1768)
Altered by Benjamin Francis (1734-1799)

Opinions differ about the worth of this hymn. Routley rates it as "really not very good, even as altered...." Brownlie, on the other hand, calls it "a first-rate hymn."

Grigg was born in humble circumstance in a year variously given as 1720 and 1728. Apparently he qualified for ministerial appointment and became assistant pastor at Silver Street Presbyterian Church, London, in 1743. This seems to have been his only ecclesiastical appointment. Four years later he resigned and married a woman of wealth, thereafter devoting himself to writing and preaching on occasion.

Grigg wrote approximately forty hymns but only two became well-known: "Jesus, and shall it ever be" and "Behold a Stranger at the Door." The former was said, according to the *Gospel Magazine* (April, 1774) to have been written when Grigg was ten. It was published in seven 4-line stanzas in the author's *Four Hymns on Divine Subjects Wherein the Patience and Love of Our Divine Savior Is Displayed,* 1765. In the original form the verses are crude and have been subjected to considerable alteration in various hymn collections.

Benjamin Francis, a Baptist minister, altered the text for inclusion in Rippon's *Selection of Hymns from the Best Authors...,* 1787.

The alterations can be noted by comparison with the original.

> Jesus! and shall it ever be!
> A mortal man ashamed of Thee?

This hymn entered Free Methodist hymnody in 1883 in the same form as in our present hymnal but with an additional stanza after stanza 2:

> Ashamed of Jesus! just as soon
> Let midnight be ashamed of noon;
> 'Tis midnight with my soul til He,
> Bright Morning Star, bid darkness flee.

The six-stanza form was repeated in 1910 and 1951.

365 Give Me the Faith Which Can Remove
Charles Wesley (1707-1788)

This hymn is found in Charles Wesley's *Hymns and Sacred Poems,* Vol. I, Part II, 1749, in eight 6-line stanzas. There it is entitled "For a Lay Preacher." Stanzas used in our hymnal are 3, 5, 6, 7. The hymn opens with these lines:

> O that I was as heretofore
>   When first sent forth in Jesu's name
> I rush'd through every open door,
>   And cried to all, 'Behold the Lamb!'
> Seized the poor trembling slaves of sin,
> And forced the outcasts to come in.

This hymn entered Free Methodist hymnody in 1883 using stanzas 3, 4, 5, and 7. Omitted in 1910 and 1951, it is now restored in 1976.

EATON was composed by Zerubbabel Wyvill (1763-1837) and is derived from his anthem *Two Hymns, and two dismissions selected and composed for the General Thanksgiving* for the celebration on June 1, 1802, of the Treaty of Amiens. Originally *Eaton* was a long-meter tune with the last two lines being repeated.

366 Rise Up, O Men of God
William Pierson Merrill (1867-1954)

Nolan R. Best, editor of *The Continent,* in 1911, suggested to Merrill that there was an urgent need for a brotherhood hymn. Shortly afterwards Merrill came across an article by Gerald S. Lee entitled "The Church of the Strong Men." Evidently the article, following closely on the suggestion by Nolan Best, furnished the inspiration for the hymn. Merrill wrote, "I was on one of the Lake Michigan steamers, going back to Chicago for a Sunday at my own church, when suddenly this hymn came up, almost without conscious thought or effort.

Under the title "To the Brotherhood," it was printed in *The Continent* for February 16, 1911, a Presbyterian publication. Later it was included in *The Pilgrim Hymnal,* 1912.

Dr. Merrill was one of the outstanding preachers of the Presbyterian church and a brilliant scholar. Following his pastorates in Philadelphia and Chicago he became the pastor of the Brick Presbyterian Church in New York City where he had a long and distinguished ministry.

FESTAL SONG was composed by William Henry Walter (1825-1893) and appeared first in the Protestant Episcopal hymnal, published by J. I. Tucker, *The Hymnal Revised and Enlarged,* 1894. There it was set to a hymn by William Hammond, "Awake and sing the song." Apparently the first association of this tune with Merrill's hymn was in Shephard's *Hymns of the Centuries,* 1911.

367 O Master, Let Me Walk with Thee
Washington Gladden (1836-1918)

Dr. Gladden, a Congregational minister, wrote this hymn under the title "Walking with God" for inclusion in *Sunday Afternoon* (March, 1879), a periodical of which he was editor. Originally it had three 8-line stanzas. At the time, he had no thought that it would become a hymn, but Gladden's friend, Dr. Charles H. Richards, saw its hymn possibilities and included stanzas 1 and 3 in his *Christian Praise,* 1880. Most hymnbook editors have followed Richards's example and omitted stanza 2, judging it unsuitable for public worship. It reads:

> O Master, let me walk with Thee
> Before the taunting Pharisee;
> Help me to bear the sting of spite,
> The hate of men who hide Thy light,
> The sore distrust of souls sincere
> Who cannot read Thy judgments clear,
> The dullness of the multitude
> Who dimly guess that Thou art good.

H. Augustine Smith reminds us that the poem was published in a devotional column called "The Still Hour," giving thereby some indication of the place and time when the hymn should be used. "It is distinctively a prayer hymn ... and a prayer of dedication to service. It is admirably adapted to moments of quiet consecration, when the congregation ... is in the hushed, reverent mood of prayer and dedication."

Gladden served as pastor of the First Congregational Church of Columbus, Ohio, for thirty-two years beginning 1882.

This hymn did not enter Free Methodist-Wesleyan hymnody until 1951.

MARYTON was composed by Anglican clergyman Henry Percy Smith (1825-1898), Canon of Gibralter from 1892 until his death. It was Gladden's desire that his hymn be sung to this tune. The tune was first published in Arthur Sullivan's *Church Hymns with Tunes,* 1874, set to the text "Sun of my soul, Thou Saviour dear."

368 When We Walk with the Lord
John H. Sammis (1846-1919)

This text was written in response to a request from Daniel B. Towner by John H. Sammis, a Presbyterian minister, who during his later years was associated with the Bible Institute of Los Angeles. Sammis was born in Brooklyn, New York. At age twenty-two he moved to Logansport, Indiana. Later he was involved in YMCA work in the state. Still later he attended Lane and McCormick seminaries and was ordained as pastor in the Presbyterian denomination.

The text with its tune appeared first in *Hymns Old and New,* 1887.

This hymn entered Free Methodist-Wesleyan hymnody in 1951.

TRUST AND OBEY was composed for this text by Daniel Brink Towner (1850-1919) a native of Rome, Pennsylvania, the birthplace of Philip Bliss. He possessed a fine baritone voice and was associated with Dwight L. Moody and other evangelists as a singer in campaigns both in the United States and abroad. He served for many years as head of the music department of Moody Bible Institute. A doctor of music degree was conferred on him in 1900 by the University of Tennessee.

Towner described the origin of this song:

> Some years ago I conducted the music in a revival meeting for Dwight L. Moody in Brocton, Massachusetts. One night a young man arose and in his testimony he said, "I'm not quite sure but I am going to *trust,* and I am going to *obey*." I sent the line to Reverend J. H. Sammis, a Presbyterian minister, with a request that he write a poem on the subject. He wrote the hymn, and the tune was born. (Quoted by Ira D. Sankey, *My Life and the Story of the Gospel Hymns).*

369 Trust in the Lord with All Your Heart
Thomas Obadiah Chisholm (1866-1960)

(See comments at Nos. 43 and 301.)

LOVELESS was composed by Wendell Phillips Loveless (b. 1892) in 1937 and included in his *Radio Songs and Choruses,* 1937.

370 Come, Ye Disconsolate

Thomas Moore (1779-1852)
Stanza 3 probably by Thomas Hastings (1784-1872)

Moore, a native of Dublin and a Roman Catholic, wrote thirty-two sacred songs which he published in his *Sacred Songs,* 1816. Most of them were written to popular airs of several countries.

The text of this hymn has undergone a number of changes. Some were made in later printings of the same book. For example, 1:2 in 1816 read: "Come, at God's altar, fervently kneel," and in the 1824 edition, "Come, at the shrine of God, fervently kneel."

Most American hymnals have adopted the changes presumably made by Thomas Hastings and included in Hastings's and Lowell Mason's *Spiritual Songs for Social Worship,* 1831. These changes include the present form of 1:2. The most radical change is in stanza 3 which Hastings replaced with one of his own.

The original form read:

> Come, ask the infidel what boon he brings us,
> What charm for aching hearts he can reveal.
> Sweet is that heavenly promise Hope sings us —
> "Earth has no sorrow that God cannot heal."

Stanza 2 was also altered. Originally it read:
> 2:2 *Hope, when all others die,* fadeless and pure,
> 2:3 Here speaks the Comforter, *in God's name* saying,

Moore is perhaps better known as a writer of ballads and other poems. For example, he wrote "The Last Rose of Summer," "Believe Me, If All Those Endearing Young Charms," "The Harp that Once Through Tara's Halls," and "Oft in the Stilly Night."

The hymn entered Free Methodist hymnody in 1883 in its present form.

CONSOLATOR, also titled CONSOLATION and ALMA, was composed by Samuel Webbe, Sr. (1740-1816), a Roman Catholic organist, and set for solo voice to "Alma redemptoris mater," in his *Collection of Motetts of Antiphons,* 1792. In Hastings and Mason, *Spiritual Songs for Social Worship,* 1831, it was arranged for solo and duet and set to the present text.

371 There Is No Sorrow, Lord, Too Slight

Jane Fox Crewdson (1809-1863)

The author, a native of Cornwall, produced four volumes of

poetry during an extended illness. Her hymns have come from these works. "There is no sorrow" is taken from *A Little While and Other Poems* written a short time before the author's death and published posthumously in 1864. The hymn bore the title "Divine Sympathy."

Originally the opening line read "There is no sorrow, Lord, too light." An early publication changed "sorrow" to "grief" and others changed "light" to "slight." Among modern hymnals *Songs of Praise* uses the word "slight" and *Hymns of Faith and Life* follows suit. Another very brief hymn by Mrs. Crewdson is worth quoting:

> O Savior, I have nought to plead,
>   In earth beneath or heaven above,
> But just my own exceeding need,
>   And Thy exceeding love.
>
> The need will soon be past and gone,
>   Exceedng great, but quickly o'er;
> The love unbought is all Thine own
>   And lasts for evermore.

ST. BERNARD was adapted from Heinrich Lindenborn's *Neues Gott und dem Lamm geheiligtes Kirchen- und Haus Gesangbuch der ... Tochter Sion,* Cologne, 1741, in *Easy Hymn Tunes Adapted for Catholic Schools,* 1851, edited by John B. Richardson (1816-1879), a talented Roman Catholic church musician. Much of his active musical life was spent in Liverpool.

372   Zion Stands with Hills Surrounded
Thomas Kelly (1769-1855)

This hymn, based on Psalm 125:2, was published in the author's *Hymns on Various Passages of Scripture,* second edition, 1806, in five 6-line stanzas. Originally, the opening line read: "Zion stands *by* hills surrounded." It was entitled "The Security of the Church."

The omitted stanzas are:

> 3. Zion's friend in nothing alters,
>   Though all others may and do:
>   His is love that never falters,
>   Always to its object true.
>   Happy Zion!
>   Crowned with mercies ever new.
>
> 4. If, thy God should show displeasure,
>   'Tis to save, and not destroy:

> If He punish, 'tis in measure,
>   'Tis to rid thee of alloy.
>   Be thou patient:
>   Soon thy grief shall turn to joy.

This hymn has appeared in all Free Methodist hymnals since 1883 in its present form.

ZION was composed in 1830 by Thomas Hastings (1784-1872). It appeared in *Spiritual Songs for Social Worship,* 1832, edited by Hastings and Mason. There it is in trio form in the key of E. It was written to accompany another Kelly hymn which appeared in the first edition (1804) of Kelly's hymnal:

> On the mountain's top appearing,
>   Lo! the sacred herald stands,
> Welcome news to Zion bearing,
>   Zion, long in hostile lands:
>   Mourning captive,
>   God himself will loose thy bands.

The present form of the melody is thought to have been made by Hastings also. It appears in his *Church Melodies,* 1858.

373 Light of the World

Charles Wesley (1707-1788)

This hymn is a cento from two Charles Wesley hymns taken from his *Hymns and Sacred Poems,* Vol. I, Part I, and from Vol. I, Part II, both published in 1749.

Our stanzas 1 and 2 are stanzas 3 and 2 respectively from a hymn in five 6-line stanzas beginning:

> Are there not in the labourer's day
> Twelve hours, wherein he safely may
>   His calling's works pursue?
> Though sin and Satan still are near,
> Nor sin nor Satan can I fear
>   With Jesus in my view.

Our stanzas 3 and 4 are stanzas 4 and 6 respectively from a hymn in six 6-line stanzas beginning:

> But can it be, that I should prove
> For ever faithful to Thy love,
>   From sin for ever cease?
> I thank Thee for the blessed hope!
> It lifts my drooping spirit up,
>   And gives me back my peace.

HULL is called an American Melody in two British hymnals. In the British *Wesleyan Tune-Book*, 1876, it is called "Old Melody." Very little is known of its origin other than a statement in *The Music to the Church Hymnary* by Cowan and Love: ". . . it is quite uncertain whether it was originally the melody of a secular song or of a hymn tune." Then a melody is quoted from *The American Musical Miscellany* set to a song called "The Indian Philosopher." Although rhythmically this tune differs from that of *Hull*, the melodic similarity is marked.

374 O for a Faith that Will Not Shrink
William Hiley Bathurst (1796-1877)

This hymn was published in the author's *Psalms and Hymns for Public and Private Use*, 1831, in six 4-line stanzas under the title "The Power of Faith." Our hymnal omits two stanzas. They read:

> 4. That bears unmov'd the world's dread frown,
>   Nor heeds its scornful smile;
>   That sin's wild ocean cannot drown,
>   Nor its soft arts beguile.
>
> 5. A faith that keeps the narrow way
>   Till life's last spark is fled,
>   And with a pure and heavenly ray
>   Lights up the dying bed!

This hymn has been in all Free Methodist hymnals since 1883. In 1883 the text followed exactly that of the Methodist hymnal of 1849 with its alterations of the original text.

Bathurst, whose family name originally was Bragg, was for thirty-two years an Anglican rector. He resigned the Rectory in 1852 because he could not reconcile his doctrinal views with the *Book of Common Prayer* and retired to private life. His literary output was extensive and included more than two hundred hymns, of which only this one is in common use.

EVAN. (See comments at No. 334.)

375 Thou Hidden Source of Calm Repose
Charles Wesley (1707-1788)

This hymn appears in Charles Wesley's *Hymns and Sacred*

Poems, Vol. I, Part II, 1749, in four 6-line stanzas under the title "For the Morning."

The only alteration from the original is:

    3:3 The *medicine* of my . . .

All Free Methodist hymnals since 1883 have included this hymn.

SELENA. (See comments at No. 152.)

376 'Tis So Sweet to Trust in Jesus
Louisa M. R. Stead (c. 1850-1917)

This text was written in 1882 or earlier, since it was copyrighted in that year by the composer of the tune, William J. Kirkpatrick (1838-1921), and published in *Songs of Triumph,* 1882, compiled by Kirkpatrick and John R. Sweney.

Louisa M. R. Stead was a native of Dover, England. From early age she wanted to be a foreign missionary. She came to America in 1871. While living with friends in Cincinnati she attended a camp meeting in Urbana, Ohio. There she offered herself as a missionary candidate but was not accepted because of poor health.

A few years later she married a Mr. Stead. In 1880, while picnicing on Long Island Sound, her husband was drowned while attempting to rescue a young boy from the surf. It is conjectured that this experience and the difficulties encountered in raising a small daughter on limited financial resources inspired the writing of the song.

About 1890 Mrs. Stead married Robert Wodehouse, a native of South Africa. Mr. Wodehouse was ordained as a Methodist minister, and he and his wife were appointed as missionaries at Umtali, Southern Rhodesia.

Mrs. Wodehouse died January 18, 1917, at Penkridge. According to Ernest K. Emurian, her "final resting place was chiseled out of solid rock on the side of Black Mountain near her African home." *(Famous Stories of Inspiring Hymns.)*

This song entered Free Methodist-Wesleyan hymnody in 1951.

377 A Mighty Fortress Is Our God

Martin Luther (1483-1546)
Translated by Frederick H. Hedge (1805-1890)

This powerful paraphrase of Psalm 46 was written by Martin Luther in 1529. Julian surmises that it was written for the Diet of Speyer (Spires) when the German princes met on April 20, 1529, to protest formally "the revocation of their liberties and thus gained the name of Protestants." It was first published in four 9-line stanzas in Klug's *Geistliche Lieder,* 1529. Later it appeared in both Low German and High German forms.

The earliest High German text extant, dates from 1531. Julian quotes it in full. The first stanza is as follows:

> Ein' feste Burg ist unser Gott,
>   ein gute wehr und waffen.
> Er hilfft uns frey aus aller Not
>   die uns jetzt hat betroffen.
>   Der alt böse Feind
>   mit Ernst ers jetzt meint,
>   gross Macht und viel List
>   sein grausam Rüstung ist,
> Auf Erd ist nicht sein's Gleichen.

Julian gives the key thoughts in each stanza in these words:

1. "we see our stronghold and its besiegers."
2. "our weakness, our Savior's power and might."
3. "The vanity of the Prince of this World."
4. "whatever earthly goods we lose we have our true treasure in heaven."

Stanza 4 has caused scholars some problems. While the first three stanzas correspond to the three strophes of Psalm 46 (separated by the word *Selah),* stanza 4 seems to bear little relation to the psalm.

There is in this hymn what Erik Routley calls, perhaps unfairly, "a good deal of that heroic blustering and holy boastfulness that was in Martin Luther the quality so greatly loved by his friends and detested by his enemies...." *(Hymns and Human Life)*

There have been many translations of the German text into English. The earliest was probably that of Miles Coverdale in his *Goostly Psalmes and Spiritualle Songes* (c. 1543). The one quite generally used in Britain is that made by Thomas Carlyle, opening with the line "A safe stronghold our God is still." This translation is perhaps the most faithful to the original. It was printed in *Fraser's Magazine,* 1831.

In United States hymnals, the favored version seems to be that of Dr. Frederick Henry Hedge. It appeared first in Dr.

W. H. Furness's *Gems of German Verse,* 1852, and then a year later in Hedge's *Hymns for the Church of Christ,* 1853. Dr. Hedge was a Unitarian minister, serving churches in Maine, Rhode Island, and Massachusetts. During part of this time he was a professor at Harvard University.

Luther has often been likened to Ambrose of Milan because of his restoration of congregational singing in public worship and for providing hymns in the language of the German people.

Johann Walther, a composer of Luther's day, said: "It is to my certain knowledge that that holy man of God, Luther, prophet and apostle to the German nation, took great delight in music.... I spent many a delightful hour with him in singing...."

A frequently quoted statement written by Luther appeared in the preface to Walther's collection of hymns:

> I am not of the opinion that all sciences should be beaten down and made to cease by the Gospel, as some fanatics pretend, but I would fain see all the arts, and music in particular, used in the service of Him who hath given and created them.

Luther played both the lute and the flute and often used the former to accompany his singing.

All Free Methodist hymnals since 1883 have included the Hedge version of this hymn.

EIN' FESTE BURG is generally attributed to Luther also. It accompanies the text in Rauscher's *Geistliche Lieder,* 1531. This chorale melody is so directly connected with the Reformation movement that composers often quote it when they want to allude to that movement musically. Some of the better known compositions that make use of the chorale are: *Les Huguenots* (Meyerbeer); Reformation Symphony, fifth movement (Mendelssohn); *Kaisermarsch* (Wagner); *Fest Ouvertüre* (Nicolai). J. S. Bach wrote a cantata (No. 80) based on the chorale and used parts of it in other compositions as well.

An early form of the melody is as follows:

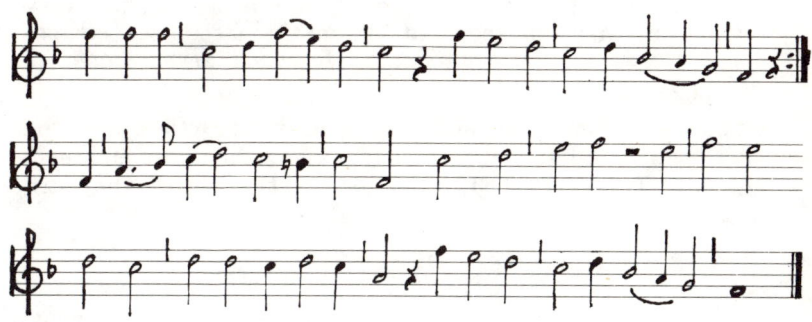

A polyphonic setting of *Ein feste Burg* by Michael Prätorius (1571-1621)

378   O the Deep, Deep Love of Jesus
Samuel Trevor Francis (1835-1925)

The author of this hymn was a London merchant. He wrote numerous hymns, some of which were included in the *Enlarged London Hymn Book*, 1873, and in his *Gems from the Revised Version with Poems*, 1891. For many years Francis engaged in open-air preaching services. He also traveled extensively in other countries.

This is the first appearance of this hymn in a Free Methodist-Wesleyan hymnal.

EBENEZER also called TON-Y-BOTEL was composed by Thomas John Williams (1869-1944) as part of an anthem "Golen yn y Glyn" ("Light in the Valley"). Its first use as a hymn tune was in *Llawlyfr Moliaint*, 1890.

The tune became extremely popular in Wales and in the words of a London daily paper:

> ... marched from one Welsh village to another long before printed copies of it were to be obtained. It was learnt by ear. One day a congregation in one town sang it; next day it would be heard more inland; and the next in the very wilds of the snow-covered mountain fastnesses. (From Lightwood, *The Music of the Methodist Hymn-Book*, p. 359*f*).

At about this time a legend sprang up to the effect that the tune had been found sealed in a bottle along the coast of Lleyn, thus the title TON-Y-BOTEL (tune in a bottle), a title that still sticks.

379 In Heavenly Love Abiding
Anna Laetitia Waring (1820-1910)

This fine hymn, under the title "Safety in God," was published first in *Hymns and Meditations, by A. L. W.*, 1850, a small booklet containing nineteen hymns. It is based on Psalm 23:4.

Bishop Frank Houghton in his book *Amy Carmichael of Dohnavur*, 1953, records that Bishop Parkenham Walsh sent her this hymn in September, 1949. She kept it by her in her last days "and she rejoiced especially in the last verse ..." beginning "Green pastures are before me."

Miss Waring was originally associated with The Society of Friends but later became a communicant in the Church of England. She was a thorough student and at one time learned Hebrew so she could study the Old Testament poetry in the original.

This hymn entered Free Methodist-Wesleyan hymnody in 1951.

SEASONS is attributed to Felix Mendelssohn (1809-1847).

380 Lord, Thou Hast Searched Me
Psalm 139, from The Psalter, 1912

This is one of three metrical versions of Psalm 139 included in *The Psalter*, 1912, of The United Presbyterian Church. There it is entitled "A Vision of God."

It is included in Free Methodist-Wesleyan hymnody for the first time.

TENDER THOUGHT is attributed to Ananias Davisson (1780-1857) in his *Kentucky Harmony,* 1816. There it is set to a text beginning "Arise, my tender thoughts arise, / To torrents melt my streaming eyes."

The melody is in the natural minor mode.

381 All the Way My Saviour Leads Me
Fanny Jane Crosby (1820-1915)

This song with the scripture text Deuteronomy 32:12 was published first in *Brightest and Best,* 1875, a Sunday school collection compiled by William H. Doane and Robert Lowry.

It entered Free Methodist-Wesleyan hymnody in 1951. In *Hymns of Faith and Life* the repetition of the last line is omitted. (See also comments at No. 42.)

ALL THE WAY was composed by Robert Lowry (1826-1899) for this text. It had been sent to him by the author.

382 He Giveth More Grace
Annie Johnson Flint (1862-1932)

The author of this hymn was born in Vineland, New Jersey. Left an orphan at an early age, she was adopted by a childless couple. After her public school education she attended normal school in Trenton and then taught school for three years. By this time she was afflicted so severely by arthritis that within five years she was unable to walk. She learned about the cures effected at the Sanatorium in Clifton Springs, New York, and went there. The disease was too far advanced to respond to treatment but she continued to live in Clifton Springs until her death.

Miss Flint began writing poetry when she was about nine years of age. Her real talent was music she thought and it was some time before she realized that poetry was the ministry to which God was calling her from the very beginning. She said,

> Verse-making was so easy and so pleasant to do that it had never seemed a work or a duty. It appeared so small a thing that I held it of no importance. I was like the Syrian general who would not have shrunk from doing some great or difficult task, but despised the seven dippings in the Jordan. (From R. V. Bingham, *The Life of Annie Johnson Flint*)

MITCHELL was composed in 1933 by Hubert Mitchell. In a personal letter to the author he described the circumstances as follows:

> I wrote the music in 1933. I was just getting ready to leave for Indonesia as a missionary to work among aboriginals of the interior of the island of Sumatra. I was having a season of prayer in the River Lake Tabernacle in Minneapolis, Minnesota. I saw this poem on the wall of the pastor's

study. It intrigued me deeply, and, as I read it over and over again, the latter part of the chorus came singing into my mind... "He giveth and giveth and giveth again."

I walked around the auditorium of the church singing the refrain ... and then within about one-half hour, the whole verse and chorus came to me as from the Lord. I hastily wrote it down as I played it over several times on the piano. I sang it in some of my meetings held throughout Kansas and California. Later on, an evangelist by the name of Loren Fox picked it up and began to sing it in his meetings. Ere long, the Lillenas Publishing Company asked that they might publish it and I granted their request.... It has been translated into Portuguese, Swedish, and a few other languages.

Mr. Mitchell and his family were forced out of Indonesia in 1942. He returned to Los Angeles and served with a number of Christian organizations. At the close of World War II he went to Calcutta where he was instrumental in launching Youth for Christ in India, Ceylon, and Singapore. Later he became full-time director of Overseas Youth for Christ International.

At the present time Mr. Mitchell heads Go-Ye Fellowship, located in Los Angeles.

383 O Love That Wilt Not Let Me Go
George Matheson (1842-1906)

The author of this hymn, a minister in the Church of Scotland, composed this hymn in 1882. It was published in the Church of Scotland magazine *Life and Work* (January, 1883), and a year later in *The Scottish Hymnal*. It has been called a "devotional masterpiece" by Erik Routley.

Matheson's own account of its writing leaves some unanswered questions but also reveals something of his frame of mind as he wrote:

> My hymn was composed in the manse of Innellan, on the evening of the 6th June, 1882. I was at that time alone. It was the day of my sister's marriage, and the rest of the family were staying overnight in Glasgow. Something had happened to me, which was known only to myself, and which caused me the most severe mental suffering. The hymn was the fruit of that suffering. It was the quickest bit of work I ever did in my life. I had the impression rather of having it dictated to me by some inward voice than of working it out myself. I am quite sure that the whole work was completed in five minutes, and equally sure that it

never received at my hands any retouching or correction.... The Hymnal Committee of the Church of Scotland desired the change of one word. I had written originally "I climbed the rainbow in the rain." They objected to the word "climb" and I put in "trace."

Matheson lost his eyesight in his youth but still managed a fruitful career as scholar, minister, and writer. The popular story that his best-known hymn was inspired by the rejection by his fiancée because of his impending blindness cannot be verified. The nature of his mental distress was not disclosed and it is just as well to avoid speculation.

In appearance, Matheson resembled General Grant. In the pulpit he became a giant, honored and esteemed, in spite of his blindness. Among the honors that came to him was an invitation to Balmoral to preach before Queen Victoria.

Matheson died in 1906 and was buried in the family vault in Glasgow.

ST. MARGARET was composed in 1884 for this text by Dr. Albert Lister Peace (1844-1912), at that time organist of Glasgow Cathedral and musical editor of *The Scottish Hymnal,* 1885. Just as the text had been written in a few minutes, so the composer said the tune came to him quickly and he wrote it down at once. The significance of the tune title is not known.

384 If Thou but Suffer God to Guide Thee
Georg Neumark (1621-1681)
Translated by Catherine Winkworth (1827-1878)

Although Neumark wrote a number of hymns the one beginning "Wer nur den lieben Gott lässt walten" has been called "classical and imperishable." It was published first in the author's *Fortgepflantzer musikalisch-poetischer Lustwald,* 1657, in seven 6-line stanzas, but written about 1641.

Neumark, en route as a young man to Königsberg to matriculate in the university, was set upon by highwaymen and robbed of all his possessions except his prayer book and some money sewed up in his clothes. Virtually penniless he sought vainly for employment. When after two or three months of great anxiety and poverty he was employed as a tutor, he wrote this hymn based on Psalm 55:22. It was entitled "A Song of Comfort: God will care for and help everyone in His own time." He described the circumstances as follows:

> This good fortune coming suddenly, and as if fallen from heaven, greatly rejoiced me, and on that very day I

composed to the honour of my beloved Lord the here and there well-known hymn "Wer nur den lieben Gott" . . . and had certainly cause enough to thank the Divine compassion for such unlooked for grace shown to me. . . .

Later in life Neumark became court poet, librarian, and registrar at Weimar, where he died.

Catherine Winkworth made two excellent translations of the hymn. The first was included in her *Lyra Germanica,* Series I, 1855, beginning "Leave God to order all thy ways." The second is the one we have chosen. It was printed in her *Chorale Book for England,* 1863. Both translations render all seven stanzas of the German original. For comparison purposes stanzas 1, 3, and 7 of Catherine Winkworth's first translation read as follows:

> Leave God to order all thy ways,
>   And hope in Him whate'er betide,
> Thou'lt find Him in the evil days
>   Thy all-sufficient strength and guide;
> Who trusts in God's unchanging love,
> Builds on the rock that nought can move.
>
> Only thy restless heart keep still,
>   And wait in cheerful hope; content
> To take whate'er His gracious will,
>   His all-discerning love hath sent.
> Doubt not our inmost wants are known
> To Him who chose us for His own.
>
> Sing, pray, and swerve not from His ways,
>   But do thine own part faithfully,
> Trust His rich promises of grace,
>   So shall they be fulfill'd in thee;
> God never yet forsook at need
> The soul that trusted Him indeed.

This hymn entered Free Methodist-Wesleyan hymnody in 1951. Stanzas used are 1, 3, and 7.

NEUMARK, also called BREMEN, was composed by Neumark probably at the same time he wrote the text. It was published with the text in 1657. Johann Sebastian Bach used the melody as the basis for his Cantata No. 166 composed in about 1725. Mendelssohn used it in his *St. Paul* with the text "To Thee, O Lord, I yield my spirit." We have used the Bach harmonization from Cantata No. 166.

385 I Must Have the Saviour with Me
Fanny Jane Crosby (1820-1915)

This song was written under the name "Lizzie Edwards" which was one of many pen names used by Fanny Crosby. It was copyrighted in 1884 by John J. Hood. (See comments at No. 42 also.)

The Free Methodist-Wesleyan hymnal of 1910 was the first official Free Methodist-Wesleyan hymnal to include this song.

PRESENCE was composed by John R. Sweney (1837-1899) evidently for this text.

386 O Safe to the Rock that Is Higher than I
William Orcutt Cushing (1823-1902)

This song was written in Moravia, New York, in 1876, according to the author. He described its composition in these words:

> It must be said of this hymn that it was the outgrowth of many tears, many heart conflicts and soul yearnings, of which the world can know nothing. The history of many battles is behind it. But the occasion which gave it being was the the call of Mr. Sankey. He said: "Send me something to help me in my Gospel work." A call from such a source, and for such a purpose, seemed a call from God. I so regarded it, and prayed, "Lord, give me something that may glorify Thee." It was while thus waiting that "Hiding in Thee" pressed to make itself known. Mr. Sankey called forth the tune, and by his genius gave the hymn wings, making it useful in the Master's work.

This hymn has been in all Free Methodist hymnals since 1883.

HIDING IN THEE was composed by Ira David Sankey for this text and first appeared in *Welcome Tidings*, 1877, compiled by Robert Lowry, William H. Doane, and Sankey.

387 Loved with Everlasting Love
George Wade Robinson (1838-1877)

Nothing has been discovered concerning the writing of this hymn. The author is known to have been born in Ireland, educated at Trinity College in Dublin and at New College, London. He served a number of Congregational churches in Ireland and England. He died at Southhampton. He published two volumes of poems, *Songs in God's World* and *Loveland.*

This is the first inclusion in a Free Methodist-Wesleyan hymnbook.

EVERLASTING LOVE was composed by James Mountain (1843-1933), presumably for this text in about 1876. He was educated for the ministry of the Countess of Huntingdon's Connexion. Later he became a Baptist minister. Further education was obtained at Heidelberg and Tübingen. He is said to have been influenced by the visit of Moody and Sankey to England. Among his publications was *Hymns of Consecration and Faith,* 1876.

388 Be Not Dismayed Whate'er Betide
Civilla Durfee Martin (1866-1948)

The circumstances that inspired this song written in 1904 and first published in *Songs of Redemption and Praise,* 1905, are difficult to verify. At least four accounts are given, one attributed to Mrs. Martin, another to her husband, a third reported by Homer Rodeheaver, and a fourth by Charles H. Gabriel. The common element in the four stories is that it was written during a period of illness.

GOD WILL TAKE CARE OF YOU was composed by Walter Stillman Martin (1862-1935), husband of the author of the text. Martin was first a Baptist minister but later became identified with the Disciples of Christ. After a period of time teaching Bible in Atlantic Christian College he engaged in Bible conference and evangelistic work across the nation.

389 God Hath Not Promised Skies Always Blue
Annie Johnson Flint (1862-1932)

(See comments at No. 382.)

WHAT GOD HATH PROMISED was composed presumably in 1919, the year the composer William Marion Runyan (1870-1957) copyrighted it.

390 Saviour, Like a Shepherd Lead Us
Attributed to Dorothy Ann Thrupp (1779-1847)

This children's hymn has been attributed to both Henry F. Lyte and Dorothy Ann Thrupp but without certain evidence for either author. Its first appearance was in Miss Thrupp's *Hymns for the Young*, fourth edition, 1636, in four 6-line stanzas. Miss Thrupp, prior to editing her songbook, contributed poems to Carus Wilson's *Friendly Visitor* and *Children's Friend*, two London religious weeklies, under the pen name of "Iota."

It has been included in all Free Methodist hymnals since 1883.

BRADBURY, also called SHEPHERD, was composed in 1859 by William Batchelder Bradbury (1816-1868) for this text and included in the composer's *Oriola*. Bradbury's tune required the repetition of the fifth and sixth lines of the hymn. Our arrangement modifies the tune so as to remove the repetition.

391 O Thou, to Whose All-Searching Sight
Nicolaus Ludwig von Zinzendorf (1700-1760)
Translated by John Wesley (1703-1791)

"Seelenbräutigam, O du Gottes-Lamm!" was written in September, 1721, and first published in *Sammlung geist- und lieblischer Lieder,* 1725, in eleven 6-line stanzas. Wesley's free translation in six four-line stanzas is based on stanzas 1, 2, 10, and 11 of Zinzendorf and stanza 12 of Freylinghausen's "Wer ist wohl wie du." The translation appears in Wesley's *Psalms and Hymns,* 1738, and in *Hymns and Sacred Poems,* Part II, 1739, under the title "The Believer's Support."

In *Hymns of Faith and Life* we use Wesley's stanzas 1, 3, 4, and 5. The ommitted stanzas are:

> 2. Wash out its stains, refine its dross,
>   Nail my affections to the cross!
>   Hallow each thought; let all within
>   Be clean, as Thou, my Lord, art clean.
>
> 6. If rough and thorny be the way,
>   My strength proportion to my day;
>   Till toil, and grief, and pain shall cease,
>   When all is calm, and joy, and peace.

Our stanzas 1 and 2 are based on Zinzendorf's stanzas 1 and 2. Stanza 4 is based on stanzas 10 and 11. Our stanza 3 (Wesley's fourth) is based on stanza 12 of Freylinghausen's "Wer ist wohl wie du," as indicated above.

Zinzendorf's hymn was included also in the Moravian *Gesang-Buch der Herrnhut,* 1735, a copy of which is in the Wesley archives at City Road Chapel.

In 3:1 Wesley had written "head" originally but in later editions of his hymnal he changed it to "soul." Line 4 would be better understood if he had not made the change. In 1:3 Wesley wrote "pants" instead of "yearns."

The 1883 and 1910 hymnals included this hymn using Wesley's stanzas 1, 2, 4, 5, and 6. The 1951 hymnal omitted the hymn.

ROCKINGHAM (MASON), sometimes called ROCKINGHAM NEW, was composed by Lowell Mason in 1830. He published it in *The Choir,* 1832.

392 Rock of Ages! Cleft for Me
Augustus Montague Toplady (1740-1778)
Altered by Thomas Cotterill (1779-1823)
and in *The Methodist Hymn Book Supplement,* 1830

This hymn was first printed in its entirety, four 6-line stanzas, in the *Gospel Magazine* for March, 1776, of which the author was editor. (An abbreviated form of stanza 1 had appeared in the same magazine for October, 1775.) Toplady's object in writing the hymn was to support his argument with John Wesley against the doctrine of holiness. It was appended to a curious article entitled "A remarkable Calculation: Introduced here, for the sake of the spiritual improvement subjoined. Questions and answers, relative to the national Debt." At the end of the article came the hymn under the title, "A Living and Dying Prayer for the Holiest Believer in the World."

From 1776 to 1810 the hymn had limited use. Then it became increasingly popular and in the process underwent numerous textual changes. Toplady himself made later alterations. Those made by Thomas Cotterill and by the editors of *The Methodist Hymn Book Supplement,* 1830, have had long-standing acceptance among Methodists and have been adopted in our present hymnal.

For comparison purposes Toplady's authorized text as printed in his *Psalms and Hymns For Public and Private Worship,* 1776, is given below:

A Prayer, Living and Dying

1. Rock of ages, cleft for me,
   Let me hide myself in Thee!
   Let the water and the Blood

>   From Thy riven side which flow'd
>   Be of sin the double cure;
>   Cleanse me from it's guilt and pow'r.
>
> 2. Not the labors of my hands
>   Can fulfill Thy Law's demands:
>   Could my zeal no respite know,
>   Could my tears for ever flow,
>   All for sin could not atone:
>   Thou must save, and thou alone.
>
> 3. Nothing in my hand I bring;
>   Simply to Thy Cross I cling;
>   Naked, come to Thee for dress;
>   Helpless, look to Thee for grace;
>   Foul, I to the Fountain fly:
>   Wash me, Savior, or I die!
>
> 4. While I draw this fleeting breath —
>   When my eye-strings break in death —
>   When I soar to worlds unknown —
>   See thee on thy judgment throne —
>   Rock of ages, cleft for me,
>   Let me hide myself in Thee!

The term "Rock of Ages" is not found in the King James Version of the Bible but a literal translation of Isaiah 26:4 would read as follows: "Trust ye in the Lord for ever; for the Lord Jehovah is the Rock of Ages." The great hymn writers of the eighteenth century knew their Bible very well and drew a number of figures from their literal renderings of the original texts. The figure of the "Rock of Ages" was used by John Newton in the first stanza of his "Glorious Things of Thee Are Spoken" and the figure of a "rock" as a place of shelter and security crops up in a number of other hymns. In fact in Charles Wesley's *Hymns on the Lord's Supper,* 1745, one hymn (No. 27) opens with this line: "Rock of Israel, cleft for me." The preface to this book is made up of extracts from a treatise by Dr. Daniel Brevint, entitled "The Christian Sacrament and Sacrifice," in which there is this petition: ". . . O Rock of Israel, Rock of Salvation, Rock struck and cleft for me, let those two streams of *blood* and *water* which once gushed out of Thy side bring down *pardon* and *holiness* into my soul. . . ."

The theological controversy out of which this hymn grew led to such excesses as Toplady's cruel description of the venerable Wesley:

> Whereunto shall I liken Mr. John Wesley? And with what shall I compare him? I will liken him to a low and puny tadpole in divinity, which proudly seeks to disembowel a high mighty whale in politics.

Elsewhere he calls him "Pope John."

Wesley's rejoinders were scarcely more charitable in tone and indicated something of the intensity of his feelings. In the preface to his sermon on "Free Grace" he wrote, "I dare not speak of the deep things of God in the spirit of a prize-fighter or a stage player." Elsewhere he said, "Mr. Augustus Toplady I know well, but I do not fight with chimney sweeps. He is too dirty a writer for me to meddle with."

It is well to withhold judgment on the character of both antagonists. Psalm 76:10 reads, "Surely the wrath of men shall praise thee ..."(RSV), and perhaps this is such an example. In *Songs of Praise Discussed,* Percy Dearmer records Toplady's reported words as he lay dying. When someone suggested that he would recover, Toplady said, "No, no, I shall die. No mortal could endure such manifestations of God's glory as I have done, and live." A few hours earlier he had said, "My heart beats every day stronger and stronger for glory. Sickness is no affliction, pain no curse, death itself no dissolution."

In Toplady's 1776 *Collection* he included such Wesley hymns as "Come, Thou Long Expected Jesus," "Arise, My Soul, Arise," and "Soldiers of Christ, Arise." John Wesley for his part included "Rock of Ages" in the first edition of his *Collection of Hymns for the People Called Methodists,* 1780.

Toplady's tomb is in the exterior wall of the Whitefield Memorial Chapel on Tottenham Court Road, London. He had personally requested to be buried there. The plaque reads:

>Within
>THESE HALLOWED WALLS
>AND NEAR THIS SPOT
>ARE INTERRED
>THE MORTAL REMAINS
>OF THE REVD
>AUGUSTUS MONTAGUE
>TOPLADY
>VICAR OF BROAD HEMBURY
>DEVON
>BORN 4TH NOVR 1740
>DIED 11TH AUGST 1778
>AGED 38 YEARS
>HE WROTE
>"ROCK OF AGES CLEFT FOR ME
>LET ME HIDE MYSELF IN THEE"

All Free Methodist hymnals since 1883 have included this hymn using the same form of the text.

TOPLADY was composed by Thomas Hastings (1784-1872) and published in *Spiritual Songs for Social Worship,* 1831, compiled by Hastings and Lowell Mason. There it is arranged as a trio in the key of D.

393 My Hope Is Built on Nothing Less
Edward Mote (1797-1874)

The author of this hymn was born in London. He was converted through the preaching of the Reverend J. Hyatt, of Tottemham Court Road Chapel, and subsequently became a Baptist minister. Although he wrote approximately one hundred hymns, only this one is in current use. It was written about 1834 and published in the author's *Hymns of Praise, A New Selection of Gospel Hymns, Combining All the Excellencies of our Spiritual Poets, with many Originals,* 1836. In its original form it was in six 4-line stanzas with refrain and began with the words, "Nor earth, nor hell my soul can move." Our hymn begins with stanza 2.

The circumstances surrounding the writing of the hymn were given by the author in the *Gospel Herald* and quoted by Julian:

> One morning it came into my mind ... to write an hymn on the "Gracious Experience of a Christian." As I went up Holborn I had the chorus,"On Christ the solid Rock I stand, / All other ground is sinking sand."
>
> In the day I had four first verses complete, and wrote them off. On the Sabbath following I met brother King as I came out of Lisle Street Meeting ... who informed that his wife was very ill, and asked me to call and see her. I had an early tea, and called afterwards. He said that it was his usual custom to sing a hymn, read a portion, and engage in prayer, before he went to meeting. He looked for his hymnbook but could find it nowhere. I said, "I have some verses in my pocket; if he liked, we would sing them." We did; and his wife enjoyed them so much, that after service he asked me, as a favour, to leave a copy of them for his wife. I went home, and by the fireside composed the last two verses, wrote the whole off, and took them to sister King....

The alterations are as follows:

> 1:3 *'midst all the hell I feel within,*
> 1:4 *On his completed work I lean;*
> 2:2 ... *Upon* unchanging grace;
> 2:3 ... *rough* and stormy gale,
> 3:2 ... in the *sinking* flood
> 4:1 when *I shall launch in worlds unseen,*
> 4:2 ... *be found in him,*

The omitted first and fifth stanzas read:

> 1. Nor earth, nor hell, my soul can move,
>   I rest upon unchanging love;
>   I dare not trust the sweetest frame,
>   But wholly lean on Jesus' name;
>   Refrain

5. I trust his righteous character,
   His council, promise, and his power;
   His honor and his name's at stake
   To save me from the burning lake;
   Refrain

Note that lines 3 and 4 of the original stanza 1 have been incorporated into stanza 1 of the present version.

This hymn has appeared in all Free Methodist hymnals since 1883. Three stanzas were used in 1883 and four stanzas thereafter.

MELITA. The Hymnal Commission rejected the traditional tune for this hymn as being unworthy of the text. Their choice of MELITA by John Bacchus Dykes (1823-1876) is a happy one. This tune was written for the text, "Eternal Father, Strong to Save," known in America as "The Navy Hymn," and was included in *Hymns Ancient and Modern,* 1861. Melita is the ancient name for the island of Malta. (See Acts 28:1.)

MELITA was heard many times on the occasions of President Kennedy's funeral and burial.

394 Joys Are Flowing Like a River
Manie Payne Ferguson (b. 1850)

This song was written by the founder of the Peniel Mission in Astoria, Oregon. Haldor Lillenas in *Modern Gospel Song Stories* gives the information that the inspiration for writing these lines came to Mrs. Ferguson when "after a period of earnest seeking she entered into the experience of perfect love so clearly taught in the Scriptures."

The author together with her husband T. P. Ferguson founded a number of "Peniel Missions" along the Pacific Coast with branches in Egypt and China. Mrs. Ferguson was a native of Carlow, Ireland.

Our 1951 hymnal was the first Free Methodist-Wesleyan hymnal to include this song.

BLESSED QUIETNESS, also called HOLY QUIETNESS, was published in *Echoes from Beulah.* The date of writing is uncertain. The copyright seems to have been secured by L. L. Pickett of Wilmore, Kentucky, in 1897, but this likely refers to the arrangement of the music. James M. Kirk and T. C. O'Kane are also mentioned as arrangers of the music.

BLESSED QUIETNESS appears to have been composed by W. S. Marshall about whom nothing is known. The date of 1876 is given in *The Hymnal* of the Evangelical United Brethren Church (1957) as the date of composition.

395   I Know Not Why God's Wondrous Grace
Daniel Webster Whittle (1840-1901)

(See comments at No. 233.)

EL NATHAN, the pseudonym of Daniel Whittle, has been chosen by a number of hymnbook editors as the name for this tune. James McGranahan (1840-1907) composed the music for the text in about 1883, the year text and music were published in *Gospel Hymns No. 4*. (See also comments at No. 91.)

396   I Never Walk Alone, I Have the Saviour
Alfred Henry Ackley (1887-1960)

Words and music for this song were written by Ackley about 1952, the year they were copyrighted by the Rodeheaver Company.

This is the first inclusion in a Free Methodist-Wesleyan hymnal.

397   O Holy Saviour, Friend Unseen
Charlotte Elliott (1778-1871)

This hymn was written soon after the death of the author's father, Charles Elliott, and published in her *Invalid's Hymn Book*, 1834, in nine 4-line stanzas. It bore the title "Clinging to Christ." A second version appeared two years later in the author's *Hours of Sorrow, Cheered and Comforted*, 1836. With a number of variations we have followed the original text using stanzas 1, 5, 6, and 7.

    1:1 Holy Savior, Friend Unseen
    1:3 ... life's *varying* scene
    4:4 ... that *rests on* thee.

Except for 1910, this hymn has been included in Free

Methodist hymnals since 1883 but with different centos. (See also comments at No. 253 and No. 296.)

FLEMING (INTEGER VITAE) was composed in 1811 by Friedrich Ferdinand Flemming (1778-1813) for male voices to the text, "Integer vitae Scelerisque purus," the famous ode of Horace. The composer was educated as a doctor and practiced medicine successfully in Berlin but probably was best known for having written this tune.

398 Commit Thou All Thy Griefs

Paul Gerhardt (1607-1676)
Translated by John Wesley (1703-1791)

This hymn and the following one are centos of John Wesley's translation of "Befiehl du deine Wege," by Paul Gerhardt. (For further comments on Gerhardt see information included at Nos. 128, 156, and 398.)

Gerhardt's hymn is in twelve 8-line stanzas and is in the form of an acrostic on Luther's version of Psalm 37:5 with each word of the psalm verse becoming the initial word of a stanza, e.g., "Befiehl dem Herren deinen Wege und hoffe auf ihn, er wirds wohl machen," becomes:

1. *Befiehl* du deine Wege,
2. *Dem Herren* musst du trauen
3. *Dein'* ew'ge Treu' und Gnade,
4. *Weg'* hast du allerwegen,
5. *Und* ob gleich alle Teufel
6. *Hoff,* o du arme Seele,
7. *Auf,* auf, gib deinem Schmerje
8. *Ihn,* ihn lass tun und walten,
9. *Er* wird zwar eine Weile
10. *Wird's* aber sich befinden,
11. *Wohl* dir, du Kind der Treue!
12. *Mach* End', O Herr, mach Ende.

W. G. Pollack in *The Handbook to the Lutheran Hymnal,* 1942, gives an interesting analysis of the twelve stanzas of the German hymn.

    1- 5 "The Invitation"
    6- 8 "The Exhortation"
    9-11 "The Assurance"
      12 "The Prayer for Endurance"

Gerhardt's hymn probably was written in 1653 while the author was serving his first pastorate in the small Bavarian village of Mittenwalde and was published first in the Berlin edition of Crüger's *Praxis pietatis melica,* 1653.

John Wesley's excellent translation which appeared first in his *Hymns and Sacred Poems,* Part II, 1739, changes the meter of the German so that the traditional tune for Gerhardt's text cannot be used. It is in sixteen 4-line stanzas. Our No. 398 uses stanzas 1-4, and 13. Our No. 399 uses stanzas 9-12, 14, and 16.

The omitted stanzas are:

5. Thy everlasting truth,
     Father, Thy ceaseless love
   Sees all Thy children's wants, and knows
     What best for each will prove.

6. And whatsoe'er Thou will'st,
     Thou dost, O King of Kings;
   What Thy unerring wisdom chose
     Thy power to being brings.

7. Thou everywhere hast sway,
     And all things serve Thy might;
   Thy every act pure blessing is,
     Thy path unsullied light.

8. When Thou arisest, Lord,
     What shall Thy work withstand?
   When all Thy children want Thou giv'st
     Who, who shall stay Thy hand?

15. Thou, seest our weakness, Lord.
      Our hearts are known to Thee;
    O, lift Thou up the sinking hand,
      Confirm the feeble knee!

Our hymnals of 1883 and 1910 used ten stanzas divided into two hymns. The hymnal of 1951 combined the ten stanzas in one hymn of five 8-line stanzas. In 1976 we have used 11 stanzas divided into two hymns.

DONCASTER or **BETHLEHEM** was composed by Samuel Wesley (1766-1837) son of Charles Wesley and father of Samuel Sebastian Wesley. Young Wesley was a precocious musician. When only three years of age he could play and extemporize on the organ. Along with his brother Charles he gave a series of subscription concerts in his father's Marylebone home attended by distinguished guests. His uncle John mentioned attending one such recital and commented that he did not feel at home in the company of such lords and ladies.

Had it not been for an unfortunate accident in 1787, Samuel might well have become one of England's greatest musicians. As it was he is credited with being the first in England to bring wide recognition to the music of J. S. Bach.

The tune DONCASTER is from J. B. Sales' *Psalms and Hymns for the Service of the Church...*, 1837. Melodically the skip of a seventh at the end of the second line is unusual in a hymn tune.

399 Give to the Winds Thy Fears
Paul Gerhardt (1607-1676).
Translated by John Wesley (1703-1791)

(See comments at No. 398.)

LEBANON. (See comments at No. 282.)

400 The Lord Is My Shepherd
Words and music by Ralph E. Hudson (1843-1901)

Text and music were presumably written in 1885, the year Hudson copyrighted them. Ralph Hudson was a lifelong resident of Ohio, having been born in Napoleon and dying in Cleveland. Following service in the Civil War he taught music at Mount Vernon College, Alliance, Ohio. He became a publisher in Alliance and produced four songbooks: *Salvation Echoes*, 1882; *Gems of Gospel Song*, 1884; *Songs of Peace, Love and Joy*, 1885; and *Songs of the Ransomed*, 1887. He was a licensed Methodist Episcopal Church preacher.

This is the first inclusion of this song in a Free Methodist-Wesleyan hymnbook.

401 O Love Divine, that Stooped to Share
Oliver Wendell Holmes (1809-1894)

Educated as a physician the author of this text practiced medicine in Boston for some time. He was elected to the chair of anatomy at Harvard in 1847. Although a distinguished educator he became best known for his work as an essayist, poet, and novelist. He was one of the founders of the *Atlantic Monthly*. This hymn was written in 1849 and published in the *Atlantic Monthly* for November 1859, in *The Professor at the Breakfast Table*, under the title "Hymn of Trust."

Holmes seems to have rebelled against the stern Calvinism of his minister father and became a member of a Unitarian congregation.

This is the first inclusion in a Free Methodist hymnal. (See comments at No. 105 also.)

ROLLER was composed in 1974 by Gilbert Roller (b. 1927), professor of music at Spring Arbor College for twenty-five years and presently chairman, Division of Fine Arts, Asbury College. It was submitted anonymously to the editors of *Hymns of Faith and Life* and was one of two original tunes accepted for inclusion.

Dr. Roller is a graduate of Greenville College and earned his Ph.D. degree in music at Michigan State University.

402 The Lord My Pasture Shall Prepare
Paraphrase of Psalm 23 by Joseph Addison (1672-1719)

This is the first of five hymns written by Mr. Addison and published by him in *The Spectator* in the space of three months. This one was in the issue of Saturday, July 26, 1712, and accompanied his article entitled "Divine Providence."

In the original broadsheet for that day the hymn was introduced with these words:

> David has very beautifully represented this steady reliance on God Almighty in his twenty-third psalm, which is a kind of pastoral hymn, and filled with those allusions which are usual in that kind of writing. As the poetry is very exquisite, I shall present my readers with the following translation of it.

Canon C. S. Phillips in *Hymnody Past and Present* calls this the "beautiful 'classically-embroidered' version of Psalm 23...." Louis F. Benson regarded Addison as "a delightful writer," and said that "a gentle wind still blows over the 'verdant landscape' of his Psalm," but he agreed with Canon Douglas that Addison was "a great deal more fond of adjectives than David was" (*Studies of Familiar Hymns,* Second Series).

Addison declined to take Holy Orders, choosing rather a career in law, politics, and literature. Although he died at the comparatively early age of forty-seven, he had gained distinction in all three areas. Lord Macauley said of him that "since his time the open violation of decency has always been considered amongst us a sure mark of a fool."

H. A. Taine in his *History of English Literature* said:

> The most cruel pamphleteers respected him; his uprightness, his talent, seemed exalted by common consent above

discussion. He lived in abundance, activity, and honors, wisely, and usefully, amid the admiration and constant affection of learned and distinguished friends, ... amid the applause of all good men and all the cultivated minds of England.

This hymn appeared in the hymnals of 1883 and 1910. It was omitted in 1951.

RAKEM was composed by Isaac Baker Woodbury (1819-1858), a writer of hymn tunes, sacred and secular songs, and glees. He was widely known in the New England area as a choral conductor.

403   Lead Us, Heavenly Father, Lead Us
James Edmeston (1791-1867)

This hymn was written for the children of the London Orphan Asylum and published in the author's *Sacred Lyrics, Set Two,* 1821, in three 6-line stanzas. Called by Erik Routley "one of our classics" *(Hymns and Human Life),* it has become a favorite wedding hymn, particularly in England. It was sung at the wedding of King George VI and at other royal weddings.

Edmeston, an active layman in the Church of England, was a practicing architect and surveyor throughout his professional life but found time to write many hymns, estimated at two thousand. Only two are currently in use, this one and "Saviour, Breathe an Evening Blessing." It is said that he endeavored to write a new hymn every Sunday and then would read it at family worship that day.

Hymns of Faith and Life is the first Free Methodist-Wesleyan hymnal to include this hymn.

This hymn was written to be sung to the tune LEWES, written by Dr. John Randall and published in leaflet form about 1774. DULCE CARMAN was discussed at No. 300.

404   How Firm a Foundation
"K" in John Rippon's *A Selection of Hymns,* 1787

This hymn of great assurance appeared in John Rippon's *Selection of Hymns from the Best Authors,* 1787, in seven 4-line stanzas under the title "Exceeding Great and Precious Promises." The authorship has never been established. In Rippon's *Collection* it is given as K_____. John Julian was certain the writer was an unknown person by the name of Keen, some say Robert Keen, precentor in Rippon's church.

The original text in Rippon's *Collection* has these renderings:

1:4 *You, who unto Jesus for refuge have fled*
2:2 *I*, I am . . .
3:2 The rivers of *woe* shall not *thee* overflow

Rippon adds a note to 5:4, "Agreeable to Dr. Doddridge's translation of Heb. 13:5."

The omitted stanzas in Rippon read:

2. In every Condition, in Sickness, in Health,
In Poverty's Vale, or abounding in Wealth;
At Home and Abroad, on the Land, on the Sea,
As thy Days may demand, shall thy Strength ever be.

6. E'en down to old age all my people shall prove
My sovereign, eternal, unchangeable love;
And when hoary hairs shall their temples adorn,
Like lambs they shall still in My bosom be borne.

One of the characteristics of Rippon's *Collection* is the large number of meters employed. In his preface he mentions that Patrick's *Psalms* uses only three measures and Dr. Watts uses only nine. He reported that he consulted more than ninety volumes of hymnbooks, hymns, psalms, and so forth from both Great Britain and America.

He wrote:

My enquiry has not been, *whose* Hymns shall I choose; but *what* hymns; and hence it will be seen, that Churchmen and Dissenters, Watts and Tate, Wesley and Toplady, England and America sing side by side, and very often join in the same Triumph using the same Words. And when Christ has been the Subject of the Song, we have been ready to say,

Europe, and *Asia,* shall resound,
With *Africa,* his Fame;
And thou, *America,* in songs,
Redeeming Love proclaim.

FOUNDATION was attributed erroneously to Anne Steele in some nineteenth-century collections. Actually this pentatonic tune is an early American melody, composer unknown. The first published appearance is said to have been in Joseph Funk's *Genuine Church Music (Harmonia Sacra),* 1832. Later appearances were in William Walker's *Southern Harmony,* 1835, under the title *The Christian's Farewell;* in William Caldwell's *Union Harmony. . . ,* 1837; and in *The Sacred Harp,* 1844, where it was called BELLEVUE and credited to Z. Chambless.

405 I Know I Love Thee Better, Lord
Frances Ridley Havergal (1836-1879)

This text seems to have been published posthumously, probably by Ralph E. Hudson (1843-1901) who composed the tune usually associated with it. Its first publication may have been in Hudson's *Gems of Gospel Song,* 1884. At any rate the song was copyrighted by Hudson but the date is uncertain. It is given variously as 1881 and 1883, and the renewal date as 1918. (See also comments at No. 294.)

406 My Shepherd Will Supply My Need
Paraphrase of Psalm 23 by Isaac Watts (1674-1748)

This paraphrase of Psalm 23 by Isaac Watts is contained in his *Psalms of David Imitated in the Language of the New Testament, and Apply'd to the Christian State and Worship,* 1719, in six 4-line stanzas. Except for combining stanzas and changing "mine" to "my" in 3:3, the hymn is just as published by Watts.

In Watts's hymnal there is a note appended to the hymn saying, in part, that the oil mentioned in 2:8 "in the Sense and Language of the New Testament, must signify the communications of the Holy Spirit, which is call'd the Anointing...." 3:7 and 8 seem to allude to the parable of the Prodigal Son.

RESIGNATION is an American Folk Hymn found in William Walker's *Southern Harmony,* 1835. It has also been attributed to F. Lewis's *Beauties of Harmony* (c. 1828) and to Joseph Funk's *Genuine Church Music,* 1832. The arrangement was made for *Hymns of Faith and Life* by the editor.

407 Nothing Between My Soul and the Saviour
Words and music by Charles Albert Tindley (1851-1933)

Tindley, son of slave parents, through incredible perseverance and considerable native ability achieved an education and was ordained to the Methodist ministry. He served a number of appointments in the Delaware Annual Conference. William J. Reynolds in *Hymns of Our Faith* informs us that in 1902 Tindley became pastor of the Calvary Methodist Church of Philadelphia where he had earlier served as janitor. When that church was relocated and rebuilt it was renamed Tindley Temple Methodist Church.

Tindley wrote both words and music of a number of gospel songs. The music for this song which we have named TINDLEY was arranged by F. A. Clark (dates unknown) and was copyrighted by C. A. Tindley in 1905.

408   He that Is Down Needs Fear No Fall
John Bunyan (1628-1688)

This text appears in Part 2 of *The Pilgrim's Progress,* 1684, as the song of the shepherd boy "in very mean cloaths but of a fresh and well-favoured countenance...."

Christiana and her children had descended into the Valley of Humiliation. Mr. Great-heart described it to them as "The best and most fruitful piece of ground in all these parts." He said,

> Behold how green the valley is; also how beautified with lilies. (Sol. II.1). I have known many labouring men that have got good estates in this Valley of Humiliation (for "God resisteth the proud, but giveth grace to the humble;" James IV.6, I Peter V.5)....

It was then they saw the boy feeding his father's sheep and heard his song. Mr. Great-heart said, "I will dare say this boy lives a merrier life, and wears more of that herb called heart's-ease in his bosom, than he that is clad in silk and velvet."

This is the first appearance of this hymn in a Free Methodist-Wesleyan hymnal.

(See comments also at No. 234.)

SOLOMON is adapted from the aria, "What tho' I trace each herb and flower," in Handel's oratorio *Solomon* composed in 1748.

409   Stand Up, Stand Up for Jesus
George Duffield, Jr. (1818-1888)

This hymn, originally in six 8-line stanzas, was born out of a tragic incident that occurred during the great revival of 1858 known as "the work of God in Philadelphia." The circumstances were given by Duffield in *Lyra Sacra Americana,* 1868, and later in a letter dated May 29, 1883. I quote from the letter:

> "Stand up for Jesus" was the dying message of the Rev. Dudley A. Tyng to the Young Men's Christian Association

and the ministers associated with them in the Noonday Prayer Meeting during the great revival. . . .

A very dear personal friend, I knew young Tyng as one of the noblest, bravest, *manliest* men I ever met. . . . The Sabbath before his death he preached in the immense edifice known as Jayne's Hall, one of the most successful sermons of modern times. Of the five thousand men there assembled, at least one thousand, it was believed, were "slain of the Lord." His text was Exodus 10:11, and hence the allusion in the third [second] verse of the hymn.

The following Wednesday [Tuesday, April 13, 1858?], leaving his study for a moment, he went to the barn floor, where a mule was at work on a horse-power shelling corn. Patting him on the neck, the sleeve of his silk study gown caught in the cogs of the wheel, and his arm was torn out by the roots! His death occurred in a few hours. . . .

The following Sunday Duffield, a Presbyterian clergyman, preached from Ephesians 6:14 and the hymn was written as a concluding exhortation. It was printed first on a flyleaf for Sunday school children and later in the *Church Psalmist,* 1859.

Dudley Atkins Tyng was rector of the Church of the Epiphany, Philadelphia, until forced out because of his strong antislavery views. He was known as an effective evangelistic preacher.

In *Hymns of Faith and Life* stanzas 2 and 5 are omitted. They read:

   2. Stand up, stand up for Jesus!
      The solemn watchword hear;
   If while ye sleep he suffers,
      Away with shame and fear.
   Where'er ye meet with evil,
      Within you or without,
   Charge for the God of battles,
      And put the foe to rout.

   5. Stand up! — stand up for Jesus,
      Each soldier to his post;
   Close up the broken column,
      And shout through all the host!
   Make good the loss so heavy
      In those that still remain,
   And prove to all around you
      That death itself is gain.

Duffield served Presbyterian pastorates in Brooklyn, New York; Bloomfield, New Jersey; Philadelphia, Pennsylvania; Adrian, Michigan; Galesburg, Illinois; and Saginaw, Ann Arbor, and Lansing in Michigan.

This hymn entered Free Methodist-Wesleyan hymnody in 1910.

WEBB also known as GOODWIN was composed by George James Webb (1803-1887) as a musical setting for a secular text "Tis Dawn, the Lark Is Singing," first published in the composer's *Odeon,* 1837, but written in 1830. Although prominent in musical circles in the Boston and New York City areas he is known today for this one tune now associated with "Stand up for Jesus" and with "The Morning Light Is Breaking." As far as is known William B. Bradbury was responsible for adapting the tune to Duffield's hymn when he published it in his *Golden Chain,* 1861.

At one time Webb was organist at Old South Church in Boston. He helped organize the Boston Academy of Music and served as president of the famed Handel and Haydn Society for three years.

410 Soldiers of Christ, Arise

Charles Wesley (1707-1788)

This hymn in sixteen 8-line stanzas based on Ephesians 6:11-18, is taken from *Hymns and Sacred Poems,* Vol. I, Part II, 1749, a volume published by Charles Wesley without the prior knowledge of his brother John. "Hymns for Believers" is the general title given to the first forty-three hymns in Part II.

It is certain that John approved of many of the hymns because he inserted them in his 1780 *Collection.* According to Frank Baker, noted authority on Wesley, this hymn was included in the first two editions of John Wesley's *Character of a Methodist,* 1742.

On March 13, 1790, in his eighty-seventh year, John Wesley wrote, "If we do not take care we shall degenerate into milk-sops. Soldiers of Christ, arise!"

No modern hymnal prints all sixteen stanzas. Our cento is made up of stanzas 1, 2, 7, 13, and 16. A portion of stanza 11 suggests that the armor needs to be cared for continually and that courage ought to be accompanied by humility.

> To keep your armor bright,
>   Attend with constant care,
> Still walking in your Captain's sight,
>   And watching unto prayer;

One of the marks of Wesley's genius was his ability to take a metre such as this one and, as Rattenburg says in *The Evangelical Doctrines of Charles Wesley's Hymns,* make it "sound the bugle, blow the trumpet, beat the drum, march to the tramp of soldiers' feet." In his hands the so-called "poulters' measure" became a "metrical triumph."

This hymn has appeared in all Free Methodist hymnals since 1883, but with different centos: 1883 and 1910 — stanzas 1, 2, and 4; 1951 — stanzas 1, 2, 7, and 16. The stanza not included in 1976 reads as follows:

> 4. Leave no unguarded place,
>   No weakness of the soul,
>   Take every virtue, every grace,
>   And fortify the whole;
>   Indissolubly join'd,
>   To battle all proceed;
>   But arm yourselves with all the mind
>   That was in Christ your Head.

In 1951 the opening line of stanza 7 was altered to read:

> Soldiers of Christ, lay hold.

DIADEMATA is discussed at No. 183.

411 Onward, Christian Soldiers
Sabine Baring-Gould (1834-1924)

This processional hymn was written in 1864 in six 8-line stanzas by the Church of England clergyman Sabine Baring-Gould. It was written for a children's festival at Horbury Bridge near Sheffield in Yorkshire, and published in *The Church Times* for October 15, 1864.

This stirring hymn has been sung on many important occasions, among them, at the signing of the Atlantic chapter.

Although the military image may not be a popular one today it may provide a corrective to the image of a "gentle Jesus, meek and mild." As Langland wrote in *Piers Plowman,* "This gentle Jesus will *joust.*"

The processional aspect of the hymn is important also. As Routley wrote in *Hymns and the Faith* "to sing it presupposes the conviction that the church is, or ought to be, going somewhere, making headway, claiming conquests in the holy war."

The omitted fourth stanza reads:

> What the saints established
>   That I hold for true,
> What the saints believed
>   That believe I too.
> Long as earth endureth
>   Men that Faith will hold, —
> Kingdoms, nations, empires,
>   In destruction rolled.

The author commented years later that he had written the

song in great haste without intending it for publication. "Whitmonday is a great day for school activities in Yorkshire," he wrote,

> and one Whitmonday it was arranged that our school should join its forces with that of a neighboring village. I wanted the children to sing when marching from one village to another but couldn't think of anything quite suitable, so I sat up at night resolved to write something myself. I am afraid some of the rhymes are faulty. Certainly, nothing has surprised me more than its popularity.

That popularity no doubt was due in part to the stirring tune composed in 1871 by Sir Arthur Seymour Sullivan (1842-1900).

Sabine Baring-Gould was a prolific writer. It is said that at one time the list of books associated with his name in the British Museum exceeded that of any other author.

All Free Methodist-Wesleyan hymnals since 1910 have included this hymn.

ST. GERTRUDE was first published in the *Musical Times* for December, 1871. It was composed for this text for inclusion in *The Hymnary,* 1872, of which Sullivan was the editor. There is no church saint by the name of Gertrude. The tune was composed during a visit to the home of Mrs. Gertrude Clay-Ker-Seymer. As someone facetiously remarked, the composer complimented his hostess and sainted her at the same time.

Although Sullivan's reputation is worldwide because of the operettas he wrote in collaboration with Sir William Gilbert, he himself would have placed the emphasis elsewhere. The late Dr. Ernest Kroeger told me once that Sullivan predicted he would ultimately be best known for having composed this tune.

Note that the soprano melody in measures 1 and 2 becomes the tenor part in measures 5 and 6 and that the tenor part in measures 1 and 2 becomes the soprano part in measures 5 and 6 — an interesting bit of double counterpoint. (See also comments at No. 165.)

The first tune to be associated with this text was ST. ALBANS, adapted from the slow movement of Haydn's *Symphony in D* and included in the 1868 appendix of *Hymns Ancient and Modern.*

412 Christian, Dost Thou See Them?

St. Andrew of Crete (660-732)
Translated by John Mason Neale (1818-1866)
Altered in *The Parish Hymn Book,* 1863

Something of the importance of Dr. Neale to the field of Christian hymnody may be derived from the amount of space in Julian's *Dictionary of Hymnology* devoted to him and his work — nearly twelve columns. This is all the more remarkable in view of his frail health and his position as warden of obscure Sackville College (Almshouse) in East Grinstead where his annual salary was twenty-seven pounds.

Judged from the impact of his voluminous writings and his influence on Christian hymnody, Dr. Neale was a giant in the High Church Movement in England during the nineteenth century.

Dr. Neale was an impressive scholar whose translations from the Latin and the Greek have earned him a prominent place in all modern hymnals. He was also endowed with a sense of humor that allowed him to use his language skills to confound a colleague and friend, John Keble. An anecdote will illustrate. Keble had invited Dr. Neale to assist him and the Bishop of Salisbury with their new hymnal. While working on the project at Hursley Mr. Keble left the room for a few moments. When he returned Neale said, "Why, Keble, I thought you told me that the *Christian Year* was entirely original." Keble protested that it was. "Then how comes this?" and Dr. Neale showed him the Latin of one of Keble's hymns. While Keble had been absent Neale had taken one of the hymns and translated it into Latin.

It was in his translations from the Greek that Dr. Neale made his greatest contribution to hymnody for here he was breaking new ground. With his publication of *Hymns of the Eastern Church,* 1862, the general public soon made favorites of such hymns as "The Day of Resurrection," "Christian, Dost Thou See Them?" "Art Thou Weary?" and "The Day Is Past and Over."

"Christian, Dost Thou See Them?" is found in Neale's *Hymns of the Eastern Church,* 1862, in four 8-line stanzas, under the heading "Stichera for the Second Week of the Great Fast." Since no Greek original for this has been discovered it is likely that the hymn is Dr. Neale's own work rather than a translation. In view of his scrupulous scholarship and personal integrity scholars have been puzzled by this fact. A clue is found in the preface to the third edition of *Hymns of the Eastern Church* in which Neale wrote that "Art Thou Languid?" and two of the other hymns "contain so little from the Greek, that they ought not to have been included in the collection; in any future edition they shall appear as an appendix." This makes the ascription to Andrew of Crete exceedingly dubious.

Andrew, Archbishop of Crete, was a native of Damascus, it is thought, a resident for a time of the monastery at Mar Saba, and then of the island of Crete. He is known to have used hymns as a weapon in combating heresy. He is credited with inventing the Greek Canon, a long liturgical poem made up of nine odes and sung principally at the Office of Lauds. The nine odes were: 1. Song of Moses (Exodus 15), 2. Song of Moses (Deuteronomy 32), 3. Song of Hannah, 4. Song of Habakkuk, 5. Isaiah 26:9-20, 6. Jonah's Prayer, 7. The earlier part of the Prayer of the Three Children, 8. The remainder of the Prayer of the Three Children (Benedicite), and 9. The *Magnificat* and *Benedictus*. In practice the second Ode is generally sung only at Lent.

The most celebrated Canon is the Great Canon in four parts and consisting of 250 stanzas requiring three hours for its performance.

Modern hymnals, particularly those in this country, have revised Neale's text at the following points:

    1:3 How the *troops of Midian*
    1:4 *Prowl and prowl around?*
    2:7 *Smite them by the virtue*
    2:8 *Of the Lenten fast.*

This hymn entered Free Methodist-Wesleyan hymnody in 1910. (See also comments at No. 7.)

ST. ANDREW OF CRETE was composed for this text by John Bacchus Dykes (1823-1876) for the 1868 appendix to the first edition of *Hymns Ancient and Modern*. It makes use of contrasting minor and major sections such as Dykes used also in his tune *Vox Dilecti*.

413 Lead On, O King Eternal
                        Ernest Warburton Shurtleff (1862-1917)

The author of this text was a Congregational minister in California, Massachusetts, and later, in Minnesota. Shurtleff went to Europe in 1905 where he organized the American Church in Frankfort, Germany. Later on he went to Paris where he was in charge of the Students' Atelier Reunions, Academy Vitti. His best-known poem was written as a parting hymn to his classmates at Andover Theological Seminary and printed in his *Hymns of the Faith*, 1887.

Except for one word the hymn is printed without alteration. Originally 2:7 began "But deeds of love, ..."

This hymn entered Free Methodist-Wesleyan hymnody in 1951.

LANCASHIRE was discussed at No. 171.

414 Through the Night of Doubt and Sorrow
Bernhardt Severin Ingemann (1789-1862)
Translated by Sabine Baring-Gould (1834-1924)

The author of this hymn was professor of the Danish Language and Literature in Denmark for forty years. During his lifetime his collected works extended to thirty-four volumes. Of his few hymns translated into English only one has enjoyed wide acceptance. It is "Igjennem Nat og Traengsel," dated 1825, published in 1855, and translated as "Through the Night of Doubt and Sorrow" by Sabine Baring-Gould for the Sunday school at Horbury Bridge where he was curate.

Baring-Gould's translation was printed in *The People's Hymnal*, 1867, and later in improved form in *Hymns Ancient and Modern*, 1875, where it is rendered in eight 4-line stanzas and set to the tune *St. Oswald*.

Ingemann compiled two hymnbooks. The first *Morgonsalmer* appeared in 1822 and the second *Höimessesalmer (High Mass Hymns)* in 1825. It was from this latter collection that Baring-Gould's translation was made.

This hymn entered Free Methodist-Wesleyan hymnody in 1976.

ST. ASAPH is one of two tunes bearing this title. This one was composed in 1872 by William Samuel Bambridge (1842-1923) for this text and published in *Church Hymns and Tunes*, 1874. It was originally called *Thanksgiving* and the reason for changing the name is uncertain.

415 My Soul, Be on Your Guard
George Heath (c. 1745-1822)

This hymn, written by an Independent minister in England, was published in his *Hymns and Poetic Essays Sacred to the Public and Private Worship of the Deity...*, 1781, under the title of "Steadfastness."

It seems that the writer failed to heed his own admonition for he was dismissed from his parish "for cause" and later on became a Unitarian minister.

There have been numerous alterations in the text, most of them at an early date. Originally, these lines read:

1:3 *An host of sins* ...
3:2 *Nor once at ease sit* down
3:3 *Thy arduous work* will not be done
3:4 Till *thou hast got thy* crown
4:1 *Then presevere till death*
4:2 *God will the work applaud*
4:3 *Reveal his love* at *thy last* breath
4:4 *And take to his* abode

This hymn in substantially its present form has been in all Free Methodist hymnals since 1883. In 1883 and 1910 the opening line of stanza four read, "Then persevere till death." In 1976 "thee" and "thou" were replaced with "you" and "your."

LABAN, also called CONFLICT, was composed in 1830 by Lowell Mason (1792-1872) and published in his *Spiritual Songs for Social Worship*, 1832.

416 Fight the Good Fight
John Samuel Bewley Monsell (1811-1875)

The author of this text was born and educated in Ireland and served there and in England as a clergyman in the Anglican Church. His career came to an untimely close when he died as a result of a falling stone from the roof of his church during remodeling. His hymns number about three hundred but not many of them have continued in common use.

This hymn, under the title "Fight of Faith" was published in the author's *Hymns of Love and Praise for the Church's Year*, 1863, but written much earlier. Originally stanza 3 read:

Cast care aside, upon thy Guide
Lean, and his mercy will provide;
Lean, and the trusting soul shall prove
Christ is its life, and Christ is its love.

An analysis of this text will prove rewarding. Note what is said about Christ. Note also the imperatives.

Contrary to some wags it is not a wedding hymn.

This hymn entered Free Methodist-Wesleyan hymnody in 1951.

PENTECOST was composed about 1864 by William Boyd

(1847-1928) as a tune for "Veni Creator" at the request of Sabine Baring-Gould for use at Horbury where he was curate. It was published in *Thirty-two Hymn Tunes, Composed by Members of the University of Oxford,* 1868. It was not until 1874 that the tune became associated with the Monsell text in Sullivan's *Church Hymns.*

The tune has essentially a range of only four notes. Apparently the title was chosen by Boyd, for when he was asked by the *Musical Times* for permission to print a facsimile of the tune, Boyd replied, "With pleasure. It is only four notes! And I will write the heading 'Pen-tecost,' because 'Pen' is the first syllable of my wife's name and she is very fond of the tune."

The association of tune and text has an interesting history which Boyd recounted in the *Musical Times,* XLIX (1908), 786-8:

> One day as I was walking along Regent Street, I felt a slap on my back, and turning round I saw my dear old friend Arthur Sullivan. "My dear Billy," he said, "I've seen a tune of yours which I must have." (He was then editing *Church Hymns.*) "All right," I said, "Send me a cheque and I agree." No copy of the book, much less a proof was sent to me, and when I saw the tune I was horrified to find that Sullivan had assigned it to "Fight the good fight!" We had a regular fisticuffs about it, but judging from the favour with which the tune has been received, I feel that Sullivan was right in so mating words and music.

417 The Son of God Goes Forth to War
Reginald Heber (1783-1826)

This hymn written for St. Stephen's Day was published in the author's posthumous *Hymns written and adapted to the Weekly Church Service of the Year,* 1827, in eight 4-line stanzas. The allusion to St. Stephen's martyrdom in stanza 2 is unmistakable. The collection consists of 570 hymns by Heber, twelve by Milman, and twenty-nine by other writers.

All of Heber's hymns were written during the period when he was Vicar of Hodnet and before his service as Bishop of Calcutta.

Two of the original quatrains have been omitted. They are:

> 6. They met the tyrant's brandished steel
>   The lion's gory mane;
> They bowed their necks, the death to feel:
>   Who follows in their train?
>
> 7. A noble army, men and boys,
>   The matron and the maid,
> Around the Savior's throne rejoice,
>   In robes of light arrayed.

This hymn has been in Free Methodist-Wesleyan hymnals since 1910. In 1910 and 1951 all stanzas were included. (See also comments at No. 38.)

ALL SAINTS NEW was composed by Henry Stephen Cutler (1824-1902) for this text. It was published in *Hymnal with Tunes, Old and New,* 1872, edited by J. Ireland Tucker. The word "new" has been added to the tune title to distinguish it from another tune known as *All Saints.*

Cutler served a number of churches in Boston, New York City, Providence, and Philadelphia as organist and choirmaster. According to Ernest K. Emurian he may have been the first to introduce vestments for American church choirs.

418   Once to Every Man and Nation

James Russell Lowell (1819-1891)
Adapted by William Garrett Horder (1841-1922)

The author of this text was not primarily a hymnwriter although he was a poet of considerable reputation. Harvard professor, U.S. Minister to Spain and to Great Britain, Lowell's influence was widely felt. In 1845 he published a poem, ninety lines in length (eighteen 5-line stanzas) under the title "The Present Crisis." It began with the line "When a deed is done for freedom," and was a protest against what he considered to be an unjust war with Mexico. The poem was printed in the Boston *Courier,* December 11, 1845.

To W. Garrett Horder, the distinguished nineteenth-century British hymnal editor, goes the credit for discovering the hymn possibilities in Lowell's poem. He took sixteen long lines, altered some and rearranged others, and published the result in his *Hymns, Supplemental to Existing Collections,* 1894.

The arrangement is as follows:

Stanza 1 is Lowell's fifth with this line omitted: "Parts the goats upon the left hand, and the sheep upon the right," and line 5 altered by our Hymnal Commission. Originally, "Some great cause, *God's new Messiah,*" leaves the singer confused.

Stanza 2 is Lowell's eleventh with this line omitted, "Doubting in his object spirit, till his son is crucified."

Stanza 3 is made up of the first two lines of Lowell's thirteenth and the first two lines of his eighteenth with "heretics" changed to "martyrs" and "Christ's bleeding feet I track" changed to "Christ, Thy bleeding feet we track."

Stanza 4 consists of the third line of Lowell's sixth and

lines 3-5 of his eighth with lines 3 and 4 reading originally, "Truth forever on the scaffold, wrong forever on the throne."

This is the first Free Methodist-Wesleyan hymnal to include the hymn.

EBENEZER (TON-Y-BOTEL) is discussed at No 378.

419 Am I a Soldier of the Cross?

Isaac Watts (1674-1748)

This hymn in six 4-line stanzas was appended to the third volume of Watts's *Sermons,* published 1721-24, and intended to accompany a sermon on I Corinthians 16:13. It bore the title "Holy Fortitude." Stanzas 5 and 6 were omitted in Spurgeon's *Our Own Hymnbook...,* 1866, a practice followed by a number of hymnal editors.

Originally 5:4 read "and seize it with their eye."

All Free Methodist hymnals have included this hymn, printing all six stanzas.

ARLINGTON, also called ARTAXERXES, was arranged as a hymn tune by Ralph Harrison (1748-1810) and published in his *Sacred Harmony,* Vol. I, 1784. The melody is derived from a theme in the Overture to the opera *Artaxerxes* composed by Thomas Augustine Arne (1710-1778) which was produced in London in 1762.

Although overshadowed by Handel, Arne would likely be considered the foremost native English composer of the eighteenth century. He composed operas and oratorios and was for many years composer for David Garrick at the Drury Lane Theater in London. Later he was composer to all the principal London theaters.

He wrote liturgical music for the Roman Catholic Church of which he was a communicant. Possibly his best-known work is the patriotic song "Rule, Britannia." He is buried in St. Paul's Covent Garden. A memorial plaque is mounted on a wall of the sanctuary.

Harrison was a Unitarian clergyman from 1777 until his death in 1810. He was an educator, author, and composer as well.

420 Sound the Battle Cry
William Fiske Sherwin (1826-1888)

Text and music of this song were written by Sherwin and published in *Bright Jewels,* 1869, which he and Robert Lowry compiled. The *Companion to the Song Book of the Salvation Army* mentions two occasions when this song was used with great effect, one while marching along Nevsky Prospekt in Petrograd (now Leningrad) in 1917 and the other at an International Salvationist Youth Congress in Royal Albert Hall, London, in 1950 when it was sung as the opening song for a worldwide BBC broadcast. (See comments at No. 211 also.)

421 Faith of Our Fathers! Living Still
Frederick William Faber (1814-1863)

This hymn appeared in two forms, one for England in four 6-line stanzas, and the other for Ireland in seven 6-line stanzas, in the author's *Jesus and Mary;* or *Catholic Hymns for Singing and Reading,* 1849. In the preface Faber states that he "has had a double end in view in the composition" of the hymns; "first, to furnish some simple and original hymns for singing; secondly, to provide English Catholics with a hymnbook for reading, in the simplest and least involved metres...."

Later he writes:

> There is scarcely anything which takes so strong a hold upon people as religion in metre, hymns or poems on doctrinal subjects. Every one, who has had experience among the English poor, knows the influence of Wesley's hymns and the *Olney Collection*.... Catholics even are said to be sometimes found poring with a devout and unsuspecting delight over the verses of the Olney hymns, which the author himself can remember acting like a spell upon him for years strong enough to be for long a counter influence to very grave convictions, and even now to come back from time to time unbidden into the mind.

Although Faber became a minister of the Anglican Church after graduating from Oxford, the influence of the Oxford movement and his admiration for John Henry Newman persuaded him to defect to the Roman Catholic Church three years later. Some of his hymns written prior to his defection and some written afterwards, with suitable alterations, have found their way into Protestant hymnals; and most collections contain two or three. Many of Faber's hymns are criticized because of their sentimentality.

Although written with overt political overtones, as Routley aptly points out, this particular hymn "is another example of a hymn of controversy rising above the sound of the battle." *(Hymns and Human Life.)*

Our version of Faber's hymn uses stanzas 1, 2, and 4 of the English version without alteration. Our stanza 4 is a much-altered version of stanza 3. The original reads as follows:

> Faith of our Fathers! Mary's prayers
> Shall win our country back to thee;
> And through the truth that comes from God
> England shall then indeed be free.
> Refrain

This hymn entered Free Methodist-Wesleyan hymnody in 1910 in a three-stanza form. In 1951 the present four-stanza version was used. (See also comments at No. 32.)

ST. CATHERINE is one of two hymn tunes by this name. The more familiar of the two is the one found in Part II of *The Crown of Jesus Music,* 1864, edited by Henri Frederick Hemy (1818-1888). The tune, probably by Hemy, was set to the words beginning "Sweet Saint Catherine, maid most pure," and headed "St. Catherine, Virgin and Martyr."

The hymn arrangement was made by James George Walton (1821-1905) using sixteen measures of the original and adding eight measures of his own and printed in his *Plain Song Music for the Holy Communion Office,* 1874.

St. Catherine, according to Eusebius, was seized by the Emperor Maxentius for "adulterous purposes," during a visit to Alexandria. Because of her "heroic firmness" she preserved chastity but suffered exile and loss of all her property.

422 Hark! The Voice of Love and Mercy
Probably by Jonathan Evans (c. 1748-1809)

The authorship of this hymn cannot be assigned clearly to Jonathan Evans; but Julian, who examined the evidence, favors Evans. Its earliest appearance was in George Burder's *Collection of Hymns from Various Authors, intended as a Supplement to Dr. Watts . . . ,* 1784, in five 6-line stanzas.

In its original form the hymn was intended for Holy Communion or for Good Friday. By omitting the original stanza 4, the hymn is suitable for general use. The omitted stanza reads:

> Happy souls, approach the table,
> Taste the soul-reviving food!

Nothing half so sweet and pleasant
As the Savior's flesh and blood.
"It is finished!"
Christ hath borne the heavy load.

ST. THOMAS (HOLYWOOD) comes from John Francis Wade's *Cantus Diversi*, 1751, the same manuscript which contains *Adeste Fideles*. (See comments at No. 121). In Wade's book ST. THOMAS is set to the Latin hymn "Tantum ergo sacramentum."

In the *Anglican Hymn Book* the harmonization is ascribed as being chiefly by Vincent Novello (1781-1861).

423 May the Mind of Christ, My Saviour
Kate Barclay Wilkinson (1859-1928)

According to the *Anglican Hymn Book*, this text dates from about 1912 and the author's first name is given as "Katie." All the other sources consulted give the name as "Kate." It appears that the publication date is 1925 in *Golden Bells*.

This is the first appearance in a Free Methodist-Wesleyan hymnal.

ST. LEONARDS is the name given to several tunes, all in different meters. This one was composed by A. Cyril Barham-Gould (1891-1953). The date assigned to it is 1925 when it appeared with this text in *Golden Bells*.

424 As Yearns the Deer for Cooling Streams
Psalm 42, paraphrased by Nahum Tate (1652-1715)
and Nicolas Brady (1659-1726)
Adapted by Gaetano Raphael ("Anthony G.") Petti, (b. 1932)

Psalm 42 as rendered by Tate and Brady in their *New Version of the Psalms...*, 1696, was in six 8-line stanzas. The authorized text seems to be the edition published by J. Hodgkin in 1698.

The modernized version used in our hymnal was made by the British hymnwriter and editor Anthony G. Petti and published in the *New Catholic Hymnal*, 1971, edited by Petti and Geoffrey Laycock.

The *New Version* was a distinct improvement over the so-called *Old Version* of Sternhold and Hopkins. A comparison of similar portions of Psalm 42 as rendered in three early versions is instructive:

Like as the hart doth pant and bray the well-springs to obtain;
So doth my soul desire alway with Thee, Lord, to remain.
My soul doth thirst, and would draw near the living God of might;
Oh, when shall I come and appear in presence of his sight?
For I did march in good array with joyful company;
Unto the temple was our way to praise the Lord most high;
My soul, why art thou sad always and fretst thus in my breast?
Trust still in God, for him to praise I hold it ever best.
(John Hopkins in *Old Version*, 1562, lines 1-4 and 9-12).

1. Like as the hart for waterbrooks in thirst doth pant and bray;
    So pants my longing soul, O God, that come to thee I may.

2. My soul for God, the living God, doth thirst; when shall I near
    Unto thy countenance approach, and in God's sight appear?

5. With them into God's house I went, with voice of joy and praise;
    Yea with the multitude that kept the solemn holy days.

6. O why art Thou cast down, my soul? Why in me so dismay'd?
    Trust God, for I shall praise him yet, his count'nance is mine aid.

(*Scottish Psalter*, 1650, stanzas 1, 2, 5, 6)

1. As pants the hart for cooling streams
    When heated in the chase,
   So longs my soul, O God, for Thee,
    And thy refreshing grace.

2. For thee, my God, the living God,
    My thirsty soul doth pine:
   O when I shall behold thy face,
    Thou majesty divine?

6. Why restless, why cast down, my soul?
    Hope still, and thou shalt sing
   The praise of him who is thy God
    Thy health's eternal spring.

Tate And Brady *Doxology:*
   To Father, Son, and Holy Ghost,
    The God whom we adore,
   Be glory, as it was, is now,
    And shall be ever more. Amen.
        (*New Version,* 1698)

Omitted stanzas in the *New Version* are these:

3. Tears are my constant food, while thus
   Insulting foes upbraid,
   "Deluded wretch, where's now thy God?
   And where his promised aid?"

4. I sigh, where'er my musing thoughts
   Those happy days present,
   When I with troops of pious friends
   Thy temple did frequent;

5. When I advanced with songs of praise,
   My solemn vows to pay,
   And led the joyful sacred throng
   That kept the festal day.

7. My soul's cast down, O God, but thinks
   On thee, and Sion still;
   From Jordan's bank, from Hermon's heights,
   And Missar's humbler hill.

8. One trouble calls another on,
   And gath'ring o'er my head,
   Fall spouting down, till round my soul
   A roaring sea is spread.

9. But when thy presence, Lord of life,
   Has once dispelled this storm,
   To thee I'll midnight anthems sing
   And all my vows perform.

10. God of my strength, how long shall I
    Like one forgotten mourn?
    Forlorn, forsaken, and exposed
    To my oppressor's scorn.

11. My heart is pierc'd, as with a sword,
    Whilst thus my foes upbraid,
    "Vain boaster, where is now thy God?
    And where his promised aid?"

The *Tate and Brady* version was introduced into Free Methodist-Wesleyan hymnody in 1951. (See also comments at No. 12.)

SPOHR was not originally written as a setting for this text. That honor goes to ST. ANNE written in 1708. SPOHR was adapted by James Stimpson as a setting for this text from the opening measures of an anthem composed in about 1834 by Louis Spohr (1784-1859) as a part of his oratorio *Calvary*. Spohr's original title was "Das Heiland's letzte Stunden." The anthem from which this tune is derived is for solo and chorus. The solo is sung by Mary to a text beginning, "Though all thy friends prove faithless."

Spohr's oratorio is said to have been performed first at Kassell, Germany, on Good Friday, 1835.

425 Yield Not to Temptation
Horatio Richmond Palmer (1834-1907)
Arranged by Lawrence R. Schoenhals (b. 1912)

This song, both words and music, was written in 1868 and published in *Sabbath School Songs* the same year and in 1874 in the author's *Songs of Love for the Bible*.

Dr. Palmer wrote a number of works on the theory of music. He served as musical editor of hymnbooks and contributed a number of tunes. He is said to have edited more than fifty publications. "Yield Not to Temptation" is probably his best-known song. His musical education was gained in Germany and Italy. For many years he directed the New York City Choral Union. In 1880 the University of Chicago conferred on him the doctor of music degree.

This arrangement of the music appeared first in our 1951 hymnal.

426 Open My Eyes that I May See
Clara H. Scott (1841-1897)

Words and music for this song were written by Clara H. Scott and published by E. A. Hoffman and H. F. Sayles in *Best Hymns No. 2*, 1895.

The tune is also called SCOTT and OPEN MY EYES.

This song was introduced into Free Methodist Wesleyan hymnody in 1951.

427 More About Jesus Would I Know
Eliza Edmunds Hewitt (1851-1920)

The author of this text was an invalid for much of her adult life. Although bedfast she was able to write extensively for Sunday school publications. She collaborated with John R. Sweney in writing a number of gospel songs. Her physical condition improved in the latter part of her life and she was able to be active in Sunday school work.

This song may be dated by the copyright obtained by Sweney

in 1887. It was published in *Glad Hallelujahs,* 1887, compiled by W. J. Kirkpatrick and Sweney.

The 1951 hymnal was the first Free Methodist-Wesleyan hymnal to include this song. (see also comments at No. 245.)

SWENEY was composed for this text by John R. Sweney (1837-1899).

428   I Thirsted in the Barren Land of Sin
John W. Peterson (b. 1921)

Words and music were written presumably in about 1950, the year they were copyrighted.

429   He Leadeth Me: O Blessed Thought
Joseph Henry Gilmore (1834-1918)

This hymn was written by a young Baptist minister, son of a New Hampshire governor, and first published in the Boston *Watchman and Reflector,* in 1862.

Young Gilmore, a recent graduate of Brown University and Newton Theological Seminary, was supplying the pulpit of the First Baptist Church in Philadelphia for a couple of Sundays in March, 1862. At the midweek service on March 26, he gave an exposition of Psalm 23. The words "He leadeth me" took hold on him, and later, in the parlor of his host, Deacon Wattson, he scribbled the hymn on a piece of paper and handed it to his wife. Some months later she sent it to the *Watchman and Reflector* where it was printed. Evidently William B. Bradbury noticed it and with modifications wrote the music for the text.

Gilmore did not know his hymn had been set to music until 1865 when he was in Rochester to preach at Second Baptist Church. Thumbing through their hymnal he discovered the hymn printed therein. According to Gilmore's own account, the refrain originally had only two lines. Bradbury added two more lines to the refrain: "His faithful follower I would be, / For by His hand He leadeth me." Bradbury published the hymn in his *Golden Censor: A Musical Offering to the Sabbath Schools of Children's Hosannas to the Son of David,* 1864. The tune was called AUGHTON originally.

Deacon Wattson's home has given way to the office building once occupied by the United Gas Improvement Company. The company on June 1, 1926, placed a bronze plaque on the side of the building, giving a brief account of the writing of "He Leadeth Me." The location is Broad and Arch streets in Philadelphia, but the plaque has been removed.

Gilmore subsequently became professor of English and logic (1868-1918) at Rochester University. He died in Rochester.

Our 1951 hymnal was the first Free Methodist-Wesleyan hymnal to include this hymn.

430 Deeper, Deeper in the Love of Jesus
Charles P. Jones

This song was copyrighted by Jones in 1900. In some songbooks R. E. Winsett is listed as the owner.

431 Talk with Us, Lord, Thyself Reveal
Charles Wesley (1707-1788)

This hymn appears in the Wesleys' *Hymns and Sacred Poems,* 1740, in six 4-line stanzas under the title "On a Journey," and with stanza 1 reading as follows:

> Savior, who ready art to hear,
>   (Readier than I to pray)
> Answer my scarcely utter'd Prayer,
>   And meet me on the way.

Stanza 1 was omitted in John Wesley's *Collection of Hymns for the Use of the People Called Methodists,* 1780, and slight textual alterations were made. This is the form used in our hymnbook except for the omission of stanza 3:

> Here then, my God, vouchsafe to stay,
>   And bid my heart rejoice;
> My bounding heart shall own thy sway,
>   And echo to thy voice.

The stanza beginning "With thee conversing ..." is reminiscent of these lines from Milton's *Paradise Lost,* Book IV; Eve's tribute to Adam:

> With thee conversing, I forget all time,
> All seasons and their change; all please alike.

Some hymnals alter the opening line to read "Speak to us, Lord. ..."

This hymn has been in all Free Methodist hymnals since 1883.

WALDRONS was composed by Charles Edward Miller (b. 1856).

432 Come, Thou My Light that I May See
Hugh Thompson Kerr (1871-1950)

The author of this text was born in Elora, Ontario, Canada, on February 11, 1871. He died on June 27, 1950. He served as pastor of the Shadyside Presbyterian Church in Pittsburgh, Pennsylvania. He was the author of a number of children's story-sermons, *The Gospel in Modern Poetry, The Christian Sacraments,* and others.

OMBERSLEY was discussed at No. 339.

433 Lord Jesus, Think on Me
Bishop Synesius of Cyrene (c. 375-430)
Translated by Allen William Chatfield (1808-1896)

This somewhat quaint hymn is the tenth of a series of ten odes written over a period of years by Synesius, the "eloquent and philosophic" bishop of Ptolemais, now Acre near Haifa. All are printed in the *Anthologia Graeca Carminum Christianorum,* 1871. Synesius was a native of Cyrene. Julian states that his "pedigree extended through seventeen centuries," and in the words of the historian Gibbon, "could not be equalled in the history of mankind." Synesius had not wanted to become bishop but as Gibbon again comments, "The philosophic bishop supported with dignity the character which he had assumed with reluctance."

Chatfield translated the ten odes of Synesius and published them in his *Songs and Hymns of Earliest Greek Christian Poets* ..., 1875. His translation of the tenth ode was in five stanzas originally. In a later edition (1876) he added four more stanzas of four-lines each.

Of his translation of the tenth ode Chatfield claimed to have taken some liberties. He wrote, "It may be considered a paraphrase or amplification, rather than an exact translation of the original."

Our hymnal uses stanzas 2, 3, 4, 5, 6, and 7 of the 1876 expanded version.

This hymn entered Free Methodist-Wesleyan hymnody in 1951.

SOUTHWELL. See comments at No. 149.

434 Our God Is Love, and All His Saints
Attributed to Thomas Cotterill (1779-1823)

This hymn in four 4-line stanzas was traced by John Julian to Thomas Cotterill's *Selection of Psalms and Hymns for Public and Private Use ...*, eighth edition, 1819. It bears the title "For Christian Love." He contends that the hymn was not by Cotterill but later writers attribute it to him.

Cotterill was appointed perpetual curate of St. Paul's in Sheffield. There his considerable interest in hymnody brought him the support and collaboration of James Montgomery. It also brought him into conflict with his ecclesiastical superiors. Nevertheless his influence on English hymnody, particularly the later hymnals, was far-reaching.

This hymn was included in the 1883 and 1910 hymnals. Omitted in 1951, it is restored in 1976. (See also comments at No. 392.)

BALLERMA, written in a pentatonic (5-tone) scale, has been credited to François Hippolyte Barthélémon (1741-1808) as a setting of a poem "Belerma and Durandarte" in a novel entitled *The Monk*, 1795. The arrangement as a hymn tune seems to have been made by Robert Simpson (1790-1832). It was discovered in manuscript form among his papers after his death.

435 What Wondrous Love Is This
American Folk Hymn

This text is attributed by William Hauser, in *The Hesperian Harp*, 1848, to a Methodist minister by the name of Alexander Means. An older text is given in George Pullen Jackson's *Spiritual Folk-Songs of Early America*.

This is the first appearance in a Free Methodist-Wesleyan hymnal.

WONDROUS LOVE is attributed to Christopher, not otherwise identified, in William Walker's *The Southern Harmony*, 1835. The melody is in the Dorian mode.

436 I Have a Song that Jesus Gave Me
Words and Music by Elton Menno Roth (1891-1951)

This song was written in about an hour, according to the author, on a hot afternoon in 1923. Its first printing was in *Campaign Melodies*, 1924.

437 More Love to Thee, O Christ
Elizabeth Payson Prentiss (1818-1878)

This hymn was written about 1856, growing out of intense physical suffering and personal sorrow over the death of the author's two children. It was published first in leaflet form in 1869. In 1873 it was included in Hatfield's *Church Hymn Book*.

According to the author's husband:

> Like most of her hymns, it is simply a prayer put in the form of verse. She wrote it so hastily that the last stanza was left incomplete, one line having been added in pencil when it was printed. She did not show it, not even to her husband, until many years after it was written; and she wondered not a little that, when published, it met with so much favor.

The 1910 hymnal was the first Free Methodist-Wesleyan hymnal to include this hymn. The third stanza was omitted. All four stanzas are included in 1951 and 1976.

MORE LOVE TO THEE was composed by William Howard Doane (1832-1915) for this text and published first in his *Songs of Devotion*, 1870.

438 Saviour, Teach Me, Day by Day
Jane Eliza Leeson (1809-1881)

The author of this children's hymn published several books of hymn poems, most of them for children. This particular hymn was included in her *Hymns and Scenes of Childhood* or *A Sponsor's Gift*, 1842, in four 8-line stanzas. It entered Free Methodist-Wesleyan hymnody in 1951.

Miss Leeson's dates are given variously as (1807-1882), and (1809-1881). Probably the latter dates are correct.

Perhaps her most popular hymn is "Loving Shepherd of Thy sheep," in three 8-line stanzas, but both hymns are rightly regarded as outstanding examples of children's hymnody.

An excerpt in a generally accepted version adopted by *Hymns Ancient and Modern* as early as 1875 reads as follows:

> 1. Loving Shepherd of Thy sheep,
>   Keep Thy lamb, in safety keep.
>   Nothing can Thy power withstand,
>   None can pluck me from Thy hand.
>
> 4. Loving Shepherd, ever near,
>   Teach Thy lamb Thy voice to hear;
>   Suffer not my steps to stray
>   From the straight and narrow way.
>
> 5. Where Thou leadest I would go,
>   Walking in Thy steps below,
>   Till before my Father's throne
>   I shall know as I am known.

POSEN was arranged from George C. Strattner (1650-1705) by Johann Anastasius Freylinghausen (1670-1739).

439   Rejoice, Ye Pure in Heart
Edward Hayes Plumptre (1821-1891)

This processional hymn was written in May, 1865, for the 1865 Peterborough Choral Festival. It was published in the same year, with music by Novello, and without music, in the second edition of the author's *Lazarus, and Other Poems*. Originally there were eleven 4-line stanzas.

1:3 Your *orient banners* wave ... was changed to "festal banner" when the hymn was included in the 1868 Appendix to *Hymns Ancient and Modern*.

Omitted stanzas read:

> 3. Yes onward, onward still,
>   With hymn, and chant, and song,
>   Thro' gate, and porch, and column'd aisle,
>   The hallow'd pathways throng.
>
> 5. Your clear Hosannas raise,
>   And Alleluias loud;
>   Whilst answering echoes upward float,
>   Like wreaths of incense cloud.
>
> 6. With voice as full and strong
>   As ocean's surging praise,
>   Send forth the hymns our fathers loved,
>   The psalms of ancient days.
>
> 7. Yes, on, through life's long path,
>   Still chanting as ye go,

> From youth to age, by night and day,
>   In gladness and in woe.
>
> 9. At last the march shall end,
>   The wearied ones shall rest,
>   The pilgrims find their Father's house,
>   Jerusalem the blest.
>
> 10. Then on, ye pure in heart,
>   Rejoice, give thanks, and sing;
>   Your festal banner wave on high,
>   The Cross of Christ your King.

Plumptre was an influential theologian, preacher, scholar, and author. He held many academic and ecclesiastical appointments. He was a member of the Old Testament Company for the Revision of the Authorized Version of the Bible.

This hymn entered Free Methodist-Wesleyan hymnody in 1951.

MARION was composed in 1883 by Arthur Henry Messiter (1834-1916) for this text and included in his musical edition of the *Hymnal, 1889 (Hymnal with Music As Used in Trinity Church).* The tune was named for the composer's mother.

440 Fairest of Ten Thousand
Oswald Jeffray Smith (b. 1889)

The music for this song was written in 1933. Dr. A. H. Ackley, the composer, sent the manuscript to Dr. Smith asking him to supply the text. Ackley suggested the title "The Song of the Soul Set Free." The completed song was copyrighted in 1938 and has since become a great favorite with choirs and congregations. Dr. Smith regards it as one of his best songs.

THE SONG OF THE SOUL SET FREE was composed by Alfred Henry Ackley (1887-1960). (See comments above.)

441 Peace, Perfect Peace
Edward Henry Bickersteth (1825-1906)

This hymn was written in 1875 by Edward H. Bickersteth, Bishop of Exeter and first printed in *Songs in the House of Pilgrimage,* n.d., a small tract of five Bickersteth hymns.

On a Sunday morning in August, 1875, Bickersteth was listening to a sermon preached by Canon Gibbon, Vicar of

Harrowgate, from the text Isaiah 26:3. He was moved by the preacher's explanation that in the Hebrew the words we translate "perfect peace" were really "peace, peace." That afternoon he visited a relative who was dying and found him considerably depressed and troubled. Drawing on the inspiration of the morning sermon Bickersteth took a sheet of paper and wrote out the hymn and read it to the dying man. The perfection implied in the repetition of the word "peace" in the Hebrew, he expressed in the opening phrase of each stanza "Peace, perfect peace."

The omitted fourth stanza reads:

> Peace, perfect peace, with loved ones far away?
> In Jesus' keeping we are safe and they.

Note that the first line of each of the first five stanzas is in the form of a question. The second line in each case gives the answer. The hymn, thus, may be sung with good effect in responsive fashion.

All Free Methodist-Wesleyan hymnals since 1910 have included this hymn.

PAX TECUM was composed in rudimentary form by George Thomas Caldbeck (1852-1918) and given to Bishop Bickersteth at the time (1877) he was bringing out *The Hymnal Companion*. The music editor of that volume, Dr. Charles Vincent (1852-1934), is responsible for the arrangement and harmonization.

442 There's a Peace in My Heart
Words and music by Anne S. Murphy (d. 1942)

Mrs. Will H. Murphy wrote this song in about 1908. It was copyrighted in that year by J. M. Harris. The usual title by which this gospel song is known has been chosen as the tune title, CONSTANTLY ABIDING.

443 Lord of Our Life
Philip Pusey (1799-1855)
Based on Matthäus Apelles von Löwenstern (1594-1648)

The German original of this hymn opens with the line "Christe, du Beistand deiner Kreuzgemeine." It was published in 1644 in four 4-line stanzas under the title "Sapphic Ode: For Spiritual and Temporal Peace." The Thirty Years' War occurred during the author's lifetime and undoubtedly influenced the writing of the hymn.

Pusey's paraphrase was written in 1834, as he stated to his brother, Dr. Edward B. Pusey, to portray the state of the Church of England "assailed from without, enfeebled and distracted within, but on the eve of a great awakening." (Quoted in Canon Liddon's *Life of Edward Bouverie Pusey*). In five 4-line stanzas it was contributed to A. R. Reinagle's *Psalm and Hymn Tunes*, 1840.

The omitted second stanza reads:

> See round thine ark the hungry billows curling!
> See how thy foes their banners are unfurling!
> Lord, while their darts envenomed they are hurling,
> Thou canst preserve us.

Philip Pusey was a layman, a leading public figure, a distinguished member of the House of Commons. Disraeli praised "his lineage," "his rare accomplishments" and "his fine abilities."

This hymn entered Free Methodist-Wesleyan hymnody in 1951.

FLEMING (INTEGER VITAE). (See comments at No. 397.)

444 When Peace like a River

Horatio Gates Spafford (1828-1888)

The author of this text was an attorney, first in New York State and then in Chicago. In 1873, upon the advice of the family doctor, he scheduled a European trip for his wife and their four daughters. He had expected to accompany the family but last-minute business affairs prevented his going.

In mid-ocean the French steamer *Ville de Havre,* carrying the Spaffords collided with an English sailing vessel, the *Lockearn,* and within a few minutes sank. The Spafford daughters perished but Mrs. Spafford was saved. She and the other survivors were landed at Cardiff in Wales where she cabled her husband, "Saved alone."

It is said that shortly thereafter Mr. Spafford on board another ship near the scene of the tragedy wrote this hymn. Ira D. Sankey records in his *Autobiography* that the song was not written until some three years later. Additional material may be found in the book, *Our Jerusalem* (1950), written by another Spafford daughter, Bertha Spafford Vester.

Dwight L. Moody wrote, "While living in Chicago, Mr. and

Mrs. Spafford became much interested in the Second Coming of Christ, and decided to go to Jerusalem ... and there await the coming of the Lord. Mr. Spafford died not long afterwards." The Spaffords and their friends established the American Colony in Jerusalem.

IT IS WELL was composed for this text by Philip Paul Bliss (1838-1876) and appeared first in *Gospel Hymns No. 2,* 1876, compiled by Ira D. Sankey and Bliss. (See also comments at No. 218.)

445 Coming to Jesus, My Saviour, I Found
Words and music by Haldor Lillenas (1885-1959)

This song was presumably written about 1923, the year it was copyrighted by the composer.
This is the first appearance of this song in a Free Methodist-Wesleyan hymnal.

446 Dear Lord and Father of Mankind
John Greenleaf Whittier (1807-1892)

This hymn is a cento from Whittier's seventeen-stanza poem "The Brewing of Soma," 1872, beginning with stanza 12. Probably the first hymnal editor to use it in a hymnal was W. Garrett Horder in his *Worship Song,* 1884.
Quaker poets like Whittier were not used to congregational singing in their services. Whittier is said to have remarked that "two hundred years of silence had taken all the 'sing' out of the Quakers." Still Quaker writers in their masterful writing of devotional verse instinctively employ that lyrical quality which is so essential in a good hymn.
The two stanzas that precede our hymn give something of the context:

> 10. As in that child-world's early year,
>   Age after age has striven
>   By music, incense, vigils drear,
>   And trance, to bring the skies more near,
>   Or lift men up to heaven!
>
> 11. And yet the past comes round again,
>   And new doth old fulfill;
>   In sensual transports wild as vain

> We brew in many a Christian fane
> The heathen Soma still!

Whittier declares that emotional ecstacy brought about by drinking an intoxicating beverage brings no one closer to God. It simply mistakenly substitutes emotional excitement for a religious experience.

Although Whittier's poems have been successfully adapted as hymns for congregational use he did not regard himself as a hymnwriter. He wrote, "I am really not a hymnwriter, for the good reason that I know nothing of music. Only a few of my pieces were written for singing. A good hymn is the best use to which poetry can be devoted, but I do not claim that I have succeeded in composing one." Most hymnologists would protest that Whittier's assessment of himself was too modest. They would place him in the front rank among nineteenth-century American hymnwriters.

An omitted stanza, following stanza 3, reads:

> With that deep hush subduing all
>   Our words and works that drown
> The tender whisper of Thy call,
> As noiseless let Thy blessing fall,
>   As fell Thy manna down.

Stanza 5 has been altered from Horder's version as follows:

> 5:1 ... *pulses* of desire
> 5:3 ... *its heats expire;*

This hymn entered Free Methodist-Wesleyan hymnody in 1951.

REST was composed by Frederick Charles Maker (1844-1927) for this text and was included first in G. S. Barrett's *Congregational Church Hymnal,* 1887. Maker was born in Bristol, England, and a resident there all his life. He was an organist and music professor. Interestingly he was at one time organist of the Milk Street *Free Methodist* Church. (See also comments at No. 155.)

447 Jesus, Priceless Treasure

Johann Franck (1618-1677)
Translated by Catherine Winkworth (1827-1878)

The German hymn of which this is a translation began "Jesu meine Freude" and it in turn was modeled in all probability after a song in Heinrich Alberti's *Arien,* 1641, which began "Flora meine Freude, meiner seele Weide." It was published first in Johann Crüger's *Praxis Pietatis Melica*, 1653.

At first some of the older Lutherans considered it too intensely emotional to be suitable for congregational use. In a later period Bishop Christopher Wordsworth and others objected to the use of "Jesus, Lover of My Soul" in public worship for a similar reason. The intrinsic merit of the hymn overcame objections and it became immensely popular. Peter the Great ordered it translated into Russian in 1724.

Catherine Winkworth's translation appeared in her *Chorale Book for England,* 1863, and another translation in her *Christian Singers of Germany,* 1869, in six 9-line stanzas. Our three-stanza hymn is taken from the latter source.

This hymn entered Free Methodist-Wesleyan hymnody in 1951.

JESU MEINE FREUDE is the traditional German melody for this text and was printed with it in Crüger's *Praxis*. Johann Sebastian Bach was fond of the melody and incorporated it in several cantatas and in four organ works. The present harmonization is a composite one derived from Bach's Motet, No. 3 (1723) and Cantata No. 81 (1724).

448 There Is a Place of Quiet Rest
Words and Music by Cleland Boyd McAfee (1866-1944)

The author and composer of this hymn was a Presbyterian minister. It was written in 1901 and published by Lorenz Publishing Company in *The Choir Leader* (October, 1903).

It entered Free Methodist-Wesleyan hymnody in 1951.

449 Like a River Glorious
Frances Ridley Havergal (1836-1879)

This hymn was published, text only, in the author's *Loyal Responses,* 1878, in three 8-line stanzas together with refrain. It had been written earlier in November, 1874. (See also comments at No. 294.)

This is the first inclusion in a Free Methodist-Wesleyan hymnal.

WYE VALLEY was composed for this text by the Reverend

James Mountain (1844-1933). It was published in his *Hymns of Consecration and Faith,* 1876, under the title "Perfect Peace."

450 When I Can Read My Title Clear
Isaac Watts (1674-1748)

This hymn appeared first in Watts's *Hymns and Spiritual Songs,* Book II, 1707, in four 4-line stanzas under the title "The Hope of Heaven, Our Support Under Trials on Earth." Through the years a number of textual changes have been made. In *Hymns of Faith and Life* the text has been restored to its original form except for 4:3 which read in the first edition "Nor dares a wave of trouble roll." Later editions altered the line as we have it.

It is interesting to observe, as noted by Josiah Miller in *Singers and Songs,* 1869, that William Cowper refers to the first two lines of stanza 1 in his poem on truth, published in 1782, where he compares the position of Voltaire to that of the humble, but believing housewife, who

> Just knows, and knows no more, her Bible true —
> A truth the brilliant Frenchman never knew:
> And in that charter *reads with sparkling eyes,*
> *Her title to a treasure in the skies.*

All Free Methodist hymnals since 1883 have included this hymn.

(See also comments at No. 6.)

LINGHAM is an example of the style of hymn tune known as a "fuguing tune," popular in the eighteenth century.

451 In the Cross of Christ I Glory
Sir John Bowring (1792-1872)

The theology contained in this hymn has been criticized by some, but when considered in the light of Galatians 6:14, "God forbid that I should glory, save in the cross of our Lord Jesus Christ," the criticism seems unfair. At any rate most hymnals now include it.

Because it was written by a Unitarian, H. A. L. Jefferson said that for a long time "there was a nervous dread of adopting these fine verses, although they express a faith as real as any Evangelical Christian could wish or express." *(Hymns in Christian Worship.)*

It was published in the author's *Hymns,* 1825, in five 4-line stanzas. Since stanza 5 is a repetition of stanza 1 we have omitted it in our hymnal.

The opening lines of this hymn are inscribed on Bowring's tombstone.

All Free Methodist hymnals since 1883 have included the hymn. (See also comments at No. 70.)

RATHBUN was composed in 1849 for this text by Ithamar Conkey (1815-1867). The composer was organist and choir director of the Central Baptist Church, Norwich, Connecticut. The first publication of the tune was in Henry W. Greatorex's *Collection of Psalm and Hymn Tunes,* 1851, where it was set to William A. Muhlenberg's "Savior Who Thy Flock Art Feeding."

The title RATHBUN was given to the tune by Conkey as a compliment to his leading soprano, Mrs. Beriah S. Rathbun.

452 Thou My Everlasting Portion

Fanny Jane Crosby (1820-1915)

This song was written by Fanny Crosby to be sung to music composed by Silas Vail. It was published with the music in *Songs of Grace and Glory for Sunday School,* 1874, compiled by Vail and William F. Sherwin

This is the first Free Methodist-Wesleyan hymnal to include this song.

(See comments at No. 42.)

CLOSE TO THEE was composed by Silas Jones Vail (1818-1884) in 1874 apparently with no text in mind. He took the music to Fanny Crosby and played it for her on the piano. She exclaimed, "That chorus says 'Close to Thee'!" She thereupon wrote the text now associated with the tune. Vail was a successful businessman who wrote and published a number of gospel songs. The tune title comes from the first line of the refrain which has been omitted in our hymnal.

453 Servant of God, Well Done

Charles Wesley (1707-1788)

This hymn was appended to John Wesley's sermon delivered at the funeral of George Whitefield at Whitefield's two chapels in London, the Tabernacle on Tottenham Court Road and at

Moorsfield, November 18, 1770. (Whitefield died on September 30, 1770, in Newburyport, Massachusetts, and is buried in that city.) It was published in *Funeral Hymns,* Third Series, in four 8-line stanzas.

In John Wesley's *Journal* he commented, "In every place I wish to show all possible respect to the memory of that great and good man."

This hymn forms a part of Charles Wesley's *Elegy on the Death of the Reverend George Whitefield.*

James Montgomery also wrote a hymn with the same opening line:

> Servant of God, well done!
>   Rest from thy loved employ;
> The battle fought, the victory won,
>   Enter thy master's joy.

All Free Methodist hymnals since 1883 have included this Wesley hymn but *Hymns of Faith and Life* is the first to use it in its original 8-line form.

DINBYCH is derived from *Llyfr Tonau Cynulleidfaol,* 1870 edition, originally published in 1859, by Dr. Joseph Parry (1841-1903).

454   Must Jesus Bear the Cross Alone?

Thomas Shepherd (1665-1739) and others
Stanza 4 by Charles Beecher (1815-1900)

The history of this hymn is a bit obscure. In various forms it appeared in Henry Ward Beecher's *Plymouth Collection,* 1855; in Thomas Shepherd's *Penetential Cries,* 1693; and in George N. Allen's *Oberlin Social and Sabbath School Hymn Book,* 1844. Allen (1812-1877) was a music professor at Oberlin College.

Stanza 1 is considerably altered from Shepherd's collection where it read as follows:

> Shall Simon bear the Cross alone,
>   And other Saints be free?
> Each saint of Thine shall find his own
>   And there is one for me.

Stanza 2 is said by John Julian to be found in a missionary collection published at Norwich, England, about 1810. Both stanzas 2 and 3 are found in Allen's collection and in slightly altered form in *The Plymouth Collection,* the form generally used today.

Stanza 4 seems to be the work of Charles Beecher, brother of

Henry Ward Beecher. It and two other stanzas were printed in the *Plymouth Collection,* in addition to the three noted earlier.

It is interesting that our 1951 hymnal was the first Free Methodist-Wesleyan hymnal to include it.

MAITLAND, also called *CROSS AND CROWN,* was composed by George Nelson Allen (1812-1877) for this text for the *Oberlin Social and Sabbath School Hymn Book,* 1844, which he edited. Apparently there is no significance to the title.

455 Be Still, My Soul, Before Thy God
Wilson T. Hogue (1852-1920)

This hymn was written by Wilson T. Hogue, Bishop of the Free Methodist Church, President of Greenville College, editor of *The Free Methodist,* and author. The date of its writing has not been determined. It has been a part of Free Methodist-Wesleyan hymnody since 1910.

HESPERUS, also called QUEBEC, was discussed at No. 100.

456 On a Hill Far Away
Words and music by George Bennard (1870-1958)

The author of this song was at one time a Salvation Army officer and later a minister and evangelist in the Methodist Episcopal Church. In his retirement years he lived near Reed City, Michigan, where he died on October 10, 1958.

The circumstances surrounding the writing of "The Old Rugged Cross" in 1913 were described by the author in George W. Sanville's *Forty Gospel Hymn Stories,* 1943 (By permission of The Rodeheaver Co., owner):

> I was praying for a full understanding of the cross, and its plan in Christianity. I read and studied and prayed. I saw Christ and the Cross inseparably. The scene pictured a method, outlined a process, and revealed the consummation of spiritual experience. It was like seeing John 3:16 leave the printed page, take form, and act out the meaning of redemption.... While watching this scene with my mind's eye, the theme of the song came to me, and with it the melody; but only the words of the theme, "The Old Rugged Cross," came. An inner voice seemed to say, "Wait!"

It was not until a couple of weeks later that Bennard felt moved to complete the song. He sent the manuscript to Charles H. Gabriel who returned it with the prophetic statement, "You will hear from this song." And, indeed, its popularity has exceeded that of most gospel songs.

457 My Hope Is in the Lord
Words and music by Norman John Clayton (b. 1903)

This song was written in 1945 and published in that year in the author's *Word of Life Melodies, No. 2*. Clayton was for many years organist for the Word of Life Rallies conducted by Jack Wyrtzen.

This song was introduced in Free Methodist-Wesleyan hymnody in 1951.

WAKEFIELD seems to have been assigned as tune title by the editor of *Hymns for the Living Church*. Clayton's mother's name was Mary Alice Wakefield.

458 As Jacob with Travel Was Weary One Day
English Carol (c. eighteenth century)
Adapted by Gaetano Raphael G. Petti (Anthony G. Petti) (b. 1932)

This song is based on the story recorded in Genesis 28:10-22 in which Jacob dreams of a ladder reaching from earth to heaven. *The Oxford Book of Carols* (1964 ed.) makes the interesting comment that "this is apparently a carol to which new words were fitted under the influence of the Methodist revival...."

This is the first appearance of this carol in a Free Methodist-Wesleyan hymnal.

JACOB'S LADDER is a traditional English melody made familiar by Sir John Stainer in 1871. The arrangement is by Geoffrey Newton Stephen Laycock (b. 1927) associated with Anthony Petti in editing the *New Catholic Hymnal*, London, 1971.

459 Let Saints on Earth in Concert Sing
Charles Wesley (1707-1788)

This is a considerably altered cento from hymn No. 1 in five 8-line stanzas in Wesley's *Funeral Hymns, Second Series*, 1759.

The 1883 *Free Methodist Hymn Book* makes two hymns out of the five stanzas with some rearrangement of lines and alteration of text. The 1910 *Free Methodist Hymnal* also divides the original hymn into two hymns, but with no alterations of the original text. The 1951 Free Methodist-Wesleyan hymnal omits the hymn entirely.

Wesley's hymn opens with these lines:

> Come, let us join our friends above
> > That have obtained the prize,
> And on the eagle-wings of love
> > To joys celestial rise:

Then follows our first printed stanza with the first line altered from the original:

> Let all the saints terrestrial sing.

Our stanzas 2 and 3 are the original stanza 2. Our stanza 4 is derived from the original stanza 3, lines 1-4, which reads:

> Ten thousand to their endless home
> > This solemn moment fly;
> And we are to the margin come,
> > And we expect to die.

Our stanza 5 is an altered version of the original stanza 5, lines 4-8. The original reads:

> O that we now might grasp our Guide!
> O that the word were given!
> Come, Lord of Hosts, the waves divide,
> And land us all in heaven!

Our stanza 5 is found in two contemporary British hymnals, e.g., *The Church Hymnary,* third edition, 1973, and the *Anglican Hymn Book,* 1965, and is very much like the text in the 1883 *Free Methodist Hymn-Book* where it reads:

> Lord Jesus, be our constant guide:
> > And, when the word is given,
> Bid death's cold flood its waves divide,
> > And land us safe in heaven.

John Wesley upon noting Isaac Watts's tribute to Charles Weley's "Wrestling Jacob," remarked, "Oh, what would Dr. Watts have said if he had lived to see my brother's two exquisite *Funeral Hymns,* beginning, 'How happy every child of grace' and 'Come, let us join our friends above' "?

It was this latter hymn that John Wesley and the congregation in Staffordshire were singing at the time Charles died.

Some regard this hymn as Charles's masterpiece. At any rate it has been often quoted.

BELMONT cannot be assigned with certainty to any composer. It seems to have been derived from a melody in William Gardiner's *Sacred Melodies,* 1812, set to the text beginning, "Come hither all ye weary souls." In a later publication Gardiner claimed the composition as his own.

BELMONT in its present form was included in *Psalms and Hymn-Tunes,* 1854, for use in St. Mary's Church, Islington. Of some interest is the fact that the editor of this hymnal was Charles Severn, organist of the church and brother of the Severn who was Keats's friend and who is buried next to Keats in the American Cemetery in Rome.

460   Abide with Me! Fast Falls the Eventide
Henry Francis Lyte (1793-1847)

Leading off from a main street in Nice, France, is an arcade on which is affixed a small sign with an arrow and the words "English Church." The arcade opens up on a churchyard and beyond this a small Anglican chapel. In the center of the churchyard among a number of graves is an unpretentious monument in the form of a cross. On the base is engraved these words, "Abide with me, fast falls the eventide." This marks the grave of Henry Francis Lyte.

Lyte, the beloved Anglican minister at Lower Brixham in Devonshire, England, had gone to southern France because of failing health and died there less than two months after his arrival. His planned destination was Rome, but he got no further than Nice.

The date of the composition of this hymn is in dispute. Some think it was written as early as 1820 and others in the summer of 1847. The latter date seems more probable. Its first publication in America was in Henry Ward Beecher's *Plymouth Collection,* 1855. In England it had been published in 1850 in *Remains of Henry Francis Lyte* and soon became immensely popular. Few hymnals omit it.

It should be noted that this is not an "evening hymn." The opening line refers to life's evening.

In the original there were eight stanzas. Those omitted in our hymnal are 3, 4, and 5:

> 3. Not a brief glance, I beg, a passing word;
>   But as thou dwelst with Thy disciples, Lord, —
>   Familiar, condescending, patient, free, —
>   Come not to sojourn, but abide with me.
>
> 4. Come not in terror as the King of Kings,
>   But kind and good, with healing in Thy wings,

Tears for all woes, a heart for every plea, —
Come, Friend of sinners, and thus bide with me.

5. Thou on my head in early youth didst smile;
And, though rebellious and perverse meanwhile,
Thou has not left me, oft as I left Thee,
On to the close, O Lord, abide with me.

A few alterations have been made through the years, but we have adopted only two:

1:2 The darkness *thickens* . . .
5:2 *Shine* through the gloom . . .

It is widely reported that in 1915, a few hours before she was martyred in Belgium, Nurse Edith Cavell joined with the British chaplain in repeating the hymn.

As a funeral hymn it is not surpassed. It was sung at the funeral services of Field-Marshall Haig (February 3, 1928), Rudyard Kipling (January 23, 1936), King George VI (February 11, 1952). Appropriately, it was sung at the memorial services for Edith Cavell on May 15, 1919.

EVENTIDE by William H. Monk (1823-1889) was composed for this text for the first edition of *Hymns Ancient and Modern,* 1861, of which Monk was musical editor. Lyte had composed a tune for his hymn but it was decidedly inferior to *Eventide.* Undoubtedly this tune has contributed much to the popularity of the hymn.

461 Ten Thousand Times Ten Thousand

Henry Alford (1810-1871)

This hymn was written by the Dean of Canterbury Cathedral as a 'Processional for Saints' Days" and was first published in the magazine *Good Words* (VIII, March, 1867) and later in the same year in the author's *Year of Praise,* 1867, in three 8-line stanzas. A fourth stanza was added in 1870 presumably by Alford, and the four-stanza hymn was sung at his funeral on January 17, 1871.

Although Alford, a noted New Testament scholar, was never privileged to visit the Holy Land, this inscription appears on his tomb, *Diversorium viatoris proficientis Hierosolymam* (the inn of a pilgrim traveling to Jerusalem).

This hymn entered Free Methodist-Wesleyan hymnody in 1910.

ALFORD was composed by John Bacchus Dykes (1823-1876)

for this text for the 1875 edition of *Hymns Ancient and Modern.* There it is in the key of B flat! In our hymnal we have used Dykes's harmonization without alteration but have lowered the pitch to the key of G.

462 For All the Saints

William Walsham How (1823-1897)

Bishop How's enormously popular hymn was first published in Earl Nelson's *Hymn for Saints' Days, and Other Hymns, by a Layman,* 1864, in eleven 3-line stanzas with refrain. It is a commentary on the article in *The Apostles' Creed* which reads, "I believe in the Communion of Saints."

Erik Routley contends that faith is the quality essential to sainthood. Therefore, he believes that the second line of stanza 1 is the most important line in the hymn and that "the rest is background and scenery" *(Hymns and the Faith).*

The omitted stanzas are 3, 4, 5, 9, and 10 which read:

3. For the Apostles' glorious company.
   Who, bearing forth the cross o'er land and sea,
   Shook all the mighty world, we sing to Thee.

4. For the Evangelists, by whose blest word,
   Like fourfold streams, the garden of the Lord
   Is fair and fruitful, be Thy name adored.

5. For Martyrs, who, with rapture-kindled eye,
   Saw the bright crown descending from the sky,
   And died to grasp it, Thee we glorify.

9. The golden evening brightens in the west;
   Soon, soon to faithful warriors comes their rest;
   Sweet is the calm of Paradise the blest.

10. But lo, there breaks a yet more glorious day;
    The Saints triumphant rise in bright array:
    The King of Glory passes on His way.

The form of the text in stanzas 2 and 4 is that found in *Hymns Ancient and Modern.* It is said that Bishop How reluctantly sanctioned these alterations shortly before his death.

The hymn entered Free Methodist-Wesleyan hymnody in 1951.

SINE NOMINE, literally "without a name," was assigned by the composer Ralph Vaughan Williams (1872-1958) apparently as a tongue-in-cheek comment on hymn tune titles in general. It was composed for this text for inclusion in the *English Hymnal,* 1906. The late Canon C. S. Phillips called it a noble tune. Opinions differ. B. L. Manning, in *The Hymns of Wesley and Watts*, spoke of it as "a feeble dance tune." Another (Dr. C. Henry Phillips, *The Singing Church: An Outline of the Music Sung by Choir and People*, 1945) said, "The words have strength in their own right but Vaughan Williams's tune gives them exultation." Present-day congregations seem to agree with this latter assessment. (See also comments at No. 98.)

463 Jesus Christ, My Sure Defense

Luise Henriette von Brandenburg (1627-1667)
Translated by Catherine Winkworth (1827-1878)

The author of the beautiful German original of this hymn "Jesus, meine Zuversicht," is thought to have been Electress of Brandenburg and mother of King Friedrich I of Prussia. The hymn is based on Job 19:25-27 and I Corinthians 15:35 ff. It appeared first in *D. M. Luther's und anderer vornehmen geistreichen und gelehrten Männer Geistliche Lieder und Psalmen . . .*, edited by Christoph Runge in 1653, in ten 6-line stanzas.

The German original has been highly praised as "first rank," as "an acknowledged masterpiece of Christian poetry," and as a "treasure among the hallowed songs of the Evangelical Church."

Miss Winkworth's translation follows the original meter and is in seven 6-line stanzas, omitting stanzas 4, 5, of the original. It is printed in her *Chorale Book for England*, 1863.

The 1951 Free Methodist-Wesleyan Hymnal *(Hymns of the Living Faith)* was the first of our hymnals to include this hymn.

GROSSER GOTT, WIR LOBEN DICH gets its name from the opening line of the German hymn associated with this tune in the *Katholische Gesangbuch*, 1774. In subsequent hymnals the tune went through a number of melodic and rhythmic changes. The form of the melody used here is essentially that found in *Allgemeines Choral-Buch für kirchen, Schulen . . . von Johann Schicht . . .*, 1819.

Another form of the melody with the title *Hursley* is discussed at No. 214.

464 Love Divine, So Great and Wondrous

Frederick A. Blom (1867-1927)
Translated by Nathaniel Carlson (1879-1957)

Nathaniel Carlson was born in Gothenberg, Sweden. He immigrated to the United States and served as a minister in the

Evangelical Free Church. He translated many Swedish songs into English. He produced *Songs of Trust and Triumph* which went through three editions between 1929 and 1932.

This is the first inclusion in a Free Methodist-Wesleyan hymnal.

PEARLY GATES was composed by Elsie Ahlwen (b. 1905) in about 1930, presumably for this text.

465 We Shall See His Lovely Face
Words and Music by Norman John Clayton (b. 1903)

Stanza 1 along with the music was copyrighted in 1943 by Norman J. Clayton. Stanzas 2 and 3 were added two years later. Clayton was for a number of years associated with Jack Wyrtzen in the Word of Life ministry as organist. Later he formed his own music publishing company and still later joined the editorial staff of the Rodeheaver Company.

466 In Heaven Above
Laurentius Laurentii Laurinus (1573-1655)
Revised by John Åstrom (1767-1844)
Translated by William Maccall (1812-1888)

The Swedish hymn "I himmelen, i himmelen" was written in 1620 upon the death of Laurinus's wife and may have been appended to the funeral sermon delivered by a fellow pastor. At any rate, when the sermon was printed three years later, it along with two other poems was included. Originally there were seven stanzas.

The revision by John Åstrom was made for the 1814 edition of Wallin's Swedish *Psalmbok*.

The English translation was made by a Scottish minister, author, and linguist, William Maccall. He translated a number of hymns from the Danish, from the Russian, and from the Swedish. The latter were published in his *Hymns of Sweden Rendered into English*, 1868.

This is the first inclusion in a Free Methodist-Wesleyan hymnal.

HAUGE is a traditional Norwegian melody now generally accepted in this country as the tune for this text.

467 Christ Is Made the Sure Foundation

From the Latin (c. seventh century)
Translated by John Mason Neale (1818-1866)

"Urbs beata Hierusalem, dicta pacis visio," called by Archbishop Trench, "this rugged but fine old hymn," dates probably from the sixth or seventh century. It is based on I Peter 2:5; Revelation 21, and Ephesians 2:20. The earliest extant manuscripts date from the eleventh century.

The Latin hymn is often divided to form two hymns. Neale translated it as one hymn in *Medieval Hymns and Sequences,* 1851, and in revised form and in two parts in *Hymnal Noted,* 1852. Our hymn, with its doxology, begins with stanza 5, "Angularis fundamentum lapis Christus missus est." In its Latin form from earliest times it was used for the dedication of a church. Likewise Neale's translation is appropriate for a similar occasion.

Among the alterations are the following:

2:4 Hear Thy *servants* ...
4:5 *Consubstantial, co-eternal*

This hymn entered Free Methodist-Wesleyan hymnody in 1910.

REGENT SQUARE. (See Comments at No. 119)

468 I Know Not What the Future Hath

John Greenleaf Whittier (1807-1892)

This is a cento from the poem "The Eternal Goodness" (dated 1865) and contained in the author's *Tent on the Beach, and Other Poems,* 1867. The complete poem consisting of twenty-two stanzas begins with these lines:

O friends! With whom my feet have trod
The quiet aisles of prayer.

Our five stanzas are 16, 17, 22, 19, and 20, in that order.

This hymn entered Free Methodist-Wesleyan hymnody in 1910 using a cento beginning with the stanzas:

I bow my forehead to the dust
 I veil mine eyes for shame,
And urge, in trembling self-distrust,
 A prayer without a claim.

> No off'ring of my own I have.
> Nor works my faith to prove:
> I can but give the gifts He gave
> And plead His love for love.

The hymnal of 1951 used the same cento as 1910. (See also comments at No. 226.)

COOLING was composed by Alonzo Judson Abbey (1825-1887) and was first published in *The American Choir*, 1858.

469, 470 God Be with You Till We Meet Again
Jeremiah Eames Rankin (1825-1904)

The author, a New England Congregational minister, wrote this song for use by his own congregation, at that time First Congregational Church of Washington, D.C. He described the circumstances:

> It was written as a Christian good-bye, and first sung in the First Congregational Church of which I was minister for fifteen years. We had Gospel meetings on Sunday night, and our music was intentionally of the popular kind. I wrote the first stanza, and sent it to two gentlemen for music. The music which seemed to me best suited to the words was written by W. G. Tomer, teacher of public schools in New Jersey. ... After receiving the music ... I wrote the other stanzas.

The song was published in the author's *Gospel Bells*, 1880. The Methodists quickly adopted the song and soon it was translated into a number of languages. Its use as a benediction hymn was for many years widespread. It was sung at the interment of the wife of President Rutherford Hayes.

Rankin wrote a number of other hymns but this one became the most popular. After serving a number of pastorates he became president of Howard University.

RANDOLPH was composed by Ralph Vaughan Williams (1872-1958) and included with this text in the *English Hymnal*, 1906.

GOD BE WITH YOU was composed for this text by William G. Tomer (1833-1896). It was revised by Dr. J. W. Bischoff, blind organist in Dr. Rankin's church in Washington. The refrain has been omitted in our hymnal.

471 Saviour, Again to Thy Dear Name
John Ellerton (1826-1893)

This hymn was originally written at Crewe Green in six 4-line stanzas for the Nantwich Choral Association festival of 1866. The author later revised and abridged it for the Appendix to *Hymns Ancient and Modern,* 1868. Still later he collaborated as coeditor with Bishop How and others in producing the S.P.C.K. *Church Hymns,* 1871. Another version of the hymn was included in this hymnal and this is the form we have used in *Hymns of Faith and Life.*

The original (1866) stanzas 4 and 6 read as follows:

4. Grant us Thy peace — the peace Thou didst bestow
   On Thine Apostles in Thine hour of woe;
   The peace Thou broughtest when at eventide
   They saw Thy pierced Hands, Thy wounded Side.

6. Thy peace in life, the balm of every pain
   Thy peace in death, the hope to rise again;
   In that dread hour speak Thou the soul's release
   And call it, Lord, to Thine eternal peace.

A facsimile of the 1871 version in the author's handwriting may be found opposite page 92 in the historical edition of *Hymns Ancient and Modern.* A photograph of the author appears opposite page 56 in the same source.

The practice of singing a hymn at the conclusion of a service of worship can be traced to the Last Supper where Matthew records: "And when they had sung a hymn, they went out into the Mount of Olives."

ELLERS was composed by Edward John Hopkins (1818-1901) for unison singing with a different accompaniment for each stanza for the 1869 edition of the Reverend Robert Brown-Borthwick's *Supplemental Hymn and Tune Book.* It is called originally BENEDICTION.

472 Christ from Whom All Blessing Flow
Charles Wesley (1707-1788)

This hymn, with an opening line reminiscent of Ken's "Praise God, from Whom All Blessings Flow," is part of a six-part hymn of thirty-nine 8-line stanzas on the Communion of Saints. Our hymn is taken from Part IV and uses stanzas 1, 3*a*, 4*a*, and 5*b*. The original is found in Wesley's *Hymns and Sacred Poems,* Part II, 1740.

The *Free Methodist Hymnal,* 1883, included this hymn but it was omitted in 1910 and 1951.

VIENNA, also called RAVENNA and ST. BONIFACE, was composed in 1797 by Justin Heinrich Knecht (1752-1817) and included in the Stuttgart *Voll Ständige Sammlung ... für das neue wirtembergische Landgesangbuch,* 1799, of which he was coeditor with J. F. Christmann.
The harmonization is by Henry Havergal (1793-1870).

473 Built on the Rock
Nicolai Frederik Severin Grundtvig (1783-1872)
Translated by Carl Döving (1867-1937)

This hymn, appearing for the first time in a Free Methodist-Wesleyan hymnal, was written in 1837 by Grundtvig, generally regarded as one of the three greatest Danish hymnwriters. Because of the author's outspokenness and evangelical fervor he was frequently involved in theological controversy and at odds with church authorities. In due time his worth was recognized and in 1861 the honorary title of bishop was conferred on him by King Frederick VII.

In addition to Grundtvig's ecclesiastical and hymnwriting efforts, he exerted such great leadership in the field of education that he has been called "the father of the public school in Scandinavia."

Carl Döving was a native of Norway. As a young man he came to the United States. After college and seminary training he served a number of Norwegian Lutheran congregations. As a member of the committee appointed by three Norwegian synods to produce an English hymnal *The Lutheran Hymnary* (1913), Döving made a number of translations of German and Scandinavian hymns, including this one.

KIRKEN DEN ER ET, a tune in the Dorian mode was composed for this text by Ludwig Mathias Lindeman (1812-1887) and first published in Wilhelm Andreas Wexel's *Christelige Psalmer,* 1840.

474 We Gather Together

Netherland Folk Song
Translated by Theodore Baker (1851-1934)

The anonymous Dutch hymn "Wilt heden nu treden voor God den Heere" is thought to have been written early in the seventeenth century in recognition of the weakening of Spain's political control and the Catholic church's religious domination. Its first publication was in Adrian Valerius's *Neder-landtsch Gedenckclanck*, 1626. An American edition was published by William Rohlfing and Sons, 1895.

The English translation was included in Coenraad V. Bos's *Dutch Folk-songs*, 1917, but apparently made in 1894.

KREMSER is named for Edward Kremser (1834-1914), director of the Vienna Männergesangverein, who published *Sechs Altniederländische Volkslieder*, 1877, all taken from Valerius's book. One of the six tunes is *Kremser*, arranged for male chorus and orchestra.

475 How Lovely Are Thy Dwellings Fair
Paraphrase of Psalm 84 by John Milton (1608-1674)

Milton's literary fame rests on his excellence in forms other than hymns. In all, he produced nineteen psalm paraphrases, only two of which have been widely used, this one and "Let Us with a Gladsome Mind" (Psalm 136). Milton's paraphrases of Psalms 80 to 88 were made in 1648 directly from the Hebrew. He attempted to make them as literal as possible, printing the Hebrew words in the margin, and every word not in the original he printed in italics.

During the latter part of his life Milton lived near Bunhill Fields in London. He is buried in the Church of St. Giles, Cripplegate.

Psalm 84 is in twelve stanzas of irregular length of which we print 1, 4, 5, 7, and 12. Stanzas 4 and 5 are of two lines each and are combined as stanza 2 in our hymnal.

The italicized words and phrases in Milton's original paraphrase are the following:

    1:3 ... *pleasant* ...
    1:4 *Where thou dost dwell so near!*
    3:2 *With joy and gladsome cheer,*
    3:3 *Till* ... *our* ... *at length*
    4:1 ... *God* ... *that reign'st on high,*
    4:2 ... *truly* ...
    4:3 ... *only* ...

The omitted stanzas are remarkably literal translations:

2. My soul doth long and almost die
     Thy courts, O Lord, to see;
   My heart and flesh aloud do cry,
     O living God, for thee.

3. There even the sparrow, *freed from wrong,*
     Hath found a house of *rest;*
   The swallow there, to lay her young,
     Hath built her *brooding* nest;
   Even *by* thy alters, Lord of Hosts,
     They find their safe abode;
   And home they fly from round the coasts
     Toward thee, my King, my God.

6. They pass through Baca's *thirsty* vale,
     That dry and barren ground,
   As through a fruitful watery dale
     Where springs and showers abound.

8. Lord God of Hosts, hear *now* my prayer,
     O Jacob's God, give ear:

9. Thou, God, our shield, look on the face
     Of thy anointed *dear.*

10. For one day in thy courts *to be*
      Is better, *and more blest,*
    Than *in the joys of vanity*
      A thousand days *at best.*
    I in the temple of my God
      Had rather keep a door
    Than dwell in tents *and rich abode*
      With sin *for evermore.*

11. For God, the Lord, both sun and shield,
      Gives grace and glory *bright;*
    No good from them shall be withheld
      Whose ways are just and right.

This is the first inclusion in a Free Methodist-Wesleyan hymnal.

BISHOPTHORPE was composed about 1786 and usually credited to Jeremiah Clark (c. 1670-1707) and first published in *Select Portions of the Psalms of David for the Use of Parish-Churches.* ... The first edition is undated. The second edition is dated 1786. According to *Hymns Ancient and Modern* the musical contents of the two editions are the same. Thus the tune may date somewhat earlier than 1786.

476 I Love Thy Kingdom, Lord
Timothy Dwight (1752-1817)

This hymn in eight 4-line stanzas is found in *The Psalms of David ... By I. Watts, D.D. A New Edition in which the Psalms omitted by Dr. Watts are versified, local passages are altered, and a number of Psalms are versified anew.... By Timothy Dwight ..., 1800.* It is taken from Dwight's third version of Psalm 137 and was written while he was president of Yale College. Stanzas included in *Hymns of Faith and Life* are 1, 2, 5, 6, and 8.

The omitted stanzas read:

3. If e'er to bless Thy sons
   My voice or hands deny,
   These hands let useful skill forsake,
   This voice in silence die.

4. Should I with scoffers join
   Her altars to abuse?
   No! Better far my tongue were dumb
   My hand its skill should lose.

7. Jesus, Thou Friend Divine,
   Our Savior and our King,
   Thy hand from every snare and foe
   Shall great deliverance bring.

All Free Methodist hymnals since 1883 have included this hymn.

Dr. J. Edwin Orr has pointed out the significance of revival movements on college campuses as a part of the general Evangelical Awakenings of 1790-1830. Timothy Dwight, grandson of Jonathan Edwards, ascended to the presidency of Yale at a most strategic time. His chapel messages and especially his baccalaureate address of 1796 were used by the Holy Spirit in bringing about social and religious changes of major proportions. It is said that during the year 1802 alone one third of the Yale students made a profession of faith. At the same time, under Dwight's leadership, academic standards were significantly raised, proof that piety and learning need not be mortal enemies.

ST. THOMAS. (See comments at No. 20.)

477 We Are One in the Spirit
Words and music by Peter Scholtes (b. 1938)

This song was written, presumably, about 1966, the year it was copyrighted.

478 In Christ There Is No East or West
John Oxenham (William Arthur Dunkerley) (1852-1941)

The author of this hymn, William Arthur Dunkerley, wrote under the name John Oxenham. The circumstances surrounding the writing of the hymn are given by the author as follows:

> The hymn was written as part of "The Pageant of Darkness and Light," which proved the chief attraction at the London Missionary Society's exhibition, 'The Orient in London," in 1908. I was asked to do the book, [and] Harris L. McCunn set it all to charming music. Hugh Moss staged it.... The four sections of the pageant were North America, Africa, the South Seas, and India. "No East or West" was in the latter.

The hymn was first published in the author's *Bees in Amber*, 1913. The first American hymnal to include it seems to have been *Hymns of the Living Age*, 1923, compiled by H. Augustine Smith, where it is set to the tune *St. Peter*. It entered Free Methodist-Wesleyan hymnody in 1951.

It is a prophetic hymn. As Erik Routley in *Hymns and Human Life* says, "If it bypasses all the problems and ignores all the difficulties, it is none the less a hymn of good hope and sound aspiration." And Albert E. Bailey adds, "Let us continue to sing this hymn. It may sting us into repentance and action." *(The Gospel in Hymns)*

ST. PETER (See comments at No. 143.)

479 Blest Be the Tie That Binds
John Fawcett (1740-1817)

The author of this hymn was originally a Methodist although he was converted at age sixteen under the ministry of George Whitefield. He later became a Baptist and was ordained as a Baptist minister.

An honorary doctor of divinity degree was conferred on Fawcett in 1811 by Brown University.

Dr. Fawcett seems to have been greatly beloved by his congregation. This hymn, published in the author's *Hymns adapted to the circumstances of Public Worship and Private Devotion*, 1782, may have been written in 1772 when his parishioners with "love and tears" prevailed on him to stay rather than bow to the "attractions of a London pulpit."

This hymn under the title of "Brotherly Love" had six 4-line stanzas originally but it is usually abridged. The omitted sixth stanza reads:

> From sorrow, toil, and pain,
>   And sin we shall be free
> An perfect love and friendship reign
>   Through all eternity.

DENNIS (See comments at No. 66.)

480 Rescue the Perishing
Fanny Jane Crosby (1820-1915)

This song was published in Doane's *Songs of Devotion for Christian Associations,* 1870, under the heading "Home Missions." According to the author it was written in 1869, out of her experiences in New York mission work. The subject "Rescue the Perishing" had been supplied by Mr. Doane a few days before the inspiration to write the song came to Fanny Crosby. It is based on Luke 14:23.

This song was printed in the 1883 Free Methodist Hymnal in the section headed "Social Worship," just thirteen years after the song's first publication. It was omitted in 1910 and restored in 1951.

RESCUE was composed by William Howard Doane (1832-1915) for this text.

481 We Have Heard the Joyful Sound
Priscilla Jane Owens (1829-1907)

This text was written for a Sunday school mission anniversary in Baltimore where Miss Owens was a public schoolteacher. She was for fifty years deeply interested in Sunday school work and wrote a number of hymns for children's services. The words of this song were originally sung to the tune of the chorus "Vive le Roi" in Meyerbeer's opera *Les Huguenots.*

JESUS SAVES was composed for this text by William J. Kirkpatrick (1838-1921) and published in *Songs of Redeeming Love,* 1882, edited by Sweney, McCabe, O'Kane, and Kirkpatrick

482 To Worship, Work, and Witness
Henry Lyle Lambdin (b. 1892)

This contemporary hymn was published in *The Mission of The Church,* 1969, by the Hymn Society of America. The author is a native of Tennessee. Educated at Carson-Newman, New York University, and Drew University, he served a number of Methodist churches in New York and New Jersey as pastor and was a district superintendent for six years.

Dr. Lambdin became Professor of Homiletics in The School of Theology of Drew University in 1951 and served until his retirement in 1963. He was a member of the Committee on New Hymns for *The Methodist Hymnal* of 1932.

WEBB was discussed at No. 409.

483 We've a Story to Tell to the Nations
Words and music by Henry Ernest Nichol (Colin Stern) (1862-1926)

The words and music of this hymn were written and published by the author in 1896. Many of his songs with original tunes were published in leaflet form under the pseudonym of "Colin Stern" derived from the letters in his last and middle names respectively.

This hymn entered Free Methodist-Wesleyan hymnody in 1951.

484 So Send I You
E. Margaret Clarkson (b. 1915)

This song was written in about 1937 when the author was twenty-two years of age. It was published in a magazine two years later. Miss Clarkson wrote another version of the hymn in 1963.

TORONTO is assigned as the tune name because Miss Clarkson is a resident of that city. It was composed for this text by John W. Peterson (b. 1921) and first published, according to the composer, in *Melody-Aire Low Voice Songs,* 1954. Peterson was born near Lindsborg, Kansas. During World War II he was a military pilot serving in the China-Burma theater. After the war he graduated from Moody Bible Institute and from the American Conservatory of Music. His many gospel songs and cantatas have made him well known in church circles everywhere.

485 The Whole Wide World for Jesus
J. Dempster Hammond

This hymn which has appeared in all Free Methodist-Wesleyan hymnals since 1910 was probably written about 1880, the year it was copyrighted by John J. Hood.

Nothing is known about the author except that he evidently was a minister.

THE WHOLE WIDE WORLD was composed by William James Kirkpatrick (1838-1921) presumably about 1880. In early hymnbooks Kirkpatrick is named as the owner of the copyright. One early songbook *(The Finest of The Wheat,* 1890) gives the copyright date as 1885.

486 Forth in Thy Name, O Lord, I Go
Charles Wesley (1707-1788)

This hymn is taken from Wesley's *Hymns and Sacred Poems, Vol. I, Pt. 2,* 1749, in the section entitled "Hymns for Believers." This particular hymn carries the added phrase "Before Work." It is in six 4-line stanzas. Of these we have chosen stanzas 1, 2, 5, and 6.

The omitted stanzas read:

> 3. Preserve me from my calling's snare,
>   And hide my simple heart above,
> Above the thorns of choking care,
>   The gilded baits of worldly love.
>
> 4. Thee may I set at my right hand,
>   Whose eyes mine inmost substance see,
> And labour on at Thy command,
>   And offer all my works to Thee.

John Wesley omitted stanza 3 in the "Large Hymnbook" of 1780.

Originally 2:4 read "And prove thine acceptable will." It was altered in the *Leeds Hymn Book,* 1853, to read "And prove Thy good and perfect will," a rendering we have adopted.

Faithfulness in the pursuit of daily tasks is the theme of this fine hymn.

It was included in the first Free Methodist hymnal (1883); omitted in 1910 and 1951; and now restored in 1976.

KEBLE was composed by John Bacchus Dykes (1823-1876) for the John Keble hymn "Sun of My Soul," hence the title. It was written for inclusion in the 1875 edition of *Hymns Ancient and Modern.*

487 The Vision of a Dying World
Ann Ortlund (b. 1923)

This hymn won first prize in the contest to secure a theme hymn for the World Congress on Evangelism in Berlin in 1966. It was printed in the July, 1966, issue of *Christianity Today,* under the title "Macedonia."

ALL SAINTS NEW (See comments at No. 417.)

488 Heralds of Christ
Laura Sherer Copenhaver (1868-1940)

The author of this hymn, a gifted lecturer and educator in the United Lutheran Church, wrote it in 1894 when she was prevented from keeping a speaking engagement because of illness. She tells the story of the writing of this missionary hymn in these words:

> In writing "Heralds of Christ" I was moved with a sense of unity with all the builders of the King's highway in other lands and ages. Missionaries and ministers were frequent guests at the college, and the missionaries were especially interesting to me. Romance hung about them. (Quoted in E. E. Ryden, *The Story of Christian Hymnody)*

The college referred to is Marion College, Marion, Virginia, where Mrs. Copenhaver served as professor of English literature.

The omitted third stanza reads:

> Where once the crooked trail in darkness wound
> Let marching feet and joyous song resound;
> Where burn the funeral pyres, and censers swing,
> Make straight, make straight the highway of the King.

Ernest K. Emurian calls "Heralds of Christ" the "finest missionary hymn of the twentieth century." *(Famous Stories of Inspiring Hymns)*

This hymn entered Free Methodist hymnody in 1951. Interestingly enough, it was not included in the hymnody of the author's church until its appearance in *Service Book and Hymnal,* 1958.

NATIONAL HYMN *(See comments at No. 24.)*

489   O Master of the Waking World
Frank Mason North (1850-1935)

This hymn by Methodist hymnwriter Frank Mason North was written in 1927 in five 6-line stanzas and published in *The Church School Journal,* January, 1928. Dr. North's own account of its writing is given in the Methodist *Companion to the Hymnal:*

> In 1927 Dr. Henry H. Meyer was moved to give emphasis to World Service in the first issue of *The Church School Journal* for 1928. He asked me to write a hymn. My unrelenting interest in the Missionary Movement refused to let me excuse myself. I was in constant touch with men and women who were giving their lives to the work of missions, — who was I, that I should not at least try to put into verse what was in their hearts, and mine, and, if the verse could be sung, so much the better.... This hymn was the result.

The omitted second stanza reads:

> On every side the walls are down,
>   The gates swing wide in every land,
> The restless tribes and races feel
>   The pressure of Thy pierced hand;
> Thy way is in the sea and air,
> Thy world is open everywhere.

Dr. North was a native of New York. From 1892-1912 he was secretary of the New York City Missionary Society. He became corresponding secretary of the Methodist Board of Foreign Missions in 1912 and served until 1924.

Hymns of Faith and Life is the first Free Methodist-Wesleyan hymnal to include this hymn.

MELITA *(See comments at No. 393.)*

490   Christ Is the World's True Light
George Wallace Briggs (1875-1959)

The author of this hymn was a gifted Anglican clergyman, poet, and musician. He was Canon and Vice-dean of Worcester Cathedral. The title given to it by Briggs was "The Light of The World." The first publication to include it was *Songs of Praise,* 1931, a book that included sixteen hymns and seven hymn tunes by Briggs, an unusual representation of works by a contemporary writer.

This is the first appearance in a Free Methodist-Wesleyan hymnal.

O GOTT, DU FROMMER GOTT, also called DARMSTDAT and WAS FRAG ICH NACH DER WELT, was probably composed by Ahasuerus Fritsch (1629-1701) and was published in the composer's *Himmels-Lust und Welt-Unlust,* second edition, 1679. The harmonization is by Johann Sebastian Bach (1685-1750) in his *Cantata No. 64,* 1723.

491 Make Us, O God, a Church that Shares
H. Victor Kane

This contemporary hymn by H. Victor Kane of Binghamton, New York, was published in 1971 by The Hymn Society of America.

Thi is the first appearance in a Free Methodist-Wesleyan hymnal.

FOREST GREEN is an English folk song, "The Ploughboy's Dream," transcribed by Ralph Vaughan Williams at Forest Green, Surrey, in 1903. He arranged it as a hymn tune and included it in *The English Hymnal,* 1906, of which he was musical editor.

492 Facing a Task Unfinished
Frank Houghton (1894-1972)

This hymn by a veteran British missionary to India was written in 1931, according to the author's widow Dorothy Houghton. She said it was written at the time they were appealing for 200 new missionaries to go to China.

Hymns of Faith and Life is the first Free Methodist-Wesleyan hymnal to include it. It was quoted by Dr. Arthur Climenhaga in the tribute he delivered at the funeral of Dr. Cornelius Haggard, president of Azusa Pacific College, August 21, 1975.

LANGLOFFAN is an old Welsh melody of unknown origin. It is found in Daniel Evans's *Hymnau a Thonaw...,* 1865. The major mode form of this tune is named *Llanfyllin* which appears to have been made for the Canadian *Book of Common Praise,* 1938.

493 O Zion, Haste

Mary Ann Thompson (1834-1923)

The author of this hymn, Mary Ann Faulkner, was born in London, England, but lived most of her life in Philadelphia. There she married John Thompson, librarian of the Free Library of Philadelphia. "O Zion, Haste," her best-known hymn, grew out of an experience in 1868 when one of her children was critically ill with typhoid fever. As she kept her vigil at the bedside she said that the words of Faber's hymn "Hark, Hark, My Soul" came with particular meaning to her. Her missionary hymn follows the same meter. She could not write a satisfactory refrain at first and it was not until three years later that she finished the hymn by writing the refrain which now forms a part of it.

Mrs. Thompson's hymn was published in *The Hymnal Revised and Enlarged...*, 1892, of the Protestant Episcopal Church.

The omitted third stanza reads:

> 'Tis Thine to save from peril of perdition
>   The souls for whom the Lord His life laid down.
> Beware lest slothful to fulfill thy mission,
>   Thou lose one jewel that should deck His crown.

This hymn entered official Free Methodist-Wesleyan hymnody in 1951, although it had appeared in gospel songbooks published by the Free Methodist Church as early as 1923.

TIDINGS was composed in 1875 by James Walch (1837-1901), an English church musician and businessman. He wrote it as a setting for "Hark, Hark, My Soul." It was published in *The Hymnal Companion to the Book of Common Prayer,* second edition, 1877.

494 Through All the World

Bryan Jeffery Leach (b. 1931)

The author of this hymn is now a free-lance speaker and writer. He was born in England where he received his education in private schools and at a seminary affiliated with the University of London. After coming to the United States he finished his seminary education at North Park and served a number of Covenant churches as minister. He was a member of the commission that produced the *Covenant Hymnal.*

"Through All the World" was published in 1970 by The Hymn Society of America. It had been written for a missionary conference held at Calvary Baptist Church in New York City.

CONRAD was composed for this text by Paul Frederick Liljestrand (b. 1931). Since 1972 he has been chairman of the Music Department of Nyack College. The tune was named for the composer's father, Conrad Liljestrand.

495 Christ for the World We Sing
Samuel Wolcott (1813-1886)

The origin of this hymn is interesting. Samuel Wolcott, minister of the Plymouth Congregational Church in Cleveland, Ohio, attended a meeting of the Young Men's Christian Association of Ohio in early February, 1869. Over the pulpit was emblazoned the motto "Christ for the World and the World for Christ." Having served briefly as a missionary to Syria, Wolcott was still filled with missionary zeal. On the way home from the service he wrote this hymn.

The first publication seems to have been in William H. Doane's *Songs of Devotion for Christian Associations,* 1870. It has been in Free Methodist-Wesleyan hymnals since 1910.

MOSCOW (ITALIAN HYMN) (See comments at No. 55.)

496 Lord, Speak to Me, that I May Speak
Frances Ridley Havergal (1836-1879)

This hymn was written April 28, 1872, at Winterdyne, Bewdley, and first printed in leaflet form in the same year. The heading in the original manuscript was "A Worker's Prayer. 'None of us liveth to himself' (Romans XIV. 7)." It was published in the author's *Under the Surface,* 1874.

Routley spoke of Miss Havergal as "a woman of great saintliness, and one gathers that she had the rare and happy gift of being able to influence everybody whom she met for the better without leaving them with a sense of patronage." *(Hymns and Human Life)*

The text of this hymn is described by Bailey as "not

institutional nor social; it is personal, inner, evangelical, evangelistic, saintly." *(The Gospel in Hymns)*

Originally there were seven 4-line stanzas. The omitted stanzas read:

> 2. O lead me, Lord, that I may lead
>   The wandering and the wavering feet;
> O feed me, Lord, that I may feed
>   Thy hungering ones with manna sweet.

> 5. O give thine own sweet rest to me,
>   That I may speak with soothing power
> A word in season, as from Thee,
>   To weary ones in needful hour.

It has been pointed out that this hymn is full of action verbs: speak, lead, feed, strengthen, teach, fill, give, use.

This hymn entered Free Methodist-Wesleyan hymnody in 1910.

CANONBURY is an arrangement from the composition for piano "Nachstucke, Opus 23, No. 4," composed in 1839 by Robert Schumann (1810-1856).

497 O Grant Us Light, that We May Know
Lawrence Tuttiett (1825-1897)

The author of this hymn was an ordained clergyman in the Church of England serving as vicar of Lea Marston, Warwickshire, and then as rector of St. Andrews, Scotland. He was an author of prose works and several collections of poetry.

Originally "Grant Us Light, that We May Know" was included in the author's *Germs of Thought on the Sunday Services,* 1864, in six 4-line stanzas. In W. Garrett Horder's *Congregational Hymn Book,* 1884, it begins "*O* Grant Us, . . ."

The omitted stanzas read:

> 4. O grant us light, in grief and pain,
>   To lift our burdened hearts above,
> And count the very cross a gain,
>   And bless our Father's hidden love.

> 5. O grant us light, that we may trace
>   A pledge of life in seeming death;
> And own the grave a resting-place
>   Nor dread at last to sleep beneath.

Hymns of the Living Faith was the first Free Methodist-Wesleyan hymnal to include this hymn.

CANONBURY (See comments at No. 496.)

498 Creator of the Universe
J. Donald Hughes (b. 1932)

The author of this contemporary hymn is a native of California. The hymn was published in 1955 by The Hymn Society of America under the heading "A Student's Hymn."

NOEL is an English traditional melody adapted and extended by Sir Arthur Sullivan (1842-1900) as a setting for "It Came Upon the Midnight Clear" in his *Church Hymns with Tunes*, 1874. The tune bears some resemblance to that associated with the carol "Dives and Lazarus," in the *Oxford Book of Carols*, No. 57, which begins with this stanza:

> As it fell out upon one day,
> Rich Dives made a feast,
> And he invited all his friends
> And gentry of the best.

499 Our Father in Heaven, Creator of All
Thomas Wistar

No information on the author of this text has been located. The hymn has been included in all Free Methodist-Wesleyan hymnals since 1910.

ALMA MATER also called POLAND was composed by Thomas Koschat (1845-1914). It is often associated with the text "The Lord is my Shepherd."

500 Lord, Who Didst Choose in Galilee
William Watkins Reid (b. 1890)

This hymn was published by The Hymn Society of America in a pamphlet *Ten New Hymns on the Ministry*, 1966. The author is an editor, columnist, and retired public relations executive of the United Methodist Board of Missions.

MELITA (See comments at No. 393.)

501 The Church's One Foundation
Samuel John Stone (1839-1900)

This hymn is one of twelve hymns written by Anglican clergyman Samuel J. Stone, based on the twelve articles of "The Apostles' Creed" and published in his *Lyra Fidelium*, 1866. This particular hymn is a commentary on Article IX: "The holy catholic Church; the communion of saints."

Stone was prompted to write the series of hymns on "The Apostles' Creed" because of the theological controversy that arose over the publication of *The Pentateuch and Book of Joshua, Critically Examined* by Bishop John William Colenso of South Africa. Bishop Robert Gray of Capetown vigorously opposed Colenso's nontraditional method of biblical interpretation and deposed him from office. Stone supported Gray's action.

Matthew Arnold (1822-1888) criticized Bishop Colenso for his "speculative confusion" in his essay *The Function of Criticism*.

Stanza 3 is often ommitted in modern hymnals because it is thought it too closely identified with the Colenso-Gray controversy. We have included it because we believe it has a present-day application.

There are three forms of the hymn: (1) the original in seven 8-line stanzas; (2) the revised form in five 8-line stanzas for the *Appendix* to *Hymns Ancient and Modern*, 1868 (the form used in *Hymns of Faith and Life)*; and (3) a ten-stanza version prepared for processional use in Salisbury Cathedral. Later, this form was sung in 1888 as a processional in Canterbury Cathedral, Westminster Abbey, and St. Paul's Cathedral, when all the bishops of the Lambeth Conference assembled.

All Free Methodist-Wesleyan hymnals since 1910 have included this hymn.

AURELIA, also called GOLDEN, was composed by Samuel Sebastian Wesley, grandson of Charles Wesley, as a setting for "Jerusalem, the Golden." It was printed in Kemble's *Selection of Psalms and Hymns*, 1864, of which Wesley was the musical editor. The name AURELIA is derived from *aurum*, the Latin word for "gold," and is said to have been suggested by Wesley's wife. The Latin original of "Jerusalem the golden" begins "Urbs Sion aurea."

502 Glorious Things of Thee Are Spoken
John Newton (1725-1807)

This hymn was first published in the author's *Olney Hymns*,

Book I, 1779, in five 8-line stanzas. There it is headed "Zion, or the City of God, Isaiah XXXIII: 27, 28," and scripture references are given for several of the lines of the text, e.g.,

    1:1 Psalm 87:3
    1:4 Psalm 132:14
    1:5 Matt. 16:16
    1:7 Isaiah 26:1
    2:2 Psalm 46:4
    3:2 Isaiah 4:5-6

The omitted fourth stanza reads:

> Blest inhabitants of Zion,
>   Wash'd in the Redeemer's blood!
> Jesus, whom their souls rely on,
>   Makes them kings and priests to God: (Rev. 1:6)
> 'Tis his love his people raises
>   Over self to reign as kings
> And as priests, his solemn praises
>   Each for a thank-off'ring brings.

Olney Hymns is arranged in three books: I. On Select Texts of Scripture; II. On Occasional Subjects; and III. On the Progress and Changes of Spiritual Life. There are 348 hymns, sixty-seven of them by William Cowper. These had been sung originally either in the church or at the prayer meetings at the Great House at Olney. (See further comments at No. 143.)

All Free Methodist hymnals since 1883 have included this hymn.

AUSTRIAN HYMN. (See comments at No. 236.)

503 Thou, Whose Purpose Is to Kindle
David Elton Trueblood (b. 1900)

This hymn was written about 1967 and published as a poem in the author's *Incendiary Fellowship,* 1967, where it is entitled "Baptism by Fire."

This is the first inclusion in a Free Methodist-Wesleyan hymnal.

HYFRYDOL. (See comments at No. 97.)

504 The City Is Alive, O God
William Watkins Reid, (b. 1890)

This hymn was written about 1969 and published in *Nine Missions of the Church Hymns,* 1969, by The Hymn Society of America.

This is the first inclusion in a Free Methodist-Wesleyan hymnal.

FOREST GREEN (See comments at No. 491.)

505 Jesus, Thou Divine Companion
Henry Van Dyke (1852-1933)

Dr. Van Dyke, the author of this hymn dignifying honest labor, had a long and distinguished career, serving at various times as a Presbyterian minister, university teacher of English literature, diplomat, Navy chaplain in World War I, and author.

This hymn was written in 1909, based on an earlier poem published in 1898. It was published in *Hymns of the Kingdom of God,* 1910, where it was set to the tune BEECHER.

This is the first inclusion in a Free Methodist-Wesleyan hymnal.

PLEADING SAVIOUR, also called SALTASH, is an old camp meeting tune often sung to a text beginning "Now the Savior stands a-pleading," sometimes attributed to John Leland (1754-1841). The tune with this text may be found in Joshua Leavitt's *Christian Lyre,* 1830. The tune was published later in the *Plymouth Collection,* 1855. The present arrangement is by Ralph Vaughan Williams (1872-1958) for *The English Hymnal,* 1906, of which he was music editor.

506 Where Cross the Crowded Ways of Life
Frank Mason North (1850-1935)

This hymn was written in 1903 and is based on a sermon preached by Dr. North on Matthew 22:9 translated "Go ye therefore into the parting of the highways."

It was written at the suggestion of Caleb T. Winchester, professor of English literature at Wesleyan University and one of the editors of the 1905 *Methodist Hymnal.* Winchester deplored the scarcity of modern missionary hymns and urged Dr. North to help make up for this lack.

Dr. North accepted the challenge and the result was "A Prayer for the Multitudes," published first in *The Christian City* (June, 1903) of which North was the editor, and then in the *Methodist Hymnal,* 1905.

The library of Drew University has a number of full and partial versions of the hymn which give insight into the process of development. The six stanzas printed in our hymnal follow the version in the 1905 *Methodist Hymnal* without alteration except for the omission of stanza 3 which reads:

> 3. From tender childhood's helplessness,
> From woman's grief, man's burdened toil,
> From famished souls, from sorrow's stress,
> Thy heart has never known recoil.

In singing this hymn it is well not to omit any stanzas. Note that stanza 5 is a continuation of stanza 4.

This hymn entered Free Methodist-Wesleyan hymnody in 1951. (See also comments at No. 489.)

GERMANY, also known as GARDINER, FULDA, and WALTON, appeared first in William Gardiner's (1770-1853) *Sacred Melodies. . . ,* Vol. II, 1815. Gardiner attributed the tune to Beethoven, a composer for whom he had the greatest admiration. No clear-cut identification with any composition by Beethoven has ever been established.

507 O God, Thy Summons Still Is Heard
Rolland W. Schloerb (1893-1958)

This hymn entered Free Methodist-Wesleyan hymnody in 1951. It was written in either 1937 or 1938, according to the author's widow, Edith G. Schloerb. Mr. Schloerb graduated from Northwestern College (now North Central College) and from the Evangelical Seminary. He served as a chaplain in World War I. Further education was pursued at Northwestern University, Union Seminary, and the University of Chicago. He was minister of the First Evangelical Church of Naperville, Illinois, for seven years and then served for thirty years as one of the ministers of the Hyde Park Baptist Church (now Hyde Park Union Church) until his sudden death on March 15, 1958.

DALEHURST was composed by Arthur Cottman (1842-1879.)

508 O Holy City, Seen of John
Walter Russell Bowie (1882-1969)

This powerful hymn of social concern was written in 1909 and published in *Hymns of the Kingdom of God,* 1910, edited by Henry Sloane Coffin and A. W. Vernon. The author was a native of Virginia, rector of two Episcopalian churches in Virginia and from 1923-1939, rector of Grace Episcopal Church in New York City. He is said to have declined the bishopric because he felt his work in New York was still unfinished.

Dr. Bowie was a hospital chaplain in France in World War I, a seminary professor, an author, a champion of social righteousness, and a preacher of considerable reputation. He was a member of the committee that prepared the Revised Standard Version of the Bible in 1946.

It was during Bowie's first rectorship in Greenwood, Virginia, that this hymn was written. The imagery of the hymn is taken from Revelation 21-22. There were five stanzas originally. The omitted stanza reads:

> Hark, how from men whose lives are held
>   More cheap than merchandise,
> From women struggling sore for bread,
>   From little children's cries,
> There swells the sobbing human plaint
>   That bids Thy walks arise!

E. E. Ryden *(The Story of Christian Hymnody)* eloquently states:

> This is the Christian challenge to every follower of the humble Servant of Jehovah to emulate Him in service and love, to bring something of the joy and blessedness of heaven into the drab days of cheerless human lives, and to begin to build even here on earth the walls of the City of God.

This is the first inclusion in a Free Methodist-Wesleyan hymnal.

MORNING SONG is called CONSOLATION in Ananias Davisson's *Kentucky Harmony,* 1816, where it is attributed to "Dean." It is headed "Flat Key on A," i.e., Aeolian Mode, and is set to Isaac Watts's *Morning Song,* "Once more, my soul, the rising day salutes thy waking eyes."

An earlier source of the tune is said to be John Wyeth, *A Repository of Sacred Music,* Part II, 1813. Our harmonization was made by C. Winfred Douglas for *The Hymnal,* 1940.

509 Blessed Jesus, Here Are We

Stanza 1 Benjamin Schmolck (1672-1737)
Translated by Charles Winfred Douglas (1867-1944)
Stanzas 2, 3, Alan R. Harley (b. 1941)

This hymn apparently was first published in Benjamin Schmolck's *Heilige Flammen der himmlisch-gesinnten Seele* ... third edition, 1706, in seven 6-line stanzas beginning "Liebster Jesu, wir sind hier deinem Worte nach zu leben," and entitled "Seasonable Reflections of the Sponsors on Their Way with the Child to Baptism."

The entire first stanza reads in German:

> Liebster Jesu, wir sind hier,
>   Deinem Worte nach zu leben;
> Dieses Kindlein kommt zu dir,
>   Weil du den Befehl gegeben:
> Dass man sie zu Christo führe,
> Denn das Himmelreich ist ihre.

Schmolck lived in Silesia, the region between modern Poland and Czechoslovakia. His ministry as a Lutheran pastor was greatly hampered by the effects of the Counter-Reformation and the restrictions imposed by the peace of Westphalia (1648). Schmolck's hymns and spiritual songs numbered more than nine hundred and were greatly loved throughout Germany.

Schmolck's hymn is not to be confused with one having the same opening line and written by Tobias Clausnitzer (1619-1684).

This hymn has been translated a number of times. Our translation for stanza 1 was made by C. Winfred Douglas in 1939. Stanzas 2 and 3 are original and are the work of the Reverend Alan R. Harley, Free Methodist minister now residing in Australia.

Stanza 1 was included in *Hymns of the Living Faith,* 1951. Stanzas 2 and 3 were written in 1971 for *Hymns of Faith and Life.*

DESSAU (LIEBSTER JESU) was composed by Johann Rudolph Ahle (1625-1673) in 1664 and appeared first in his *Neue geistliche auf die Sonntage ... Andachten.* The harmonization is by Johann Sebastian Bach (1685-1750).

510, 511 When I Survey the Wondrous Cross

Isaac Watts (1674-1748)

This is unquestionably the most popular of Watts's many hymns. It was published first in his *Hymns and Spiritual Songs,*

1707, in five 4-line stanzas. There 1:2 read "where the young Prince of Glory dy'd." This was changed in the second edition (1709) as we have printed it.

5:2 read, "That were a present far too small." The alteration to "offering" seems to have been made first in Hugh Stowell's *Selection of Psalms and Hymns Suited to the Services of the Church of England,* 1831. The original fourth stanza was bracketed in the 1709 edition, indicating that it might be omitted. George Whitefield did so in the 1757 *Supplement* to his *Collection of Hymns for Social Worship,* a practice generally followed to this day.

The original stanza 4 read:

> His dying Crimson, like a Robe,
>   Spreads o'er His Body on the Tree;
> Then am I dead to all the Globe,
>   And all the Globe is dead to me.

Watts headed the hymn with these words: "Crucifixion to the World, by the Cross of Christ. Gal. VI. 14."

At the time John Julian edited his famous *Dictionary of Hymnology,* he judged this hymn "in popularity and use" as "one of the four which stand at the head of all hymns in the English language." The others are: "Awake, My Soul, and with the Sun" (Ken), "Hark! the Herald Angels Sing" (C. Wesley), and "Rock of Ages, Cleft for Me" (Toplady).

Matthew Arnold regarded this as the "finest hymn in the English language" and was heard to repeat the third stanza shortly before his sudden death.

Robert Bridges is quoted as saying that "this hymn stands out at the head of the few English hymns which can be held to compare with the best old Latin hymns of the same measure."

In Erik Routley's commentary on this hymn *(Hymns of the Faith),* he mentions the imaginative use of adjectives and the simplicity of style. Others have drawn attention to the fact that the majority of the words are one-syllable words. There are only thirteen two-syllable words and only three three-syllable words: "offering," "sacrifice," and "amazing."

All Free Methodist hymnals since 1883 have included this hymn.

HAMBURG is based on a Gregorian Chant, Tone I, and was written by Lowell Mason in 1824 while he was in Savannah, Georgia. As first sung it was set to the hymn "Sing to the Lord with Joyful Voice," Watts's paraphrase of Psalm 100. It was printed first in the *Boston Handel and Haydn Society Collection of Church Music,* 1825.

ROCKINGHAM OLD, also called ROCKINGHAM, appeared

in its present form first in Dr. Edward E. Miller's *Psalms of David with Tunes,* 1790. Miller (1735-1807) based his hymn on a tune called *Tunbridge* (10.11.10.11.) in a book entitled *A Second Supplement to Psalmody in Miniature, Containing an Addition of new Hymn-tunes, Chiefly used at the Lock Tabernacle, Tottenham Court, Lady Huntingdon's and Mr. Wesley's Chaples, Dissenting Meetings . . . many of which are not in any other collection,* n.d., (probably later than 1783) edited by Aaron Williams (1731-1776).

Miller had a copy of the above book and had made a notation under the tune *Tunbridge,* "would make good long M."

512   In Memory of the Saviour's Love
Thomas Cotterill (1779-1823)
Stanza 2, Anonymous

This is a cento (stanzas 3, 5, and 6) from Cotterill's "Bless'd with the Presence of Their God," published first in six 4-line stanzas in *A Selection of Psalms and Hymns for Public and Private Use,* 1805, sometimes known as the *Uttoxeter Selection* after the editor, Jonathan Stubbs, curate at Uttoxeter. There it was headed "For the Sacrament." Our cento seems to have been used first in Richard Whittingham's *Selection of Psalms and Hymns,* 1835. Originally the first line read "In memory of *His dying* love."

The second stanza has been used in Church of the Brethren hymnals since 1852. "Brethren, We Are" was modified to read "As Brethren All" in the 1964 *Methodist Hymnal,* a change we have adopted also.

This hymn entered Free Methodist-Wesleyan hymnody in three-stanza form in 1951.

ST. PETER (See comments at No. 143.)

513   Alas! And Did My Saviour Bleed?
Isaac Watts (1674-1748)

This hymn was first published in the first edition of Watt's *Hymns and Spiritual Songs,* 1707, in six 4-line stanzas. It bore the title "Godly Sorrow Arising from the Sufferings of Christ." In the enlarged edition of the same work, 1709, stanza 2 was bracketed. Such stanzas, according to the explanation in the preface, "may be left out in singing without disturbing the sense."

The omitted stanza reads:

> Thy Body slain, sweet *Jesus,* thine,
>   And bath'd in its own Blood,
> While the firm mark of Wrath Divine
>   His soul in Anguish flood?

In 1709 and later editions the last two lines of this stanza read:

> While all expos'd to Wrath divine
>   The glorious sufferer stood?

All Free Methodist hymnals since 1883 have printed this hymn, but with occasional alterations. Watts wrote:

> 1:4 For such a worm as I (Also FM 1883, 1910, 1951)

Except for this line, our 1976 hymnal restores Watts's original language.

MARTYRDOM, also called AVON, was discussed at No. 319.

514 Sing, My Tongue, the Glorious Battle

Venantius Honorius C. Fortunatus (c. 535-600)
Translated by John Mason Neale (1818-1866) and others

This is a translation of the Latin hymn beginning 'Pange lingua gloriosi proelium certaminis," regarded by John Julian as "one of the finest of the Latin Medievel Hymns, and perhaps the best of its author."

Neale translated the original ten stanzas plus doxology for his *Medieval Hymns and Sequences,* 1851, as did a number of other poets. *Hymns of Faith and Life* uses stanzas 1, 4, 6, 7, and 11.

According to legend the *Pange lingua* was written in celebration of the reception of a relic of the True Cross, given by Emperor Justin II to Queen Rhadegunda for her convent of Saint Croix at Poitiers on November 19, 569.

In the post-Reformation church, passion hymns have tended to be sombre and full of sorrow. This hymn instead sounds a note of victory.

This is the first appearance in a Free Methodist-Wesleyan hymnal. Note also that our hymnal includes a translation of the Swedish version of *Pange lingua* at No. 181.

ST. THOMAS (HOLYWOOD). (See comments at No. 422.)

515 Let Us Break Bread Together
Traditional Spiritual

This spiritual probably dates from mid-nineteenth century. It was not published until the twentieth century, however.

516 'Twas on That Night
John Morison (1749-1798)
In Scottish *Translations and Paraphrases*, 1781

The Scottish *Translations and Paraphrases* were originally prepared by a committee appointed by the General Assembly of 1742 of the Church of Scotland. Dr. John Morison, parish minister of Canisbay, Caithness, was added on May 26, 1781, to the committee appointed by the General Assembly of 1775 to revise the *Translations and Paraphrases* of 1745. The result was *Translations and Paraphrases in Verse, of Several Passages of Sacred Scripture,* 1781. Morison is credited with seven of the paraphrases in the 1781 collection, including " 'Twas on That Night." It is a version of Matthew 26:26-29 and originally had six 4-line stanzas.

The omitted stanza 6 reads:

> With love to man this cup is fraught,
> Let all partake the sacred draught;
> Through latest ages let it pour
> In memory of My dying hour.

ROCKINGHAM OLD. (See comments at No. 323 and No. 511.)

517 Bread of the World in Mercy Broken
Reginald Heber (1783-1826)

This hymn in two 4-line stanzas by Bishop Heber was published posthumously from his manuscript collection in *Hymns Written and Adapted to the Weekly Church Service of the Year,* 1827, and headed "Before the Sacrament." It was written during his vicarage at Hodnet, Shropshire, 1807-1823.

EUCHARISTIC HYMN was composed in 1868 by John Sebastian Bach Hodges (1830-1915) for this text while he was rector of Grace Episcopal Church in Newark, New Jersey. It was published in his *Book of Common Praise,* 1869.

518 Here, O My Lord, I See Thee Face to Face
Horatius Bonar (1808-1889)

Dr. Bonar wrote this hymn in 1855 at the request of his older brother Dr. John James Bonar, minister of St. Andrew's Free Church, Greenock, Scotland. It was printed first in leaflet form and then in the author's *Hymns of Faith and Hope,* First Series, 1857, under the heading "This Do in Remembrance of Me." There were ten 4-line stanzas originally. We have used stanzas 1, 2, 3, 5, and 7. The omitted stanzas read:

> 4. Too soon we rise. The symbols disappear;
>   The feast, though not the love, is past and gone;
>   The bread and wine remove, but Thou art here;
>   Nearer than ever; still my shield and sun.
>
> 6. I have no wisdom, save in Him who is
>   My wisdom and my teacher, both in one;
>   No wisdom can I lack while Thou art wise,
>   No teaching do I crave, save Thine alone.
>
> 8. I know that deadly evils compass me,
>   Dark perils threaten, yet I would not fear,
>   Nor poorly shrink, nor feebly turn to flee,
>   Thou, O my Christ, art buckler, sword, and spear.
>
> 9. But see, the pillar-cloud is rising now,
>   And moving onward through the desert-night;
>   It beckons, and I follow, for I know
>   It leads me to the heritage of light.
>
> 10. Feast after feast thus comes and passes by;
>   Yet, passing, points to the glad feast above,
>   Giving sweet foretaste of the festal joy,
>   The Lamb's great bridal feast of bliss and love.

TOULON, also called OLD 124TH, is found in the *Genevan Psalter* of 1551 where it is associated with Psalm 124. Although the composer is not given, it is possibly the work of Louis Bourgeois. In the *Old Version* (Sternhold and Hopkins) it was set to the same Psalm, using a 5-line verse in Whittingham's version of the Psalm. The shortened 4-line form of the melody is generally called TOULON.

519 According to Thy Gracious Word
James Montgomery (1771-1854)

This communion hymn was first published in Montgomery's *Christian Psalmist,* 1825, in six 4-line stanzas, under the heading "This Do in Remembrance of Me, Luke 22:19."

The omitted third stanza reads:

> Gethsemane can I forget?
>   Or there Thy conflict see,
> Thine agony and bloody sweat,
>   And not remember Thee?

Montgomery has been discussed elsewhere but it is well to be reminded of his place in Christian hymnody. Routley's assessment is probably correct when he says, "Without any question, on the verdict of posterity, Montgomery was the greatest of Christian lay hymnwriters." Later he writes:

> In doctrine, Montgomery's surviving hymns hold the balance, in their congregational and churchmanlike emphasis, between the cosmic impersonality of Watts and the fiery experience of Wesley. *(Hymns and Human Life)*

All Free Methodist hymnals since 1883 have included this hymn. In 1883 and 1910 all six stanzas were printed.

DUNDEE (FRENCH) (See comments at No. 67.)

520 Thy Law Is Perfect, Lord of Light
James Montgomery (1771-1854)

This paraphrase of Psalm 19 appeared in Montgomery's *Songs of Zion,* 1822. All Free Methodist hymnals since 1883 have included it.

BALLERMA. (See comments at No. 434.)

521 God's Word Is Our Great Heritage
Nicolai Frederik Severin Grundtvig (1783-1872)
Translated by Ole G. Belsheim (1861-1925)

Grundtvig, who was discussed at No. 473, is spoken of as the poet of Whitsuntide. His hymns also reflect a profound belief in the Word of God as the rule and guide for the believer.

This hymn is not found in many contemporary hymnals but is included here for the first time in Free Methodist-Wesleyan hymnody as a strong hymnic affirmation of our high view of Scripture.

EIN' FESTE BURG was discussed at No. 377.

522 O Word of God Incarnate
William Walsham How (1823-1897)

Bishop How's hymn based on Psalm 119:105 was written for and published in the 1867 *Supplement* to *Psalms and Hymns* which he compiled in collaboration with Thomas Baker Morrell. There it was headed "For the commandment is a lamp; and the law is light; and reproofs of instruction are the way of life" (Proverbs 6:23). In all, Bishop How wrote fifty-four hymns, all of them written while he was rector at Whittington, a village on the Welsh border made famous as the probable birthplace of Dick Whittington, Lord Mayor of London. How's tomb and memorial cross are in the churchyard at Whittington.

MUNICH is the work of an unknown composer. Its first appearance in complete form was in the *Neuvermehrtes Gesangbuch,* Meiningen, 1693, where it was set to Johann Heermann's "O Gott, du frommer Gott." Felix Mendelssohn (1809-1847) adapted and harmonized the melody for the chorale "Cast thy burden upon the Lord" in his oratorio *Elijah,* 1846. (See hymn No. 565.)

523 Holy Bible, Book Divine
John Burton, Sr. (1773-1822)

This hymn in four 4-line stanzas first appeared in Burton's *Youth's Monitor in Verse, a Series of Little Tales, Emblems, Poems and Songs,* 1803. In a later publication it was signed "Nottingham — J. B." Burton, a Baptist layman, was a resident of Nottingham until 1813 when he moved to Leicester.

This hymn entered Free Methodist-Wesleyan hymnody in 1951. We have restored the original text in the 1976 hymnal.

ALETTA was composed by William Batchelder Bradbury (1816-1868) for the Toplady hymn beginning "Weary sinners, keep thine eyes on the atoning sacrifice." It was published with this text in *The Jubilee,* 1858.

524 Break Thou the Bread of Life
Stanzas 1 and 4 by Mary Artemisia Lathbury (1841-1913)
Stanzas 2 and 3 by Alexander Groves (1843-1909)

The Chautauqua movement was founded by Dr. John H.

Vincent, later Bishop Vincent, and the first encampment was held on the shores of Lake Chautauqua in upstate New York in the summer of 1877. At this time Dr. Vincent asked his secretary, Mary A. Lathbury, to write a "study song" for the "Chautauqua Literary and Scientific Circle" which could be sung at every session. She quickly produced a two-stanza hymn.

Two additional stanzas were written by Alexander Groves and published in the *Wesleyan Methodist Magazine* (England) September, 1913. We have followed the lead of some British hymnals in inserting Groves's stanzas after stanza 1 of the original hymn.

The hymn entered Free Methodist-Wesleyan hymnody in 1951, although it appeared as early as 1924 in four-stanza form in *Inspirational Songs,* a gospel song collection produced by The Free Methodist Church. (See also comments at No. 211.)

BREAD OF LIFE was composed for this text by William Fiske Sherwin (1826-1888), musical director of the Chautauqua Institution. The first hymnal to include the hymn and tune was *The Calvary Selection of Spiritual Songs,* 1878, edited by Charles S. Robinson and Robert S. MacArthur.

525 Break Forth, O Living Light of God
Frank von Christierson (b. 1900)

This hymn was published by The Hymn Society of America in *Ten New Bible Hymns,* 1952. It was written for the celebration of the Revised Standard Version of the Bible. (See also comments at No. 179.)

ST. STEPHENS. (See comments at No. 32.)

526 O Father, Who at Sundry Times
Alan Reginald Harley (b. 1941)

This original hymn was submitted anonymously by the Reverend Alan R. Harley for publication in *Hymns of Faith and Life.* Dr. Harley is a native of Brighton, England. He became a member of the West Ontario Conference of the Free Methodist Church in 1964 and served a number of churches in that conference.

Dr. Harley has engaged in preaching missions to the Middle East, Australia, Hong Kong, and the United Kingdom.

527 This Is the Day the Lord Hath Made
Isaac Watts (1674-1748)

This is Watts's paraphrase of Psalm 118:24-26 published in his *Psalms of David Imitated in the Language of the New Testament,* 1719, in five 4-line stanzas under the heading "Hosanna; the Lord's Day; or, Christ's Resurrection, and Our Salvation." In a footnote Watts refers to Revelation 1:10 for stanza 1 and Matthew 21:9 for stanza 3. According to Watts "The *word* Hosanna *signifies,* save, we beseech." This footnote was omitted in the second edition.

This hymn entered Free Methodist-Wesleyan hymnody in 1951.

EPWORTH was composed by the gifted Charles Wesley II (1757-1834) eldest son of the hymnwriter Charles Wesley. It is found in Part III of *The Psalmist,* 1838. Young Charles was born in Bristol. After the family moved to London, he and his brother Samuel gave a series of subscription concerts in the Marylebone home of their father. John Wesley in his *Journal* mentions attending one of these.

Young Wesley seems to have been highly regarded by the king, George III, and he played for him at Windsor Castle on many occasions. His father opposed his accepting a public appointment else he might well have become organist at St. George's Windsor. After his father's death when Charles would have welcomed an appointment at St. Paul's Cathedral or Westminster Abbey, his application was greeted by the remark, "We want no Wesleys here." He did serve as organist at some other churches including the Marylebone Parish Church in which churchyard he was buried as was his father before him.

528 This Is the Day of Light
John Ellerton (1826-1893)

This hymn by John Ellerton was written in 1867 and published in Dean Howson's *Selection of Hymns for Special Services and Festivals in Chester Cathedral.*

In Ellerton's *Hymns Original and Translated,* 1888, there is another stanza, now generally omitted:

> 5. This is the day of Bread,
>   The Bread that Thou dost give;
>   For us today Thy feast is spread
>   That hung'ring souls may live.

There is one alteration:

5:1 This is the *first of days*

Canon Ellerton served rather obscure country parishes but his name lives on in his beautiful hymns while the names of many of his more distinguished contemporaries are largely forgotten. H. A. L. Jefferson says that "in editing, revising, and translating he was one of the most potent influences in Anglican hymnody in the nineteenth century." *(Hymns in Christian Worship)*

It is significant that Ellerton refused to protect his hymns by copyright, declaring that if they were "counted worthy to contribute to Christ's praise in the congregation, one ought to feel very thankful and humble."

ST. MICHAEL (OLD 134TH). (See comments at No. 195.)

529 O Perfect Love

Dorothy Blomfield Gurney (1858-1932)
Stanza 4 by John Ellerton (1826-1893)

This hymn for Holy Matrimony was composed in 1883 for Dorothy Blomfield's sister's forthcoming marriage. It was written on a Sunday evening in a quarter of an hour to fit Dykes's hymn tune "Strength and Stay." The author's account of its history was given several years later and is recorded in some detail in John Brownlie's *Hymns and Hymn Writers of the Church Hymnary* and elsewhere.

The family had been singing hymns and had just sung No. 12, "O Strength and Stay," in *Hymns Ancient and Modern* when the author's sister remarked that this was her favorite tune. She wished that "the words were suitable to a wedding." Urged on by her sister, Dorothy took the hymnbook into the library and a few minutes later emerged with the completed hymn. It gained almost immediate popularity in London as a wedding song.

Our stanza 4 is the doxology from John Ellerton's "O Strength and Stay," a paraphrase of the Latin hymn "Rerum Deus tenax vigor," the hymn text referred to above.

Our 1951 hymnal was the first Free Methodist-Wesleyan hymnal to include this hymn.

SANDRINGHAM is the title given to the hymn-tune version of the anthem Sir Joseph Barnby (1838-1896) composed for this text in 1889 for the marriage of the Duke of Fyfe to Princess Louise of Wales. Although Dorothy Blomfield intended her hymn to be sung to Dykes's tune, SANDRINGHAM has become the accepted tune in virtually all hymnals produced in America and Great Britain since text and tune were wedded in John Stainer's *Church Hymnary,* 1898.

530 Be Present at Our Table, Lord

John Cennick (1718-1755)
Stanza 2 altered by Edward Henry Bickersteth (1825-1906)

This metrical grace for giving thanks at mealtime appeared in John Cennick's *Sacred Hymns for the Children of God, In the Days of Their Pilgrimage,* 1741. Stanza 1 was hymn No. 130 and headed "Before Meat." Stanza 2 was hymn No. 131 and headed "After Meat." Originally it read:

> We bless Thee, Lord, for this our Food;
> But more for Jesu's Flesh and Blood;
> The *Manna* to our Spirit's giv'n,
> The Living Bread sent down from Heav'n;
> Praise shall our Grateful Lips employ,
> While Life and Plenty we enjoy;
> Till worthy, we adore Thy Name,
> While banqueting with Christ, the Lamb.

The present version of stanza 2 dates from Bickersteth's *Christian Psalmody, A Collection of Above 700 Psalms, Hymns and Spiritual Songs,* 1833, although the author is unknown. It may date much earlier than this printed version.

All Free Methodist hymnals since 1883 have included this grace.

HEBRON is one of two hymn tunes by this name. This one is by Lowell Mason (1792-1872) and is taken from the Boston *Handel and Haydn Society Collection of Church Music,* 1830, edited by Mason.

531 We Thank You, Lord, for this Our Food

James E. Wilson

This table grace was composed by the conductor of the Greenville College Concert Choir for use by his choir. It was written to fit the tune HERR JESU CHRIST from the *Pensum Sacrum,* c. 1648. The harmonization is that of one of the 371 chorales of Johann Sebastian Bach (1685-1750).

532 The Grace of Life Is Theirs
Frederick Pratt Green (b. 1903)

The author of this hymn is a retired British Methodist clergyman. He turned his attention to hymn writing in 1967 when he was appointed to the committee to prepare a supplement to the British Methodist hymnbook. This book, entitled *Hymns and Songs*, was published in 1969. It contains 104 hymns, canticles, and psalms. Eight are by Green, more than by any other writer.

This hymn under the title "Christian Marriage" is contained in a small volume *26 Hymns* by F. Pratt Green, first published in 1971 by Epworth Press, London.

GOPSAL was written about 1749 by George Frederick Handel. The story of how it came to light is most interesting. In 1826, Samuel Wesley, Charles Wesley's son, was granted permission to review the music manuscript collection in the Fitzwilliam Museum at Cambridge. In the course of his work there, he discovered three hymn tunes written by Handel and in his own handwriting. All three were set to Charles Wesley's hymns, leading Samuel to write to his wife that "my dear father's poetry must have highly delighted Handel...."

The three hymns were: "Sinners, Obey the Gospel-word"; "O Love Divine, How Sweet Thou Art"; and "Rejoice, the Lord Is King." The tune accompanying the latter hymn is the one we now call GOPSAL. Its name derives from what was formerly the residence of Charles Jennens, compiler of the libretto for Handel's *Messiah*.

533 Happy the Home When God Is There
Henry Ware, Jr. (1794-1843)

This hymn was published first in Mrs. Herbert Mayo's *Selection of Hymns and Poetry for the Use of Infant and Juvenile Schools and Families*, third edition, 1846, in four 4-line stanzas, under the title "The Happy Home."

The author of this hymn graduated with honors from Harvard. Subsequently he was licensed to preach by the Boston Unitarian Association and latter became the ordained pastor of the Second Church, Boston. Here he was copastor with Ralph Waldo Emerson. A number of his hymns are rated as excellent and enjoy considerable usage, particularly among American Unitarians.

Originally 3:4 read: "And live but for the skies." In *Hymns of*

Faith and Life we have followed the alteration adopted in the 1935 Methodist hymnal.

All Free Methodist hymnals since 1883 have included this hymn.

ST. AGNES was disussed at No. 101.

534 Like as a Mother Comforteth
William Marion Runyan (1870-1957)

(See Comments at No. 43.)

BEATITUDO was discussed at No. 314.

535 I Sing a Song of the Saints of God
Lesbia Scott (b. 1898)

This song was written for the author's own three children and included in her *Everyday Hymns for Children* with this intention, according to Leonard Ellinwood in *The Hymnal 1940 Companion:*

> ... not for publication, but ... as an expression of the faith we were trying to give the children. Most of them came in response to the children's own demands. "Make a hymn for a picnic," "Make a hymn for a foggy day," and (this one) was meant for use on Saints' days, to impress the fact that sainthood is a living possibility today.

Subsequently the Morehouse-Gorham Company obtained copies of the hymns and published them in 1929.

There are two slight changes in the third stanza.

GRAND ISLE was composed for this text in 1940 by John Henry Hopkins (1861-1945), an Anglican rector in New England. In retirement after 1929 he lived at Grand Isle, Vermont, on Lake Champlain, hence the title of this tune.

536 Lamb of God, I Look to Thee
Charles Wesley (1707-1788)

This is part of a two-part hymn in the Wesleys' *Hymns and Sacred Poems,* 1742. Part I in seven 4-line stanzas begins "Gentle

Jesus, meek and mild." Part II also in seven 4-line stanzas begins "Lamb of God, I look to Thee."

Stanzas included here from Part II are 1, 2, and 7. Our only alteration is in 2:3 where we have substituted "merciful" for "pitiful."

The opening line of Part I was characterized by George Bernard Shaw as a "sniveling travesty," a harsh judgment not shared necessarily by many other critics.

GENTLE JESUS was composed for this text by Martin Fallas Shaw (1875-1958) and published in *Additional Tunes and Settings in Use at St. Mary's, Primrose Hill,* 1915.

537 Jesus Loves Me! This I Know
Anna Bartlett Warner (c. 1820-1915)

The author, who also wrote under the pen name "Amy Lothrop," lived much of her life on Constitution Island in the Hudson River near West Point. She taught a Bible class for many years in the chapel of the United States Military Academy.

This children's song entitled "The Love of Jesus" is included in *Say and Seal,* 1859, a best-selling religious novel written in collaboration with the author's sister Susan. One of the fictional characters, Johnny Fax, is taught the song by his Sunday school teacher just before the lad's death.

Some years later Miss Warner wrote, "For the time being Johnny Fax was so intensely real, so vividly in my heart, that the hymn was written for *him,* as if he had been a living child."

The 1976 hymnal is the first Free Methodist-Wesleyan hymnal to include this song although *Light and Life Songs* No. 2, 1914, included it. There it is described as "The favorite Hymn of China."

JESUS LOVES ME was composed for this text in 1861 by William Batchelder Bradbury (1816-1868) and published in *The Golden Chain.*

538 Tell Me the Stories of Jesus
William Henry Parker (1845-1929)

The author of this hymn composed a number of hymns for Sunday school anniversaries of the Chelsea Street Baptist Church, New Basford, Nottingham. These were generally printed at first on hymn sheets. This one was written in six 8-line stanzas for the anniversary of 1885. Apparently the first hymnal to include it was the *Sunday School Hymnary,* 1905.

It entered Free Methodist-Wesleyan hymnody in 1951. Omitted stanzas read:

> 3. Tell how the sparrow that twitters
>   On yonder tree,
>   And the sweet meadow-side lily
>   May speak to me;
>   Give me their message,
>   For I would hear
>   How Jesus taught us
>   Our Father's care.
>
> 5. Into the city I'd follow
>   The children's band,
>   Waving a branch of the palm tree
>   High in my hand;
>   One of His heralds,
>   Yes, I would sing
>   Loudest hosannas:
>   Jesus is King

STORIES OF JESUS was written in 1903 for this text by Frederic Arthur Challinor (1866-1952) and submitted in a competition sponsored by the National Sunday School Union, London, as a part of its observance of its centennial year. The judge was Sir John Frederick Bridge (1844-1924), organist at Westminster Abbey. When he handed the manuscript to the secretary of the National Sunday School Union he is said to have remarked, "This is the best. A fine hymn, too. In a few years both will be sung all over the kingdom."

539   O Thou Whose Hand Has Brought Us
Frederic William Goadby (1845-1880)

The author of this hymn was a Baptist pastor in England whose untimely death cut short a promising ministry. This hymn in five 8-line stanzas appeared in the *Baptist Hymnal,* 1879, under the heading "Opening of a Place of Worship."

The omitted fifth stanza reads:

> Lord God, our fathers' helper
>   Our joy, and hope, and stay:
> Grant now a gracious earnest
>   Of many a coming day.
> Our yearning hearts Thou knowest;
>   We wait before Thy throne:

O come, and by Thy presence
    Make this new house Thine own.

The alterations are these:

    2:1 For this *new* house . . .
    2:2 Reared *at* Thine . . .
    2:3 . . . generous *bosom*
    4:1 . . . years roll *onward*
    4:5 . . . its *chiefest honour*

This is the first inclusion in a Free Methodist-Wesleyan Hymnal.

ST. THEODULPH was discussed at No. 146.

540 Another Year Is Dawning
Frances Ridley Havergal (1836-1879)

This hymn in six 4-line stanzas was written in about 1874 for a series of ornamental leaflets and cards published by Caswell, according to the author. It was first published in her *Under The Surface*, 1874.

This hymn entered Free Methodist-Wesleyan hymnody in 1910.

ELLACOMBE was discussed at No. 16.

541 Father, Let Me Dedicate
Lawrence Tuttiett (1825-1897)

This New Year's hymn in four 8-line stanzas appeared first in the author's *Germs of Thought on The Sunday Special Services*, 1864.

This is the first appearance in a Free Methodist-Wesleyan hymnal. We have interchanged stanzas 3 and 4, otherwise the text is unchanged from the original. (See further comments at No. 497.)

TOKYO is a tune in the Japanese gagaku mode, composed in 1958 by Isao Koizumi (b. 1907).

542 O Beautiful for Spacious Skies
Katherine Lee Bates (1859-1929)

This patriotic hymn was written in 1893 by Katherine Lee Bates, a professor of English at Wellesley College, after she had journeyed to Pike's Peak in the Colorado Rockies and had visited the Chicago World's Fair. Years later Miss Bates said that her "New England eyes delighted in the wind-waved gold of the vast wheat-fields" and that from Pikes Peak she "gazed in wordless rapture. . . ." The opening lines of the hymn were inspired by these experiences. The patriotic feeling conveyed by the visit to the World's Fair can be sensed in the fourth stanza.

Stanzas 1 and 4 are direct commentaries on the author's experiences on this journey.

Miss Bates wrote the hymn after returning to Colorado Springs but it was not published until 1895 when it was included in *The Congregationalist*. She was not, however, satisfied with the original text and revised it in 1904. A further revision of stanza 3 seems to have been made as early as 1912 by the author. She wrote that it was only "after the lapse of a few years, during which the hymn had run the gauntlet of criticism, I changed the wording of the opening quatrain of the third stanza." In the 1904 version this troublesome quatrain read:

> O beautiful for glorious tale
>   Of liberating strife,
> When valiantly, for man's avail
>   Men lavished precious life!

This hymn entered Free Methodist-Wesleyan hymnody in 1951, although it had been included in the gospel songbook *Inspirational Hymns*, 1924. It is said that Miss Bates had no formal church affiliation. She is buried in Falmouth, Massachusetts. A marker was erected at the gravesite in 1959.

MATERNA was composed in 1882 by Samuel Augustus Ward (1847-1903) for the text "O mother dear, Jerusalem." Someone in 1912 brought text and music together and by so doing lifted a relatively little-known organist, choir director, and businessman from obscurity. Note that except for the fourth measure the bass line of the third score is a repetition of the soprano line of the first score.

543 O Say, Can You See

Francis Scott Key (1779-1843)

This patriotic song was written on September 14, 1814, by Francis Scott Key, a young attorney residing in Georgetown (Washington, D.C.). In brief, the circumstances were these. A physician by the name of William Beanes having earlier provided hospitality to a number of British officers now joined with a group of citizens in seizing some British soldiers who seemed bent on plundering the Maryland countryside.

The British retaliated by capturing Dr. Beanes and imprisoning him on board one of their ships. Key, in response to the entreaty of mutual friends, sailed from Baltimore, accompanied under a flag of truce by a Mr. John S. Skinner, the American commissioner for the exchange of prisoners, to try to effect the release of Beanes. Admiral Sir George Cochrane, Commander-in-chief of the British fleet in American waters, was persuaded to grant their request, but because of the impending attack on Baltimore, insisted that all be detained on board ship.

From their position at anchor they could see plainly the flag of Fort McHenry. Throughout the night of September 13 they could observe the bombardment of the fort. Early on the morning of the fourteenth they noted that the fort's flag was still waving. Key was inspired to sketch out the words of this song on the back of a letter. Whether consciously or unconsciously, he chose the meter of a popular English drinking song "To Anacreon in Heav'n." He finished the poem on the boat taking them to shore and put it in final form in his hotel room in Baltimore that night.

Although the song was widely circulated by means of broadsides, its popularity as a national song was probably not established until the time of the Civil War. It became our official national anthem by an act of Congress on March 3, 1931.

A humorous paraphrase of the song, with a satirical jab at "To Anacreon ...," was published in the *Temperance Annual and Cold Water Magazine* in 1843:

> Oh! who has not seen by the dawn's early light,
>   To his home weakly reeling,
> With eyes and nose most revolting to sight;
>   Yet still in his breast not a throb of shame feeling!
> And the plight he was in — steep'd filth to his chin,
> Gave proof through the night, in the gutter he'd been,
> While the pityable wretch would stagger along,
> To the shame of his friends, 'mid the jeers of the throng.

STAR-SPANGLED BANNER is, as indicated above, the tune of an English drinking song:

> To Anacreon, in Heav'n, where he sat in full glee,
>   A few sons of harmony sent a petition,
> That he their inspirer and patron would be;
>   When this answer arriv'd from the jolly old Grecian —
> "Voice, fiddle, and flute,
> No longer be mute,
> I'll lend you my name and inspire you to boot;
> And besides, I'll instruct you like me to intwine
> The myrtle of Venus with Bacchus's vine."
>
>   (from a 1783 publication)

The composer has not been identified with certainty but is generally believed to have been John Stafford Smith (1750-1836), an eminent English organist, singer, composer, teacher, and music historian.

544 My Country, 'Tis of Thee
Samuel Francis Smith (1808-1895)

The author of this patriotic hymn was a Baptist minister, missionary statesman, linguist, and hymnal editor. While translating some German school songs for Lowell Mason he was attracted to a tune set to some patriotic words. Immediately he was prompted to write a patriotic hymn of his own to fit the tune. In the short space of about half an hour he had written the hymn, now known as "America."

Smith was not aware at the time that the British had already used this tune for their patriotic song "God Save the King." The German hymn that was Smith's inspiration was "Gott segne Sachsenland" by Siegfried August Mahlmann.

The hymn was first sung in Park Street Church, Boston, on July 4, 1831, by a children's choir directed by Lowell Mason. The first collection to include it was Lowell Mason's *Choir, or Union Collection of Church Music,* 1832.

Smith was a classmate of Oliver Wendell Homes at Harvard, graduating in 1829. At the thirtieth class reunion in 1859 Holmes wrote this poem:

> And there's a nice youngster of excellent pith—
> Fate tried to conceal him by naming him Smith;
> But he shouted a song for the brave and the free—
> Just readon his medal, "My Country, of thee!"

Originally there were five stanzas but the author removed the third because of the derogatory reference to British tyranny. It read:

> No more shall tyrants here

> With haughty steps appear,
> And soldier-bands;
> No more shall tyrants tread
> Above the patriot dead —
> No more our blood be shed
> By alien hands.

AMERICA is the work of an anonymous composer. It appeared in the *Thesaurus Musicus* (c. 1744), but is thought to have been composed somewhat earlier. It is not known whether the tune is of German or English origin.

545 O Canada

Adolphe B. Routhier (1839-1920)
Translated by Robert Stanley Weir (1856-1926)

This patriotic hymn was written by Routhier at the request of the lieutenant governor of Quebec to be sung at a national festival in Quebec City in 1880. Routhier was a distinguished jurist in Quebec.

According to Stanley L. Osborne in *If Such Holy Song* Weir's translation was published in Montreal in 1908. A number of revisions of the concluding lines have been proposed since then. In 1972 the Canadian parliament approved the following:

> From far and wide, O Canada,
> We stand on guard for thee.
> God, keep our land glorious and free
> O Canada, we stand on guard for thee.

O CANADA is based on a melody composed by Calixa Lavallée (1842-1891) for this text.

546 God Save Our Gracious Queen

Attributed to Henry Carey (d. 1743)

This adaptation of "God Save the King" has a rather complicated history. It is thought to have had its origin in a Latin chorus or hymn dated 1688. Carey became acquainted with it about 1740 and made a translation. Through the years there have been a number of variations of the text. Orginally there were two stanzas. Stanza 3 (our second) was added about 1745. (Julian's *Dictionary of Hymnology* gives an excellent summary of the historial research on this hymn.)

GOD SAVE THE QUEEN was discussed at No. 544.

547 God Bless Our Native Land
Stanza 1 by Charles Timothy Brooks (1813-1883)
and John Sullivan Dwight (1813-1893.)
Stanza 2 by Dwight
Stanza 3 by William Edward Hickson (1803-1870)

The origin of this hymn is traced in detail in Julian's *Dictionary of Hymnology*. In brief, it is one of several translations of the "Sachsenlied" by Siegfried Augustus Mahlmann (1771-1826) which was published in the *Zeitung für die elegante Welt*, 1815, mentioned in connection with our hymn No. 544. The first stanza of the German original reads:

Gott segne Sachsenland,
Wo fest die Treue stand
In Sturm und Nacht!
Ew'ge Gerechtigkeit,
Hoch über'm meer der Zeit,
Die jedem Sturm gebeut,
Schütz uns mit Macht!

Our stanza 1 is from a translation made by the Reverend C. T. Brooks, Unitarian minister, while he was a student at Harvard Divinity School. John Sullivan Dwight, son of President Timothy Dwight of Yale, altered the last two lines of stanza 1 and added a second stanza exactly as we have it in *Hymns of Faith and Life*.

Our stanza 3 is taken from the version written in 1836 by an English boot manufacturer, William E. Hickson, as a replacement for "God save our gracious King." Hickson's hymn is in four 7-line stanzas of which our stanza 3 is his fourth.

This hymn has been in Free Methodist hymnals since 1883.

SERUG is taken from Samuel Sebastian Wesley's *European Psalmist*, 1872, but it is in all probability of earlier origin.

548 God, Who Art the Lord of Harvest
David Elton Trueblood (b. 1900)

This hymn was copyrighted in 1954 by the author. *Hymns of Faith and Life,* according to Dr. Trueblood, is the first hymnal to include it.

SICILIAN MARINER'S HYMN, also called SICILY, may have come from Italy but the evidence is sketchy. In the *Historical Companion to Hymns Ancient and Modern* the tune and the text beginning "O sanctissima, O Piissima" were said to have been collected by J. G. Herder in Italy sometime during the last decade of the eighteenth century. Both were printed in his *Stimmen der Völker in Liedern,* 1807, under the heading "An die Jungfrau Maria. Ein sicilianische Schifferlied."

In England the tune was printed in the Reverend W. D. Tattersall's *Improved Psalmody,* 1794, with Merrick's rendering of Psalm 19.

549 Come, Ye Thankful People, Come
Henry Alford (1810-1871)

This harvest festival hymn was written by the dean of Canterbury Cathedral and published in his *Psalms and Hymns, adapted for the Sundays and Holidays throughout the year* . . . , 1844. Since that time the hymn has been considerably altered, sometimes by the author himself and sometimes by others. In particular, the version included in *Hymns Ancient and Modern,* was repudiated by Alford.

Alford made what he termed as the authorized version in his *Poetical Works of Henry Alford,* 1865, and then proceeded to make more extensive alterations in his hymnal *The Year of Praise,* 1867.

We have omitted three stanzas from the 1867 version and have followed the commonly accepted alterations at the following points:

>2:1 *We ourselves are* God's own field
>4:2 *To* Thy final harvest-home
>4:7 In *God's garner* to abide;

The hymn entered Free Methodist-Wesleyan hymnody in 1951.

ST. GEORGE'S WINDSOR was composed by Sir George Job Elvey (1816-1893) for Edward H. Thorne's *Selection of Psalm and Hymn Tunes,* 1858. Elvey was the longtime organist at St. George's Chapel, Windsor, hence the title.

550 Sing to the Lord of Harvest
John Samuel Bewley Monsell (1811-1875)

Monsell's harvest hymn was published in his *Hymns of Love and Praise*, second edition, 1866, in four 8-line stanzas. There are two authorized versions of the opening line. In the author's *Parish Hymnal*, 1873, it reads, "Sing to the Lord of bounty."
This is the first appearance in a Free Methodist-Wesleyan hymnal.

WIE LIEBLICH IST DER MAIEN was composed by Johann Steurlein (1546-1613). This arrangement is by the Canadian composer and organist Healey Willan (b. 1880) and is derived from a hymn anthem on the text composed by Willan in 1958.

551 We Plow the Fields and Scatter
Matthias Claudius (1740-1815)
Translated by Jane Montgomery Campbell (1817-1878)

Claudius's poetry was published in successive parts of his *Asmus omnia sua secum portans; oder sämmtliche Werke des Wandsbecker Bothen*. This hymn is taken from part IV, 1782, in seventeen 4-line stanzas under the title "Im Anfang war's auf Erden." The stanzas that most nearly parallel our English version are 3, 5, 7, 9, 10, and 13.
The song, a so-called "Peasant's Song," is found in a sketch entitled *Paul Erdmann's Fest*. The stanzas are sung as a solo with everyone joining in on the refrain.
The translation by Miss Campbell was contributed to the Reverend C. S. Bere's *Garland of Song, or an English Liederkranz*, 1861.
Claudius had begun preparation for the Lutheran ministry but being dissillusioned with the rationalism of the university turned his attention to journalism. He became acquainted with Goethe, then living in Frankfurt, and a group of freethinking philosophers. His interest in religion waned. In 1777 he became seriously ill and, as one biographer said, realilzed the emptiness of his life. The result was a reaffirmation of his earlier faith and a resumption of his editorial work, but now with a distinctively Christian spirit.
The 1951 Free Methodist-Wesleyan hymnal was the first to include this hymn.

WIR PFLÜGEN is generally attributed to Johann Abraham Peter Schulz (1747-1800). The earliest appearance in print of this tune is in A. L. Hoppenstedt's *Lieder für Volkschulen,* second edition, 1800, where it is set to this text. No name is attached. In another publication some twelve years later Schulz's name is given as the composer. The earliest publication in the United States seems to have been in Lowell Mason's *The Seraph,* 1840.

552 The God of Harvest Praise
James Montgomery (1771-1854)

This hymn in seven 7-line stanzas was written in 1840 and published shortly thereafter in the *Sheffield Mercury.* In the *Evangelical Magazine* for November, 1840, it was printed under the heading "A Harvest Hymn for 1840."

GOD OF HARVEST was composed for this text by Dr. Charles Herbert Finney (b. 1911) for inclusion in *Hymns of the Living Faith,* 1951. Dr. Finney, longtime chairman (1950-77) of the music department of Houghton College, was a member of the Joint Hymnal Commissions for both our 1951 and 1976 hymnals.

553 Christians, We Have Met to Worship
Attributed to George Atkins (nineteenth century)

The origin of this hymn, generally given as "Brethren, We Have Met to Worship," is uncertain. It is thought to date from early nineteenth century.
This is the first inclusion in a Free Methodist-Wesleyan hymnal.

HOLY MANNA is the tune associated with this text in several contemporary hymnals. It is attributed to William Moore, compiler of *The Columbian Harmony,* 1825, which contains this tune. The title derives from the words included in the text.

554 Let All Mortal Flesh Keep Silence
From the *Liturgy of St. James* (c. fifth century)
Adapted by Gerald Moultrie (1829-1885)

This communion hymn is based on the prayer of the Cherubic Hymn from the *Liturgy of St. James,* as found in John Mason Neale and Richard F. Littledale's, *A Translation of the Primitive*

Liturgies, 1868/9. This metrical version in four 6-line stanzas was made by the Reverend Gerard Moultrie in Orby Shipley's, *Lyra Eucharistica,* second edition, 1864.

Canon C. S. Phillips gives a prose translation of the Greek text as, "Let us, who mystically represent the cherubim and sing the thrice-holy hymn to the quickening Trinity, lay by at this time all worldly cares, that we may receive the King of glory, invisibly attended by the angelic orders. Alleluia, Alleluia, Alleluia!" *(Hymnody Past and Present)*

This is the first appearance in a Free Methodist-Wesleyan hymnal.

PICARDY, also called FRENCH CAROL, is a folksong from Picardy in France. It was adapted as a hymn tune to accompany this text in the *English Hymnal,* 1906. The first printed source is *Chansons Populaires des Provinces de France...,* 1860.

555 Let Us Worship God
Adapted from Scripture by Charles H. Finney (b. 1911)

The text, based on Scripture, and the music were written in 1975 for inclusion in *Hymns of Faith and Life.* Dr. Finney served on the Joint Hymnal Commission that produced this hymnal. (See also comments at No. 552.)

556 Lord Jesus Christ, Be Present Now
From J. Neidling's *Lutherisches Handbüchlein, 1648*
Translated by Catherine Winkworth (1829-1878)

The German hymn of which this is a translation, "Herr Jesu Christ, dich zu uns wend," is found anonymously in J. Neidling's *Lutherisches Handbüchlein,* second edition, 1648. It was headed "A heartfelt petition of pious Christians for grace and the help of the Holy Spirit, during Divine service, before the sermon."

Authorship is sometimes assigned to Wilhelm II, Duke of Saxe-Weimar (1598-1662).

This translation by Miss Winkworth appears in her *Chorale Book for England,* 1863.

The omitted third stanza reads:

> Until we join the hosts that cry,
> "Holy art Thou, O Lord, most high!"
> And in the light of that blest place
> Fore'er behold Thee face to face.

HERR JESU CHRIST appeared anonymously in the appendix of *Pensum Sacrum*, 1648. It was set to this text in *Cantionale Sacrum*, 1651. (See also comments at No. 531.)

557 As We Proclaim Your Name This Hour
Paul Q. Brooks

This is the first stanza of a four-stanza hymn written in 1968 by the Reverend Paul Q. Brooks, a retired United Methodist minister in New England. It was published in 1969 by The Hymn Society of America as one of nine new hymns on *The Mission of the Church*.

According to the author in a personal letter, the hymn "was written two days before Christmas 1968 from notes after reading a printed announcement of a search for new hymns on the Mission of the Church, sponsored by The Hymn Society of America. The 'deadline' was just after Christmas . . . . My purpose was to reflect personal and group convictions in prayer form relating to the expression of faith in everyday living, to be timely as well as timeless, and, as the hymn states,

> To seek new values, redefined
> By higher motives You designed."

The stanzas omitted in our hymnal are:

> 2. Support the weak, console the sad,
>   Increase our faith and make us glad,
>   Your Love forgiving guilt and wrong
>   That we may greet each day with song.
>
> 3. May human rights be our concern
>   That men throughout the world may yearn
>   To seek new values, redefined
>   By higher motives You designed.
>
> 4. Now through companionship Divine
>   As hopes confirm and creeds refine,
>   We shall with thankful, joyful mind
>   Acknowledge You to all mankind.
>   Amen.

Ours may be the first hymnal to include this hymn.

TRURO was discussed at No. 108.

558 Send Forth Thy Light
Adapted from Psalm 43:3

This is an excerpt of a choral composition by the French composer Charles Gounod (1818-1893).

559 Search Me, O God
Psalm 139:23-24

This choral prayer was composed by Charles H. Finney (b. 1911), professor of music (1946-78) at Houghton College, for inclusion in *Hymns of the Living Faith,* 1951.

560 May the Grace of Christ Our Saviour
John Newton (1725-1807)

This short hymn consisting of one 8-line stanza was included in *Olney Hymns, Book III,* 1779. It is a paraphrase of II Corinthians 13:14.

With appropriate substitutions of personal pronouns, this hymn may be sung as a benediction following a wedding ceremony.

EVENING PRAYER was composed by Sir John Stainer (1840-1901). It appeared first in the *Church Hymnary,* 1898. It is said to have been based on the opening theme of Beethoven's "Andante in F."

561 Lead Me, Lord
Samuel Sebastian Wesley (1810-1876)

This is an excerpt from an anthem written by Samuel Sebastian Wesley, a son of Samuel and a grandson of Charles Wesley. The text is a paraphrase of Psalm 5:8 and Psalm 4:8, in the Great Bible Version.

562 Father, Give Thy Benediction
Samuel Longfellow (1819-1892)

The author of this short stanza was a younger brother of Henry Wadsworth Longfellow and a lifelong friend of Samuel Johnson. They collaborated in producing *A Book of Hymns,* 1846, and *Hymns of the Spirit,* 1864. This latter book contains "Father, Give Thy benediction."

The importance of these two Samuels to the field of hymnody is recounted in some detail in Julian and in Henry Wilder Foote's *Three Centuries of American Hymnody,* 1940. They were fellow students in Harvard Divinity School and, being dissatisfied with the available Unitarian hymnals, set about to compile one of their own. It ran to twelve editions. They are credited with introducing "Lead, Kindly light" to American hymnody and with recognizing the hymnic qualities in Whittier's poems.

Longfellow and Johnson took considerable liberties in altering texts to fit their views. A sister of a schoolmate chided them with this limerick:

> There once were two Sams of Amerique
> Who belonged to profession called cleric;
> They hunted up hymns
> And cut off their limbs
> These truculent Sams of Amerique.

ALTA TRINITA BEATA is a melody from a fourteenth-century manuscript of *Laudi Spirituali.* In its modern form it is found in the chapter on "The State of Music in 1450" in Charles Burney's *General History of Music,* 1782.

564 Create in Me a Clean Heart, O God
Carl Frank Mueller (b. 1892)

This is an excerpt from a popular anthem by the contemporary American choral composer Carl F. Mueller.

565 Cast Thy Burden upon the Lord
Julius Schubring (b. 1806)
Translated by William Bartholomew (1793-1867)

This chorale from Mendelssohn's oratorio *Elijah* is found in Part I immediately following the air for baritone sung by Elijah, "Lord God of Abraham."

The subject of the oratorio was discussed as early as 1837. Mendelssohn wrote about that time to Pastor Julius Schubring who had helped him with the libretto of *St. Paul:*

> I wish to ask your advice in a matter which is of importance to me, and I feel it will therefore not be indifferent to you either.... It concerns the selection of a subject of an oratorio, which I intend to begin next winter.... Many very apparent reasons are in favor of choosing St. Peter as the subject....

Mendelssohn then gives his reason for feeling this way. Sometime between the date of the above letter and the fall of 1838 he definitely fixed on Elijah as the subject for his next oratorio. He worked intermittently on the project and finished only days before its first performance on August 25, 1846.

Mendelssohn's feelings toward the oratorio are reflected in these excerpts from letters to Schubring:

> I figured to myself Elijah as a grand, mighty prophet, such as we might again require in our own day energetic and zealous, but also stern, wrathful, and gloomy....

> In such a character as that of Elijah, like every one in the Old Testament, except perhaps Moses, it appears to me that the dramatic should predominate, the personages should be introduced as acting and speaking with fervour; not however, for Heaven's sake, to become mere musical pictures, but inhabitants of a positive, practical world....

The libretto by Pastor Schubring in German was translated into English by William Bartholomew, sometimes spoken of as a poet-diplomat. He collaborated with Mendelssohn in preparing English texts for a number of his oratorios. Actually the first performance of the *Elijah* was in English.

This is the first inclusion in a Free Methodist-Wesleyan hymnal.

COMMITMENT is the title assigned to the chorale melody with this text. In an earlier form as found in the *Meiningisches Gesangbuch,* 1693, it is usually called *Munich.* (See comments at No. 522.) Mendelssohn adapted the tune for use in his *Elijah.*

566, 567 Glory Be to the Father (Gloria Patri)
Traditional (c. third century)

The term *Doxology* is applicable to any form of ascription of praise to the Trinity, but particularly to the *Gloria in excelsis,* known as the "Greater Doxology" and to the *Gloria Patri,* known as the "Lesser Doxology."

The language of the *Gloria Patri* derives from Christ's commission to baptize, in Matthew 28:19. In its Latin form it probably dates from the third or fourth century. In the early Western church it was customary to append the *Gloria Patri* to most psalms. This practice was observed also by users of the various versions of metrical Psalms. Isaac Watts appended approximately twenty versions in various meters to his *Hymns and Spiritual Songs.*

He wrote in the fifth edition dated 1716,

> Tho' the Latin of it, *Gloria Patri,* be retained in our nation from the Roman Church: and tho' there may be some Excesses of superstitious Honour paid to the Words of it, which may have wrought some unhappy Prejudices in weaker Christians, yet I believe it still to be one of the noblest Parts of Christian Worship.

One example by Watts, designated as Third Long Metre:

> To God the Father, God the Son,
> And God the Spirit, Three in One,
> Be Honour, Praise and Glory giv'n
> By all on Earth, and all in Heav'n.

To avoid the smothering effect of too frequent repetition, various forms of the *Gloria Patri* might well be used. The Watts example could be used with a long-metre tune. The first stanza of Horatius Bonar's hymn (No. 56) would be a welcome change also from the traditional form.

Charles Wesley wrote a number of hymns to the Trinity. Seven of them were included in *Hymns and Sacred Poems.* These along with seventeen more were published in *Gloria Patri, etc., or Hymns to the Trinity,* 1746. The following are among the shorter ones:

> II. Sing we to our God above
> Praise eternal as His love:
> Praise Him, all ye heavenly host,
> Father, Son, and Holy Ghost. (7.7.7.7.)
>
> XII. To Father, Son, and Holy Ghost,
>   One God in persons Three,
>   Give praise, ye saints and heavenly host,
>   Through all eternity. (C.M.)

There are four versions of the *Gloria Patri* written by John Newton and appended to his *Olney Hymns,* 1779. The first one can be used with a short-metre tune:

> 1. The Father we adore,
>   And everlasting Son,

>   The Spirit of His love and pow'r,
>   The glorious Three in One!
>
> 2. At the creation's birth,
>   This song was sung on high,
>   Shall sound through every age on earth,
>   And through eternity.

Gloria Patri to the Greatorex tune appeared in the 1910 hymnal and to the Meineke tune in the 1951 hymnal.

GREATOREX was composed in 1851 by Henry Wellington Greatorex (1813-1858). Greatorex was born in England and came to the United States in 1839. He served as organist in churches in Hartford, Connecticut, and in New York City. His *Collection of Psalm and Hymn Tunes, Chants, Anthems and Sentences for the Use of the Protestant Episcopal Church in America,* 1851, contained thirty-seven original tunes and a number of arrangements. The *Gloria Patri* is from this collection.

MEINEKE was composed in about 1844 by Christoph Meineke (1782-1850). Meineke was born in Germany, moved from there to England, and then in 1820 to Baltimore where he was organist at St. Paul's Episcopal Church the time of his death. He wrote *Music for the Church ... composed for St. Paul's Church,* Baltimore, 1844. *Gloria Patri* is taken from "Evening Prayer" in *Music for the Church.*

654, 655 Praise God from Whom All Blessings Flow
Thomas Ken (1637-1710)

Charles Wesley records in his *Journal* for March 14, 1744, that as he was speaking in an old upper room in Leeds, the floor gave way.

> I lost my senses, but recovered them in a moment, and was filled with power from above. I lifted up my head first, and saw the people under me, heaps upon heaps. I cried out, "Fear not! The Lord is with us. Our lives are all safe;" and then,
>   "Praise God, from whom all blessings flow."

(See comments at No. 205 and No. 210)

BULA was arranged apparently from an English or Welsh melody in about 1907 by Fannie Birdsall (1864-1926), later Mrs. George E. Bula. The first printed source of this arrangement we have been able to locate is *Missionary Hymns and Responsive*

Scripture Readings ..., 1907, compiled by the Reverend Wilson T. Hogue, Ph.D. It has been included in all Free Methodist-Wesleyan hymnals since 1910.

Another form of the melody popular about 1910 is the song for male chorus "What Did He Do?"

SELECTED BIBLIOGRAPHY

Avery, Gordon. *Companion to the Song Book of the Salvation Army* (2nd edition). London: Salvationist Publishing and Supplies, 1962.

Bailey, Albert Edward. *The Gospel in Hymns.* New York: Charles Scribner's Sons, 1950.

Balleine, G. R. *Sing with the Understanding.* London: Independent Press, Ltd., 1954.

Benson, Louis F. *The English Hymn.* New York: George H. Doran Company, 1915.

Benson, Louis F. *Studies of Familiar Hymns* (second series). Philadelphia: The Westminster Press, 1923.

Bett, Henry. *The Hymns of Methodism* (3rd edition). London: The Epworth Press, 1945.

Brownlie, John. *The Hymns and Hymn Writers of the Church Hymnary.* London: Henry Frowde, 1911.

Bucke, Emory Stevens; Gealy, Fred D., Lovelace, Austin C.; and Young, Carlton R. *Companion to the Hymnal.* Nashville and New York: Abingdon Press, 1970.

Curwen, John Spencer. *Studies in Worship-Music.* London: J. Curwen & Sons, 1880.

Douglas, Winfred. *Church Music in History and Practice,* New York: Charles Scribner's Sons, 1937.

Ellinwood, Leonard. *The History of American Church Music* (revised edition). New York: Da Capo Press, 1970.

Ellinwood, Leonard, editor. *The Hymnal 1940 Companion* (3rd revised edition). New York: The Church Pension Fund, 1951.

Emurian, Ernest K. *Famous Stories of Inspiring Hymns.* Grand Rapids: Baker Book House, 1956 (reprint 1975).

Erickson, J. Irving. *Twice-Born Hymns.* Chicago: Covenant Press, 1976.

Foote, Henry Wilder. *Three Centuries of American Hymnody.* Hamden, Connecticut: Archon Books, 1968.

Frost, Maurice. *Historical Companion to Hymns Ancient and Modern.* London: William Clowes & Sons, Ltd., 1962.

Gilman, Frederick John. *The Evolution of the English Hymn.* New York: The Macmillan Company, 1927.

Gregory, A. S. *Praises with Understanding.* London: The Epworth Press, 1936.

Hogue, Wilson, T. *Hymns That are Immortal* (2nd edition). Chicago: Free Methodist Publishing House, 1906.

Howard, John Tasker. *Our American Music* (3rd edition). New York: Thomas Y. Crowell Company, 1946.

Hustad, Donald P. *Dictionary-Handbook to Hymns for the Living Church.* Carol Stream, Illinois: Hope Publishing Company, 1978.

Jefferson, H. A. L. *Hymns in Christian Worship.* New York: The Macmillan Company, 1950.

Julian, John, editor. *A Dictionary of Hymnology.* London: John Murray, 1907. New York: Dover Publications (reprint, 1957).

Kerr, Phil. *Music in Evangelism.* Glendale, California: Gospel Music Publishers, 1939.

Lang, Paul Henry. *Music in Western Civilization.* New York: W. W. Norton, 1941.

Lightwood, James T. *The Music of the Methodist Hymn-Book.* London: The Epworth Press, 1935.

Lightwood, James T. *Hymn-Tunes and Their Story.* London: The Epworth Press, 1923.

Lillenas, Haldor. *Modern Gospel Hymn Stories.* Kansas City: Lillenas Publishing Company, 1952.

McCutchan, Robert Guy. *Hymns in the Lives of Men.* New York and Nashville: Abingdon Press, 1945.

McCutchan, Robert Guy. *Hymn Tune Names, Their Sources and Significance.* New York and Nashville: Abingdon Press, 1957.

McCutchan, Robert Guy. *Our Hymnody: A Manual of the Methodist Hymnal*. Nashville: Abingdon-Cokesbury Press, 1937.

MacDougall, Hamilton C. *Early New England Psalmody*. Brattleboro: Stephen Daye Press, 1940.

Manning, Bernard L. *The Hymns of Wesley and Watts*. London: The Epworth Press, 1942.

Marks, Harvey B. *Rise and Growth of English Hymnody* (revised 2nd edition). New York: Fleming H. Revell Company, 1938.

Marrocco, W. Thomas and Gleason, Harold. *Music in America*. New York: W. W. Norton & Company, Inc., 1964.

Ninde, Edwards. *The Story of the American Hymn*. New York: The Abingdon Press, 1921.

Nuelson, John L. *John Wesley and the German Hymns*. Calverley, Yorkshire: A. S. Holbrook, 1972.

Nutter, Charles S., and Tillett, Wilbur F. *The Hymns and Hymn Writers of the Church*. New York and Cincinnati: The Methodist Book Concern, 1911.

Osbeck, Kenneth W. *Singing with Understanding*. Grand Rapids, Michigan: Kregel Publications, 1979.

Osborn, G., editor. *The Poetical Works of John and Charles Wesley* (13 volumes). London: Wesleyan-Methodist Conference Office, 1868.

Patrick, Millar. *The Story of the Church's Song* (revised edition). Richmond, Virginia: John Knox Press, 1962.

Pfatteicher, Helen E. *In Every Corner Sing*. Philadelphia: Muhlenberg Press, 1954.

Phillips, C. S. *Hymnody Past and Present*. London: S.P.C.K., 1937.

Polack, W. G. *The Handbook to the Lutheran Hymnal* (2nd revised edition). Saint Louis: Concordia Publishing House, 1942.

Price, Carl F. *The Music and Hymnody of the Methodist Hymnal*. New York and Cincinnati: The Methodist Book Concern, 1911.

Rattenbury, J. Ernest. *The Eucharistic Hymns of John and Charles Wesley*. London: The Epworth Press, 1948.

Rattenbury, J. Ernest. *The Evangelical Doctrines of Charles Wesley's Hymns*. London: The Epworth Press, 1941.

Reynolds, William Jensen. *A Survey of Christian Hymnody*. New York: Holt, Rinehart and Winston, Inc., 1963.

Reynolds, William J. *Companion to Baptist Hymnal*. Nashville: Broadman Press, 1976.

Reynolds, William Jensen. *Hymns of our Faith, A Handbook for the Baptist Hymnal* (revised edition). Nashville: Broadman Press, 1967.

Routley, Erik. *Hymns and Human Life* (2nd edition). Grand Rapids: Wm. B. Eerdmans Publishing Company, 1959.

Routley, Erik. *Hymns and the Faith*. Grand Rapids: William B. Eerdmans Publishing Company, 1968.

Routley, Erik. *Hymns Today and Tomorrow*. New York and Nashville: Abingdon Press, 1964.

Routley, Erik. *The Musical Wesleys*. New York: Oxford University Press, 1968.

Ryden, E. E. *The Story of Christian Hymnody*. Rock Island, Illinois: Augustana Press, 1959.

Sankey, Ira D. *My Life and the Story of the Gospel Hymns*. New York: Harper & Brothers Publishers, 1907.

Sanville, George W. *Forty Gospel Hymn Stories* (5th edition). Winona Lake, Indiana: Rodeheaver-Hall Mack Co., 1945.

The Seven Great Hymns of the Medieval Church (3rd edition, 1866). New York: Anson D. F. Randolph, 1865.

Smith, H. Augustine. *Lyric Religion*. New York: D. Appleton-century Company, 1931.

Smith, Oswald J. *Oswald J. Smith's Hymn Stories* (revised edition). Winona Lake, Indiana: The Rodeheaver Company, 1969.

Sonneck, Oscar George Theodore. *Report on "The Star-Spangled Banner," "Hail Columbia," "America," "Yankee Doodle."* Washington: Government Printing Office, 1909.

Telford, John. *The New Methodist Hymn-Book Illustrated in History and Experience.* London: The Epworth Press, 1934.

Thurman, Howard. *Deep River.* New York: Harper & Brothers, 1955.

Wesley, John. *A Collection of Psalms and Hymns.* Charles-Town: Printed by Lewis Timothy, 1737. (Facsimile edition with additional material edited by Frank Baker and George Walton Williams. Charleston: The Dolcho Historical Society, 1964.)

INDEXES

AUTHORS, TRANSLATORS, SOURCES

Abelard, Peter 160
Ackley, Alfred Henry 396
Addison, Joseph 10, 35, 52, 402
Alexander, Cecil Frances 139, 215, 303
Alexander, James Waddell 156
Alford, Henry 461, 549
Ambrose of Milan, St. 60, 114
Andrew of Crete, St. 412
Astrom, Johan 466
Atkins, George 553

Babcock, Maltbie Davenport 65
Baker, Henry Williams 47, 107, 149
Baker, Theodore 118, 474
Bakewell, John 157
Baring-Gould, Sabine 212, 213, 411, 414
Bartholomew, William 565
Barton, Bernard 229
Bateman, Christian Henry 94
Bates, Katharine Lee 542
Bathurst, William Hiley 341, 374
Baxter, Lydia 82
Beecher, Charles 454
Befiehl du deine Wege 398, 399
Belsheim, Ole G. 521
Ben Judah, Daniel 15
Bennard, George 456
Berg, Caroline V. Sandell 49
Bernard of Clairvaux 100, 101, 156
Bevan, Emma Frances 230
Bickersteth, Edward Henry 264, 304, 441, 530
Bishop, C. 291
Blandy, E. W. 259
Bliss, Philip Paul 91, 218, 223
Blom, Fredrick A. 464
Boberg, Carl Gustaf 61
Bode, John Ernest 302
Bonar, Horatius 56, 85, 228, 281, 282, 518
Booth, William 219
Borthwick, Jane Laurie 299
Bottome, Frank 333
Bourne, George Hugh 358
Bowie, Walter Russell 508
Bowring, John 70, 451
Brady, Nicholas 12
Brandenburg, Luise Henriette von 463
Bridgers, Luther Burgess 99
Bridges, Matthew 183
Bridges, Robert Seymour 81, 158
Briggs, George Wallace 236, 490
Brooks, Charles Timothy 547
Brooks, Paul Q. 557
Brooks, Phillips 136
Budry, Edmond Louis 178
Buffum, Herbert 338
Bunyan, John 234, 408
Burton, John, Sr. 523
Byrne, Mary Elizabeth 357

Campbell, Jane Montgomery 551
Campbell, John D. Sutherland, Duke of Argyll 68
Canticle of the Sun 26
Carey, Henry 546
Carlson, Nathaniel 464
Carmichael, Ralph Richard 39, 247
Carter, Russell Kelso 231
Caswall, Edward 81, 101
Cennick, John 186, 530
Chapman, J. Wilbur 97, 145
Chatfield, Allen W. 433
Chisholm, Thomas O. 43, 301, 369
Chorley, Henry Fothergill 17
Christiansen, Avis Burgeson 88
Christierson, Frank von 179, 525
Clark, William H. 79

Clarkson, E. Margaret 484
Claudius, Matthias 551
Clausnitzer, Tobias 58
Clayton, Norman J. 457, 465
Clephane, Elizabeth Cecilia 155
Codner, Elizabeth 261
Coffin, Charles 113
Coffin, Henry Sloan 116
Collins, Henry 356
Copenhaver, Laura Sherer 488
Cory, Julia Bulkey Cady 8
Cotterill, Thomas 392, 434, 512
Cowper, William 67, 217, 222, 314, 354
Cox, Frances Elizabeth 41
Crewdson, Jane Fox 371
Croly, George 197
Crosby, Fanny J. 42, 83, 89, 90, 239, 284, 287, 311, 348, 381, 385, 452, 480
Crown of Jesus 122
Cushing, William Orcutt 232, 386

Dearmer, Percy 133, 234
Dies irae, dies illa 237
Doane, George Washington 209
Doddridge, Philip 14, 66, 73, 290
Douglas, C. Winfred 509
Doving, Carl 473
Draper, William Henry 26
Driver, J. M. 220
Dryden, John 204
Duffield, George Jr. 409
Dunkerly, William Arthur (see John Oxenham)
Dwight, John Sullivan 547
Dwight, Timothy 476

Edmeston, James 403
Elijah 563
Ellerton, John 471, 528, 529
Elliott, Charlotte 253, 296, 397
Elliott, Emily E.S. 140
Esling, Cathrine Watterman 227
Evans, Jonathan 422
Excell, Edwin Othello 266, 283

Faber, Fredrick William 32, 71, 421
Failing, George E. 199
Farjeon, Eleanor 208
Fawcett, John 479
Featherstone, William Ralph 86
Ferguson, Manie Payne 394
Findlater, Sarah Borthwick 191, 248
Finney, Charles H. 555
Fischer, William G. 45
Flint, Annie Johnson 382, 389
Fortunatus, Venantius Honorius C. 181, 514
Fosdick, Harry Emerson 25
Foster, Frederick William 23
Francis of Assisi, St. 26
Francis, Benjamin 364
Francis, Samuel Trevor 378
Franck, Johann 447

Gabriel, Charles Hutchinson 153, 154
Gerhardt, Paul 128, 156, 312, 398 399
Gibson, Evan K. 198, 202, 316
Gilmore, Joseph Henry 429
Gladden, Washington 367
Goadby, Frederic William 539
Grant, Robert 2
Green, F. Pratt 532
Grigg, Joseph 364
Groves, Alexander 524
Grundtvig, Nicolai Frederik Severin 473, 521
Gurney, Dorothy Blomfield 529

Hall, Elvina Mabel 216
Hall, George 332
Hammond, J. Dempster 485
Hanby, Benjamin Russell 129
Hankey, Arabella Catherine 45
Harley, Alan Reginald 509, 526
Harris, J.M. 102
Harris, Thoro 93
Hart, Joseph 243
Hartsough, Lewis 256
Hastings, Thomas 370
Hatch, Edwin 336
Havergal, Frances Ridley 294, 308, 405, 449, 496, 540
Hawks, Annie Sherwood 347
Hayford, Jack W. 44
Hearn, Marianne 307
Heath, George 415
Heber, Reginald 38, 54, 417, 517
Hedge, Frederick Henry 377
Heermann, Johann 158
Henderson, S. J. 271
Herbert, George 4
Herman, Nicolaus 112
Herrell, N.B. 185
Hewitt, Eliza Edmunds 245, 330, 427
Hickson, William Edward 547
Hoffman, Elisha Albright 276
Hogue, Wilson T. 142, 274, 455
Holland, Josiah G. 131
Holmes, Oliver Wendell 105, 401
Houghton, Frank 492
How, William Walsham 360, 462, 522
Hoyle, Richard Birch 178
Hubbert, Frances Martha 134
Hudson, Ralph E. 79, 295, 400
Hughes, J. Donald 498
Hull, Eleanor Henrietta 357
Hutton, Frances A. 342

Ingemann, Bernhardt S. 414
Iverson, Daniel 313
Ives, David Livingstone 169

James, Mary D. 300
John of Damascus 171, 173
Johnson, E. Gustav 61
Johnson, William 159
Jones, Charles P. 430
Jones, Lewis Edgar 235
Jones, Richard G. 34
Jones, Ruth Caye 242

"K" in J. Rippon's *Selection of Hymns* 404
Kane, H. Victor 491
Keble, John 214, 326
Kelly, Thomas 189, 372
Kempton, Lois 132
Ken, Thomas 205, 210, 654, 655
Kennedy, Benjamin Hall 87
Kerr, Hugh Thomson 432
Kethe, William 7
Key, Francis Scott 543

Lambdin, Henry Lyle 482
Landstad, Magnus Brostrup 254
Lathbury, Mary Artemisia 211, 524
Latrobe, Benjamin 251
Latta, Eden R. 258
Laurenti, Laurentius 191
Laurinus, Laurentius Laurentii 466
Leech, Bryan Jeffery 494
Leeson, Jane Eliza 438
Lemmel, Helen Howarth 246
Lillenas, Haldor 106, 292, 363, 445
Liturgy of St. James 554
Littlefield, Milton Smith 206
Logan, John 73
Longfellow, Samuel 562
Longstaff, William Dunn 331
Lowell, James Russell 418
Lowenstern, Matthaus Aqelles von 443
Lowry, Robert 175
Luther, Martin 114, 125, 130, 251, 315, 353, 377
Lutherisches Handbüchlein 556

Lynch, Thomas Toke 198
Lyte, Henry Francis 18, 309, 460

Maccall, William 466
MacDuff, John Ross 190
Mackay, William Paton 345
Madan, Martin 117, 157, 186
March, Daniel 361
Martin, Civilla Durfee 388
Matheson, George 305, 383
McAfee, Cweland Boyd 448
McDonald, William 265
Medley, Samuel 96
Mendelssohn, Felix 563
Mercer, William 23
Merrill, William Pierson 366
Methodist Hymn Book Supplement, The 392
Meyer, Ronald 193
Miles, C. Austin 260
Miller, John 23
Miller, Rhea Florence 362
Milton, John 475
Mitre Hymn Book 326
Mohr, Joseph 123
Monsell, John Samuel Bewley 416, 550
Montgomery, James 20, 36, 64, 110, 119, 150, 195, 342, 350, 519, 520, 552
Moore, Thomas 370
Morison, John 516
Morris, Lelia Naylor 275, 321
Mote, Edward 393
Moultrie, Gerard 554
Munster Gesangbuch 74
Murphy, Anne S. 442

Neale, John Mason 7, 107, 116, 146, 171, 173, 176, 264, 412, 467, 514
Neander, Joachim 63
Neumark, Georg 384
Neumeister, Erdmann 230
Newell, William Reed 250
Newton, John 143, 269, 502, 560
Nichol, Henry Ernest 483
Nicholson, James L. 329
Nicolai, Philipp 111
Neidling, Johann 556
Nitschmann, Johann 323
Noel, Caroline Maria 98
North, Frank Mason 489, 506

Oakeley, Frederick 121
Ogden, William Augustus 221
Olivers, Thomas 15
Olson, Ernst William 49
Orr, J. Edwin 318
Ortlund, Anne 487
Ovens, W. G. 188
Owens, Priscilla Jane 481
Oxenham, John (Pseud. for W.A. Dunkerly) 478

Palmer, Horatio Richmond 425
Palmer, Ray 100, 268
Pang lingua, gloriosi praclium 181
Parish Hymn Book 412
Park, Edward A. 248
Parker, William Henry 538
Pearce, Almeda J. 192
Perronet, Edward 75, 76, 77
Peterson, John W. 84, 187, 285, 428
Petti, Anthony G. 424, 458
Pierpoint, Folliott Sandford 33
Plumptre, Edward Hayes 439
Pollard, Adelaide Addison 298
Pollock, Thomas Benson 162, 163, 164, 165, 166, 167, 168
Pope, Richard Hudson 325
Pott, Francis 180
Prentiss, Elizabeth Payson 437
Prudentius, Aurelius Clemens 107
Psalter 37, 380
Psalteriolum Cantionum Catholicarum, Cologne 116
Pusey, Philip 443

Rankin, Jeremiah Eames 469, 470
Reed, Andrew 196
Reed, Eliza Holmes 334
Reid, William Watkins, Jr. 500, 504
Reynolds, William M. 114
Rinkhart, Martin 9
Rippon, John 75, 76, 77
Rippon's *Selection of Hymns* 404
Rist, Johann 126
Rix, Edwin J. 31
Roberts, Daniel Crane 24
Roberts, Gladys Wescott 188
Robinson, George Wade 387
Rossetti, Christina Georgina 124, 138
Roth, Elton Menno 436
Routhier, Adolphe B. 545
Rowley, Francis Harold 103
Runyan, William Marion 534
Russell, Arthur Tozer 112, 126

Sacred Harp, The 269
Sammis, John H. 368
Sankey, Ira David 103
Sargent, Edward H. Gladstone 297
Sarum Primer 343
Schloerb, Rolland W. 507
Schmolck, Benjamin 299, 509
Scholtes, Peter 477
Schubring, Julius 565
Schutz, Johann Jakob 41
Schwedler, Johann Christoph 87
Scott, Clara H. 426
Scott, Lesbia 535
Scott, Sir Walter 237
Scottish Paraphrases 73
Scottish Psalter 29, 30
Scriven, Joseph Medlicott 352
Seiss, Joseph Augustus 74
Shepherd, Thomas 454
Sherwin, William Fiske 420
Shurtleff, Ernest Warburton 413
Simpson, William John Sparrow 161
Sleeper, William True 252
Smith, Oswald J. 174, 289, 306, 440
Smith, Samuel Francis 544
Smith, Walter Chalmers 3
Sqaeth, Harriet R. 118
Spafford, Horatio Gates 444
Splendor paternae gloriae 60
Stead, Louisa M.R. 376
Stennett, Samuel 95
Sterne, Colin 483
Stocking, Jay Thomas 141
Stockton, John Hart 244
Stokes, Elwood Haines 202
Stone, Samuel John 501
Stork, Charles Wharton 21
Stowe, Harriet Beecher 207
Stowell, Hugh 349
Swain, Joseph 48
Synesius of Cyrene, Bishop 433

Tappan, William Bingham 148
Tate, Nahum 12, 127
Tate and Brady, *New Version of the Psalms* 12, 424
Tersteegen, Gerhard 22, 23, 248, 322
The Yigdul 15

Theodulph of Orleans 146
Thomas of Celano 237
Thompson, Will Lamartine 240
Thomson, Mary Ann 493
Threlfall, Jeannette 147
Thring, Godfrey 183
Thrupp, Dorothy Ann 390
Tindley, Charles A. 407
Toplady, Augustus Montague 157, 243, 392
Troutbeck, John 126
Trueblood, David Elton 503, 548
Tucker, F. Bland 160
Tuttiett, Lawrence 497, 541

United Presbyterian Book of Psalms 40, 72

Van Deventer, Judson W. 310
Van Dyke, Henry 5, 505
Veni Redemptor gentium 114

Wade, John Francis 121
Walford, William W. 351
Wallin, Johann Olof 21
Walton, W. Spencer 279
Ware, Henry, Jr. 533
Waring, Anna Laetitia 379
Warner, Anna Bartlett 537
Watson, George D. 316
Watts, Isaac 6, 11, 16, 27, 50, 53, 59, 62, 115, 194, 200, 406, 419, 450, 510, 511, 513, 527
Webb, Benjamin 144
Wer nur den lieben Gott lasst walten 384
Weir, Robert Stanley 545
Weissel, Georg 108
Wells, Marcus M. 201
Wesley, Charles 1, 19, 28, 46, 80, 92, 104, 109, 117, 152, 172, 177, 182, 184, 186, 200, 203, 224, 225, 238, 241, 249, 257, 263, 266, 267, 272, 273, 277, 278, 280, 288, 304, 317, 319, 320, 324, 327, 328, 335, 339, 340, 344, 346, 365, 373, 375, 410, 431, 453, 459, 472, 486, 536
Wesley, John 11, 22, 27, 50, 53, 59, 204, 270, 312, 322, 323, 391, 398, 399
Wesley, Samuel 151
Whately, Richard 38
Whitefield, George 117
Whitfield, Fjederick 78
Whittier, John Gjeenleaf 226, 446, 468
Whittle, Daniel Webster 233, 395
Wilkinson, Kate Barclay 423
Williams, Clara Tear 255
Williams, Peter 69
Williams, William 69
Wilson, James E. 531
Winkworth, Catherine 9, 58, 63, 108, 111, 128, 130, 315, 353, 384, 447, 463, 556
Wirf dein Anlicgan auf den Herrn 565
Wistar, Thomas 499
Wolcott, Samuel 495
Woodhull, Alfred Alexander 13
Wordsworth, Christopher 51, 57, 135, 337

Young, John Freeman 123

Zinzendorf, Nicolaus L. von 270, 323, 391

COMPOSERS, ARRANGERS, AND SOURCES

Abbey, Alonzo Judson 468
Ackley, Alfred Henry 396, 440
Ackley, Bentley DeForest 174, 306
Agincourt Song, The 144
Ahle, Johann Rodolph 509
Ahlwen, Elsie 464
Allen, Chester G. 83
Allen, George Nelson 454
Arne, Thomas Augustine 419
Atkinson, Frederick Cook 197
Attwood, Thomas 204

Bach, Johann Sebastian 37, 112, 114, 126, 128, 130, 146, 156, 158, 228, 251, 254, 353, 384, 447, 490, 509, 521, 531, 539
Bain, James Leith 30
Baker, Henry Williams 100, 264, 270, 455
Bambridge, William Samuel 414
Barham-Gould, A. Cyril 423
Barnby, Joseph 81, 213, 307, 322, 356, 529
Barthélemon, François Hippolyte 205, 304, 434, 520
Beethoven, Ludwig van 5, 179
Bennard, George 456

Billings, William 120
Bliss, Philip Paul 218, 223, 308, 444
Bohemian Brethren's *Kirchengesänge,* 41
Bortniansky, Dimitri S. 290, 312
Bourgeois, Louis 6, 7, 655, 656
Boyd, William 416
Bradbury, William Batchelder 148, 253, 261, 351, 390, 429, 523, 537
Bridgers, Luther Burgess 99
Bula, Fannie B. 654

Caldbeck, George Thomas 441
Calvary, Spohr 257, 344
Campbell, Thomas 273
Caniadau y Cyssegr 3
Cantica Spiritualia 142, 199
Cantionale Sacrum 556
Carmichael, Ralph Richard 39, 247
Carr, Benjamin 94
Carter, Russell Kelso 231
Chadwick, George Whitefield 286
Challinor, Frederic A. 538
Choral Book for England, The 63
Choralgesänge, J. S. Bach 228
Chorister's Companion, The 288
Christian Lyre, The 243, 309, 361, 505
Christmas Oratorio, J. S. Bach 126, 128, 130, 156
Clark, F.A. 407
Clark, Jeremiah 475
Clayton, Norman J. 457, 465
Collection of Hymns and Sacred Poems, A 12
Columbian Harmony 553
Conkey, Ithamar 451
Converse, Charles Crozat 352
Cottman, Arthur 507
Creation, The 35
Croft, William 59, 80
Crotch, William 195
Crucifixion, The 161
Crüger, Johann 9, 104, 158, 200, 447
Cummings, William Hayman 117
Cutler, Henry Stephen 417, 487, 526

Damon, William, *Booke of Musicke* 151
Damon, William, *Psalmes* 149, 433
Darwall, John 46, 62, 184
Davies, H. Walford 343
Davisson, Ananias, *Kentucky Harmony* 380
Doane, William Howard 42, 82, 311, 348, 437, 480
Douglas, Charles Winfred 107, 234, 508
Driver, J.M. 220, 221
Dunbar, C.R. 295
Dykes, John Bacchus 47, 54, 101, 164, 281, 296, 314, 327, 393, 412, 461, 486, 489, 500, 533, 534

Ebeling, Johann Georg 128
Edson, Lewis, Sr. 288
Elijah 563, 565
Ellis, J. 219
Ellor, James 77
Elvey, George Job 183, 410, 549
Essay on the Church Plain Chant, An 121, 300, 403
Este, Thomas, *The Whole Book of Psalms* 324
Evans, David 208
Excell, Edwin Othello 283

Finlay, Kenneth George 134, 212
Finney, Charles H. 310, 552, 555, 559
Fischer, William Gustavus 45, 265, 272, 329
Flemming, Friedrich F. 397, 443
Freylinghausen, J. A. 438
Funk, Joseph, *Genuine Church Music (Harmonia Sacra)* 404

Gabriel, Charles Hutchinson 153, 154
Gall's, Christian *As Hymnodus Sacer,* Leipzig 354
Gardiner, William, *Sacred Melodies* 2, 459, 506
Gatty, Nicholas C. 57
Gauntlett, Henry John 72, 139
Gawler, W., *Hymns and Psalms* 141
Geistliche Kirchengesänge Cologne 26, 118
Geistliche Lieder, Leipzig 130
Geistliches Gesangbüchlein, Wittenberg 114
Genevan Psalter 195, 518, 528, 655

Gerig, Richard E. 169
Gesangbuch . . . der Herzogl. Wirtembergishen katholischen Hofkapelle 16, 147, 540
Giardini, Felice de 55, 495
Gibbons, Orlando 53, 162
Gladstone, William Henry 339, 432
Gläser, Carl Gotthelf 1
Gordon, Adoniram Judson 86, 279
Goss, John 18
Gottschalk, Louis Moreau 196
Gounod, Charles F. 558
Gower, John Henry 215
Grant, David 29
Grape, John Thomas 216
Greatorex, Henry Wellington 209, 249, 274, 566
Greiter, Mattaeus 27
Grenoble Antiphoner 263
Gruber, Franz 123

Haleliwiah Drachefn 103, 109, 186, 503
Hallelujah, The 225
Handel, George Frederick 115, 127, 177, 178, 408, 532
Harding, James Procktor 207
Harkness, Robert 97, 291
Harrington, Karl Pomeroy 131
Harris, John M. 102
Harris, Thoro 93
Harrison, Ralph 419
Hartsough, Lewis 256
Hassler, Hans Leo 156
Hastings, Thomas 95, 349, 372, 392
Hatton, John 194
Havergal, William Henry 334, 374, 472
Haydn, Franz Joseph 35, 236, 502
Haydn, Johann Michael 64, 191
Hayford, Jack W. 44
Helmore, Thomas 116
Hemy, Henri Frederick 421
Herman, Nicolaus 112
Herrell, N.B. 185
Hervey, Frederick Alfred John 167
Hewitt, James, *Harmonia Sacra* 127
Hickman, Roger M. 289
Hodges, John S.B. 517
Holbrook, Joseph Perry 278, 299
Holden, Oliver, *Union Harmony* 75
Holst, Gustav Theodore 138
Hooker, Gordon E. 332
Hopkins, Edward John 471
Hopkins, John Henry 535
Hudson, Ralph E. 79, 255, 400, 405
Hughes, John 25, 69
Hullah, John Pyke 222
Hymnbook, The 98
Hymn Tunes of the United Bethren 36

Ingalls, Jeremiah 272
Irvine, Jessie Seymour 29
Iverson, Daniel 313

Jackson, Robert 336
Jacob, Gordon 30
Jarman, Thomas 450
Johnson, Norman E. 61
Jones, Charles P. 430
Jones, J. Lloyd 345
Jones, Lewis Edgar 235
Jones, Ruth Caye 242
Jones, William 32, 525
Joseph, Georg 199
Jude, William Herbert 303
Judson, Alfred 292

Katholisches Gesangbuch, Vienna 214, 463
Kempton, Lois 132
Kentucky Harmony 380, 508
Kirchengesangbuch, Darmstadt 58
Kirk, James M. 394
Kirkpatrick, William James 79, 89, 245, 284, 301, 330, 333, 376, 481, 485
Knapp, Phoebe Palmer 287
Knapp, William 14, 96, 315
Knecht, Justin Heinrich 472
Kocher, Conrad 33

Koizumi, Isao 541
Koschat, Thomas 499
Kremser, Edward 8, 474

Lane, Spencer 342
Laudi Spirituali 562
Lausanne Psalter 64, 191
Lavallee, Calixa 545
Laycock, Geoffrey 458
Lemmel, Helen Howarth 246
Liljestrand, Paul F. 494
Lillenas, Haldor 106, 363, 445
Lindeman, Ludvig Mathias 473
Lindenborn, Heinrich, *Tochter Sion,* Cologne 371
Lobegesang, Mendelssohn, 9
Loes, Harry Dixon 88
Loveless, Wendell P. 369
Lowry, Robert 175, 347, 381
Luther, Martin 377, 521
Lvov, Alexis Feodorvich 17
Lyon, Meyer (Leoni) 15
Lyra Davidica 172

Main, Hubert Platt 309, 361
Maker, Frederick Charles 155, 446
Malan, H. A. César 87
Mann, Arthur Henry 302
Marsh, Charles Howard 145
Marshall, W.S. 394
Martin, George Clement 320
Martin, George William 267, 305
Martin, W. Stillman 388
Mason, Lowell 1, 66, 110, 115, 217, 227, 268, 334, 341 346, 374, 391, 415, 479, 510, 530
Mason and Webb's *Cantica Laudis* 360
Matthews, Timothy Richard 140
McAfee, Cleland Boyd 448
McGranahan, James 91, 233, 395
Meineke, Christoph 567
Mendelssohn, Felix 9, 117, 206, 354, 379, 522, 563, 565
Messiter, Arthur Henry 439
Meyer, Ronald 193
Miles, C. Austin 260
Miller, Charles Edward 431
Miller, Edward 323, 511, 516
Mitchell, Hubert 382
Monk, William Henry 33, 34, 180, 189, 264, 460
Moore, William 553
Morris, Lelia Naylor 275, 321
Morris, Reginald Owen 124
Mountain, James 387, 449
Mozart, Wolfgang Amadeus 294
Mueller, Carl F. 564
Murphy, Anne S. 442
Murray, James R. 125
Musical Monitor 13, 105

Nägeli, Johann Georg 66, 479
Neander, Joachim 23, 190
Neumark, Georg 384
Neu-vermehrtes Gesangbuch, Meiningen 522
Nichol, Henry Ernest 483
Nicolai, Philipp 111
Norris, John Samuel 259
Novello, Vincent 422

Oakeley, Herbert Stanley 19
Ogden, William Augustus 221
Oliver, Henry Kemble 248, 364
Ovens, W.G. 188
Owen, William 358

Palestrina, Giovanni Pierluigi da 180
Palmer, Horatio R. 425
Paris Antiphoner 85
Paris Processional 116
Parker, Edwin Pond 196
Parry, Joseph 277, 328, 453
Pattison, Olive 355
Peace, Albert Lister 383
Pearce, Almeda J. 192
Pensum Sacrum 531, 556

Perkins, Henry S. 258
Peterson, John W. 84, 187, 285, 428, 484
Piae Cantiones 60, 107, 129, 133, 176
Pope, Richard Hudson 325
Praetorius, Michael 60, 118, 176
Praxis Pietatis Melica, Berlin 104, 200
Prichard, Rowland Hugh 97, 103, 109, 186, 503
Psalmodia Evangelica 108, 557
Psalmodia Sacra, Gotha 72
Purday, Charles Henry 68

Quaile, Robert Newton 51

Ramsey, Robert 2-fold Amen 656
Ravenscroft's *Psalter* 67
Read, Daniel 237
Redhead, Richard 150, 198, 340
Redner, Lewis Henry 136
Reed, Ephraim 13, 105
Reinagle, Alexander Robert 143, 478, 512
Richardson, John B. 371
Rix, Edwin J. 31
Roberts, John, *Caniadau y Cyssegr* 3
Roller, Gilbert 401
Röntgen, Julius 157
Rostockerhandboken 21
Roth, Elton Menno 436
Rudd, William H. 78
Runge's *Geistliche Lieder und Psalmen,* Berlin 34
Runyan, William Marion 43, 389

Sankey, Ira David 232, 386
Sargent, Edward H. Gladstone 297
Sateren, Leland B. 159
Scheffler's *Heilige Seelenlust* 142
Schein, Johann Hermann 254
Schmelli's *Musikalisches Gesangbuch* 238
Schlesische Volkslieder 74
Schoenhals, Lawrence R. 56, 95, 120, 170, 201, 202, 218, 227, 266, 269, 313, 316, 320, 346, 351, 357, 406, 425
Scholtes, Peter 477
Schop, Johann 126
Schultes, Wilhelm A.F. 350
Schulz, Johann Abraham Peter 551
Schumann, Robert, *Nachtstucke* 496, 497
Schumann, Valten, *Geistliche Lieder* 22, 353
Scott, Clara H. 426
Scottish Psalter 52, 67, 226, 519
Shanks, D.M. 338
Shaw, Geoffrey, 133, 135
Shaw, Martin 536
Shea, George Beverly 362
Sheppard, Franklin Lawrence 65
Sherwin, William Fiske 211, 420, 524
Shore, William 249
Shrubsole, William 76
Simpson, Robert 434, 520
Singing Master's Assistant, The 120
Smart, Henry Thomas 119, 171, 413, 467
Smith, Henry Percy 367
Smith, John Stafford 543
Smith's R.A., *Sacred Music* 319, 513
Solomon 408
Southern Harmony 406, 435
Spohr, Louis 257, 344, 424
Stainer, John 161, 337, 560, 656
St. Alban's Tune Book 165
St. John Passion 146, 158, 539
St. Matthew Passion 156, 158
Stebbins, George Coles 239, 252, 298, 331
Steurlein, Johann 550
Stockton, John Hart 244, 276
Stokes, Walter 224
Stralsund Gesangbuch 63
Strassburger Kirchenamt 27
Strattner, George C. 438
Sullivan, Arthur Seymour 165, 173, 203, 305, 411, 498
Swedish *Koralbok* 181
Sweetser, Joseph E. 326
Sweney, John R. 90, 202, 385, 427

Tallis, Thomas 40, 210
Tans'ur, William 10, 11, 160
Tattersall's *Psalmody* 548
Teschner, Melchior 146, 539

Thesaurus Musicus 544, 546
Thompson, Will Lamartine 240
Tindley, Charles A. 407
Tomer, William Gould 470
Tourjée, Lizzie Shove 71
Towner, Daniel Brink 250, 271, 368
Tromble, William W. 89, 113, 193

Union Harmony 75

Vail, Silas Jonas 452
Vincent, Charles John 441
Virginia Harmony 269
Vulpius, Melchior 37

Wade's, Cantus Diversi 422
Wade, John Francis 514
Wainwright, Robert 28
Walch, James 493
Walter, William Henry 366
Walther's, Johann, Geistliches Gesangbüchlein 251
Walton, James George 421
Ward, Samuel Augustus 542
Warren, George William 24, 488
Webb, George James 409, 482
Webbe, Samuel, Sr. 370
Weber, Carl Maria von 70, 209, 249, 274, 299

Weedin, Winfield Scott 310
Weisse, Michael 56
Wells, Marcus M. 201
Werner, Johann, Choralbuch 92
Wesley, Charles, Jr. 527
Wesley, Samuel 398, 527
Wesley, Samuel Sebastian 501, 561
Wesley, Samuel Sebastian, European Psalmist 547
Wetzel, Richard D. 355
Whinfield, Walter Grenville 4
Wilkes, John Bernard 36
Willan, Healey 550
Williams, Aaron 20, 476
Williams, A., The New Universal Psalmodist 20, 50
Williams, A., Supplement to Psalmody 323, 511
Williams, Ralph Vaughn 26, 98, 243, 462, 469, 491, 504, 505
Williams, Robert 182
Williams, Thomas John 378, 418
Williams, Thomas, Psalmodia Evangelica 557
Willis, Richard Storrs 74
Wilson, Hugh 319, 513
Wilson, James E. 230
Woodbury, Isaac Baker 152, 203, 375, 402
Work, John W. 137
Wyeth, John, Repository of Sacred Music, Part II 48, 280
Wyvill, Zerubbabel 365

Zeuner, Heinrich Charles 229
Zundel, John 282, 335, 399

ALPHABETICAL INDEX OF TUNES

S.M. (Short Meter)
C.M. (Common Meter)
Ref. (with Refrain)
L.M. (Long Meter)
D. (Doubled)
Irr. (Irregular)

A Flag to Follow-
7 6 7 6 D. Ref. 285
Aberystwyth-7 7 7 7 D. 277
Ackley-11 10 11 10 Ref. 396
Adeste Fideles-Irr. 121
Aletta-7 7 7 7 523
Alford-7 6 8 6 D. 461
All Saints New-
C.M.D. 417, 487, 526
All That Thrills My Soul-
8 7 8 7 Ref. 93
All the Way-8 7 8 7 D. 381
Allen-Irr. 83
Alma Mater-11 11 11 11 499
Almsgiving-8 8 8 4 296
Alta Trinita Beata-8 7 8 7 562
Amazing Grace-C.M. 269
America-6 6 4 6 6 6 4 544
Angel's Song (Song 34)-L.M. 53
Angel's Story-7 6 7 6 D. 302
Angelus-L.M. 142, 199
Antioch-C.M. 115
Ar Hyd Y Nos-
8 4 8 4 8 8 8 4 38
Arfon-7 7 7 7 D. 241
Arlington-C.M. 419
Assam-Irr. 262
Assurance-9 10 9 9 Ref. 287
At Calvary-9 9 9 4 Ref. 250
Attwood (Veni Creator)-
8 8 8 8 8 8 8 204
Aurelia-7 6 7 6 D. 501
Aus Tiefer Not-
8 7 8 7 8 8 7 251
Austrian Hymn-
8 7 8 7 D. 236, 502
Away in a Manger-
11 11 11 11 125
Azmon-C.M. 1
Avon (Martyrdom)-C.M. 319

Ballerma-C.M. 434, 520
Balm in Gilead-Irr. 293
Bangor-C.M. 10, 160
Beatitudo-C.M. 314, 327, 534

Beecher-8 7 8 7 D. 335
Belmont-C.M. 459
Bentley-7 6 7 6 D. 222
Bishopthorpe-C.M. 475
Blessed Be the Name-
C.M. Ref. 79
Blessed Quietness-8 7 8 7 Ref. 394
Blessed Redeemer-9 9 9 9 Ref. .. 88
Bliss-6 6 6 6 8 6 308
Bourne-10 10 10 10 Ref. 245
Boylston-S.M. 346
Bradbury-8 7 8 7 8 7 390
Bradford-C.M. 177
Bread of Life-6 4 6 4 D. 524
Breath of Calvary-
8 7 8 7 Ref. 332
Breslau-L.M. 354
Brother James' Air-
(Marosa) C.M. 30
Bryn Calfaria-8 7 8 7 4 7 7 ... 358
Bula-L.M. 654
Bunessan-5 5 5 3 D. 208

Caithness-C.M. 52
Canonbury-L.M. 496, 497
Canterbury (Song 13)-
7 7 7 6 162
Carmichael-11 7 11 7 Ref. 247
Chapman-11 10 11 10 Ref. 145
Charity-7 7 7 5 337
Chautauqua-7 7 7 7 4 Ref. 211
Christ Arose-11 10 Ref. 175
Christmas-C.M. 127
Christmas Song-
6 6 6 6 12 12 131
Christus, Der Ist Mein Leben-
C.M. 37
Clarendon-7 6 7 6 8 8 Ref. 279
Clayton-7 6 6 5 D. 465
Cleansing Fountain-C.M.D. 217
Coffin-S.M. 113
Comforter-12 12 12 6 Ref. 333
Coming Again-7 7 7 7 Ref. 187
Commitment-Irr. 565

Conrad-14 12 12 14 494
Consecration-Irr. 313
Consolator-11 10 11 10 370
Constantly Abiding-
12 8 12 9 Ref. 442
Converse-8 7 8 7 D. 352
Cooling-C.M. 468
Coronae-8 7 8 7 4 7 189
Coronation-C.M. 75
Cranham-Irr. 138
Creation-L.M.D. 35
Crimond-C.M. 29
Cross of Jesus-8 7 8 7 161
Cushing-11 10 11 10 Ref. 232
CWM Rhondda-8 7 8 7 8 7 .. 25, 69

Dalehurst-C.M. 507
Darlington-5 5 11 D. 225
Darwall's 148th-
6 6 6 6 8 8 .... 46, 62, 184
Davis-6 6 9 D. 280
Davis-11 8 11 8 48
Dennis-S.M. 66, 479
Deo Gracias-L.M. 144
Dessau (Liebster Jesu)-
7 8 7 8 8 8 509
Deus Tuorum Militum (Grenoble)
L.M. 263
Diadem-C.M. 77
Diademata-S.M.D. 183, 410
Dinbych-S.M.D. 328, 453
Divinum Mysterium-
8 7 8 7 8 7 107
Dix-7 7 7 7 7 7 33
Dominica-S.M. 19
Dominus Regit Me-
8 7 8 7 47
Doncaster-S.M. 398
Draw Me Nearer-
10 7 10 7 Ref. 311
Driver-Irr. 220
Duke Street-L.M. 194
Dulce Carmen-8 7 8 7 8 7 300, 403
Dunbar-8 8 8 8 6 295
Dundee (French)-C.M. .. 67, 73, 519
Dunfermline-C.M. 226

page 403

Easter Hymn-
   7 7 7 7 with Alleluias 172
Eaton-8 8 8 8 8 8 365
Ebenezer (Ton-Y-Botel)-
   8 7 8 7 D. 378, 418
Ein' Feste Burg-
   8 7 8 7 6 6 6 6 7 ..... 377, 521
Eisenach-8 8 8 8 8 8 254
El Nathan-C.M. Ref. 395
Elijah-Irr. 563
Ellacombe-7 6 7 6 D. ... 147, 540
Ellacombe-C.M.D. 16
Ellers-10 10 10 10 471
Ellesdie-8 7 8 7 D. 309, 361
England's Lane-7 7 7 7 7 7 .. 135
Epworth-C.M. 527
Erindale-8 8 8 4 31
Ermuntre Dich-
   8 7 8 7 8 8 7 7 126
Es Ist Ein Ros'-
   7 6 7 6 6 7 6 118
Eucharistic Hymn-9 8 9 8 517
Evan-C.M. 334, 374
Even Me-8 7 8 7 3 261
Evening Prayer-8 7 8 7 560
Eventide-10 10 10 10 460
Everlasting Love-
   7 7 7 7 D. 387

Faithful Guide-7 7 7 7 D. 201
Faithfulness-
   11 10 11 10 Ref. 43
Federal Street-L.M. 248, 364
Festal Song-S.M. 366
Fill Me Now-8 7 8 7 Ref. 202
Fillmore-8 8 8 8 8 8 272
Finney-Irr. 559
Finney-5 7 20 5 555
Flemming (Integer Vitae)-
   8 8 8 6 397
Flemming (Integer Vitae)-
   11 11 11 5 443
Forest Green-C.M.D. 491, 504
Fortitude-11 11 11 12 Ref. ... 425
Foundation-11 11 11 11 404
Fountain-L.M. Ref. 258
Freuen Wir Uns All in Ein-
   8 7 8 7 56

Galilee-8 7 8 7 303
Gentle Jesus-7 7 7 7 536
Gerald-C.M.D. 257, 344
Gerig-Irr. 169
Germany-L.M. 506
Glenfinlas-6 5 6 5 .... 134, 212
Gloria (Iris)-7 7 7 7 Ref. 122
Gloria Patri (Greatorex)-Irr. .. 566
Gloria Patri (Meineke)-Irr. .. 567
Glorious Freedom-
   10 9 10 9 Ref. 292
Glory to His Name-
   9 9 9 5 Ref. 276
Go Tell It on the Mountain-
   Irr. 137
God Be in My Head-Irr. 343
God Be with You-9 8 8 9 470
God of Harvest-6 6 4 6 6 6 4 .. 552
God Save the Queen-
   6 6 4 6 6 6 4 546
God Will Take Care of You-
   C.M. Ref. 388
Gopsal-6 6 6 8 8 8 532
Gordon-11 11 11 11 86
Gräfenberg-C.M. 104, 200
Grand Isle-Irr. 535
Greenland-7 6 7 6 D. 64, 191
Greenwood-S.M. 326
Grenoble-L.M. 263
Grosser Gott, Wir Loben Dich-
   7 8 7 8 7 7 463

Hamburg-L.M. 510
Hankey-7 6 7 6 D. Ref. 45
Hanover-10 10 11 11 80
Hauge-8 6 8 6 8 6 466
Hayford-13 13 13 13 Ref. 44

He Abides-Irr. 338
He Hideth My Soul-
   11 8 11 8 Ref. 89
He Is Able to Deliver Thee-
   10 10 10 10 Ref. 221
He Keeps Me Singing-
   9 7 9 7 Ref. 99
He Leadeth Me-L.M. Ref. 429
He Rose Triumphantly-
   6 6 6 6 Ref. 174
He's Everything to Me-Irr. 39
Hebron-L.M. 530
Hendon-7 7 7 7 7 87
Henley-11 10 11 10 227
Hermitage-6 7 6 7 124
Herr Jesu Christ-L.M. ... 531, 556
Hervey's Litany-7 7 7 6 167
Herzliebster Jesu-
   11 11 11 5 158
Hesperus (Quebec)-L.M. 100, 270, 455
Hickman-9 9 9 9 Ref. 289
Hiding in Thee-
   11 11 11 11 Ref. 386
His Yoke Is Easy-Irr. 400
Holiness-6 5 6 5 D. 331
Holiness unto the Lord-
   10 10 10 10 Ref. 321
Holy Faith-8 8 8 8 8 8 320
Holy Manna-8 7 8 7 D. 553
Holywood (St. Thomas)-
   8 7 8 7 8 7 .... 422, 514
Hudson-C.M. Ref. 405
Hull-8 8 6 D. 373
Hursley-L.M. 214
Hyfrydol-8 7 8 7 D.
   .... 97, 103, 109, 186, 503
Hymn to Joy-8 7 8 7 D. 5, 179

I Am Coming, Lord-
   S.M. Ref. 256
I Do Believe-C.M. 266
Ich Halte Treulich Still-
   S.M.R. 238
In Babilone-8 7 8 7 D. 157
In My Heart There Rings a
   Melody-Irr. 436
In Times like These-Irr. 242
Integer Vitae (Flemming)-
   8 8 8 6 397
Integer Vitae (Flemming)-
   11 11 11 5 443
Irby-8 7 8 7 8 8 139
Iris (Gloria)-7 7 7 7 Ref. 122
Irish-C.M. 12
It Is Well-11 8 11 9 Ref. 444
Italian Hymn (Moscow)-
   6 6 4 6 6 6 4 .... 55, 495

Jacob's Ladder-Irr. 458
Jesu, Meine Freude-
   6 6 5 6 6 5 7 8 6 447
Jesus, I Come-Irr. 252
Jesus Is Calling-10 8 10 7 Ref . 239
Jesus Loves Me-7 7 7 7 Ref. .. 537
Jesus Paid It All-
   6 6 7 7 Ref. 216
Jesus Saves-7 6 7 6 7 7 6 ... 481
Jewett-8 6 5 6 5 299
Jones-10 5 10 5 Ref. 430
Judas Maccabeus-
   5 5 6 5 6 5 6 5 178
Judea-11 11 11 11 Ref. 120
Just as I Am-8 8 8 6 307

Keble-L.M. 486
King's Weston-6 5 6 5 D. 98
Kirken Den Er Et-
   8 8 8 8 8 8 8 473
Kremser-12 11 12 11 .... 8, 474
Kum Ba Yah-Irr. 359

Laban-S.M. 415
Lambeth-C.M. 350

Lancashire-7 6 7 6 D. 171, 413
Lasst Uns Erfreuen-
   8 8 4 4 8 8 26
Last Hope (Mercy)-7 7 7 7 ... 196
Lauda Anima-8 7 8 7 8 7 18
Laudes Domini-6 6 6 6 6 6 81
Lebanon-S.M.D. 282, 399
Lebbaeus-7 7 7 6 165
Lemmel-9 8 9 8 Ref. 246
Lenox-6 6 6 6 8 8 288
Leominster-S.M.D. 267, 305
Leoni-6 6 8 4 D. 15
Let Us Break Bread-10 10 Ref. . 515
Liebster Jesu (Dessau)-
   7 8 7 8 8 8 509
Light of the World-
   11 8 11 8 Ref. 218
Lingham-C.M. 450
Litany of the Passion-
   7 7 7 6 164
Llanfair-7 7 7 7 with Alleluias . 182
Llangloffan-7 6 7 6 D. 492
Lobe Den Herren-14 14 4 7 8 .. 63
Lobt Gott, Ihr Christen-C.M. . 112
Loveless-8 7 8 7 Ref. 369
Lux Fiat-11 10 11 10 558
Lyons-10 10 11 11 2

Madrid (Spanish Hymn)-
   6 6 6 6 D. 94
Maitland-C.M. 454
Manchester New-C.M. 28
Maori-10 10 10 10 318
Margaret-Irr. 140
Marion-S.M. Ref. 439
Marlee-6 6 6 6 8 8 159
Martyrdom (Avon)-C.M. 319
Maryton-L.M. 367
Materna-C.M.D. 542
Meditation-C.M. 215
Melita-8 8 8 8 8 8 .. 393, 489, 500
Mendebras-7 6 7 6 D. 110
Mendelssohn-7 7 7 7 D. Ref. . 117
Mendon-L.M. 13, 105
Mercy (Last Hope)-7 7 7 7 ... 196
Merrial-6 6 5 6 5 213
Message-10 8 8 7 7 Ref. 483
Metzler-(Redhead No. 66) C.M. 340
Meyer-Irr. 193
Miles' Lane-C.M. 76
Mit Freuden Zart-8 7 8 7 8 8 7 . 41
Mitchell-12 11 12 11 Ref. 382
Monkland-7 7 7 7 36
More Love to Thee
   6 4 6 4 6 6 4 4 437
Morecambe-10 10 10 10 197
Morning Hymn-L.M. 205, 304
Morning Song-8 6 8 6 8 6 508
Morning Star-11 11 10 207
Moscow (Italian Hymn)-
   6 6 4 6 6 6 4 .... 55, 495
Mueller-Irr. 564
Munich-7 6 7 6 D. 522
My Jesus, I Love Thee-
   11 11 11 11 219
My Redeemer-8 7 8 7 Ref. 91
My Saviour's Love-8 7 8 7 Ref. 154

National Hymn-
   10 10 10 10 .... 24, 488
Near the Cross-7 6 7 6 Ref. .. 348
Near to the Heart of God-
   C.M. Ref. 448
Nearer Home-S.M.D. 203
Need-6 4 6 4 Ref. 347
Neumark-9 8 9 8 8 8 384
New Name in Glory-
   9 8 9 7 Ref. 260
Nicaea-11 12 12 10 54
Noel-C.M.D. 498
Nottingham-7 7 7 7 294
Nun Danket-6 7 6 7 6 6 6 6 9
Nun Komm, Der Heiden Heiland
   7 7 7 7 114

page 404

O Canada-Irr. 545
O Gott, Du Frommer Gott
  6 7 6 7 6 6 6 6 490
O It Is Wonderful-
  13 13 13 13 Ref. 153
O Quanta Qualia-10 10 10 10 85
O Store Gud-11 10 11 10 Ref. ... 61
Oaksville-C.M. 229
Old Hundredth-L.M. 6, 7
Old 112th-8 8 8 8 8 8 22
Old 113th-8 8 8 8 8 8 27
Old 134th (St. Michael)-
  S.M. 195, 528
Oldbridge-8 8 8 4 51
Olive's Brow-L.M. 148
Olivet-6 6 4 6 6 4 268
Ombersley-L.M. 339, 432
Ortonville-C.M. 95
Othello-C.M. Ref. 283
Ovens-Irr. 188

Pardon-Irr. 271
Passion Chorale-7 6 7 6 D. 156
Pax Tecum-10 10 441
Peace-10 10 10 6 286
Pearce-11 10 11 10 192
Pearly Gates-8 7 8 7 Ref. 464
Pen Y Bryn-Irr. 345
Penitence-6 5 6 5 D. 342
Pentecost-L.M. 446
Peterson-11 6 11 6 84
Picardy-8 7 8 7 8 7 554
Pleading Savior-
  8 7 8 7 243
Pleading Saviour-
  8 7 8 7, D. 505
Pollard-5 4 5 4 D. 298
Pope-Irr. 325
Posen-7 7 7 7 438
Power in the Blood-
  10 9 10 8 Ref. 235
Precious Name-8 7 8 7 Ref. 82
Presence-8 7 8 7 Ref. 385
Promise-C.M. Ref. 275
Promises-11 11 11 9 Ref. 231
Puer Nobis-7 6 7 7 133
Puer Nobis Nascitur-L.M. .. 60, 176

Quebec (Hesperus)-
  L.M. 100, 270, 455

Rakem-8 8 8 8 8 8 402
Randolph-9 8 8 9 469
Rathbun-8 7 8 7 451
Ratisbon-7 7 7 7 7 7 .... 34, 92
Ravendale (Stokes)-8 8 6 D. 224
Redeemed-9 8 9 8 Ref. 284
Redhead No. 76-
  7 7 7 7 7 7 .... 150, 198
Redhead No. 66 (Metzler)-C.M. 340
Refuge-7 7 7 7 D. 278
Regent Square-
  8 7 8 7 8 7 .... 119, 467
Repouso Tranquilo-Irr. 132
Rescue-6 5 10 D. Ref. 480
Resignation-C.M.D. 406
Resonet in Laudibus-
  7 7 8 8 Ref. 129
Rest-8 6 8 8 6 446
Retreat-L.M. 349
Riddarholm (Upp, Min Tunga)-
  8 7 8 7 181
Rockingham (Mason)-L.M. 391
Rockingham Old-L.M. 323, 511, 516
Roller-L.M. 401
Rondinella-10 9 10 9 Ref. 301
Russian Hymn-11 10 11 10 17

Sagina-8 8 8 8 8 8 273
St. Agnes-C.M. 101, 533
St. Andrew of Crete-6 5 6 5 D. . 412
St. Anne-C.M. 59
St. Asaph-8 7 8 7 7 7 414
St. Augustine-S.M. 228
St. Bernard-C.M. 371

St. Catherine-8 8 8 8 8 421
St. Christopher-7 6 8 6 8 6 8 6 . 155
St. Chrysostom-
  8 8 8 8 8 8 .... 322, 356
St. Dunstan's-6 5 6 5 6 6 5 234
St. Denio-11 11 11 11 3
St. Elizabeth-5 5 7 5 5 8 74
St. Gertrude-6 5 6 5 D. 411
St. George's, Windsor-
  7 7 7 7 D. 549
St. John's, Hoxton-6 6 6 6 297
St. Kevin-7 6 7 6 D. 173
St. Leonard's-8 7 8 5 423
St. Louis-8 6 8 6 7 6 8 6 136
St. Margaret-8 8 8 8 6 383
St. Martin's-C.M. 11
St. Michael (Old 134th)-
  S.M. 195, 528
St. Michel's-C.M.D. 141
St. Peter-C.M. 143, 478, 512
St. Petersburg-L.M. 290
St. Petersburg-8 8 8 8 8 312
St. Stephen-C.M. 32, 525
St. Theodulph-7 6 7 6 D. .. 146, 539
St. Thomas-S.M. 20, 50, 476
St. Thomas (Holywood)-
  8 7 8 7 7 7 .... 422, 514
Sandon-10 4 10 4 10 10 68
Sandringham-11 10 11 10 529
Satisfied-8 7 8 7 Ref. 255
Schumann-S.M. 360
Seasons-7 6 7 6 D. 379
Selena-8 8 8 8 8 8 .... 152, 375
Serug-6 6 4 6 6 6 4 547
Seymour-7 7 7 7 .... 209, 249, 274
Shea-11 11 11 10 Ref. 362
Sherwin-Irr. 420
Showers of Blessing-
  8 7 8 7 Ref. 233
Sicilian Mariner's Hymn-
  8 7 8 7 8 7 548
Sine Nomine-10 10 10 4 462
Slane-10 10 9 10 357
Solomon-C.M. 408
Song 13 (Canterbury)-7 7 7 6 ... 162
Song 34 (Angel's Song)-L.M. 53
Southwell-S.M. 149, 433
Spanish Hymn (Madrid)-
  6 6 6 6 D. 94
Spohr-C.M. 424
Springs of Living Water-
  12 10 12 10 Ref. 428
Star-Spangled Banner-Irr. 543
Stephanos-8 5 8 3 264
Stille Nacht-Irr. 123
Stockton-C.M. 244
Stories of Jesus-
  8 4 8 4 5 4 5 4 538
Stuttgart-8 7 8 7 72
Such Love-10 10 10 8 Ref. 291
Surrender-8 7 8 7 Ref. 310
Swedish Litany-7 7 7 6 163
Sweet Hour-L.M.D. 351
Sweney-L.M. Ref. 427

Tallis' Canon-L.M. 40, 210
Tender Thought-L.M. 380
Ter Sanctus-8 8 10 10 21
Terra Patris-S.M. 65
The Lord's Prayer-Irr. 355
The Old Rugged Cross-Irr. 456
The Saviour's Name-C.M. Ref. ... 78
The Song of the Soul Set Free-
  Irr. 440
The Unveiled Christ-
  8 7 8 7 Ref. 185
The Whole Wide World-
  7 6 7 6 D. Ref. 485
They'll Know We Are Christians-
  Irr. 477
Thompson-11 7 11 7 Ref. 240
Tidings-11 10 11 10 Ref. 493
Tindley-Irr. 407
To God Be the Glory-
  11 11 11 11 Ref. 42
Tokyo-7 5 7 5 D. 541
Ton Y Botel (Ebenezer)-
  8 7 8 7 D. 378, 418

Toplady-7 7 7 7 7 7 392
Toronto-11 10 11 10 Ref. 484
Toulon-10 10 10 10 518
Trentham-S.M. 336
Truro-L.M. 108
Trust-8 7 8 7 206
Trust and Obey-6 6 9 D. Ref. ... 368
Trust in Jesus-8 7 8 7 Ref. 376
Trusting-7 7 7 7 265
Truth-Irr. 426
Tryggare Kan Ingen Vara-L.M. ... 49
Tucker-8 3 8 3 D. 316
Tugwood-L.M. 57

Universal Praise-
  10 4 6 6 6 6 10 4 4
Unsearchable Riches-
  10 7 10 7 Ref. 90
Unser Herrscher-8 7 8 7 8 7 190
Uxbridge-L.M. 341

Vater Unser-8 8 8 8 8 8 .... 22, 353
Veni Creator (Attwood)-
  8 8 8 8 8 8 204
Veni Emmanuel-8 8 8 8 8 116
Victory (Palestrina)-8 8 8 4 ... 180
Vienna-7 7 7 7 472
Vom Himmel Hoch-L.M. 130
Vox Dilecti-C.M.D. 281

Wachet Auf Ruft Uns Die Stimme-
  Irr. 111
Wakefield-6 6 6 6 Ref. 457
Waldrons-C.M. 431
Wareham-L.M. 14, 96, 315
Warum Sollt Ich-8 3 3 6 D. 128
Webb-7 6 7 6 D. 409, 482
Wellesley-8 7 8 7 71
Were You There?-Irr. 170
Wesley-Irr. 561
What God Hath Promised-
  9 9 9 9 Ref. 389
Where He Leads Me-8 8 8 9 259
Whiter than Snow (Fischer)-
  11 11 11 11 Ref. 329
Whiter than Snow (Kirkpatrick)-
  10 10 10 10 Ref. 330
Wie Lieblich Ist er Maien-
  7 6 7 6 D. 550
Wilmot-8 7 8 7 70
Wilson-7 7 7 7 230
Winchester Old-C.M. 324
Windham-L.M. 237
Windsor-C.M. 151
Wir Glauben All 'n Einen Gott-
  8 7 7 7 7 58
Wir Pflugen 7 6 7 6 D. Ref. 551
With Thy Spirit Fill Me-
  7 7 7 6 Ref. 306
Witness-C.M.D. Ref. 363
Wonderful Grace-Irr. 106
Wonderful Peace (Lillenas)-
  10 8 10 5 Ref. 445
Wonderful Saviour-
  10 9 10 9 Ref. 102
Wondrous Love-12 9 12 9 435
Woodworth-L.M. 253
Words of Life-Irr. 223
Wrestling Jacob-8 8 8 8 8 8 317
Wunderbarer König-
  6 6 8 D. 3 3 6 6 23
Wye Valley-6 5 6 5 D. Ref. 449

Yigdal-(Leoni) 6 6 8 4 D. 15

Zion-8 7 8 7 4 7 372

page 405

SCRIPTURAL REFERENCES IN HYMNS

GENESIS
1:1 .... 3, 38
1:5 528
1:9-31 16
2:7 336
3:15 220
5:24 314
17:1 17
18:18 494
20:7 331
20:8, 11 527
27:38 261
28:11 458
28:15 73
28:17 22
32:26 323
32:29 317
33:20, 22 73

EXODUS
3:14 .... 15, 193
13:14 252
15 173
15:11 321
15:21 96
16:4 553
16:7 208
19:5 368
20:8 528
20:11 37
25:22 349
28:36 321
32:33 260
33:14 .... 19, 39, 48, 244
33:15 385
33:22 .... 89, 377
34:21 528

LEVITICUS
6:13 304
8:35 346
26:35 346

NUMBERS
22:12 474

DEUTERONOMY
6:5 405
6:6, 7 496
8:3, 16 530
30:14 521
33:25 382

JOSHUA
24:15 .... 418, 533

I SAMUEL
.... 256
10:24 546

II SAMUEL
7:22 61
12:13 225
22:2 473

I KINGS
8:56 275
10:7 405
19:12 446

I CHRONICLES
16:9 96
16:11 557
16:29 .... 5, 567
16:31 59
17:16, 17 269
28:9 329
29:11 20
29:12 62
29:14 360

II CHRONICLES
7:14 .... 547, 350
15:15 290

16:9 .... 359, 68
20:20 58
29:30b 556
30:8 298

NEHEMIAH
5:19 433
8:10 11
9:5 20
9:6 33

JOB
1:21 .... 49, 79
5:17 455
19:25 .... 87, 177
23:8-10 468
23:12 347
29:2 314
36:29 — 37:6 67
38:4-30 5
38:7 .... 36, 65
42:3 468

PSALMS
2:12 52
3:5 207
3:8 474
4:1 359
4:7 405
4:8 .... 211, 212, 561
5:2 206
5:3 .... 81, 205, 208
5:8 .... 318, 560, 561
6:4 249
7:5 3
8 37
8:1 34
8:3, 4 .... 35, 39
8:5 189
9:9 .... 277, 278
9:11 .... 6, 181, 654
16:6 431
16:8 565
16:11 .... 100, 101, 448, 468
17 465
17:3 .... 318, 560
17:8 278
17:15 465
18:1 .... 11, 437
18:30 9
18:32 25
18:35 66
18:46 173
19 114
19:1-6 .... 33, 35, 39, 466
19:7,12 520
19:14 .... 298, 343
21:2 386
21:13 20
22:1-5 165
22:3, 4 .... 24, 421
22:6 157
22:23 .... 128, 193
22:24 167
23 (paraphrase) .. 29, 30, 47, 402
23 .... 69, 168, 282, 349, 379, 381, 396, 397, 429, 468, 475
24 (paraphrase) 108
24 .... 14, 33, 34, 65, 261, 439
25:1 556
25:5 .... 69, 429
25:7 433
25:9 .... 232, 384
25:11 .... 209, 272
26:3 44
26:8 .... 476, 539
27:1 .... 64, 92, 246, 432, 443
27:4 19
27:5 352
27:7 36
27:7, 9, 10 165
27:10 372

27:11 69
28:7 36
29:2 .... 5, 42
29:11 .... 17, 400, 441, 471
31:2, 3 392
31:3 403
31:5 284
31:19 393
32:1 272
32:6, 7 278
32:8 .... 69, 232, 474
33:1 .... 7, 88, 439
33:2 283
33:6 36
33:12 .... 21, 542, 544
34:1 .... 12, 79
34:4 286
34:18 .... 266, 282, 343, 393
34:22 277
35:28 .... 1, 69
36:7 .... 96, 448
36:9 278
37:4 .... 280, 437
37:5 .... 244, 398, 399
38:10 255
39:7 267
39:12 .... 359, 563
40:3 99
40:6 237
40:8 .... 287, 312, 334
40:17 433
42:1 .... 255, 322, 347, 424
42:2 .... 265, 323, 428
42:5 267
42:7 219
42:11 393
43:3 .... 432, 558
45:2 .... 74, 93, 95
45:7 110
46:1 377
46:4 503
46:9 17
46:10 .... 446, 554
47:1 7
47:6 .... 112, 120
48:1 .... 61, 321
48:12-14 542
48:14 .... 9, 24, 69, 391, 402
49:15 176
50:23 6
51:1 249
51:2 .... 266, 325, 520
51:3 249
51:7 .... 258, 329, 330
51:10 .... 327, 330, 503, 564
51:17 .... 254, 266
52:8 10
55:14 431
55:22 .... 267, 384, 388, 565
57:8, 9 205
59:16 207
61:2 .... 386, 392
61:8 27
62:2 392
62:11 236
63:3 96
64:1 319
65:2 563
65:9 51
66:4 4
66:16 45
67:3 .... 83, 181
68:19 .... 51, 552
71:1 399
71:4 252
71:14 69
72:6 261
72:8 194
72:15 81
72:19 .... 82, 110, 494

73:1 564
73:24 201
73:25 .... 255, 263
74:12 46
79:9 .... 235, 443
81:1 27
84:1 476
84:2 424
84:4 475
85:6 345
85:8 17
86:1 347
86:15 71
87:2, 3 .... 50, 502, 503
89:1 103
89:13, 18 24
89:16 101
89:26 563
90:1, 2 59
91 (paraphrase) 40
91:1, 2 460
91:4 .... 210, 232, 469
92:1, 2 .... 43, 208
92:13 49
93:1-4 .... 14, 80, 358
93:5 339
94:16 366
95:1 .... 7, 94
95:6 .... 16, 21, 31, 553, 555, 556
95:7, 8 248
96 16
96:1 540
96:2, 3 .... 483, 489
96:10 184
96:13 237
97:1 .... 41, 184
97:1, 6 35
97:3 237
97:9 184
98 115
98:1 .... 14, 180
98:4 115
99:5 21
100 (paraphrase) 7, 53
100 .... 16, 51
102:18 26
103 (paraphrase) 72
103:1 79
103:1-6 63
103:2 .... 18, 444
103:2, 5 552
103:17 .... 70, 162, 249
103:20-22 23
104 2
104:24 .... 13, 26, 33
104:33 16
104:34 101
105:2 96
105:40 381
105:43, 45 544
106:4 335
107:2 .... 177, 283
107:8 6
107:9 100
107:15 23
107:21, 22 33
107:29 349
108:2, 3 205
109:26 274
113 .... 13, 32, 80
116:1 405
116:5 254
116:7 33
116:15 462
117 .... 6, 21, 72, 254
118:8, 9 .... 376, 393, 397
118:14 389
118:14, 28, 29 48
118:24-26 527
119:9 307
119:12-14 496
119:18 .... 426, 520
119:30 498
119:63 474

page 406

Reference	Page(s)
119:90	43
119:94	311
119:97	45
119:103, 165	66
119:105	520, 522, 525
119:130	522, 525
119:131	255
119:132	433
119:176	282
121:1-7	68
121:4	534
122:1, 2	476, 539
125:2	372, 469
126:3	44
126:6	548
127:1, 2	210, 539
129:5	372
130 (paraphrase)	251
130:4, 5	249, 267
132:14	503
133:1	477, 479
134:2	553
137:5, 6	476
138:10	429
139	380
139:9, 10	207, 208
139:12	214, 391
139:18	207
139:23	318, 559
141:2	209, 211
143:6	166, 266
143:10	298
145:1	72
145:3	26, 146
145:6	14
145:9, 10	2
145:13	59
145:15	551
146:2	27, 41, 91
146:5	324, 393
147:1	33, 439
147:3	370
147:20	547
148 (paraphrase)	62
148:5	38
148:13	42
149:1	50
150	63, 552
150:2	83

PROVERBS

Reference	Page(s)
1:20, 21	259
1:24	241
3:5-7	369, 374, 498
3:11	455
3:13	499
3:24	210, 212, 213
4:18	432
6:23	522
8:17	285
9:10	499
10:9	396
10:22	371, 474
14:34	547
16:3	398
18:10	101
19:17	360
19:22a	362
20:28	546
23:23	499
23:26	245, 259
28:13	203
29:6	96
29:18	280

ECCLESIASTES

Reference	Page(s)
11:6	206

SOLOMON

Reference	Page(s)
2:1	118
2:16	387
8:7	219, 405, 532

ISAIAH

Reference	Page(s)
1:18	216, 330
1:24	14
2:3	223
2:5	229
4:5, 6	503
6:3	54, 211
6:5	466
6:8	256, 361
7:14	116, 117
9:3	549
9:6	82, 89, 101, 112, 117, 121, 125, 135
9:7	377, 102
11:1, 2	118
11:6	125
12:2	289, 299, 460
21:4	255
25:1	43, 220
25:4	97, 277, 377
26:1	503
26:3	369, 393, 441, 442, 446, 449
26:9	255
27:1	490
28:5	76, 270
30:29	14
32:2	155
32:17	394
33:5	332
33:20, 21, 27, 28	508
35:10	370, 371
40:1	370
40:3	488
40:8	521
40:9	488, 492
40:11	29, 402, 406
40:17	13
40:28	59, 332
40:29	199
40:31	264, 389, 564
41:10	97, 389, 500
41:13	429
41:14	91
41:20	65
42:6	490
42:12	83
42:16	391
43:1	91, 177
43:2	19, 48, 391, 397
44:3	341
44:8	99
45:22	246
48:10	372
48:16	219
48:17	413, 429
48:18	219, 449
49:7	43
49:26	14
50:4	496
50:10	393
51:9	205
52:1	205, 393
52:7	493
53	152, 159
53:3	157, 160, 185
53:4, 5	149
53:5	153, 156, 159, 161, 188
55:1	219, 240
55:7	247
56:6, 7	495
56:7	539
58	407
58:6, 7	89, 333, 508
58:11	9, 69, 255
59:19	420
59:20	116, 177
60:1, 20	206
60:16	14
60:20	373
61:1	252
61:10	270, 290, 393
62:3	76, 76
63:1	14
63:16	8
64:8	298
66:3	534

JEREMIAH

Reference	Page(s)
3:11	33
6:16	375
8:22	293
17:7	52
23:5	102
23:28	496
24:7	327
31:3	164, 291, 383
31:33	328
32:19	14
44:4	328

LAMENTATIONS

Reference	Page(s)
1:12	151, 160
3:22	163, 249
3:22, 23	43, 540
5:21	540

EZEKIEL

Reference	Page(s)
3:9	415
16:8	540
18:7	508
18:31	241
33:8-19	241
34:6, 11	282
34:26	233, 261
36:25	325
36:26	327
36:27	198, 320
37:6	336
37:14	198
40:4	426

DANIEL

Reference	Page(s)
3:17	221
5:23	336
7:9, 22	55
7:27	194
10:21	523

JOEL

Reference	Page(s)
2:13	249
2:21	544
2:26	15

AMOS

Reference	Page(s)
4:11	272

JONAH

Reference	Page(s)
2:2	256

MICAH

Reference	Page(s)
4:7	184
5:2	136
6:8	314, 452
7:8	373
7:18	31, 93, 162, 249
7:19	314

NAHUM

Reference	Page(s)
1:15	127

HABAKKUK

Reference	Page(s)
2:20	22, 23, 554
3:2	345
3:18	222

ZEPHANIAH

Reference	Page(s)
1:15	237

HAGGAI

Reference	Page(s)
2:7	109
2:9	443

ZECHARIAH

Reference	Page(s)
7:9	508
9:9	126, 146, 147
10:1	233
13:1	217, 392

MALACHI

Reference	Page(s)
2:6	426
3:1	467
3:2, 3	319
3:6	15
3:10	233
4:2	214

MATTHEW

Reference	Page(s)
1:20, 21	220
1:21	135, 480
1:23	120
2:1	119
2:1, 2, 9, 10	123
2:2	119, 133
2:4	133
2:7-11	134
2:10	128, 131
2:11	122
3:11	199, 319, 332
3:16, 17	197
4:9-13	353, 355
4:10	31
4:19	303, 316, 361
5:6	265, 524
5:7	163
5:8	326, 330
5:10-12	418
5:13-16	487
5:16	304
5:48	339
6:9-13	353, 355
6:10	296
6:11	530
6:21	138
6:32	347
6:33	245
7:7	247, 286
7:24, 25	501
8:17	352
8:19	259, 262
8:22	245
9:21	226
9:37, 38	548
10:8	360
10:16	486
10:29-31	65
10:37-39	303
10:38	309
10:42	506
11:28	223, 227, 235, 240, 248, 264
11:28-30	245, 281, 376
11:29, 30	244, 400, 536
12:8	527
12:50	164
13:3	548, 550
13:24-30	549
14:13-21	524
14:19	524
14:33	555
14:36	226
15:24	282
16:16	503
16:16, 18	501
16:18	411, 473
16:24	309, 454
17:20	365
18:3	320
18:4	120
18:12	282
18:20	19, 358, 472
19:14	125, 509, 538
20:28	116, 159, 167
21:1-11	146
21:5	151
21:6	146
21:9	146, 147, 527
21:15, 16	538
21:22	563
21:29	257
22:9	506
24:14	483, 492
24:23	453
24:44	111, 191
25:6	111
25:7-10, 13	111
25:13	187, 191, 346
25:21	453
25:21, 23	461
25:31, 32	238
25:35	508
25:40	367, 504
26:20-29	516
26:36	148, 150
26:38	160
26:39	287, 299, 334
26:41	346
26:42	296, 299
26:64	192
27	170
27:28, 29	156
27:29	519
27:46	164
27:51	151, 185

Reference	Pages
28:2	175
28:6, 7	172, 174, 179
28:9	171
28:18	75
28:18-20	333, 487
28:19, 20	500, 507
28:20	397, 468

MARK

Reference	Pages
1:17	259
2:7	125
2:17	239
4:2	538
4:26-29	549
6:31	446
8:6	551
8:12	229
8:34	302, 316
8:34-38	417
9:24	374
10:14	509, 537
10:28	309
10:38	417
11:1-10	147
13:35, 36	191
14	524
14:32-42	148, 150
14:36	299
15	170
15:46	175
16:2-20	182
16:6	174
16:12	367
16:15	486, 489, 493
16:15, 16	485

LUKE

Reference	Pages
1:15	320
1:32	135
1:33	377
1:78, 79	92, 116
2:1, 2	127
2:4-14	136
2:7	125, 130, 132, 134, 135, 140
2:7, 12-16	131
2:8	127
2:8, 9	119
2:8-14	120, 137
2:9, 10	129, 137
2:11	139
2:11, 12	127, 133, 134
2:13, 14	36, 117, 145
2:14	122, 128, 130
2:15	121
2:16	123, 134
2:20	122, 128
2:32	490
2:40, 52	139
2:74	110
3:16	110, 199
4:4	524
4:18	348, 1
5:1	538
5:4	430
5:11	407
5:32	243
6:21	255, 306
6:35	524
7:34	97
7:47	230
9:26	364
9:57	302
9:60	488, 492
10:20	260, 280
10:39	224
11:1	353
11:2	296, 299, 355
11:13	200, 202, 332
11:28	52
12:12	203
12:37	238
12:40	111, 187
14:26, 33	417
15:2	230
15:3-7	47
18:1	354
18:16	509, 537
19:10	480, 504
20:36	459
21:27	113, 187
22:14	513
22:19	512, 519
22:32	342
22:39	150
22:39-44	148
23	170
23:33	150, 250
23:34	88, 162, 422
23:43	152, 163, 230
23:46	168
24:15	472
24:26	151
24:29	211, 385, 460
24:30	515, 517
24:31, 32	182
24:34	172, 173
24:47	483, 489
24:51	182

JOHN

Reference	Pages
1:1	107, 521
1:4	105, 218, 490
1:4, 5	92
1:9	60, 432, 490
1:11	140
1:14	114, 121, 130, 138, 524
1:16	90, 281
1:17	274
1:29	151, 510, 536
1:29, 36	104
3:11	87
3:14	138
3:15, 16	480, 560
3:16	159, 291, 322, 378, 435, 484, 495
3:17	279, 485
4:10	323
4:13, 14	166
4:22	87
4:24	31, 553, 566
4:35	487
4:42	88, 256
5:8, 9	276
5:25	270
5:36	141
6:11	551
6:33	524
6:35	281, 358, 524
6:37	253
6:41	517
6:41, 50	530
6:51-58	517, 518
6:68	223
7:17	287
7:37	166, 239, 264
7:37, 38	281
7:38, 39	341
8:12	142, 206, 218, 246, 281, 490, 497
8:31, 32	368, 418
8:32	524, 543
8:32, 36	440
8:36	305
9:4	141, 365
10:1-18	47
10:3	429
10:4	361
10:11	29, 282, 288
10:11-16	402
10:14, 15	48, 390
10:16	495
10:17, 18	169
10:37	141
11:25	179, 463
11:28	259
12:15	108
12:26	302, 357, 361
12:28	541
12:35	432
12:35, 46	497
12:47	480
12:50	496
13:1	378, 383
13:7	67, 468
13:15	301, 506
14:1-3	252
14:2	227, 270, 450
14:2, 3	50, 190
14:6	142, 285, 432
14:16	198, 333, 334, 336, 338, 394
14:17	204
14:19	175
14:21	335
14:23	338
14:26	198, 203, 315
14:27	445, 471
15:4	448, 460
15:5	347, 385
15:9, 13	149
15:10	252, 379, 442
15:12	164, 476
15:13	435, 457
15:16	366
16:13	69, 196, 201, 315, 498
16:23, 24	180, 353
16:28	130
17:17	523, 525
17:21-23	472
17:26	86
18:37	361
19:16, 17	456
19:17	454
19:26, 27	164
19:28	166
19:30	167, 422
20:19	176
20:21	482, 484, 486, 506
20:21, 22	306, 332, 336
20:31	295
21:14	172
21:15	405, 438
21:17	356

ACTS

Reference	Pages
1:8	195, 199, 332, 363, 485, 491
1:11	113, 186, 187
1:14	471
2:4	202
2:17	195
2:21	289
2:23	158
2:28	280, 290, 363
2:36	84, 129, 189
2:38	243
2:39	275
2:42	515
3:1	351
3:1-6	82
3:19	261, 556
4:12	78, 143, 215, 289, 481
4:20	45
5:20	45
5:31	80, 249
7:54, 55, 59, 60	417
8:2	292
8:29	201
9:4, 5	257
9:6	310
9:31	370
10:36	75, 77
10:38	142
10:42	487
13:32	493
14:17	551
16:31	246, 293, 481
17:24	13
17:24, 26	105
17:27	93
17:28	57, 105
18:10	397
20:24	346
20:32	469
22:14, 15	80
24:16	344
26:14	256
26:18	249
26:22	14

ROMANS

Reference	Pages
1:3, 4	185, 321
1:7	535
1:16	293, 364
2:5	340
3:23-25	289
4:16	228
4:21	389
4:24, 25	188
5:2	268
5:5	200, 319, 335, 434
5:6	156
5:8	149, 215, 273, 291, 322
5:8-10	169
5:9	258, 284, 513
5:11	280, 288
5:17	269
5:20, 21	273
6:6	155
6:13	310
6:18, 22	292, 297, 507
6:19	298, 300
7:6	313
8:2	305
8:9	320
8:10	198
8:15	288
8:28, 37	12
8:29	301
8:31	49
8:33	270
8:34	172, 288
8:35	383
8:35, 37	349
8:37-39	49, 246, 387
9:17	557
9:21	298
10:9	244
10:15	492
11:26	109
11:33	70
12	365
12:1	287, 294, 305, 307, 356, 510
12:2	296
12:5	411
12:11	487, 564
13:1	546
13:11, 12	92, 324
14:7	496
14:9	154
14:10	238
14:17	196, 550
15:13	200, 290, 341
16:24	560

I CORINTHIANS

Reference	Pages
1:9	43
1:17, 18	366
1:18	510
1:23, 24, 31	451
1:28	157
1:30	8, 270
2:2	87, 152
2:13	203
3:10,11	204
3:11	393, 404, 467
3:16	57
4:5	380
4:15	357
5:7, 8	172, 512
6:20	44, 294, 541
9:19	365
9:24	416
10:3	232
10:4	242, 386, 392
10:13	342, 351, 425
10:16	515, 518
10:31	205, 557
11:23-26	515, 516, 517, 518
11:28	512, 554
12:4	472
13:13	337, 434
15:3, 4	169, 174, 288
15:10	160
15:19, 20	172, 454
15:25	102
15:27	1
15:34	503

5:35ff. 463	5:25, 26 476,	1:9 ..... 228, 341, 361	1:10 331
5:54, 55 .... 178, 180	501, 507	1:10 156	1:18, 19 .... 91, 217,
6:13 .... 346, 409, 419	5:28 532	1:12 .... 87, 385, 395	279, 284, 348
II CORINTHIANS	5:31 529	2:1 234	1:19 513
:3-5 .... 81, 222	6:6 ..... 287, 363	2:2 496	1:12 ...... 185, 373
:20 .... 231, 275	6:10 234	2:3 419	1:22 326
:14 ...... 146, 180	6:10-20 ..... 410, 412	2:3, 4 ...... 411, 413	1:25 526
:17 292	6:14 409	2:19 .... 61, 404	2:2 255
:6 ... 196, 218, 432	6:18 350	3:7, 14-15 498	2:6 467
:7 447	**PHILIPPIANS**	3:12 454	2:9 ...... 1, 229, 432
:14 176	1:9 .... 11, 437	3:15 523	2:17 546
:18 518	1:20 364	4:8 .... 413, 456	2:21 .... 153, 158,
:1 464	1:27, 28 .... 414, 415	4:18 453	301, 417
:7 396	2:1 560	**TITUS**	2:24 .... 158, 168,
:14 142	2:5 423	1:15 326	308, 312
:15 .... 174, 295, 317	2:5-11 .... 98, 339, 506	2:13 .... 191, 192	2:25 ..... 29, 239, 282
:17 540	2:6 117	3:1, 2 310	3:7 532
:7 420	2:7 .... 112, 505	3:5 .... 163, 228, 249	3:18 ... 88, 153, 161, 188
:1 321	2:8 .... 514, 519	3:5, 6 28	4:6 57
:10 282	2:9 104	3:8 .... 344, 395	4:11 541
:9 106	2:9, 10 .... 75, 77,	**HEBREWS**	5:7 ..... 66, 97, 267,
:6, 7 ...... 360, 362	78, 98, 189	1:1 .... 236, 526	316, 374, 388, 416, 532
:8 388	2:9-11 .... 82, 107, 143	1:3 .... 60, 188	5:8, 9 ... 346, 412, 415
:9 .. 97, 168, 269, 382	2:15, 16 ..... 522, 524	1:4, 9 104	5:10, 11 25
:9, 10 389	3:7, 8 .... 294, 312, 510	1:9 110	**II PETER**
:11 .... 226, 441	3:7-10 252	2:9 .... 183, 188, 189	1:3 427
:14 560	3:8 ..... 306, 427, 447	2:14 181	1:4 .... 231, 275
GALATIANS	3:9 393	3:1, 2 453	1:5 499
:4 288	3:10, 11 171	3:7, 8 247	2:15 282
:20 .... 149, 155, 273,	3:12 262	3:14 518	3:7-11 237
308, 310, 312, 322	4:1 409	4:3, 9 375	3:9 257
:8 545	4:4 .... 7, 46	4:9 .. 322, 339, 340, 448	3:11 331
:22 .... 228, 263, 267	4:6 352	4:14, 15 ... 139, 157	3:18 .. 80, 94, 427, 457
:27 507	4:7 .... 375, 444,	4:15 371	**I JOHN**
:28 .... 477, 478	445, 471, 562	4:16 347	1:3 .... 349, 459
:4 145	4:9 226	5:7, 8 308	1:3, 7 479
:6 288	4:11 408	7:25 ..... 221, 288, 342	1:5 .... 229, 274
:1 .... 292, 440	4:19 .... 90, 382	9:11-28 217	1:7 .. 216, 253, 276,
:22 445	**COLOSSIANS**	9:14 .... 265, 344	325, 329, 474, 513, 520
:22, 23 301	1:14 ...... 8, 235, 464	9:22 276	1:9 .... 43, 162,
:4 312	1:15 3	9:28 308	249, 263, 376
:25 .... 197, 200, 379	1:16 .... 38, 63, 65	10:10 154	2:5 335
:2 482	1:18 .... 357, 411	10:15 287	2:25 275
:2, 9 548	1:20 .... 217, 276, 510	10:19-25 351	3:1 .... 124, 291, 435
:10 360	1:21, 22 457	10:22 .... 311, 329	3:1-11 102
:4 ... 87, 155, 348,	1:27 .... 84, 457	10:23 .... 43, 275	3:3 344
451, 456, 510, 511, 519	2:6 452	10:37 366	3:14 99
:8 470	2:9 142	10:39 58	3:16 .... 149, 335
EPHESIANS	2:12 507	11:6 264	3:18 477
:3, 4 .... 327, 331	3:3, 4 .... 192, 312	11:13 462	3:24 198
:1 .... 217, 249, 284	3:11 81	11:24-26 453	4:9-11 .... 317, 322, 491
:3 67	3:14, 15 ..... 335, 441	11:26 90	4:17 237
:2 376	3:17 82	11:39 421	4:18 340
:2, 14 300	3:23-25 505	12:1 297	4:19 .... 86, 220,
:7-20 184	4:2 .... 346, 354	12:2 .... 142, 161, 169,	253, 405, 438, 537
:1 .... 98, 104	4:12 430	268, 300, 374, 456	4:42 74
:3 141	**I THESSALONIANS**	12:2, 3 308	5:6-10 287
:5 .... 154, 274	1:5, 6 ...... 204, 287	12:5, 6, 11 455	**JUDE**
:6 .... 90, 269	4:3, 4, 7 204	12:14 331	14 461
:8 .... 228, 243,	4:16 190	12:22 50	24 282
268, 392, 514	4:17 .... 186, 209	12:29 319	**REVELATION**
:3 .... 253, 510, 513	5:6 346	13:1 540	1:5 .... 271, 322, 358
:4, 15 478	5:17, 18 ... 51, 353, 552	13:5 ...... 384, 404,	1:6 56
:0-22 .. 242, 467, 501	5:23 ..... 49, 192, 312	442, 534	1:7 .... 186, 190
:6 305	5:24 43	13:6 500	1:10 527
:3 38	**II THESSALONIANS**	13:8 44	2:10 417
:3 450	1:10 189	13:12 .... 153, 215	3:3 187
:4-19 319	3:3 .... 43, 425	13:15 300	3:5, 18 393
:6 268	3:16 443	**JAMES**	3:20 .... 240, 247
:7-19 .... 144, 224,	**I TIMOTHY**	1:5 25	4:4 393
:06, 312, 322, 401, 430	1:1 460	1:12 86	4:8 58
:7-21 .... 28, 71	1:5 326	1:17 ... 51, 71, 229, 550	4:11 .... 65, 95
:0 .... 221, 293, 356	1:14 .... 28, 106	2:12, 18 141	5:9 ... 1, 80, 154, 177
:5 305	1:15 .... 270, 273, 480	4:6, 10 408	5:9, 10 45
:6 525	1:16 183	4:7 412	5:9, 11, 12 461
:8 ...... 174, 382	1:17 ... 3, 62, 84, 194	4:8 .... 314, 448	5:11, 12 ... 85, 121, 461
:3 413	2:3-6 .... 143, 167, 240	4:14 240	5:11, 13 .... 75, 77, 465
:3 313	4:10 74	4:18 343	5:12 .. 95, 181, 215, 451
:4 ...... 156, 452	5:4 533	5:7, 8 ..... 113, 465	5:13 178
:8 229	5:6 408	5:13 103	6:14-17 186
:9 ...... 490, 503	6:12 ..... 416, 419	5:16 352	6:23 520
:9 202	6:15 .. 55, 183, 189, 194	**I PETER**	7:9 348
, 20 103,	**II TIMOTHY**	1:3 .... 9, 179, 458	7:9-15 .... 189, 393
436, 531	1:6 304	1:3-5 .... 171, 176	7:13, 14 ..... 270, 468
		1:8 .... 11, 86,	7:14 ... 258, 330, 417
		101, 290, 397, 440	7:17 .... 403, 461

10:6	65	15:3, 4	3, 440, 541	19:16	75, 76, 84, 105	22:16	348, 44
11:15	186, 189	17:14	77	21	461	22:17	230, 25
11:17	55	19:1	85, 105, 220	21:23	490	22:17-20	18
12:11	417	19:6	172	22:3, 4	459	22:21	47
14:6	223	19:8	393	22:9	555	22:14	46
14:13	453, 462	19:12	183	22:14	50		

COMPLETE INDEX OF FIRST LINES AND TITLES

Titles are in CAPS AND SMALL CAPS.   First lines are in lower case type.

A charge to keep I have 346
A mighty fortress is our God 377
A virgin unspotted 120
A wonderful Saviour is Jesus my Lord 89
Abide with me; fast falls the eventide 460
According to Thy gracious word 519
Ah, holy Jesus, how hast Thou offended? .. 158
Alas! and did my Saviour bleed? 513
All creatures of our God and King 26
All for Jesus, all for Jesus 300
All glory, laud, and honor 146
All glory to Jesus, begotten of God 84
All hail the power of Jesus' name!
  (Coronation) 75
All hail the power of Jesus' name!
  (Miles' Lane) 76
All hail the power of Jesus' name!
  (Diadem) 77
All my heart this night rejoices 128
All my life long I had panted 255
All people that on earth do dwell 7
All praise to Him who reigns above 79
All praise to Thee, my God, this night 210
ALL THAT THRILLS MY SOUL 93
All the way my Saviour leads me 381
All to Jesus I surrender 310
All ye that pass by 225
Almighty Father, hear our prayer 563
Alone Thou goest forth 160
Am I a soldier of the cross? 419
Amazing grace! how sweet the sound 269
Amens 656
AMERICA 544
AMERICA THE BEAUTIFUL 542
And can it be? 273
Angels, from the realms of glory 119
Angels we have heard on high 122
Another year is dawning 540
Arise, my soul, arise 288
Art thou weary, art thou troubled? 264
As Jacob with travel was weary one day .. 458
As we proclaim Your name this hour 557
As yearns the deer for cooling streams ... 424
Ask ye what great thing I know 87
AT CALVARY 250
At the name of Jesus 98
Awake, my soul, and with the sun 205
Awake, my soul, in joyful lays 96
Away in a manger, no crib for a bed 125

Beautiful Saviour 74
Be not dismayed whate'er betide 388
Be present at our table, Lord 530
Be still, my soul, before thy God 455
Be Thou my vision 357
Before the great Jehovah's throne 53

Behold the Saviour of mankind 15
Beneath the cross of Jesus 15
Blessed assurance, Jesus is mine! 28
Blessed be the fountain of blood 25
Blessed Jesus, here are we 50
BLESSED QUIETNESS 39
BLESSED REDEEMER 8
Blessing and honor and glory and power .. 8
Blest are the pure in heart 32
Blest be the tie that binds 47
Bread of the world in mercy broken 51
Break forth, O beauteous heavenly light .. 12
Break forth, O living light of God 52
Break Thou the bread of life 52
BREATH OF CALVARY 33
Breathe, O mighty One from heaven 33
Breathe on me, Breath of God 33
Built on the Rock the church doth stand .. 47

"Called unto holiness," church of our God 3
Cast thy burden upon the Lord 5
Children of the heavenly Father ....
CHRIST AROSE 1
Christ for the world we sing! 4
Christ from whom all blessings flow 4
Christ is coming! let creation 1
Christ is made the sure Foundation 4
Christ is risen! raise your voices 1
Christ is the world's true light 4
"Christ the Lord is risen today" 1
Christ, whose glory fills the skies ....
Christian, dost thou see them? 4
Christians, we have met to worship 5
Cleanse me from my sin, Lord 3
CLOSE TO THEE 4
Come, Christians, join to sing ....
Come, ever blessed Spirit, come ....
Come, every soul by sin oppressed 2
Come, Holy Ghost, all-quickening fire! ...
Come, Holy Spirit, God and Lord! 3
Come, Holy Spirit, Heart's Desire 1
Come, Holy Spirit, heavenly Dove 2
Come, O Lord, like morning sunlight 2
Come, O Thou Traveler unknown 3
Come, Thou Almighty King ....
Come, Thou long-expected Jesus 1
Come, Thou my Light that I may see 4
Come unto me when shadows darkly
  gather 2
Come, ye disconsolate 3
Come, ye faithful, raise the strain ....
Come, ye sinners, poor and wretched 2
Come, ye thankful people, come ....
Come, ye that love the Lord ....
COMING AGAIN! ....

oming to Jesus, my Saviour, I found	445	God reveals His presence	23
ommit thou all thy griefs	398	God save our gracious Queen	546
Constantly Abiding	442	God that madest earth and heaven	38
radled in a manger	134	God the Omnipotent	17
reate in me a clean heart, O God	564	God Will Take Care of You	388
reator of the universe	498	God, who art the Lord of harvest	548
reator Spirit! by whose aid	204	God's Word is our great heritage	521
ross of Jesus, cross of sorrow	161	Gracious Spirit, dwell with me	198
rown Him with many crowns	183	Gracious Spirit, Holy Ghost	337
		Great God of nations	13
ay is dying in the west	211	Great God, we sing that mighty hand	14
ear Lord and Father of mankind	446	Great is Thy faithfulness	43
eep were His wounds, and red	159	Guide me, O Thou great Jehovah	69
eeper, deeper, in the love of Jesus	430		
epth of mercy! Can there be?	249	Hail the day that sees Him rise	182
own at the cross where my Saviour died	276	Hail Thou once despised Jesus	157
oxology	654, 655	Hail to the Lord's anointed	110
Draw Me Nearer	311	Happy the home when God is there	533
		Hark! the herald angels sing	117
acing a task unfinished	492	Hark! the voice of Jesus crying	361
airest of ten thousand	440	Hark! the voice of love and mercy	422
Fairest Lord Jesus	74	Have Thine own way, Lord!	298
aith of our fathers! living still	421	He Abides	338
ather, give Thy benediction	562	He giveth more grace	382
ather, I stretch my hands to Thee	266	He Hideth My Soul	89
ather, let me dedicate	541	He Is Able to Deliver Thee	221
ght the good fight with all thy might	416	He Keeps Me Singing	99
Follow Me	316	He leadeth me, O blessed thought!	429
or all the saints	462	He Rose Triumphantly	174
or God so loved this sinful world	275	He that is down needs fear no fall	408
or the beauty of the earth	33	He the Pearly Gates Will Open	464
orth in Thy name, O Lord, I go	486	He who would valiant be	234
om all that dwell below the skies	6	He's Everything to Me	39
om every stormy wind that blows	349	Heralds of Christ	488
om heaven above to earth I come	130	Here, O my Lord, I see Thee face to face	518
		Hiding in Thee	386
ve me the faith which can remove	365	His Yoke Is Easy	400
Give me thy heart"	245	Holiness unto the Lord	321
ve to the winds thy fears	399	Holy Bible, book divine	523
Gloria Patri	566	Holy Ghost, with light divine	196
Glorious Freedom	292	Holy Spirit, faithful Guide	201
orious things of thee are spoken	502	Holy, holy, holy! Lord God almighty!	54
ory be to God the Father!	56	Hosanna, loud hosanna	147
ory be to the Father (Greatorex)	566	Hover o'er me, Holy Spirit	202
ory be to the Father (Meineke)	567	How are Thy servants blest, O Lord!	52
Glory to His Name	276	How firm a foundation	404
o, tell it on the mountain	137	How gentle God's commands	66
o to dark Gethsemane	150	How lovely are Thy dwellings fair	475
d be in my head	343	How oft have I the Spirit grieved	257
d be with you till we meet again (Randolph)	469	How sweet the name of Jesus sounds	143
d be with you till we meet again (Tomer)	470	I am coming to the cross	265
d bless our native land	547	I am Thine, O Lord	311
d calling yet! Shall I not hear?	248	I can hear my Saviour calling	259
d hath not promised skies always blue	389	I gave my life for Thee	308
d hath spoken by His prophets	236	I have a song I love to sing	283
d is gone up on high	184	I have a song that Jesus gave me	436
d is love; His mercy brightens	70	I have decided to follow Jesus	262
d is my strong salvation	64	I hear my blessed Saviour say	316
d moves in a mysterious way	67	I hear the Saviour say	216
d of all power, and truth, and grace	339	I hear Thy welcome voice	256
d of concrete, God of steel	34	I heard the voice of Jesus say	281
d of grace and God of glory	25	I Know God's Promise Is True	275
d of our fathers	24	I know I love Thee better, Lord	405
		I know not what the future hath	468
		I know not why God's wondrous grace	395
		I know that my Redeemer lives	177

page 411

I Know Whom I Have Believed	395
I love Thy kingdom, Lord	476
I love to tell the story	45
I must have the Saviour with me	385
I need Thee every hour	347
I never walk alone, I have the Saviour	396
I sing a song of the saints of God	535
I sing th' almighty power of God	16
I sought a flag to follow	285
I sought the Lord	286
I stand all amazed at the love Jesus offers me	153
I stand amazed in the presence	154
I Surrender All	310
I thirst, Thou wounded Lamb of God	323
I thirsted in the barren land of sin and shame	428
I want a principle within	344
I was a wandering sheep	282
I was once a sinner, but I came	260
I will sing of my Redeemer	91
I will sing the wondrous story	103
I would be Thine; O take my heart	334
I'd rather have Jesus	362
I'll Live for Him	295
I'll praise my Maker while I've breath	27
I'm rejoicing night and day	338
If thou but suffer God to guide thee	384
Immortal, invisible, God only wise	3
Immortal love, forever full	226
In Christ there is no East or West	478
In heaven above	466
In heavenly love abiding	379
In memory of the Saviour's love	512
In My Heart There Rings a Melody	436
In tenderness He sought me	279
In the bleak midwinter	138
In the cross of Christ I glory	451
In the hour of trial	342
In the stars His handiwork I see	39
In times like these	242
It Is Well with My Soul	444
Jesus, all our ransom paid	167
Jesus, all Thy labor vast	168
Jesus, and shall it ever be	364
Jesus calls us o'er the tumult	303
Jesus Christ, my sure defense	463
Jesus, I Come	252
Jesus, I my cross have taken	309
Jesus, in Thy dying woes	162
Jesus, in thy thirst and pain	166
Jesus is tenderly calling thee home	239
Jesus, keep me near the cross	348
Jesus, lover of my soul (Aberystwyth)	277
Jesus, lover of my soul (Refuge)	278
Jesus loves me! this I know	537
Jesus, loving to the end	164
Jesus my King, my wonderful Saviour	102
Jesus, my Lord, my Life, my All	356
Jesus, my strength, my hope	267
Jesus Paid It All	216
Jesus, pitying the sighs	163
Jesus, priceless treasure	447
Jesus Saves	481
Jesus shall reign where'er the sun	194
Jesus, the name high over all	104
Jesus, the sinner's friend, to Thee	263
Jesus, the very thought of Thee	101
Jesus, Thy all-victorious love	319
Jesus, Thou divine companion	505
Jesus, Thou joy of loving hearts	100
Jesus, Thy blood and righteousness	270
Jesus, Thy boundless love to me	312
Jesus, we look to Thee	19
Jesus! what a friend for sinners!	97
Jesus, whelmed in fears unknown	165
Joy to the world! the Lord is come	115
Joyful, joyful, we adore Thee	5
Joys are flowing like a river	394
Just as I am, Thine own to be	307
Just as I am, without one plea	253
Kum ba yah, my Lord	350
Lamb of God, I look to Thee	53
Lead me, Lord	56
Lead on, O King Eternal	41
Lead us, heavenly Father, lead us	40
Let all mortal flesh keep silence	55
Let all the world in every corner sing	8
Let all together praise our God	11
Let my life speak for Thee, dear Lord	36
Let saints on earth in concert sing	45
Let us break bread together	51
Let us worship God	55
Lift up your heads, ye mighty gates	10
Light of the world	37
Like a river glorious	44
"Like as a mother comforteth"	534
Lo, God is here!	2
Lo, He comes, with clouds descending	18
Lo, how a rose e'er blooming	11
Look, ye saints, the sight is glorious!	18
Lord, enthroned in heavenly splendor	35
Lord, God, the Holy Ghost!	19
Lord, I believe a rest remains	34
Lord, I hear of showers of blessings	26
Lord Jesus Christ, be present now	55
Lord Jesus, I long to be perfectly whole	32
Lord Jesus, think on me	43
Lord of all being! throned afar	10
Lord of mercy, God of might	27
Lord of our life, and God of our salvation	44
Lord, possess me now, I pray	30
Lord, speak to me, that I may speak	49
Lord, Thou hast searched me	38
Lord, we have come to Thee	29
Lord, who didst choose in Galilee	50
Love came down at Christmas	12
Love divine, all loves excelling	33
Love divine, so great and wondrous	46
Loved with everlasting love	38
Low in the grave He lay	17
Macedonia	48
Majestic sweetness sits enthroned	5
Make me a captive, Lord	30
Make us, O God, a church that shares	49
Marvelous message we bring	18
May the grace of Christ our Saviour	56
May the mind of Christ	42
More about Jesus would I know	42

More love to Thee, O Christ	437
Morning has broken	208
Must Jesus bear the cross alone?	454
My country, 'tis of thee	544
My faith looks up to Thee	268
My God and Father, while I stray	296
My God, how wonderful Thou art	32
My God, the spring of all my joys	11
My hope is built on nothing less	393
My hope is in the Lord	457
My Jesus, as Thou wilt	299
My Jesus, I love Thee	86
My life, my love, I give to Thee	295
My Shepherd will supply my need	406
My soul, be on your guard	415
NEAR TO THE HEART OF GOD	448
Not what these hands have done	228
Nothing between my soul and the Saviour	407
Now thank we all our God	9
Now the day is over (Glenfinlas)	212
Now the day is over (Merrial)	213
O beautiful for spacious skies	542
O boundless salvation! deep ocean of love	219
O Canada!	545
O come, all ye faithful	121
O come, O come, Emmanuel	116
O Father, who at sundry times	526
O for a closer walk with God	314
O for a faith that will not shrink	374
O for a heart that is whiter than snow!	330
O for a heart to praise my God	327
O for a thousand tongues to sing	1
O for that flame of living fire	341
O God, for Thy redeeming grace	31
O God of Bethel, by whose hand	73
O God, our help in ages past	59
O God, Thy summons still is heard	507
O grant us light, that we may know	497
O happy day, that fixed my choice	290
O holy city, seen of John	508
O Holy Saviour, Friend unseen	397
O how happy are they	280
O IT IS WONDERFUL	153
O Jesus, I have promised	302
O little town of Bethlehem	136
O Lord of heaven and earth and sea	51
O Lord, our Lord, in all the earth	37
O Love Divine, by Christ revealed	142
O Love Divine, how sweet Thou art	224
O Love Divine, that stooped to share	401
O Love Divine, what hast Thou done!	152
O love, how deep, how broad, how high!	144
O Love that wilt not let me go	383
O Master, let me walk with Thee	367
O Master of the waking world	489
O Master Workman of the race	141
O mighty God, when I behold the wonder	61
O my soul, bless thou Jehovah	72
O perfect life of love	149
O perfect Love	529
O sacred Head, now wounded	156
O safe to the Rock that is higher than I	386
O say, can you see, by the dawn's early light	543
O soul, are you weary and troubled?	246

O splendor of God's glory bright	60
O spread the tidings 'round	333
O the deep, deep love of Jesus	378
O the unsearchable riches of Christ	90
O Thou in whose presence	48
O Thou, to whose all-searching sight	391
O Thou who camest from above	304
O Thou whose hand hath brought us	539
O to be like Thee! blessed Redeemer	301
O Word of God incarnate	522
O worship the King	2
O Zion, haste	493
Of the Father's love begotten	107
On a hill far away	456
On the cross of Calvary	169
Once in royal David's city	139
Once I was bound by sin's galling fetters	292
Once our blessed Christ of beauty	185
Once to every man and nation	418
One day when heaven was filled	145
ONLY TRUST HIM	244
Onward, Christian soldiers!	411
Open my eyes, that I may see	426
Our blessed Lord was slain	174
Our Father in heaven, Creator of all	499
Our Father, Thou in heaven above	353
Our Father, which art in heaven	355
Our God is love, and all His saints	434
OUR GREAT SAVIOUR	97
Out of my bondage, sorrow, and night	252
Out of the depths I cry to Thee	251
Peace, perfect peace	441
Praise God from whom all blessings (Bula)	654
Praise God from whom all blessings (Old Hundredth)	655
Praise Him! Praise Him!	83
Praise, my soul, the King of heaven	18
Praise the Saviour, now and ever	181
Praise to the Lord, the Almighty	63
Prayer is the soul's sincere desire	350
Redeemed — how I love to proclaim it!	284
Rejoice, rejoice, believers!	191
Rejoice, the Lord is King	46
Rejoice, ye pure in heart	439
Rescue the perishing	480
REVIVE US AGAIN	345
Rise up, O men of God	366
Rock of Ages! cleft for me	392
Saved by the blood of the Crucified One	271
Saved! saved! saved!	289
Saviour, again to Thy dear name	471
Saviour, like a shepherd lead us	390
Saviour of the nations, come	114
Saviour, teach me, day by day	438
Search me, O God (Finney)	559
Search me, O God (Maori)	318
Send out Thy light and Thy truth	558
Servant of God, well done!	453
SHOWERS OF BLESSING	233
Silent night, holy night	123
SINCE I HAVE BEEN REDEEMED	283
Sing, my tongue, the glorious battle	514
Sing of our God	193
Sing, O sing, this blessed morn!	135

Sing praise to God who reigns above	41
Sing them over again to me	223
Sing to the Lord of harvest	550
Sinners Jesus will receive?	230
Sinners, turn; why will you die?	241
Sleep sweetly, wee Jesus	132
So send I you	484
Softly and tenderly Jesus is calling	240
Softly now the light of day	209
Soldiers of Christ, arise	410
Sometimes a light surprises	222
Songs of praise the angels sang	36
Sound the battle cry!	420
Spirit of faith, come down	203
Spirit of God, descend upon my heart	197
Spirit of the living God	313
SPRINGS OF LIVING WATER	428
Stand up and bless the Lord	20
Stand up, stand up for Jesus!	409
Standing on the promises of Christ my King	231
Still, still with Thee	207
SUCH LOVE	291
Sun of my soul, Thou Saviour dear	214
Sweet hour of prayer!	351
Take my life and let it be	294
Take the name of Jesus with you	82
Take time to be holy	331
Talk with us, Lord, Thyself reveal	431
Tell me the stories of Jesus	538
Ten thousand times ten thousand	461
That day of wrath, that dreadful day	237
That Easter Day with joy was bright	176
That God should love a sinner such as I	291
The church's one Foundation	501
The city is alive, O God	504
THE COMFORTER HAS COME	333
The coming of our God	113
The day of resurrection!	171
The God of Abraham praise	15
The God of harvest praise	552
The grace of life is theirs	532
The King of love my Shepherd is	47
THE LIGHT OF THE WORLD IS JESUS	218
The Lord is my Shepherd. I shall not want	400
The Lord Jehovah reigns	62
The Lord my pasture shall prepare	402
The Lord's my Shepherd, I'll not want (Brother James' Air)	30
The Lord's my shepherd, I'll not want (Crimond)	29
The man who once has found abode	40
THE OLD RUGGED CROSS	456
The Saviour is waiting	247
THE SOLID ROCK	393
The Son of God goes forth to war	417
THE SONG OF THE SOUL SET FREE	440
The spacious firmament on high	35
THE STAR-SPANGLED BANNER	543
The strife is o'er, the battle done	180
The thing my God doth hate	328
THE UNVEILED CHRIST	185
The vision of a dying world	487
The whole wide world for Jesus	485
The whole world was lost in the darkness of sin	218
THE WORDS FROM THE CROSS	162–168

There is a balm in Gilead	2
There is a fountain filled with blood	2
There is a green hill far away	2
There is a name I love to hear	
There is a place of quiet rest	
There is no sorrow, Lord, too slight	
There shall be showers of blessing	
There's a peace in my heart	
There's a song in the air!	
There's a wideness in God's mercy	
THERE'S POWER IN THE BLOOD	
There's within my heart a melody	
THEY'LL KNOW WE ARE CHRISTIANS BY OUR LOVE	
Thine is the glory	
This is my Father's world	
This is the day of light	
This is the day the Lord hath made	
Thou didst leave Thy throne	
Thou hidden Love of God	
Thou hidden Source of calm repose	
Thou Judge of quick and dead	
Thou my everlasting portion	4
Thou, whose purpose is to kindle	5
Through all the changing scenes	
Through all the world let every nation sing	4
Through the night of doubt and sorrow	4
Thy law is perfect, Lord of light	5
'Tis midnight; and on Olive's brow	1
'Tis so sweet to trust in Jesus	3
'Tis the grandest theme through the ages rung	2
To God be the glory!	
To Thee, O Lord, the God of all	2
To worship, work, and witness	4
TRUST AND OBEY	3
Trust in the Lord with all your heart	3
TURN YOUR EYES UPON JESUS	2
'Twas on that night	5
Under His wings, I am safely abiding	2
Unto the hills around do I lift up	
Unto us a boy is born!	1
Up Calvary's mountain one dreadful morn	
Wake, awake, for night is flying	
Walk in the light!	2
We all believe in one true God	
We are one in the Spirit; we are one in the Lord	4
We gather together to ask the Lord's blessing	4
We give Thee but Thine own	3
We have heard the joyful sound	4
We lift our voice rejoicing	
We plow the fields and scatter	5
We praise Thee, O God, for the Son of Thy love	3
We praise Thee, O God, our Redeemer	
We shall see His lovely face	4
We thank You, Lord, for this our food	5
We worship Thee, Almighty Lord	
We've a story to tell to the nations	4
Were you there?	
What a friend we have in Jesus	3
WHAT GOD HATH PROMISED	
What is our calling's glorious hope?	
What shall I do, my God, to love	

hat various hindrances we meet	354
hat wondrous love is this	435
hen all Thy mercies, O my God	10
hen He shall come	192
hen I can read my title clear	450
en I survey the wondrous cross (Hamburg)	510
n I survey the wondrous cross (Rockingham Old)	511
n morning gilds the skies	81
n peace like a river	444
n we walk with the Lord	368
ere cross the crowded ways of life	506
ERE HE LEADS ME	259
ere shall my wondering soul begin? ...	272
ile shepherds watched their flocks / night	127
TER THAN SNOW	329

WHITER THAN THE SNOW	258
Who can cheer the heart like Jesus?	93
Who is He in yonder stall?	129
WITH THY SPIRIT FILL ME	306
Wonderful grace of Jesus	106
WONDERFUL PEACE	445
Wonderful story of love!	220
WONDERFUL WORDS OF LIFE	223
Would you be free from the burden of sin?	235
Wounded for me	188

Ye servants of God, your Master proclaim .	80
Years I spent in vanity and pride	250
Yield not to temptation	425

Zion stands with hills surrounded	372